A Real American Breakfast

A Real American Breakfast

The Best Meal of the Day, Any Time of the Day

Cheryl Alters Jamison
and Bill Jamison

WILLIAM MORROW

An Imprint of HarperCollinsPublishers

HarperCollins books may be purchased for educational, business, or sales promotional use. For information please write: Special Markets Department, HarperCollins Publishers Inc., 10 East 53rd Street, New York, NY 10022.

FIRST EDITION

Designed by Vertigo Design, NYC
Photo insert designed by Mary Austin Speaker
Photographs by Ellen Silverman
Food styling by Anne Disrude
Prop styling by Betty Alfenito

Printed on acid-free paper

Library of Congress Cataloging-in-Publication Data
Jamison, Cheryl Alters.
A real American breakfast: the best meal of the day, any time of the day /
Cheryl Alters Jamison and Bill Jamison.
p. cm.
Includes index.
ISBN 0-06-018824-3
1. Breakfasts. 2. Cookery, American. I. Jamison, Bill. II. Title.
TX733 .J35 2002
641.5'2—dc21
                                                                    2001042715

02 03 04 05 06 /QW 10 9 8 7 6 5 4 3 2 1

TO THE NEWEST BREAKFAST FAN IN OUR FAMILY,
granddaughter Bronwyn Linn Neale, who has already
established herself as a world champion applesauce eater

Contents

Acknowledgments

We're grateful to many people who have helped us in various ways with this book. First we must thank two organizations, the James Beard Foundation and the International Association of Culinary Professionals Foundation, which jointly fund the Linda D. Russo Travel Research Grant for food writers. The governing committee of the program generously awarded us a grant that allowed us to do research in the cookbook collection of the Schlesinger Library of Radcliffe College and in the menu collection of the New York Public Library. Much of the nonrecipe sidebar material in the book comes from that research.

Barbara Haber, the curator of the Schlesinger collection, provided considerable assistance in making our trip there as worthwhile as possible. Dawn Letson, Ann Barton, and the rest of the staff at the Blagg-Huey Library at Texas Woman's University also helped in the same way with additional research we did at their institution. Culinary historian Sandra Oliver aided us in an equally valuable manner by culling breakfast information from her extensive files on New England food traditions.

The gracious and grand first lady of American home cooking, Marion Cunningham, prepared wonderful waffles for us one morning and allowed us to interview her about breakfast. As the author of *The Breakfast Book* (1987), she obviously knows the subject well and gave us sound guidance. Ella Brennan and Ti Brennan Martin talked to us about New Orleans breakfast traditions one morning, and then at lunch at their Commander's Palace restaurant quizzed half of the city for us about morning food memories. We got further help from numerous other cookbook authors and culinary authorities, including Lora Brody, Cecilia Chang, John T. Edge, Sarah Fritschner, Robin Kline, Peggy Knickerbocker, Matt and Ted Lee, Jacqueline Higuera McMahan, Deborah Madison, and Elisa D'Amico-Maloberti.

Family and good friends helped us as well in various ways. Cheryl gives special thanks to her mother for fixing buckwheats or buttermilks and sometimes both every Saturday for many childhood years. Heather and J. B. Neale, our daughter and son-in-law, tasted many of the dishes with us, and their children, two-year-old Bronwyn and three-year-old Riley, often assisted with the cooking. Deborah Durham, Gayther and Susie Gonzales, Patty Karlovitz, Myrna and John Richard, and B. J. and Bob Weil lent us their appetites and advice. Nicole Curtis, Grace Graham, Jackie Imamura, and Art Pacheco helped us track down the best in ingredients, and Lynn Walters shared seeds from her garden with ours. Ed and Ellen Reid gave us a trove of American cookbooks they had inherited from a family estate. Joyce Swedlund and Flora West loaned us cookbooks that we couldn't find elsewhere, and Sanya Schick gave us some great coffee cake recipes. Tammy Blake provided help with other business that allowed us to keep focused on this project.

To get the book behind covers and on shelves, we're indebted to the talents and diligence of Carrie Weinberg, Kate Stark, Karen Ferries, Ann Cahn, Karen Lumley, Leah Carlson-Stanisic, Roberto de Vicq de Cumptich, Ellen Silverman, Anne Disrude, and Betty Alfenito. To keep egg off our face, we're particularly grateful to our editor Harriet Bell, our agent, Doe Coover, and Doe's assistant Frances Kennedy, all of whom offer substantial support in both professional and personal ways.

1

The Best Meal of the Day Any Time of the Day

"IT'S THE MOST important meal of the day," Mother used to say as she poured milk and sugar into cereal shaped like tiny doughnuts. We scoffed at the statement, partly because we did at all of Mother's admonitions, but also because the accompanying food didn't seem at all consequential.

Breakfast gained distinction only on special weekends when our parents cooked for us and ate with us, when they gave the experience significance by the way they respected and enjoyed the food. Those breakfasts were not just "important"; they were the best meals of the day, and they made those days some of the best of the year.

Most people recall such radiant dawns, but despite the memories we tend to trivialize the morning meal. We rush it, of course, even more than other meals, and usually insist on a repetitious routine that we would never follow at lunch or dinner, consuming the same few mainstays every day for years at a time. We chew silently, reading a newspaper or listening to music through headphones, with little relish or sense of sharing. If we're paying real attention to what we're eating, we're likely focused on fiber content rather than flavor, treating breakfast like a virtue tonic or a daily vitamin.

Behind this rut is a deep desire for comforting, familiar foods, embellished perhaps at times but always close to our sense of home. The phenomenally successful marketing of commercial breakfast products over the last century, and the more recent advertising blitz by giant fast-food chains, has convinced many of us that we can satisfy our longings out of a box from the grocery shelf or a sack from a drive-up snack joint. The companies competing for our breakfast bucks peddle speed and convenience, of course, but they also cater craftily to our morning wants. They package dumbed-down versions of down-home ideas in compelling ways, persuading us that we're getting the biscuits, the bagels, or the bran we crave without any toll on our time or attention.

All we sacrifice is enjoyment. We give up almost everything associated throughout human history with the pleasure of food. We experience little lust in the eating, little satisfaction in the preparation, little anticipation of gratification, little cheer in the breaking of bread with family and friends. We sell the soul of our breakfasts for the shell of somnolence.

Our lives are busy, to be sure, and we must earn the money for our daily bread before we can break it with anyone. We can't just add an hour to the other twenty-four to make room for a leisurely repast. We're forced to juggle priorities, and it seems sensible to give short shrift to something that comes along while we're still yawning.

Some of the time, yes. All of us need to eat on the run at least occasionally, whether it's to get to a morning meeting, take the kids across town to school, or catch a grimly early airline flight. The problem, as we see it, is the pervasiveness of the practice. We've settled into our rut so thoroughly that we overlook plenty of reasons and opportunities to start the day with a serious rush.

A Real American Breakfast

To recall what we're missing, take a step back in time. As personal memories may attest, the American breakfast used to be a brawny and bracing meal. Our ancestors sometimes ate meagerly, particularly when faced with the scarcity of the frontier, but even then they chose hearty foods that satisfied their appetites. The meal might have been milk and bread in rural New England or fried salt pork and corn bread in Tennessee, but it came from the land instead of a store and was fresh from the cow or the cooking pan.

More frequently, and certainly whenever possible, Americans enjoyed much bigger breakfasts, as we illustrate in scores of stories and quotes in the recipe chapters. They often had meat and something sweet—a combination peculiar to us—along with an ample selection of pancakes, biscuits, other hot breads, fish and game, eggs, grits, potatoes, and more. Anything appropriate to eat at all found a place on the American breakfast plate by the nineteenth century.

The variety and quantity stunned foreign visitors and immigrants. Some authorities say we inherited our love of substantial breakfasts from the British, but even English travelers marveled at the abundance of the American table. In the 1830s, the usually critical Harriet Martineau complimented a Massachusetts breakfast of "excellent bread, potatoes, hung beef, eggs and strong tea," and she became almost ecstatic over an Alabama morning feast of chicken, steak, pickled and fresh fish, bacon, eggs, hominy, corn bread, and buckwheat pancakes. Charles Dickens, who visited in 1842, encountered groaning boards at many breakfasts, such as one on a Pennsylvania canal boat that featured "bread, butter, salmon, shad, liver, steak, potatoes, pickles, ham, chops, black-puddings, and sausages." When he found the morning fare lacking, his complaints were often matters of pride to his hosts, particularly his attack on the common American T-bone cut as a "deformed beefsteak with a great flat bone in the centre."

A bountiful breakfast sustained the intensive work of farm families, who made up most of the country's population until recent generations. They rose early, started their daily chores, and then gathered at the table to appreciate the results of their labor. They ate dinner in the afternoon and just a light supper in the evening, leaving them eager to break their fast in the morning. In wealthier households, particularly on southern plantations, the first meal often provided an occasion for lavish entertaining. In areas that lacked inns, travelers stayed with friends and even strangers, who invariably showed their hospitality by offering guests as magnanimous a breakfast as they could manage. In cities, affluent hostesses staged elaborate "company breakfasts," which one writer at the turn of the twentieth century described as "much in favor with people of the leisure class, and also with the artist and *littérateur,* who frequently have considerable time to kill."

Almost everyone lost that luxury of time by the decades right after World War II. That hastened the decline of a toothsome breakfast, as did myriad other changes in American life. Most jobs became less physically taxing, decreasing our metabolic needs. Women found new and liberating responsibilities outside the kitchen. The more we worked away from home, the later we ate dinner, reducing our hunger for breakfast. The more we watched TV, the later we stayed up at night, making everything feel more rushed in the morning.

Despite these major lifestyle changes, and our normally feeble excuse for breakfast today, the old tradition still grabs our imagination. The contemporary buffet breakfasts in hotels, as sorry as they usually are, summon some notion of bounty. Our fascination with vintage diners and bed-and-breakfast inns comes partially from the respect they try to bestow, often successfully, on the morning meal. We'll line up deep for a good restaurant brunch, a direct descendant of those plantation and company breakfasts of the past. We haven't so much forsaken the heritage as we've forgotten how to honor it at home.

The Homey Meal

That's a troublesome paradox because breakfast is the homiest meal of all, when we most ardently seek solace in long-familiar, well-loved foods. We may want Moroccan flavors at lunch or a Thai banquet in the evening, but in the morning we yearn for simple indulgences. Our tastes strike chords from childhood, from our family, regional, and ethnic roots. However wide ranging our culinary interests, however sophisticated our palate and talents in the kitchen, we usually return home for breakfast.

This inclination translates too readily into a dull routine. If we don't make a real breakfast for ourselves, at least occasionally, we sacrifice the vitality and variety that Americans once prized. Packaged foods can never offer those qualities. Producers can't box and sack many of the most memorable morning foods, and the items they can sell must be bland enough to appeal to a mass audience. In a quest for comforting chow, we give up the robust for the robotic. None of us needs the quantity of food that our ancestors ate, but it's time to awaken ourselves to what we've lost in vibrancy.

To people concerned about the potential heaviness or unhealthiness of a solid breakfast, we offer plenty of spirited options for fruit, fish, cereals, dairy drinks, greens, and beans. To people who plead "no time," we suggest breakfast is the best time to cook for yourself and family, an occasion when one course seems ample to all and many of the favorite foods are fast and easy to prepare. Even the busiest families can usually sit down together briefly on some mornings, and they may even find it more convenient and less harried then than later in the day. Since the hour invites invigorating tastes but readily forgives flaws, it's also an opportune moment to experiment with dishes and flavors, to play creatively with a simple meal. If you're short of time or any other resource, limited by a diet or a small kitchen, on a tight budget, living alone, or waylaid in any other way from enjoying good home cooking, breakfast is your best chance to break out.

Everyone can do it occasionally. Most of us can manage it regularly, if we wish, by selecting dishes that benefit from advance preparation, that require little more than turning on the blender, or that cook quickly, as a wide variety do. The recipe chapters demonstrate how to master true wake-up foods that take less time in the morning and involve less fuss than packaged products. The ones that require more effort shine their brightest on leisurely weekends, during holidays, and when we're sharing our table with overnight guests.

Breakfast food also provides splendid succor at other meals. Omelets, pancakes, skillet-cooked potatoes, sausage, and hashes all convey their comforting message as well later in the day as in the morning. We're accustomed to turning lunch into brunch by adding bacon and eggs, but supper seems to us personally to work even better as an occasion for heartwarming dishes. Almost anytime you're cooking at home is a great time for breakfast.

If you're among the millions of people who just make do for breakfast, who get by on boxed doughnuts in one form or another, we invite you to sit down to a plateful of big, hearty regional flavors. We'll serve you real buttermilk biscuits and hash browns, a LEO scramble, a salt-cod hash, a summer-harvest strata made the night before, a great baked apple, and even in a contrarian American spirit, that T-bone that upset Charles Dickens. By the next morning's coffee break, you'll be bragging about the best meal of your day.

2

Break an Egg

IF PERFORMERS NEED to "break a leg" to be a success on stage, as the old salutation goes, American cooks must break an egg to win any standing ovations at breakfast. The first people on earth ate the eggs of wild fowl, and everyone across the globe eats chicken eggs today, but no one has ever made them the foundation of the morning meal to the same degree that we have.

While they are featured in lunch and supper in most other cultures, eggs dominate our image of a bountiful breakfast. Scrambled, poached, fried, or folded into an omelet—cooked in fact in more different ways than anywhere in the world—they signify sunrise as surely as the crow of a cock.

We've gotten jaded about our eggs, however, often accepting stale supermarket versions that taste of the shelf rather than the hen. The freshness and quality of eggs matter critically in any dish that features them. Look for the best you can buy—a bargain at any price—at farmers' markets, farm stands, and grocery stores that carry local products. The bright, bold goodness of fresh eggs provides cooks a gold mine of morning flavors. Change a step or two in the preparation and they yield an entirely new taste and texture. Change the ingredients in a scramble or omelet, or the toppings on fried or poached eggs, and you can transform a dish, personalizing it to your appetite. A good egg is a miraculous little package with an amazing power to please.

JOE'S SPECIAL

NUOVO JOE YOUR WAY

"Nuovo" Joes abound in the Bay area and elsewhere, featuring additions of tomatoes, black olives, mushrooms, pickled peppers, and Asiago, Cheddar, and other cheeses. We often cut the amount of meat to ¼ pound, just enough for background flavoring, and add extra vegetables. We've also substituted sweet or hot Italian sausage for the ground beef and escarole or chard for the spinach, using common Italian frittata ingredients that may have inspired Joe originally. Customize according to your inclinations and leftovers.

The people who count such things say that scrambles now outrank all other egg preparations in America's affections. This San Francisco creation—claimed by almost every Joe who's owned a restaurant in the Bay area—helps to explain the popularity. With the addition of ingredients as basic but as unlikely as ground beef and spinach, the namesake cook (probably Italian-American) turned straightforward scrambled eggs into a distinctive treasure of tastes. For a full sense of place, serve the eggs with good sourdough toast.   **SERVES 4**

6 large eggs

Splash or two of Tabasco or other hot pepper sauce

1 teaspoon salt or more to taste

½ teaspoon dried basil or oregano

½ teaspoon freshly milled black pepper or more to taste

1 tablespoon olive oil

1 tablespoon unsalted butter

1 medium yellow onion, diced

½ pound lean freshly ground beef, preferably chili grind (a bit coarser than hamburger grind)

¾ to 1 pound fresh spinach, preferably the crinkly savoy variety, trimmed of stems and chopped, or one 10-ounce package frozen chopped spinach, thawed and drained

Crack the eggs into a small bowl and add the Tabasco, salt, basil, and pepper. Whisk just enough to combine; you should still see large bubbles. Set aside.

Warm the oil and butter in a large skillet over medium heat until the butter melts. Add the onion and sauté until soft but not beginning to brown, about 4 minutes. Add the ground beef and continue cooking until uniformly brown, breaking the meat into small pieces as it cooks. Cover with the spinach, place a lid over the mixture, and cook for about 3 minutes, just until the spinach wilts. (If using frozen spinach, cook, covered, for 1 minute, just to take off its raw edge.)

Stir the spinach into the meat, cooking briefly to eliminate excess liquid if the mixture seems watery. Pour the egg mixture over all, stirring with a spatula from the bottom until the eggs begin to set. Remove from the heat and stir a few more times, as the eggs cook through from the residual heat. Serve immediately.

AMANA HOPPELPOPPEL

TECHNIQUE TIP

Of German heritage this hearty, chunky hodgepodge has stoked many an Iowa farmhand. It's not as well known today as in the past, but the remaining fans haven't lost any ardor. When we checked out a hoppelpoppel site on the Internet (www.wrightplace.tripod.com), a booming oompah band greeted us with its favorite recipe. Serve the scramble with applesauce or rye toast with apple butter.

SERVES 4 OR MORE

TECHNIQUE TIP

Americans may love scrambled eggs, but we don't always cook them well. In the perfect state of doneness they are fluffy soft curds, moist and tender, far removed from the dried-out mess served at most breakfast buffets. We find a few simple guidelines helpful in our own efforts.

- Whisk the raw eggs only until the yolks and whites reach a yellow tint and the bubbles in the liquid are still large. The eggs should still drop unevenly from the whisk.
- Use a pan no larger than 8 inches for up to 4 eggs. If you're scrambling up to twice as many eggs, a 10-incher should be adequate. What you want to avoid is the egg layer being so thick or thin that it overcooks or undercooks in spots.
- No matter how hurried you feel, keep the heat to medium or below. Save high heat for omelets.
- Be vigilant about stirring the eggs from the bottom with a spatula or other broad-bladed kitchen tool and then removing them from the heat shortly before they are done to your liking.
- Forget you've got a microwave.
- Don't tarry on the way to the table.

4 large eggs

2 tablespoons milk

1 to 2 tablespoons minced fresh parsley

Salt and freshly milled black pepper to taste

4 to 6 thick slices bacon, cut into 1-inch pieces

1 medium to large onion, cut into large dice

¾ pound small waxy red potatoes, boiled until tender, then cut into ¼-inch slices

Crack the eggs into a bowl and add the milk, parsley, salt, and pepper. Whisk just long enough to combine; you should still see large bubbles. Set aside.

Fry the bacon until brown and crisp in an 8-to 10-inch skillet. Remove the bacon with a slotted spoon and reserve it. Add the onion and sauté until soft but not brown, about 5 minutes. Add the potatoes and continue cooking until they are golden with some brown edges. Stir in the bacon, then pour in the egg mixture. With a spatula, turn the mixture over a couple of times to combine, scraping up from the bottom, then pat the mixture back down into a thick layer. Cover, reduce the heat to low, and cook for 5 to 7 minutes or until the eggs are lightly set but still very moist. Don't overcook. Spoon out and serve immediately.

A SIMPLY SUBLIME SCRAMBLE

Different cooks take many different routes to success in making a simple, unadorned scramble, but this approach works best for us. Plan on 2 large eggs, 1 tablespoon unsalted butter, and 1 tablespoon cream, half-and-half, or milk per person. If you have big appetites, or won't have much to accompany the eggs, add an extra egg and tablespoon of liquid for every other person. Whisk the eggs together with the cream, just until combined, seasoning generously with salt (¼ teaspoon or so per person) and freshly milled black pepper. We also like to add a dash of Tabasco or other hot pepper sauce, a little minced anchovy, or a grating of fresh horseradish.

Warm a well-seasoned, heavy-duty cast-iron skillet or a high-quality nonstick pan over medium heat. Add the butter and swirl it to cover the whole surface. Pour in the eggs and turn the heat down to medium-low. Cook, frequently stirring up from the bottom with a spatula, until they have formed curds but still look a little runny, 3 to 4 minutes. Do not overcook. Remove from the heat and stir through an additional time or two before serving immediately. A sprinkling of minced chives, scallions, tarragon, dill, chervil, or parsley over the eggs makes a nice final touch.

AMANA HOPPELPOPPEL WITH GERMAN SAUSAGE

Substitute cooked bratwurst or other wurst for the bacon. Start with 4 to 6 ounces sausage sliced into very thin half-moons, fried to crisp the edges. Depending on the sausage's fat content, you may need to use a tablespoon of oil or butter for the frying. You want enough fat left in the skillet to sauté the onion and flavor the eggs.

THE LEO

A favorite New York seafood scramble, the LEO takes its name from the first letter of the key ingredients, lox, eggs, and onions. Sautéed together, the trio taps out a luscious harmony based on the mellow richness of the eggs, the salty smokiness of the salmon, and the sweetness of the onions. Serve the LEO with a bagel or bialy.

SERVES UP TO 4

6 large eggs	1 large onion, diced
Freshly milled black pepper to taste	½ pound thinly sliced lox or nova, chopped
2 tablespoons unsalted butter	Salt to taste, optional

Crack the eggs into a bowl and add 3 tablespoons water and a generous grinding of pepper. Whisk just long enough to combine; you should still see large bubbles. Set aside.

Warm the butter in an 8- to 10-inch skillet over medium-low heat. Sauté the onion for about 8 minutes, until very soft and beginning to brown. Add the lox, just heating it through. Immediately pour in the egg mixture. Cook, frequently stirring up from the bottom with a spatula, until the eggs form soft curds and are lightly set but still look a little runny, 3 to 4 minutes. Do not overcook. Remove from the heat, then stir an additional time or two to cook through before serving immediately. Allow diners to salt to taste at the table, but the salinity of the lox should suffice for most people.

GAY ISLAND LOBSTER SCRAMBLE

Another sensuous scramble with a taste of the sea, this comes from the Maine islands. It's special-occasion fare of the highest order, a romantic way to start or end the day. Whisk together 2 tablespoons whipping cream and 1 tablespoon mayonnaise. Then add 4 eggs, salt, freshly milled pepper, and a tablespoon or two of chives. Whisk just long enough to combine; you should still see large bubbles. Warm an 8- to 10-inch skillet over medium heat, add 3 tablespoons unsalted butter, and swirl it to cover the whole surface. Pour in the egg mixture and turn down the heat to medium low. Cook, frequently stirring up from the bottom with a spatula, until the eggs have begun to form curds. Add 1 to 1½ cups cooked lobster chunks and any juices. Continue cooking until the eggs are lightly set but still a little runny, about 3 minutes longer. Do not overcook. Remove from the heat and stir an additional time or two to cook through before serving immediately.

TECHNIQUE TIP

When buying eggs, shop until the hens drop for you. We should all applaud the growing availability of real farm-fresh eggs from field-grazed chickens raised without hormones and antibiotics. Look for them anywhere you find fresh, local farm products. The shells may vary in color, depending on the variety of the hen, and the yolks are always deeper in hue. The primary difference from conventional eggs, however, is in the vibrant flavor, particularly noticeable in simple scrambles and other preparations where the egg is the major factor in taste. Good eggs cost more than average ones, because they cost more to produce, but they are still one of the best food bargains around. In the past, farm-fresh eggs were sold and stored briefly at room temperature, but unless they are literally just laid, it is better today to buy them refrigerated and keep them that way.

FROM SEA TO SHINING SEA

Seafood scrambles are hardly unique to Manhattan and Maine. During the Great Depression, the classic *Long Island Seafood Cookbook* (1939) recommended a scramble using steamed Nesconset mussels popped fresh from the shell into the eggs. Farther south, from Maryland to the Gulf of Mexico, blue crabmeat becomes the shellfish of choice. *The Historical Cookbook of the American Negro,* published by the National Council of Negro Women in 1958, features one exemplary version. Handfuls of bell pepper, celery, and onion are sautéed with bacon pieces and then rendered of drippings before ½ pound of crabmeat is added to 4 eggs, with a sprinkling of thyme and marjoram for seasoning. Out west, the Hotel Bel-Air in Los Angeles developed a specialty that tops even the Gay Island Lobster Scramble in prodigality. The kitchen cooked the eggs in butter and cream, spooned them back into their cleaned shells, placed the shells in elegant egg cups, and finished the dish with generous dollops of sevruga caviar.

BROWN-BUTTER SCRAMBLE WITH AVOCADO

SELECTIONS FROM THE BREAKFAST MENU AT THE HOTEL BALTIMORE IN BALTIMORE, 1899

Chicken Broth in Cup

Fried Rolled Eggs, Tomato Sauce

Omelet, with Mushrooms

Eggs, Meyerbeer

Shirred Eggs, Buckingham

Scrambled Eggs, with New Peas

Omelet, with Apricots

Many California recipes pair eggs with the locally grown Hass avocado. Our favorite version comes from the creative kitchen of Helen Evans Brown, whose *West Coast Cook Book* (1952) remains one of the best regional cookbooks ever published in the country. Her rendition was subtly different from most by calling for browned butter, which complements the nutty flavor of the avocado. She placed avocado slices on toast and spooned the finished eggs over them, but we add the avocados to the eggs just before they come from the stove. Serve the scramble perhaps over split and toasted English muffins or Herbed Popovers (page 342).

SERVES 4

6 large eggs

3 tablespoons heavy (whipping) cream or half-and-half

2 garlic cloves, roasted in a dry skillet until soft and minced

Splash of Cholula, or other Mexican hot pepper sauce, optional

Salt and freshly milled black pepper to taste

4 tablespoons (½ stick) unsalted butter

2 medium avocados, cut into bite-size chunks

Crack the eggs into a bowl and add the cream, garlic, Cholula if desired, salt, and pepper. Whisk just long enough to combine; you should still see large bubbles. Set aside.

Warm the butter in an 8- to 10-inch skillet over medium-low heat. Cook until the butter turns from pale yellow to light nutty brown, about 5 minutes. Immediately pour in the egg mixture. Cook, frequently stirring up from the bottom with a spatula, until the eggs form soft curds and are lightly set but still look a little runny, 3 to 4 minutes. Do not overcook. Fold in the avocados and remove from the heat. Stir an additional time or two to cook through before serving immediately.

BROWN-BUTTER SCRAMBLE WITH AVOCADO AND BACON

Adding bacon to this scramble introduces a compatible crunch to the soft texture. Use 2 to 3 slices crumbled cooked bacon. You may like a few shreds of grated sharp Cheddar as well.

FRESH GARDEN SCRAMBLE

Many vegetables work well in scrambles, particularly ones that are as local and fresh as premier eggs. Alone or in compatible combinations, consider scallions or other onions, sweet peppers or a few hotter chiles, tomatoes of multiple sizes and colors, summer squash such as zucchini or the yellow crookneck variety, a handful of baby spinach leaves, asparagus tips and tender stems, even shredded carrot, which also adds a vibrant hue and sweetness. Some options such as broccoli shine best with a handful or two of grated cheese. Cut the veggies into roughly uniform bite-size pieces. Then sauté them briefly in a couple of tablespoons of butter or olive oil over medium heat, long enough for them to become tender and for most of their water to evaporate. Add a few fresh herbs if you wish, perhaps dill, tarragon, parsley, or thyme.

NOPALITOS SCRAMBLE

In south Texas many locals scramble eggs with the sliced or diced pads of the prickly pear cactus, a tasty and unusual vegetable called *nopalitos*. You can use the canned precooked variety that only have to be drained and combined at the end of the cooking, but fresh cacti are becoming more widely available in stores that cater to a Mexican-American clientele. Boil *nopales* in salted water until soft, about 5 minutes, and dice before adding them to the almost finished eggs.

GRANTS QUIKI

Old Route 66 used to abound with down-home cafés, but few survived after Interstate 40 replaced the original highway and brought in the fast-food joints. One happy exception is the Uranium Café in Grants, New Mexico, operated by the Callahan family. The clan's specialty is the "quiki," a seemingly unpromising combination of scrambled eggs, canned hominy, and one or more choices from among chorizo, ham, green chile, and Swiss cheese. We suggested the scramble once to a journalist friend, Beverly Bundy of the Fort Worth *Star-Telegram*, who was researching a story on road food in the Southwest. She got so excited by the dish that she took digital photos and e-mailed them to colleagues so they could share the experience. Neither she nor the Callahans will mind sharing a bite with you.

SERVES UP TO 4

6 or 7 large eggs

3 tablespoons heavy (whipping) cream or half-and-half

Salt and freshly milled black pepper to taste

¼ pound Pasqual's Chorizo (page 138) or other bulk chorizo

Up to 2 tablespoons unsalted butter

One 14½- to 15½-ounce can hominy, preferably yellow, drained

Crack the eggs into a bowl and add the cream, salt, and pepper. Whisk just long enough to combine; you should still see large bubbles. Set aside.

Place the chorizo in a 10-inch skillet over medium heat. Fry until well browned and cooked through, breaking it into small pieces with a spatula as it cooks. Add enough butter to the drippings to make about 2 tablespoons of fat. When the butter is melted, add the hominy and heat through. Scoop out about ½ cup of the hominy mixture and reserve it. Reduce the heat to medium low.

Pour in the egg mixture. Cook, frequently stirring up from the bottom with a spatula, until the eggs form soft curds and are lightly set but still look a little runny, 3 to 4 minutes. Do not overcook. Remove from the heat and stir an additional time or two to cook through. Top each portion with some of the reserved hominy and serve immediately.

PASTRAMI AND EGGS

A staple at true delis, this is a grand combination of meat and eggs featuring tender shreds of gently spiced pastrami. Like the following matzoh brei, it resembles an omelet, but it's cooked like a scramble. Accompany it perhaps with toasted rye bread and dill pickles or a side of hash browns.　　**SERVES 4**

8 large eggs

Salt to taste

½ teaspoon freshly milled black pepper or more to taste

1 pound thinly sliced or shaved pastrami

Crack the eggs into a bowl and add 2 tablespoons water, salt, and pepper. Whisk just long enough to combine; you should still see large bubbles. Set aside.

Cook the pastrami in a medium skillet over medium heat for about 5 minutes, until the meat leaves a thick film of fat at the bottom of the skillet. (If the pastrami is extra-lean, and doesn't yield the proper amount of fat, add a little vegetable oil to compensate.) Pour the egg mixture over the meat and cook, lifting up around the edges, tilting the skillet so the uncooked egg runs underneath, until the eggs just begin to set, 3 to 4 minutes. Keep the meat well distributed throughout the eggs. Remove from the heat and let sit for another minute to finish cooking. Using a heatproof rubber spatula, nudge the pastrami and eggs onto a platter. Serve immediately.

SALAMI AND EGGS

Simply substitute salami for the pastrami for an equally hearty deli dish. As with the pastrami, we prefer the salami sliced extra-thin, but some fans of both combos like the meat thicker for a toothier texture.

CHIPPED BEEF AND EGGS

An old American favorite, ruined in reputation by poor supermarket and cafeteria versions, chipped beef shines in a scramble if you seek out good meat. We follow precepts that go back at least as far as *Miss Beecher's Domestic Receipt-Book,* from 1849, where Catharine Beecher recommended sautéing thin slices of the dried beef in butter until frizzled before scrambling in the eggs. You might top the scramble with a dollop of sour cream zipped up with a healthy dose of horseradish.

BRONX MATZOH BREI

A traditional Passover dish, matzoh brei has become a year-round breakfast standard for many Jewish families. Sometimes called fried matzohs, sometimes described as a Jewish French toast, it looks like an egg pancake broken into pieces for serving. Our friend Charlie Allenson, who grew up eating this regularly in the Bronx, helped us with the finer points of the preparation. It's a simple dish—not much more than unleavened bread and eggs—but one with broad appeal when made properly. Charlie says that different neighborhoods serve it in different ways, plain, with fruit preserves, or with sour cream. We favor the sour cream, with a nontraditional dash of Tabasco sauce mixed in. Charlie looks the other way when we add it.   **SERVES 4**

Four 6-inch matzoh squares, preferably salted

1 cup milk, chicken stock, or water

4 large eggs

½ to 1 small onion, minced, optional

Salt and freshly milled black pepper to taste

2 to 3 tablespoons unsalted butter or, if you happen to have it, chicken fat

Sour cream or fruit jam or preserves, optional

Break the matzohs into large flakes and soak them in the milk for about 5 minutes. Squeeze the matzohs to remove excess liquid, discarding the milk.

Crack the eggs into a medium bowl and add the onion, salt, and a generous amount of pepper. (If you bought unsalted matzohs, add a little extra salt too.) Stir the matzohs into the eggs.

Warm a 10-inch or larger skillet over medium heat and add the butter. When melted and foaming, pour the matzoh-egg mixture in and press down into a large pancake. Cook until lightly set and the bottom is golden with a few brown flecks, 2 to 3 minutes. Flip the pancake in chunks, pressing it all back down, and continue cooking until the second side is golden, 1 to 2 minutes longer. Remove from the heat while still moist looking, because the eggs will cook further from the residual heat.

Break into big chunks and serve mounded on plates with a dollop of sour cream or jam on each portion if you wish.

EGG-IN-THE-HOLE

We never knew this dish as children, when most fans develop an enduring loyalty to the innocently simple idea of an egg fried in a hole cut in a piece of bread. We first experienced it about ten years ago, when our friend Bill Kraus offered to make it for breakfast before we headed out for a day of Colorado skiing. Bill and many others call it egg-in-the-hole, but it's also known as bull's eye, toad-in-the-hole, baby-in-the-hole, knothole egg, egg-in-the-eye, picture-frame egg, and egg-on-a-raft. Multiply the recipe by the number of giggling diners.

SERVES 1

1 slice good but not too firm white, whole wheat, or brown bread

2 tablespoons unsalted butter

1 large egg

Salt and freshly milled black pepper to taste

Paprika, optional

Cut a hole at least 2 inches in diameter in the middle of the bread slice, using a biscuit cutter or knife. (You can also use a cookie cutter of similar size if the shape is simple, such as a star.)

Melt the butter in a small skillet over medium heat. Arrange the bread slice in the skillet and cook briefly until toasted golden on the bottom side. Turn the bread over and fry for 30 seconds to 1 minute. Crack the egg into a cup or saucer, then pour it into the hole and sprinkle with salt and pepper. Cover the pan and cook for just 1 minute. Uncover, reduce the heat to low, and cook for about 1 minute longer or until done to your liking. Dust with paprika, if you wish, and serve immediately.

MIGAS

Matzoh brei is just one of many egg preparations that incorporate bread, from crunchy croutons to saltine crackers. We're particularly fond of migas, a stellar Tex-Mex dish. The name derives from the Spanish word for crumbs, a reference to the tortilla chips that provide crunchy corn flavor. We serve this spicy version with warm flour tortillas.

SERVES 4

We give a specific recipe for migas that yields a great result, but fans of the dish know better than obedience to the written word. Vary your migas according to what's in the refrigerator. We sometimes add 2 to 4 slices crumbled crisp bacon or about ¼ pound chorizo, using the drippings of either in place of the butter or oil. A vegetarian friend uses drained crumbled soft tofu, sautéed in vegetable oil, to add heft to the dish. Rather than work with store-bought chips, you can start with fresh or stale corn or even flour tortillas, cut into strips and then fried briefly in a little oil until crisp. If you're pressed for time, salsa can substitute for the tomato-chile mixture. Any good melting cheese can replace the Cheddar. We've always loved the cheese as part of the mix, but some cooks leave it out entirely or just sprinkle a bit over the migas prior to serving.

9 large eggs	1 small onion, cut into thin strips
3 tablespoons water, milk, or heavy (whipping) cream	About 2½ dozen tortilla chips, broken into bite-size pieces
Salt to taste	6 to 8 ounces mild Cheddar cheese, grated (1½ to 2 cups)
1 small red-ripe tomato, preferably plum	2 tablespoons minced fresh cilantro, optional
1 fresh poblano or other large mild green chile	Extra whole tortilla chips, diced red-ripe tomato, grated Cheddar cheese, cilantro sprigs, or sour cream, optional
1 fresh jalapeño chile	
2 tablespoons unsalted butter or olive oil	

Crack the eggs into a medium bowl and add the cream and salt. Whisk just long enough to combine; you should still see large bubbles. Set aside.

Roast the tomato, poblano, and jalapeño: Either hold each on a fork directly over the flame of a gas burner or place them on a baking sheet under the broiler until browned all over and blackened in spots. The tomato skins, in particular, will probably split a bit. Place the poblano and jalapeño in a plastic bag to steam as they cool. When cool enough to handle, finely chop the tomato and its charred skin. Strip the peel off the poblano and the jalapeño, or as much as comes off easily. Slice the chiles open and remove their seeds and, if you wish, the veins that run lengthwise (which cuts the heat a bit). Slice the poblano into thin strips and mince the jalapeño.

Warm the butter in a large skillet over medium heat. Add the onion and sauté until limp, then stir in the tomato, chiles, and their juices and heat through. If they give off enough liquid to make the mixture watery, cook briefly until most of the liquid evaporates. Pour in the egg mixture and stir up from the bottom of the skillet as it cooks to your desired doneness. About a minute before the eggs are done, add the chips, stirring them in well. Remove the eggs from the heat and stir in the cheese and cilantro if desired. The dish is popular because it tastes great, not because the jumble of ingredients looks beautiful. Dress the migas with one or more of the garnishes to enhance the visual appeal if you like. Serve the migas immediately.

SCRAMBLED EGGS WITH SALSA AND CHEESE

For a simpler dish with some characteristics of migas, just make a basic scramble with the 8 eggs, cream or water, and salt. When the eggs begin to set, stir in $\frac{1}{2}$ to 1 cup prepared salsa (drained lightly if it's very soupy) and $\frac{3}{4}$ to 1 cup grated cheese, perhaps Monterey Jack or pepper Jack. Grate a little more cheese over the eggs if you wish and serve. Tangy tomatillo-based salsas are especially tasty with eggs and cheese, but tomato salsas work too.

SCRAMBLED EGGS WITH CHILI CON CARNE

A variation on the preceding variation. Substitute 1 cup warm chili con carne for the salsa, adding the cheese to the scramble and over the top.

EGG FU YUNG

Chinese cooks in western railroad and logging camps developed these small vegetable-filled egg cakes. We put the preparation into a recipe, but the creators never did, just binding almost anything on hand with eggs. Like chop suey and other improvised Chinese-American dishes, egg fu yung sometimes arouses disdain in culinary circles, but it can be delicious when made with good ingredients and a little care.   SERVES 4

SAUCE

1 tablespoon cornstarch dissolved in 1 tablespoon cold water

1 cup chicken stock

¼ cup soy sauce

1 teaspoon sugar

1 teaspoon Asian sesame oil

EGG FU YUNG

2 tablespoons peanut oil

2 teaspoons minced fresh ginger

1 garlic clove, minced

½ cup mixed chopped crunchy vegetables such as celery, water chestnuts, and bamboo shoots (see Ingredient Tip)

¼ cup chopped green bell pepper

¼ cup thinly sliced scallions

1 cup cooked crabmeat or chopped cooked shrimp, chicken, duck, or ham

Peanut oil for panfrying

6 large eggs, whisked

½ teaspoon salt

Minced fresh cilantro

In a small saucepan, combine the dissolved cornstarch, stock, soy sauce, and sugar. Bring to a boil, then reduce the heat to medium and cook briefly, just until lightly thickened. Stir in the sesame oil and keep warm over very low heat.

Heat the 2 tablespoons oil in a wok or large skillet over high heat. Stir in the ginger and garlic and cook for 30 seconds. Add the vegetables and cook until the celery is crisp-tender, about 2 minutes. Stir in the crab to heat through, then remove from the heat and scrape the mixture into a medium bowl.

Clean out the work and return it to the heat. Pour in enough oil to measure about 1 inch in depth. Heat the oil over medium-high heat until it ripples.

Stir the eggs, salt, and ½ tablespoon of the prepared sauce into the vegetable-crab mixture. Ladle about ⅓ cup at a time into the hot oil. It will spread to several inches. Cook until set and lightly browned on the bottom, about 1½ minutes, then turn and cook just until the second side is set, about 1 minute longer. Remove the egg patty with a slotted spoon and drain. Repeat with the remaining mixture, adjusting the temperature as needed to cook for the proper amount of time. You should get about 8 patties. Arrange the patties side by side on plates, spoon sauce over and around them, and top with a sprinkling of cilantro.

NINA SIMONDS'S SPICY BEAN SPROUTS

Chinese cooking authority Nina Simonds developed a lighter, more piquant contemporary version of egg fu yung that she calls simply "spicy bean sprouts." She created it for her book *China Express* (1993), which features dishes skillfully modified for today's harried cooks. Simonds starts by making very thin beaten egg "sheets" in a large skillet, using just a couple of eggs. These are stacked and cut into slivers and reserved. A tablespoon each of ginger and garlic are stir-fried with a teaspoon of hot chile paste just until fragrant, then 2 cups leek slivers are added to the pan, followed by 6 cups bean sprouts, cooked just until wilted. She then pours on a sauce mixture of ¼ cup chicken stock, 1½ tablespoons soy sauce, 1 tablespoon rice wine, 2 teaspoons sugar, 2 teaspoons Chinese black vinegar, 1 teaspoon Asian sesame oil, and 1 teaspoon cornstarch. That's all stirred together just until the sauce thickens, and then the egg slivers are mixed in. It can be served hot or at room temperature.

THE AMERICAN MELTING WOK

People often adopt unfamiliar foods when they resemble something within their own experience or when they fill a practical niche. One of the first Asian-American cookbooks, Sara Bosse and Onoto Watanna's slim *Chinese-Japanese Cook Book* (1914), tried hard to reassure its audience about the acceptability of the dishes. One of the recipes is for *foo yung dan,* which the authors describe as a Chinese omelet with "herbs" (actually celery and onion). They prepare it as a French-style folded omelet, then serve it with rice. A few decades later, The First Catholic Slovak Ladies Association of Beechwood, Ohio, wrote enthusiastically of egg *foo yong* in its 1952 *Anniversary Slovak-American Cookbook* because it was a dish that could be made without meat for religious fast days.

BACON-BASTED FRIED EGGS

It may seem passé, it may even seem deadly to some, but this is going to remain one of the finest destinies for an egg as long as there is a chicken alive on earth. You can double the recipe using a 12-inch pan or prepare it simultaneously in two smaller skillets.

It may seem passé, it may even seem deadly to some, but this is going to remain one of the finest destinies for an egg as long as there is a chicken alive on earth. You can double the recipe using a 12-inch pan or prepare it simultaneously in two smaller skillets.

SERVES 2

TECHNIQUE TIP

We follow a few simple maxims in frying eggs.

- As when scrambling eggs, keep the heat low to medium and use a well-seasoned, heavy-duty cast-iron skillet or a high-quality nonstick pan.
- Seek out very fresh eggs, which should have a high-standing yolk enveloped in white like rays around the sun. The water content of older eggs makes the white runny and the yolk more fragile in turning. Grade AA eggs have the firmest, most mounded yolks and whites.
- Break the eggs into a saucer or bowl first and then pour them from the saucer into the heated pan.
- Sprinkle the eggs with salt and pepper early in the cooking to avoid bland results.

4 thick slices bacon	Salt and freshly milled black pepper to taste
4 large eggs	

In a medium skillet over medium heat, fry the bacon until crisp and brown. Remove the bacon, drain, and reserve.

Crack each egg into a cup or saucer, then gently nudge the eggs one by one into the warm skillet, side by side. Salt and generously pepper the eggs immediately. Cook the eggs for 1 minute, sprinkling them with salt and pepper while they fry. As they cook, use a spatula to scoop up some of the bacon drippings and drizzle them over the whites. Turn the heat down to low and continue cooking and drizzling the drippings for about 1 minute longer or until done to your liking. Serve immediately, with bacon on the side.

HAM AND EGGS

Fry ham slices in the skillet over medium-high heat until a bit brown and crisp in spots. The ham will render some drippings, but not as much fat as you'll likely want for frying the eggs. Turn the heat down to medium, then add a tablespoon or more butter to the skillet and proceed as directed.

BUTTER-BASTED EGGS

Warm the skillet first, then add at least a full tablespoon of butter per egg. When the foam subsides, add the eggs and proceed as directed, spooning the butter over the whites throughout the cooking. When you take the eggs from the pan, spoon a little of the remaining butter over each egg.

OLIVE-OIL-FRIED EGGS

Use ½ to 1 tablespoon oil per egg and fry similarly. These are especially good when you also add other strong flavors, perhaps a mashed garlic clove in the oil or a little chile paste drizzled over the top.

OLIVE-OIL-FRIED EGGS WITH SPAGHETTI

Turn the previous variation into an entire meal for two, especially nice for a comforting evening supper. Fry 4 eggs in ¼ cup olive oil with a garlic clove and, if you have it, some minced fresh sage. When the eggs are softly set, with somewhat runny yolks, toss them with ½ pound freshly cooked spaghetti so that the whites tear into soft shreds and the yolks coat the pasta. Top the dish perhaps with a few toasted bread crumbs or grated Parmesan.

FRIED EGGS OVER-EASY

Instead of basting eggs in fat or oil, or in addition to it, you can flip the eggs halfway through the cooking time to finish the top side and cook the yolks more thoroughly. Turn the eggs gently with a broad spatula and be careful not to overcook.

HUEVOS RANCHEROS

It's perhaps a prejudice from the years we've lived in the Southwest and traveled in Mexico, but huevos rancheros seems to us the perfection of fried eggs. Nothing brings out the earthy freshness of an egg better to us than the piquancy of a chile salsa and the corn tang of a tortilla. Round out the ranch-style breakfast with chorizo or bacon and a side of refried pinto beans.

SERVES 4

RANCHERO SAUCE

1 tablespoon vegetable oil

1 medium onion, chopped

2 garlic cloves, minced

¾ cup chopped roasted mild green chile, preferably New Mexican or poblano, fresh or frozen

2 cups canned crushed tomatoes

1 tablespoon vinegar, preferably white

1 to 2 teaspoons sugar

½ teaspoon cumin seeds, toasted and ground

½ teaspoon salt or more to taste

⅓ cup chopped fresh cilantro

1 tablespoon fresh lime juice

Vegetable oil for panfrying

8 corn tortillas

8 large eggs

About 2 tablespoons unsalted butter

Salt and freshly milled black pepper to taste

2 ounces Monterey Jack, asadero, or mild Cheddar cheese, grated (about ½ cup)

Mexican crema (crème fraîche) or sour cream and cilantro sprigs, optional

For the sauce, warm the oil in a skillet over medium heat. Stir in the onion and garlic and cook briefly until limp, 2 to 3 minutes. Mix in the chile, tomatoes, vinegar, sugar, cumin, and salt and bring to a boil. Reduce the heat to a simmer, cover, and cook for about 15 minutes, until thickened but still spoonable. (The sauce can be made a day ahead, covered, and refrigerated. Reheat before proceeding, adding a little water if it seems stiff.) Stir the cilantro and lime juice into the sauce shortly before removing from the heat.

Heat about ¼ inch of oil in a medium to large skillet. Dip the tortillas into the oil, 1 or 2 at a time, and cook for a few seconds, until soft and pliable. Drain the tortillas and arrange 2 overlapping on each of 4 plates.

Break the eggs, 2 by 2, into cups or small bowls.

Pour out of the skillet all but enough oil to generously coat the surface. Warm the skillet again over medium heat for 1 to 2 minutes. Add 1 to 2 teaspoons of the butter and, when the foam subsides, in about 1 minute, pour in the eggs and begin to fry them, 2 to 4 at a time, depending on the skillet size. Cook for 1 minute, seasoning generously with salt and pepper while the eggs cook. As they cook, use a spatula to scoop up some of the butter to drizzle over the whites. Then turn the heat down to low and continue cooking and drizzling the butter for about 1 minute longer or until done to your liking. Repeat with the remaining eggs, adding more butter to the skillet as necessary.

Top each tortilla with a fried egg. Sprinkle a couple of tablespoons of the cheese over each serving of eggs and top with equal portions of the sauce. Serve the eggs immediately, with crema and cilantro if you wish.

HUEVOS AL BARRIO

The best riff on the ranchero theme we've tasted is huevos al barrio, served at Mejor que Nada ("Better than Nothing") in San Angelo, Texas. The restaurant tops shreds of smoky barbecued beef brisket with a warm tomato salsa spiked gently with chile and serves it alongside perfectly fried eggs and bacony refried beans. The proprietor's mother concocted the dish years ago in her home kitchen.

GERMAN-STYLE HUEVOS RANCHEROS

From the central Texas hill country, where German and Mexican traditions intermingled, we found an unusual ranchero sauce in a local cookbook called *Guten Appetit!* (1978). Credited to Mary Valenzuela, the recipe starts with a bacon and chicken stock base and adds a few potatoes for heft, an approach suggestive of hot German potato salad. Fry ½ pound chopped bacon, then remove with a slotted spoon. In the drippings, sauté a chopped onion and 2 minced garlic cloves until beginning to soften, about 3 minutes. Sprinkle in 2 tablespoons flour and stir to incorporate, cooking for another minute. Add 3 chopped medium-size tomatoes and 3 to 5 chopped mild green chiles or one 15-ounce can Ro-tel tomatoes with green chiles (a Texas favorite) and cook for 3 minutes longer. Mix in 3 cups chicken stock, ½ pound diced peeled waxy red potatoes, the reserved bacon, and salt to taste. Simmer until cooked down into a rather smooth sauce with soft potato chunks, about 30 minutes. Continue with the eggs and tortillas as directed.

BIRD'S NEST

TECHNIQUE TIP

A few basics on cooking eggs in their shells:

- Whether your goal is soft, hard, or in between, never boil a "boiled" egg, which turns the white rubbery and gives the yolk a green tint. Start with cold water and bring it to a temperature just below a full boil, when bubbles begin to break insistently around the water's edge.

- For a classic 3-minute egg, which is soft-boiled, let it sit covered in the pan for that time or a little less after you turn off the heat. A hard-boiled egg takes 15 minutes or longer in the cooling water.

- Eggs peel most easily when still warm. For easier peeling of soft-boiled or medium eggs, pierce the large end with a small straight pin prior to cooking to release air.

In researching this book, we talked to hundreds of people about their favorite breakfast dishes from the past and present. This sunny soft-boiled or coddled egg in a bowl came up often, across every geographic, ethnic, and cultural line. Like Egg-in-the-Hole (page 19), it's one of those charmingly simple comfort foods that we shouldn't forget or forsake. A Seattle acquaintance, Myra Platt, mentioned the maple syrup topping, a boarding school indulgence for her that gave the eggs some French-toast flavor. Multiply the recipe by the number of eaters.

SERVES 1

1 or 2 large eggs in the shell

1 or 2 slices soft white or whole wheat bread

Unsalted butter, softened

Salt and freshly milled black pepper to taste

Real maple syrup, optional

Cover the egg with about an inch of cold water in a small saucepan. Over medium heat, warm the egg, bringing the water to the stage just before a full boil, when bubbles begin to break insistently around the water's edge. Gently stir the egg a few times while heating, to help the yolk stay centered. Turn off the heat, cover the pan, and let it stand—about 2 to 3 minutes for runny soft-boiled or up to 5 to 8 minutes for firmer white and yolk.

While the egg stands, toast the bread and spread it generously with butter. Tear the toast into large bite-size pieces and arrange the toast in a bowl, bird's nest style.

Gently peel the egg, then arrange it over the toast with its most attractive side up. Sprinkle with salt and pepper and serve immediately. Offer maple syrup on the side if you wish.

EGGS SUR LE PLAT

"Eggs sur le plat" became particularly popular for fancy breakfasts at the turn of the twentieth century. The French name connoted elegance and referred to eggs cooked and served in the same dish, usually a plate, shallow gratin-style dish, or small skillet. Like any baked egg, it can be enhanced by cooking on a bed of ingredients with contrasting but compatible texture, color, and flavor, such as the beans and mushrooms used in this contemporary version. To simplify the preparation, we compose the dish in one large skillet, but you can spoon equal portions of beans and eggs into separate ramekins if you prefer. In choosing between the levels of suggested seasoning for the beans, bear in mind that the eggs will dilute their impact.

SERVES 4 TO 6

TECHNIQUE TIP

A baked egg for one can be as elementary as a single egg broken into a buttered dish, with just a sprinkling of salt and maybe the merest hint of fresh thyme or chives. One of the great things about baked eggs, however, is how well they lend themselves to a crowd. They can be readied in their containers a bit in advance, arranged on a baking sheet, and then popped into the oven just before you plan to serve. Our baked egg recipes double easily.

SELECTIONS FROM THE BREAKFAST MENU AT THE HOTEL PORTLAND IN PORTLAND, OREGON, 1921

NO. 1 40 CENTS

Grapenuts or Stewed Prunes or Rhubarb

Toast or Rolls

NO. 9 90 CENTS

Sliced Orange

Fresh Peaches and Cream or Strawberries and Cream

Choice of Ham or Bacon and Eggs, Boiled Eggs, Omelette Spanish,

Grilled Royal Chinook Salmon, Breakfast Steak

Hot Rolls or Toast

---

2 thick slices bacon, halved crosswise and cut into thin strips

2 tablespoons extra virgin olive oil

2 to 3 plump garlic cloves, thinly sliced

½ pound woodsy mushrooms, such as porcini or portobello, or button mushrooms, thinly sliced

4 cups cooked white beans, such as cannellini or Aztec

½ cup dry white wine

½ to 1 teaspoon dried tarragon or thyme or a combination

¼ teaspoon hot red pepper flakes or a pinch or two of cayenne pepper, optional

Salt and freshly milled black pepper to taste

4 to 6 large eggs

Preheat the oven to 350°F.

Fry the bacon in a heavy 10- to 12-inch ovenproof skillet over medium heat until light brown, with much of the fat rendered. Add the olive oil and garlic and cook for another minute. Add the mushrooms and sauté until softened, about 5 minutes. Stir in the beans, wine, tarragon, hot red pepper flakes if desired, salt, and pepper. (The mixture can be made to this point a day ahead. Cool, cover, and refrigerate, and reheat before proceeding.)

Place the skillet in the oven, uncovered, and bake for 45 minutes to 1 hour, until the liquid is thickened, reduced, and bubbly. Leave the oven on. Using a large spoon or the bottom of a cup, make 4 equal-spaced indentations in the beans (or another 1 or 2 for additional eggs). Crack an egg into each indentation and return the skillet to the oven. Bake for 8 to 12 additional minutes or until the eggs are cooked to your liking. Serve warm from the skillet.

POACHED EGGS ON CREAMY GRITS

Poaching an egg brings out its essence in the simplest and most sumptuous way. This contemporary pairing with creamy grits—an old southern favorite spreading in popularity across the country—doubles the luscious richness. We serve the dish here with a Creole sauce on top, but even if you skip that step, you've got a sublime but homey start for the day. **SERVES 4**

GRITS

2 tablespoons unsalted butter

½ teaspoon salt or more to taste

1 cup stone-ground grits, not instant or quick-cooking (see Ingredient Tip, page 320)

2 cups whole milk, half-and-half, or a combination

CREOLE SAUCE

2 tablespoons vegetable oil

1 to 2 teaspoons bacon drippings, optional

2 tablespoons unbleached all-purpose flour

1 medium onion, chopped

1 small green bell pepper, chopped

¼ cup minced celery

2 plump garlic cloves, minced

1 cup chicken stock or water

1 cup chopped canned tomatoes with juice

1 bay leaf

½ teaspoon dried thyme

Pinch or two of cayenne pepper

Salt and freshly milled black pepper to taste

EGGS

1 tablespoon white vinegar

4 to 8 large eggs

Salt and freshly milled black pepper to taste

In a large heavy saucepan, bring 1 quart water, butter, and salt to a boil. Whisk in the grits a few handfuls at a time. (They will bubble up initially.) When you have added all the grits, reduce the heat to a very low simmer and cook for 45 to 50 minutes, stirring occasionally at first and more frequently toward the end. After about 30 minutes, or when the grits begin to seem somewhat stiff and give a bit of resistance at the bottom, stir in half the milk, adding the rest about 10 minutes later. Add more salt if you wish near the end of the cooking time. When done, the grits should be slightly soupy but with enough body that they don't run all over the plate or bowl. The grits can be held briefly over low heat, with a little water or additional milk added to keep them from getting too stiff.

While the grits simmer, begin the sauce. Warm the oil in a large heavy skillet over medium heat, adding the bacon drippings if you wish for extra flavor. Sprinkle the flour into the pan drippings, stirring to combine, and cook the mixture until it's a rich, deep brown, about 5 minutes. Watch it carefully and stir frequently, because it can go quickly from the desired shade to burned. Immediately mix in the onion, bell pepper, and celery and cook until they begin to soften, about 5 minutes. Stir in the garlic and cook for another minute. Pour in the stock and tomatoes, add the bay leaf, thyme, and cayenne, and simmer the sauce for about 15 minutes. Season with salt and pepper and reserve.

When the grits and sauce are ready, poach the eggs. Fill a broad saucepan with about 2 inches of water, pour in the vinegar, and bring to a boil. Break as many eggs as will fit in your pan easily into cups or ramekins. Reduce the heat to a bare simmer, then slip the eggs into the water. We prefer to simmer the eggs gently for 30 seconds, then turn off the heat and cover for 2 to 3 minutes. When done, remove with a slotted spoon. Repeat if needed for additional eggs. Trim any ragged edges off the egg whites.

Spoon a pool of grits into 4 shallow soup bowls or plates, spoon a few tablespoons of sauce around the edge, and nestle an egg or two over the grits. Serve immediately, with the remaining sauce on the side.

POACHED EGGS VIRGINIA

Lily Haxworth Wallace, in her 1945 *Egg Cookery,* suggests serving poached eggs over Fresh Corn Fritters (page 99) rather than cornmeal grits. She tops the dish with a cream sauce enhanced with bits of chicken and country ham.

- Drain the eggs well before serving them. If working with a bunch of eggs, we spoon them onto sections of paper towel as we fish them out of the water, then gently transfer them to the finished dish.
- Eggs can be poached in a variety of liquids—cream, wine, stock, tomato juice, sauces—but keep in mind they will take on some of the color as well as the flavor of whatever you use. You may like the slight tan of a meat broth better than the purplish tint bequeathed by red wine.
- You can flavor the eggs, albeit subtly, by seasoning the poaching liquid. For example, we like using curry powder or paste in water or chicken stock. Keep in mind that you need a comparatively large amount of spice or other flavoring because of the short cooking time and the amount of liquid used.

EGGS BENEDICT

Craig Claiborne called Eggs Benedict "conceivably the most sophisticated dish ever created in America." According to most accounts, it originated in the kitchen of the old Delmonico's restaurant, which reigned over New York cuisine for nearly a century beginning in the 1820s. The restaurant had a reputation for inventing dishes—including Delmonico steaks, Delmonico potatoes, lobster Newburg, and baked Alaska—and so patrons sometimes challenged the chef with a new idea. LeGrand Benedict or his wife usually gets credit for inspiring this combination of toasted bread, Canadian bacon, poached eggs, and a buttery hollandaise sauce. Despite the eminence of the dish, the classic version can be made from start to finish in less than thirty minutes, though you should certainly feel free to imply to your family and guests that you've labored for much longer.

SERVES 2 OR 4

4 thin slices Canadian bacon (see Ingredient Tip)

HOLLANDAISE SAUCE (MAKES ABOUT 1 CUP)

3 large egg yolks

1 tablespoon fresh lemon juice

1 tablespoon water

8 tablespoons (1 stick) unsalted butter, cut into about a dozen small chunks and then softened

Salt and freshly milled white pepper to taste

Cayenne pepper to taste, optional

1 tablespoon white vinegar

4 large eggs

2 English muffins, split with a fork and toasted (see Ingredient Tip on page 38)

Cayenne pepper or paprika

It's always a smart idea to have ingredients and cooking utensils assembled before you jump into a recipe. It's especially important in this case.

Turn your oven on to 200°F to 250°F. Place your plates in the oven to warm them.

Prepare the Canadian bacon. Warm a heavy skillet over medium-high heat. Add the Canadian bacon slices and sear quickly, to brown and crisp in a few spots. Cover with foil and place in the oven.

Prepare the sauce. Combine the yolks, lemon juice, and water in a medium saucepan over low heat. Whisk continually but lightly to thicken the sauce evenly, not add air. When you can begin to see trails across the pan's bottom as you make the strokes, after 5 to 6 minutes, start whisking in the butter chunks one at a time. Whisk them in more or less continuously, but always incorporate each chunk fully before adding the next one. To avoid overheating, take the pan off the heat while incorporating about every other butter chunk. (It sounds awkward, but it's easy as you get into it.) Try to keep the mixture from adhering to the pan sides, where it can cook too quickly. The sauce is ready when it's thick, silky, and still spoonable, less than 10 minutes from start to finish. Season with salt, pepper, and cayenne if you like, just before you remove it from the heat for the last time. (You can hold the sauce up to 30 minutes in the top of a double boiler. Fill the bottom with hot tap water and then warm over the merest bit of heat.)

Fill a broad saucepan with about 2 inches of water, pour in the vinegar, and bring to a boil. Break as many eggs as will fit in your pan easily into cups or ramekins. Reduce the heat to a bare simmer, then slip the eggs into the water. We prefer to simmer the eggs gently for 30 seconds, then turn off the heat and cover for 2 to 3 minutes. When done, remove with a slotted spoon. Repeat if needed for additional eggs. Trim any ragged edges off the egg whites.

Place one or two English muffin halves on warm plates. Top with Canadian bacon, then the poached eggs. Spoon hollandaise over and around, sprinkle with cayenne or paprika, and savor immediately.

BÉARNAISE BENEDICT

Some people replace the hollandaise with a béarnaise sauce, a tasty alternative: In a medium saucepan, combine ¼ cup dry white wine, 2 tablespoons tarragon white wine vinegar, 2 tablespoons minced shallot, and 2 tablespoons chopped fresh tarragon. Reduce the mixture over medium heat until 2 tablespoons of liquid remain. Strain and reserve the liquid, discarding the solids. Return the liquid to the saucepan and whisk it together with 3 egg yolks. Warm gently over low heat, whisking continuously. Gradually add ½ cup unsalted butter in small chunks, starting when you can begin to see trails across the pan's bottom as you make the whisking strokes. Whisk in the butter chunks one at a time, more or less continuously, but always incorporating each chunk fully before adding the next one. To avoid overheating, take the pan off the heat while incorporating about every other butter chunk. Season with salt and pepper just before you are ready to remove it from the heat for the last time. The sauce is ready when it's thick, silky, and still spoonable, about 5 to 8 minutes total.

EGGS BLACKSTONE

One of the few variations on Benedict to attain an established name, the Blackstone replaces the Canadian bacon with a red-ripe tomato slice and a halved piece of bacon. If you want to embellish the notion, the tomato can be dipped in seasoned cornmeal and fried until crisp.

EGGS IN THE GRASS

The Black Dog Tavern on Martha's Vineyard offers a veggie variation on Benedict under this tag. For a home version of the dish, trade out the Canadian bacon for about 10 ounces lightly steamed asparagus. Arrange the English muffin halves side by side on each plate. Place half of the asparagus spears running across the muffin halves lengthwise. Arrange 1 or 2 poached eggs on top and ladle on the hollandaise, leaving the green "grass" growing out of both ends.

EGGS ASTORIA

Named for the Oregon town at the mouth of the mighty Columbia River, this dish substitutes chunks of hot-smoked salmon for the meat (see Ingredient Tip, page 41). We like this best with an extra-lemony hollandaise. Add the grated zest of 1 lemon and an extra teaspoon or two of lemon juice to the basic sauce.

BLENDER HOLLANDAISE

Some cooks prefer to make hollandaise in a blender, which may seem less intimidating than the traditional method. You prepare it like mayonnaise, but use melted butter to bind the emulsion instead of oil. First melt the butter, keeping it warm but not hot. In the blender, combine the egg yolks, lemon juice, salt, pepper, and cayenne. When the ingredients are well mixed, and with the motor still running, pour in the butter in a slow steady stream, blending until thick. Hollandaise made this way is typically on the thick side; thin it with water if you like.

BENEDICT BOUNTY

Few dishes have inspired more variations than Eggs Benedict. From the shameful to the splendid, versions range from McDonald's Egg McMuffin to Campton Place's San Francisco specialty with pancetta, a pesto biscuit, and a basil hollandaise. For the bread base, we've seen everything from bagels to flour tortillas, corn bread to pizza-flavored focaccia. Substitutes for the Canadian bacon, which go even further afield, include country ham, corned beef hash, oysters, lobster, salt-cod cakes, crab cakes, smoked trout, chicken breast, and, in south Florida, citrus-marinated alligator tail. For other variations, both the bizarre and the scrumptious, see Josh Karpf's Eggs Benedict website, www.foody.org/eggs/benedict.html.

ORIGINAL FARMERS' MARKET SHIRRED EGGS

TECHNIQUE TIP

Whether you call them shirred or baked eggs, the basic cooking principles are the same.

- Choose small, close-fitting individual dishes, just the size to fit the egg or eggs and any other key ingredients. We use ramekins, small gratin dishes, or even small cast-iron skillets.
- If the eggs will rest on other ingredients, warm the ingredients or at least bring them to room temperature before combining and baking. The brief cooking time won't heat through many ingredients except the eggs.
- The temperature of the egg at the time of baking will affect the number of minutes needed in the oven. We let our eggs sit briefly—10 to 20 minutes— at room temperature before cracking them into their baking dishes. Colder eggs sometimes become rubbery during their extended baking.

An egg was the first item ever sold at the Los Angeles Farmers' Market, three minutes after its July 14, 1934, opening, a fact recorded for posterity because the farmers had a betting pool on the initial sale. In those days the market vendors were actual farmers, unlike the retailers and restaurateurs that now cater to the public at the bustling intersection of Third and Fairfax. In homage to those roots, we selected a recipe from the old *The Farmers Market Cookbook* (1951), by Neill and Fred Beck, as our model for classic shirred eggs. Baked in ramekins and drizzled with cream, they can be tailored to anyone's taste with a range of additional flavorings.   **SERVES 4**

2 tablespoons unsalted butter, softened

2 tablespoons dried bread crumbs

4 thin red-ripe tomato slices from a medium tomato

4 large eggs

Marjoram, parsley, sage, thyme, or other compatible fresh or dried herb

Tabasco or other hot pepper sauce to taste, optional

¼ cup heavy (whipping) cream or half-and-half

1 slice bacon, cooked crisp and crumbled, optional

Salt and freshly milled black pepper to taste

Preheat the oven to 350°F.

Generously butter the sides and bottom of 4 individual ramekins, preferably ones that hold at least ½ cup. Divide the bread crumbs equally among the ramekins and twirl each around so that they stick to the sides and bottom. Arrange a tomato slice in the bottom of each ramekin. Break an egg into each ramekin, being careful to keep the yolks unbroken. Add a shot of hot sauce to each if you wish, then pour the cream over. Sprinkle with bacon if you wish and then season with salt and pepper. Bake the eggs for 8 to 12 minutes, depending on how firm you like your eggs. (They will continue to cook a bit after you remove them from the oven.) Serve immediately.

SHIRRED EGGS WITH LEFTOVERS

Baked eggs offer a chameleonlike ability to combine with a wealth of ingredients. A tablespoon of marinara sauce, chili, succotash, or even beef stew can form a tasty bed at the bottom of the ramekin. You can also use odd bits of leftover produce such as a handful of peas, or chopped asparagus or mushrooms cooked briefly in a little butter until tender. Cheese, even a southern pimiento cheese spread, is good under, over, or around the eggs.

In a perfect world, baked eggs are served on a plate that has the letters of the alphabet around the rim and a picture of a clown jumping over the letter X. As a side dish, buttered white toast cut up to postage-stamp size is just right, with a large glass of milk—perhaps in a jelly glass—or a cup of cocoa.

Laurie Colwin, *Home Cooking* (1988)

SHIRRED EGGS IN CLOUDS

In this preparation the egg yolk nestles in a cloud of beaten egg white. Prepare the ramekins as directed. Separate the eggs, however, and beat the whites until just stiff but still moist. Season with salt and pepper and, if you wish, fold in 1 to 2 tablespoons minced chives, parsley, chervil, or thyme. Reserving about one third of the egg white mixture, spoon the rest of it evenly into the ramekins. Make an indentation in the center of each ramekin's egg white. Gently slip a yolk into each indentation, sprinkling with a bit more salt and pepper if desired. Mound the remaining egg-white mixture equally around (but not over) the yolks, creating 4 diminutive nests. Bake the eggs for 8 to 12 minutes, depending on how firmly set you like your eggs. (They will continue to cook a bit after you remove them from the oven.) Serve immediately.

IVORY COAST BAKED EGGS

One of our favorite variations on shirred eggs comes from African roots. Mash baked yam—the true yam found in tropical produce sections rather than the sweet potato—with some milk or butter, season with salt, and spread warm, about ½ inch thick, in a shallow dish. Dust with a healthy sprinkling of dried ground red chile and drizzle with a thin glaze of palm oil (usually sold wherever you can find true yams) or melted butter. Make indentations with the spoon for the number of eggs you wish to bake, and place in a 350°F oven until cooked to your desired doneness, 8 to 12 minutes.

EGGS GOLDENROD

INGREDIENT TIP

This is one of the subtly flavored dishes where homemade butter really shines. See page 56 for our recipe.

Warmly soothing on a winter morning or a stormy evening, Eggs Goldenrod takes its name from the dusting of grated hard-boiled egg yolk over the creamy base. Also known under tags as varied as creamed eggs and egg vermicelli, the preparation appears in many major national cookbooks as far back as Fannie Farmer's original 1896 tome. It flourished particularly, it seems, in the upper Midwest, where Cheryl's mother, Betty Alters, grew up thinking of Eggs Goldenrod as one of the world's finest foods. **SERVES 4**

6 hard-boiled eggs, peeled

6 tablespoons unsalted butter (see Ingredient Tip)

3 tablespoons unbleached all-purpose flour

2½ cups whole milk

2 large egg yolks

⅛ teaspoon freshly grated nutmeg

Pinch of cayenne pepper, optional

Salt and freshly milled black pepper to taste

4 slices crisp toast

Separate the hard-boiled egg yolks from the egg whites. Dice the whites so that they are in more or less even toothsome bits, not chunky. Reserve the whites and whole yolks.

Melt the butter in a medium-size skillet over medium heat. Whisk in the flour and cook the mixture for 2 minutes. Whisk in the milk in a steady stream and cook until lightly thickened, about 5 minutes. Whisk several tablespoons of the warm mixture into the uncooked egg yolks, then whisk it back into the milk, along with the nutmeg, cayenne if desired, salt, and pepper. Simmer briefly until the sauce develops a bit more body but still pours easily from a spoon. (The dish can be made to this point up to the night before. Refrigerate the hard-boiled egg yolks and whites and the sauce, reheating the sauce before proceeding.) Stir in the hard-boiled egg whites and heat through. Arrange a piece of toast on each plate, then spoon the sauce over. Using the fine holes on a box grater, grate a shower of hard-boiled egg yolks over each plate. Serve immediately.

WAIKIKI EGGCESS

When architects in the 1980s restored the splendor of Honolulu's Moana Hotel, one of the grand dames of Waikiki, the main restaurant reopened with a selection of some dishes from its original 1901 menu. The breakfast choices included Eggs Volga, a tour-de-force preparation of poached eggs, artichoke hearts, and ham with a silky blanket of béarnaise sauce and a caviar topping. We ate it once and loved it but feared our departing plane would never get off the ground.

EGGS BENEDICT SOUFFLÉS

The bed-and-breakfast circuit offers myriad shortcut recipes inspired by Eggs Benedict. Most don't come close in flavor to the model and aren't substantially easier to make. This custardlike variation on soufflés holds its own, honoring the progenitor while staking a real claim to originality. The idea comes from Mostly Hall, a now-shuttered Cape Cod inn. **SERVES 6**

INGREDIENT TIP

Many commercial versions of English muffins taste like marshmallow bread. Traditionally toothsome, they are properly made from a soft yeast dough and then griddle-baked in rounds. English muffins should be halved before toasting, pulled apart with a fork rather than sliced with a knife, to expose more rough surface area. The best nationally available brand we've found is Wolferman's, from the Kansas City area. If you want to make your own muffins, see page 366.

SOUFFLÉS

8 large eggs

½ cup heavy (whipping) cream

1 cup grated Gruyère, Swiss, or Fontina cheese (about ¼ pound)

¾ cup minced smoky ham or Canadian bacon (about 6 ounces)

½ teaspoon dried tarragon or 2 teaspoons minced fresh chives

½ teaspoon salt

Pinch of cayenne pepper

6 English muffins, split with a fork and toasted (see Ingredient Tip)

2 recipes (about 2 cups) Hollandaise Sauce (page 32)

Fresh tarragon leaves or minced fresh chives or parsley, optional

Preheat the oven to 275°F. Butter 6 ramekins that will hold at least ¾ cup each. Cut parchment paper or wax paper circles the diameter of each ramekin and line the bottom of each.

Whisk the eggs and cream in a medium bowl until uniformly yellow. Add the cheese, ham, tarragon, salt, and cayenne. Pour the mixture into the ramekins, making sure the cheese and ham are distributed evenly. Arrange the ramekins in a larger baking dish and pour in enough warm water to come halfway up the sides of the cups. Bake uncovered for 55 to 60 minutes, until the soufflés are puffed and a thin-bladed knife inserted into the center of one comes out clean.

Remove the soufflés from the pan and run a small knife around the sides of each to loosen. (These soufflés will deflate a bit but are not as delicate as a classic version based on beaten egg whites.) Arrange an English muffin half on a warm plate and unmold the first soufflé over it. (Be sure to remove the paper if it adhered to the soufflé.) Arrange the top half of the muffin so that it is tilted partially over the soufflé like a jaunty little hat. Repeat with the additional muffins and soufflés. Top each with several generous tablespoons of sauce. Scatter tarragon over, if you wish, and serve immediately.

FARM-FRESH OMELET

TECHNIQUE TIP

With today's nonstick cookware and nonmelting rubber spatulas, it's really a breeze to have a showy and satisfying omelet on the table in minutes. Remarkably though, the results are often poor. Many omelets, especially in restaurants, are hopelessly overcooked and overloaded with ingredients. All too often, the filling and the egg are two disparate entities. Omelets are great for using up a bit of cheese here, a handful of leftover veggies there, but some thought of harmony should go into what the eggs encase, if anything at all. To end up with super results:

- Have everything ready before you start, including your guests. Omelets don't wait. While you can make only one at a time (presuming you have only one proper pan), the process goes quickly enough to serve several guests at one seating. Premeasure all the ingredients required for the number of omelets you're making and have them handy. Mix up each batch of eggs separately for the best results. Just wipe out the pan between omelets.

- We prefer to use a bit of water, rather than milk, in our egg mixture, about 1 tablespoon with two extra-large eggs per omelet. Some people prefer no extra liquid at all, especially for a rolled omelet.

- Unlike most other egg preparations, omelets should be cooked over high heat, in a

The omelet sports a French name and has European cousins such as the Italian frittata and Spanish tortilla, but Americans have adopted it with ardor. Too much ardor, perhaps, in some cases when we've filled omelets with peanut butter, grape jelly, leftover mashed potatoes, and other ingredients that would mortify a French cook. Fresh vegetables and cheese won't alarm anyone and make a much tastier filling.

SERVES 1

2 extra-large eggs

Salt and freshly milled black pepper to taste

2 tablespoons unsalted butter

1 baby leek (white and light green parts) or 2 scallions, sliced into thin half-moons

1 cup lightly packed chopped fresh spinach

¼ cup diced tomato or halved cherry tomatoes, squeezed of juice

½ cup crumbled mild creamy goat cheese or grated sharp Cheddar cheese (about 2 ounces)

Extra diced tomato or halved cherry tomatoes, a combination of red and yellow if available

Crack the eggs into a bowl and add the salt, pepper, and 1 tablespoon water. Whisk just enough to combine the yolks and whites; you should still see large bubbles. Set aside.

Warm 1 tablespoon of the butter in a 7- to 8-inch omelet pan or skillet, preferably nonstick, over medium heat. Stir in the leek and sauté until soft, about 5 minutes (scallions will take about half this time). Stir in the spinach and cook until wilted, with no watery liquid. Spoon out into a small bowl, stir in the tomatoes, and salt lightly.

Wipe out the pan. Warm it again, this time over high heat. Add the remaining tablespoon of butter, swirling to coat the entire surface thoroughly. Just when the butter begins to color, add the egg mixture and swirl it to coat the entire surface as well. Let the pan sit directly over the heat for a few seconds, until the eggs just begin to set in the bottom of the pan. Spoon the leek mixture over the egg, quickly followed by about half of the cheese. Pull the pan sharply toward you several times and then tilt the pan and use a spatula to fold the front half of the omelet over the back. Tip the omelet out onto a heatproof serving plate, neatening it with the spatula if needed.

Scatter the remaining cheese over the omelet and arrange the extra tomatoes over or on the side. Serve immediately.

pan that's hot enough to sizzle a drop of water. You have to pay close attention to the cooking, but only for a brief time. Remember that the egg will continue to cook off the heat, so remove it from the stove just before the preferred doneness.

■ Fillings should be modest in portions, cut into small pieces, and moist but not runny. Warm the filling to the temperature at which you want it to be served prior to adding it to the egg mixture. If you plan to roll the omelet rather than fold it, spoon the filling in a line from side to side, across the center of the omelet, to wrap it more easily in the egg blanket.

A BREAKFAST MENU SUGGESTION FOR A WINTER MORNING

Hominy and Milk

Broiled Pig's Feet

Baked Potatoes   Plain Omelet

Corn Bread   Toast

Rice Griddle-cakes

Maria Parloa, *Miss Parloa's Kitchen Companion* (1887)

CLASSIC CHEESE OMELET

Use any good melting cheese, about ⅓ cup finely grated, per omelet. Scatter a little additional cheese over the top before serving if you wish. We like a dash or two of Tabasco to enhance the egg mixture. You can also add up to a tablespoon of minced fresh summer savory, parsley, marjoram, or chives to either the eggs or the filling.

CHEESE AND MUSHROOM OMELET

One of our favorite variations on the Classic Cheese Omelet incorporates button mushrooms into the cheese filling. Sauté ¾ cup minced mushrooms in 1½ tablespoons butter over medium-high heat until very soft. Add salt to taste.

CHEESE OMELET WITH MESILLA VALLEY GREEN CHILE SAUCE

We like this twist on the Classic Cheese Omelet even more. Eggs and chile are a dynamic duo, particularly the green chile grown near Hatch in southern New Mexico. Make this Mesilla Valley Green Chile Sauce to serve over an omelet filled with Cheddar or Monterey Jack cheese. First warm 3 tablespoons vegetable oil in a heavy saucepan over medium heat. Add 1 large chopped onion and sauté until softened, about 5 minutes. Stir in 3 minced garlic cloves and sauté for another minute, then add 2 tablespoons flour and continue cooking for 1 to 2 minutes. Mix in 2 cups chopped roasted mild green chile, preferably New Mexican or Anaheim, fresh or frozen. Pour in 2 cups chicken stock and add a teaspoon each of salt and ground coriander. Bring the mixture to a boil, reduce the heat to a low simmer, and cook for about 15 minutes. When ready, the sauce will be thickened but still pourable. Spoon it over cheese omelets before serving and then sprinkle more grated cheese over the top. This is enough sauce for 4 to 5 omelets.

SPANISH OMELET

No more Iberian than Spanish rice, this omelet comes from the American West. Tomatoes form the core of the filling, assisted by sautéed bell peppers, onion, and, in some cases, ham, mushrooms, or a little heat in the form of fresh chile or Tabasco sauce. Homemade versions can be as delicious as some restaurant versions are dreadful. To make a basic version of the filling, warm 1 tablespoon butter in a small saucepan over medium heat, add 1 tablespoon each finely chopped onion and green or red bell pepper and cook for 1 minute. Add salt to taste and 1 cup chopped fresh or drained canned tomatoes and cook for about 5 minutes, just until the liquid is thick instead of watery. Fill the omelet with about two thirds of the mixture, saving the rest to spoon over the completed omelet before serving.

EGG-WHITE OMELET WITH VEGETABLES

If you're avoiding egg yolks for any reason, omelets can be made with just whites or with just 1 yolk to 2 or 3 whites. Whisk them together with water, salt, and pepper as directed. A pinch or two of turmeric or curry powder can add the buttery color that is lacking otherwise. You may wish to fry the omelet in safflower or other vegetable oil instead of butter. Fill it with your choice of well-sautéed vegetables. To compensate for the slight extra dryness from the loss of yolks, you may want to add a tablespoon or two of drained crumbled soft tofu.

COLUMBIA RIVER HOT-SMOKED SALMON OMELET

INGREDIENT TIP

A good mail-order source for hot-smoked salmon is Josephson's Smoke House in Astoria, Oregon (503-325-2190). The small family operation, perched at the mouth of the Columbia River, still smokes the salmon in the time-honored method over alder wood. If you have a smoker or covered grill, you can also smoke your own according to the directions on page 158.

A perfect omelette is neither greasy, burnt, nor overdone; the fire should not be too hot, as it is an object to have the whole substance heated without much browning; the perfect omelette is not thin, like a piece of fried leather, but it is thick, in order to be full and moist.

Mrs. M. E. Porter, *Mrs. Porter's New Southern Cookery Book* (1871)

Hot-smoked salmon from the Pacific Northwest—drier, smokier, and chunkier than cold-smoked nova or lox—makes a refined filling for the thinner, rolled-style omelet promoted by French-American chefs from Pierre Blot in the nineteenth century to Jacques Pépin today. The technique requires a bit more dexterity, because you scramble the egg mixture while cooking, but it becomes easy enough with practice.

SERVES 1

3 ounces hot-smoked salmon (see Ingredient Tip)

1½ ounces cream cheese, softened

1 tablespoon minced fresh chives

2 extra-large eggs

Salt to taste

⅛ teaspoon freshly milled black pepper

1 tablespoon unsalted butter

Whole fresh chives or dill sprigs, optional

In a small bowl, mix together the salmon, cream cheese, and chives. Mash the mixture enough so that some of the salmon breaks into very small bits but some texture remains.

Briefly whisk together the eggs, 1 tablespoon water, salt, and pepper just enough to combine the yolks and whites.

Over high heat, warm a 7- to 8-inch omelet pan or skillet, preferably non-stick. Add the butter to the pan, swirling to coat the entire surface. Just when the butter begins to foam, add the egg mixture and swirl it to cover the entire pan as well. With a fork, scramble the eggs rapidly as they cook, simultaneously tilting the pan back and forth so that the eggs run under and cook in multiple layers, rather than just a single mass. When the eggs firm in the bottom of the pan but are still a bit moist on top, spoon the salmon mixture across the center of the eggs. Pull the pan sharply toward you several times and then tilt the pan so that the front half of the omelet begins to roll over the back. Use a spatula to help shape the eggs into a loose cylinder. Tip the omelet out onto a warm serving plate, neatening it with the spatula if needed. Garnish with chives if you wish and serve immediately.

LOX OMELET

Cold-smoked salmon, such as lox, makes a silkier and saltier omelet filling than the hot-smoked cousin. We prefer it mixed with fried cubed potatoes and onions, just heated through, as done in exemplary fashion at the Barney Greengrass deli on Manhattan's Upper West Side. Reduce the amount of salmon to 2 ounces chopped lox and mix it with about ½ cup warm fried potatoes with onions. Eliminate the cream cheese or reduce it to a tablespoon or less.

CAPE COD SMOKED BLUEFISH OMELET

Substitute flaked smoked bluefish (or smoked mackerel) for the salmon. The more assertive flavor allows for other savory additions. Add about ½ teaspoon freshly grated or prepared horseradish as you whisk the eggs, and if you have a good lemon pepper blend, use ¼ to ½ teaspoon of it rather than the smaller amount of regular pepper.

OMELET À LA WASHINGTON

In his *Hand-Book of Practical Cookery* (1867), Pierre Blot suggested an omelet to honor the memory of George Washington. The dish featured four different four-egg omelets served on a single plate overlapping each other. He made one *au naturel* without a filling, another stuffed with apples, a third flavored with herbs, and a final version with asparagus or sorrel, depending on the season. The French immigrant said, "This omelet, or rather these omelets, were a favorite dish with the Father of his Country; they were very often served on his table when he had a grand dinner."

BURNT SUGAR–ORANGE OMELET

Our version of this omelet is modeled on one suggested by Mary Lincoln, the first director of the influential Boston Cooking School in the early 1880s. It's a little different from most because, at the end, you put it briefly under the broiler to scorch the sugar, a result Lincoln attained with a red-hot poker. Cheryl especially likes this omelet because it reminds her of a favorite Austrian college dish, Salzburger nockerln, which is something of a cross between a sweet omelet and a soufflé.

SERVES 1

1 medium orange	1 tablespoon unsalted butter
2 extra-large eggs	1 to 2 tablespoons orange marmalade
1 tablespoon confectioners' sugar	
Salt to taste	Fresh mint sprigs, optional

Peel off enough zest from the orange to measure 2 minced teaspoons. Peel off the remaining peel and pith from the orange and halve it. Squeeze 1 tablespoon of juice from one half and reserve. Slice the other half neatly between the membranes into sections and halve the sections.

Heat the broiler.

Crack the eggs into a bowl and add the orange juice, 1 teaspoon of the sugar, and the salt. Whisk just enough to combine the yolks and whites.

Over high heat, warm a 7- to 8-inch omelet pan or skillet, preferably non-stick. Add the butter to the pan, swirling to coat the entire surface thoroughly. Just when the butter begins to color, add the egg mixture and swirl it to coat the entire surface as well. Let the pan sit directly over the heat for a few seconds, until the eggs just begin to set in the bottom of the pan. Sprinkle the orange sections over it. Pull the pan sharply toward you several times and then tilt the pan and use a spatula to fold the front half of the omelet over the back. Tip the omelet out onto a heatproof serving plate, neatening it with the spatula if needed.

Sprinkle the top of the omelet evenly with the remaining sugar. Place under the broiler for about 1 minute, just until the sugar begins to melt and brown in spots. Spoon the marmalade on the side or over the omelet. Serve immediately, garnished with mint if you wish.

BURNT SUGAR–LEMON OMELET

Replace the orange with a large lemon and the orange marmalade with store-bought lemon curd.

APPLE AND CHEESE OMELET

A legendary Chicago restaurant, Lou Mitchell's, earned an enviable reputation on an omelet stuffed with apples and cheese. For a home version, prepare a basic 2-egg omelet, either rolled or folded, with about ⅓ cup finely grated medium to sharp Cheddar for the filling. Top with ½ recipe Fried Apples (page 000) and scatter more cheese over the top.

SOUFFLÉD BURNT SUGAR–ORANGE OMELET

Most any omelet can be turned into a souffléd or puffy omelet, which looks elegant and tastes lighter on the tongue. We especially like the treatment for this fancy fruit omelet.

Preheat the oven to 350°F. Separate the eggs and beat the egg whites with ⅛ teaspoon cream of tartar until just stiff. In another bowl, whisk the egg yolks with the orange juice, sugar, and salt as directed, but beat them longer, until the yolks form thick ribbons. Fold the whites into the yolks. Melt the butter in the skillet, then gently spoon or pour in the egg mixture, smoothing the top without compacting it. Cook first on the stovetop over medium-high heat just until the bottom is set and very lightly colored, 4 to 5 minutes. Top the omelet with the remaining sugar. Immediately move to the oven and bake for 8 to 10 minutes, until a thin knife inserted near the center comes out clean.

The omelet soufflé can be served flat, just inverted onto a platter, with the marmalade topping it, or can be folded over a filling of the marmalade. To serve folded, slice with a thin knife across the center from side to side, cutting into the omelet but not all the way through. Add the marmalade to either half, then use a spatula to tip one half over the other. In either case, serve immediately.

SHORT LIST OF OTHER PERSONAL FAVORITES FOR OMELET FILLINGS

- Chopped artichoke hearts with tarragon and Brie
- Louisiana red beans
- Creamy goat cheese or Taleggio with mint
- Blue cheese with toasted walnuts or crumbled bacon
- Smoked whitefish salad, capers, and chives
- Zucchini blossoms and mild Cheddar
- Fresh mozzarella with fresh sage leaves and a sprinkling of hot red pepper flakes
- Caramelized onions
- Paul Prudhomme's fried diced sweet potatoes with tasso ham

ARTICHOKE AND SPINACH FRITTATA

TECHNIQUE TIP

Unlike an omelet, a frittata can be expanded successfully to accommodate the number of diners. Plan on 1 to 2 eggs per person, depending on the amount of additional ingredients. A frittata for one or two can be made in a pan as small as 6 inches, and you can feed a group of eight from a 10- to 12-inch skillet. Frittatas cook best over medium heat and are usually started on the stovetop and finished in the oven.

At least in name, the Italian frittata reached American shores much later than the omelet. But even in the early nineteenth century, American cooks made open-face omelets in the hearth in a similar style, flavoring the dish perhaps, as Catharine Beecher suggested, with the "remnants of ham, cut fine," "sweet herbs," or "fine cut onion." Easier to make than an omelet, but just as inviting, the frittata really thrives with other choice ingredients such as Italian cheese, mushrooms, spinach, and artichoke hearts.

SERVES 6

6 large eggs

2 tablespoons milk or water

Salt and freshly milled black pepper to taste

A splash of Tabasco or other hot pepper sauce, optional

6 ounces Fontina or provolone cheese, grated (about 1½ cups)

3 tablespoons olive oil

½ pound mushrooms, thinly sliced

1 medium onion, halved and thinly sliced

¾ pound fresh spinach, chopped, or one 10-ounce package frozen spinach, thawed and squeezed dry

Two 6-ounce jars marinated artichoke hearts, drained and thinly sliced

Preheat the oven to 350°F.

In a medium bowl, whisk together the eggs, milk, salt, pepper, Tabasco, and cheese until uniformly yellow. Set aside.

Warm the oil in a 10- to 12-inch ovenproof skillet over medium heat. Add the mushrooms and sauté until they have begun to soften, about 3 minutes. Add the onion and continue cooking until both vegetables are very soft, another 5 to 7 minutes. Add the spinach and stir to combine. If using fresh spinach, cover the skillet until it wilts, about 3 minutes longer. Add the artichoke hearts, then pat the mixture down smoothly in the skillet. Reduce the heat to medium-low.

Pour the egg mixture over the vegetable mixture and stir gently in the pan. Continue heating until the bottom is set, about 3 minutes longer, lifting the edges and tilting the skillet to allow uncooked egg to flow to the bottom. Cover and transfer the skillet to the oven. Bake until set to your liking, 12 to 15 minutes. Serve hot or chilled, sliced into wedges.

MIXED MUSHROOM FRITTATA

Eliminate the onion, spinach, and artichoke hearts. Add 1 tablespoon butter to the olive oil and in it sauté 1 pound thinly sliced mushrooms, preferably a mix of portobello or cremini with chanterelle, porcini, oyster, shiitake, or button mushrooms. Use the Fontina or provolone or try Brie, Muenster, or a buttery Gouda. Add a few tablespoons of chopped ham to the mushrooms or a teaspoon of Dijon mustard to the egg mixture if you like.

BROCCOLI-CHEESE FRITTATA

Use sharp Cheddar instead of Fontina. Eliminate the olive oil, mushrooms, spinach, and artichoke hearts. Replace the olive oil with 2 tablespoons butter and sauté the onion in it. When soft, mix in 1½ to 2 cups chopped cooked broccoli. For a more substantial dish, also add ½ to 1 cup leftover cooked rice.

LOUISE STEWART'S ANTIPASTO FRITTATA

Louise Stewart at the Grant Corner Inn in Santa Fe created a popular dish by combining her favorite antipasto flavors with eggs. She mixes about 1 cup quartered artichoke hearts or bottoms with ¼ cup olive oil, 1 tablespoon red wine vinegar, and 1 minced garlic clove and lets the mixture sit for 30 minutes. Then she drains the liquid into a skillet and simmers 2 ounces slivered salami in it. The artichoke mixture then goes into the pan along with ½ cup each of black olives and peas (we skip the peas ourselves). She sprinkles 1½ cups grated mozzarella over the veggies, then pours 6 beaten eggs over it all and cooks over medium-low heat on the stovetop until set.

PASTA FRITTATA

If you like the antipasto frittata, you may love the pasta frittata, usually made in Italian-American homes with pasta left over from the night before. Mix into the eggs about 4 ounces cooked pasta per 4 eggs. We especially like long strands of linguine or spaghetti, but any variety will do. The pasta can be with or without sauce, though it shouldn't be drenched in liquid. Add a good handful of shredded mild soft cheese such as mozzarella or Fontina, then, if you wish, a couple finely grated tablespoons of a more pungent cheese such as Parmesan or pecorino. Also consider other complementary ingredients, such as minced fresh basil or oregano, slivered artichoke hearts, sautéed mushrooms, bits of bell pepper, sliced Italian sausage, or prosciutto.

SHORT LIST OF OTHER PERSONAL FAVORITES FOR FLAVORING FRITTATAS

- Asparagus tips with morels
- An armload of sorrel, simmered with a bit of water until it nearly dissolves
- Slivered artichoke hearts or bottoms with oregano or tarragon
- Eggplant chunks with red bell peppers
- Thinly sliced red waxy potatoes or mashed russets, garlic, and rosemary
- Corn kernels and diced green chile with Teleme or Monterey Jack cheese
- Zucchini, garlic, and prosciutto, bacon, or pancetta
- Butter-sautéed figs with Teleme cheese and maybe prosciutto or pancetta

RANCHO TORTILLA ESPAÑOLA

The Spanish tortilla, unlike the Mexican, is a densely layered stack of egg-enriched potatoes. In the home country, cooks often prepare it in the evening as a tapa and then might serve leftovers in the morning. In the land of egg breakfasts, American cooks usually turned the tables, making it in the morning and reserving any remnants for snacks later in the day. This version is similar to one Jacqueline Higuera McMahan's grandmother made as a California rancho staple. She kept cooked potatoes in the icebox, ready to go, and often used her own home-cured ranch olives.

SERVES 6

2 (about 1 pound) medium potatoes, preferably Yukon Gold or German Butterball

2 tablespoons olive oil

1 tablespoon unsalted butter

1 medium leek (white and light green parts), split lengthwise, cleaned well, and cut into thin half-moons

1 red bell pepper, roasted over an open flame or in the broiler, peeled, and sliced into thin strips

¼ cup Kalamata or other briny black olives, pitted and sliced

8 large eggs

Salt and freshly milled black pepper to taste

Splash or two of Tabasco or other hot pepper sauce

2 to 3 tablespoons grated Manchego or Parmesan cheese, optional

Extra virgin olive oil

Cover the potatoes with salted water and bring to a boil. Cook until just tender when pierced with a fork, about 20 minutes. (They should retain some firmness.) Drain. When cool enough to handle, peel and slice very thin. (The potatoes can be cooked a day ahead and refrigerated.)

Preheat the oven to 350°F.

Warm the olive oil in a heavy 10-inch skillet, preferably nonstick, over medium heat. Add the butter and, when melted, stir in the leek. Sauté the leek until beginning to soften, about 2 minutes. Add the potato slices and sauté until lightly colored and glistening with oil, turning them carefully to coat all of them. Stir in the bell pepper and olives and pat the mixture back down in a solid layer.

In a large bowl, whisk the eggs, a generous amount of salt and pepper, and the Tabasco until uniformly yellow. Pour the eggs over the potato mixture and let the mixture sit for about 1 minute. Then stir it up from the bottom with a spatula and pat it all back down. Sprinkle on the cheese if you wish. Cook for 2 minutes longer, then transfer the skillet to the oven.

Bake for 5 to 7 minutes, until set and beginning to pull away from the skillet's edges. Remove from the oven and drizzle a little of the extra-virgin oil around the edge, then loosen around the edge with a spatula or knife. Cool for several minutes, then slide the tortilla out onto a serving platter. Cut into wedges and serve, drizzled with a bit more oil. Serve warm or at room temperature. (Don't let it sit out, though, for a long time.) Any leftovers can be served chilled later in the day with a glass of sherry or red wine or the following day on a crusty roll, perhaps with a dollop of store-bought Romesco sauce.

THOSE WERE THE YEARS

One of the most fascinating American publications on eggs is a small pamphlet written in 1921 by the maître de cuisine at San Francisco's St. Francis Hotel, Victor Hirtzler, for the Poultry Producers of Central California. Hirtzler's *Tempting Ways to Serve Eggs* includes a shirred dish with foie gras terrine, truffles, and brown gravy, and poached eggs "Moscow," with the cooked eggs chilled, drained of yolk, refilled with caviar, and fried in "very hot swimming lard."

BASQUE PIPERRADA

Basques from the Pyrenees in northern Spain and southwestern France settled the rugged intermountain West, in a rough triangle from southern Idaho to Bakersfield, California, to southern Nevada. Mostly sheepherders, the immigrants lived an isolated frontier life that helped preserve a tradition of simple, hearty dishes such as *piperrada* or *pipérade.* Marcelino Ugalde, a specialist in Basque studies at the University of Nevada, provided the inspiration for this version, heady as usual with peppers and onions. Serve with fried potatoes.

SERVES 4 TO 6

2 green bell peppers

1 red bell pepper

3 tablespoons olive oil

4 to 6 large thin slices prosciutto, Serrano ham, or country ham (1 per serving)

1 large onion, cut into thin matchsticks

2 plump garlic cloves, minced

6 large eggs

Salt and freshly milled black pepper to taste

Preheat the broiler.

Place the peppers on a baking sheet and broil, several inches from the heat, for 10 to 15 minutes turning the peppers every few minutes, until lightly charred on all sides. Transfer the peppers to a plastic bag and set aside until cool enough to handle. Pull the skin off the peppers and discard it and the seeds. Slice peppers into ¼-inch strips, reserving their juice. (This step can be done a day ahead if you wish. Wrap and refrigerate the peppers until needed.)

Warm 1 tablespoon of the oil in a heavy 9- to 10-inch skillet over medium heat. Add the prosciutto, a couple of slices at a time. Fry until the edges just begin to crisp, turning once, about 1 minute. Keep the prosciutto warm.

Pour the remaining oil into the skillet, let it heat for a minute, then add the onion and cook until soft, about 5 minutes. Add the garlic and sauté until the vegetables are very soft and the onion begins to brown in spots, 4 to 5 minutes longer. Add the peppers and their juice and cook for another minute or until the juice has evaporated.

Whisk together the eggs and a generous amount of salt and pepper in a large bowl. When uniformly yellow, pour the eggs over the pepper mixture. Let the mixture sit for about 1 minute, then use a spatula to raise the sides of the egg mixture and let the more liquid portion run under. Continue raising the mixture and patting it back down, until lightly set, 5 to 6 minutes total. While cooked like a stovetop frittata, this is served more like a scramble. Arrange a prosciutto slice on each plate, spoon the *piperrada* over each, and serve.

RIO GRANDE EGG PUFFS

The descendants of Spanish colonial settlers in the Rio Grande Valley of northern New Mexico serve these fritters traditionally as a meatless Lenten dish. Also called *tortas* and *torrejas,* they feature a tempura-crisp surface and a soothing center that melts away in the heat of a robust chile sauce. **SERVES 6**

RIO GRANDE RED CHILE SAUCE

1 tablespoon vegetable oil

2 tablespoons minced onion

2 garlic cloves, minced

¾ cup ground dried mild red chile, preferably New Mexican, or ancho

½ teaspoon salt or more to taste

FRITTERS

6 large eggs

6 tablespoons unbleached all-purpose flour

Scant ½ teaspoon baking powder

½ teaspoon salt

Vegetable oil for panfrying

For the sauce, warm the oil in a large saucepan over medium heat. Add the onion and garlic and sauté until soft, about 3 minutes. Stir in the chile, breaking up any lumps. Gradually pour in 1 quart water, stirring to combine. Bring the sauce to a boil, then reduce the heat to a simmer. Cook for about 15 minutes, stirring occasionally, until it coats a spoon thickly. (The sauce can be made up to several days ahead, then cooled, covered, and refrigerated. Reheat before proceeding.)

Separate the eggs, placing the whites in a nonplastic mixing bowl and the yolks in a separate medium bowl. Whisk the yolks lightly, just to combine, then add the flour, baking powder, and salt.

Beat the egg whites with a mixer on high speed until they are stiff but not dry. Gently fold the yolk mixture into the whites. It's fine to have a few streaks remaining.

Heat 1 inch of oil to 375°F in a large heavy skillet or Dutch oven. Drop a large spoonful of the batter gently into the oil. Within seconds it should puff up to about double in size. Fry briefly until golden-brown and crisp, turning as needed to cook evenly. Remove with a slotted spoon and drain. Cut into the fritter to verify that it has cooked through but is still moist with a nearly melting center. Adjust the oil temperature a bit if necessary to get the desired result. Fry the remaining fritters a few at a time until all the batter is used. Spoon chile sauce on a platter and arrange the fritters over it. Serve immediately, passing any remaining sauce separately.

A BREAKFAST MENU SUGGESTION FOR LENT

Oat Meal Mush with Whipped Cream

Broiled Oysters

Beauregard Eggs

Muffins

Coffee or Chocolate

Pomegranates

Sarah Tyson Rorer,
Philadelphia Cook Book (1886)

Eggs are among the most nutritious articles of food substances. . . . Their free use cannot be too highly recommended to the delicate, to hard brain workers, and to families generally.

The Picayune's Creole Cook Book (1901)

3

Dairy Delights

FOR MOST AMERICANS,
breakfast is downright deficient
without one or more dairy
products. We want milk in our
cereal, cream in our coffee, butter
on our toast, and yogurt with our
fruit. When we're thinking
healthy, we might go for a
smoothie.

If we're inclined instead to hearty, we might opt for one of many beloved breakfast cheese dishes, which range in taste, texture, and tradition from blintzes to enchiladas.

Americans inherited their love of dairy foods from the original British settlers, who brought a solidly entrenched dairy culture from the old country. The first American cookbooks usually dwelled at length on how to process your own butter and cheese at home, skills that ranked in importance then with bread making. Cooks today generally let commercial producers do the work, but that old, elementary expertise is still the essential starting point if you want to explore the wonders of the dairy world. We cover those basics early in the chapter and then move quickly to traditional and contemporary preparations, aiming to summon the breadth of the subject without trying to milk it dry.

CREAMY COTTAGE CHEESE

Cottage cheese gained a reputation in recent decades as a bland diet food, but it actually makes a tasty morning cheese when freshly prepared. You do most of the work in advance, following the old technique of warming milk, stirring the liquid as curds begin to form—like scrambling eggs—and then draining the cheese. Eat it with fresh fruit, toast, or Heavenly Hash Browns (page 305) or in Old-Fashioned Blintzes (page 69), or make it a slightly chilled filling in a Classic Cheese Omelet (page 40). When you've got it, you'll find many ways to flaunt it.

MAKES ABOUT 4 CUPS

1 gallon whole milk

1 cup buttermilk or yogurt with active cultures

¾ teaspoon salt or more to taste

⅓ to ½ cup heavy (whipping) cream, half-and-half, or whole milk

Strawberry or other fruit preserves or minced herbs such as chives, parsley, or lovage, optional

Make sure your utensils, surfaces, and hands are scrupulously clean. Combine the milk and buttermilk in a large heavy saucepan. Warm to 115°F over medium-low heat, stirring gently every few minutes. Set aside to cool to room temperature, cover, and let the mixture stand for 22 to 24 hours, until a soft, thick custardlike curd forms. With a large thin spoon, slice through the curd from side to side in opposite directions at about ½-inch intervals. Then scoop the spoon down into the custard to about half its depth and pull it through the curd horizontally to help form the small curds common to cottage cheese. Let it sit undisturbed for 10 to 15 minutes.

Warm uncovered again over the lowest heat, bringing the mixture back, over 20 to 30 minutes, to 115°F. Hold the temperature there for another 30 to 40 minutes, so that it is heated for at least 1 hour altogether. Turn off the heat occasionally if needed to maintain the proper temperature. During this time the curds will sink and separate from the liquid whey.

Arrange 2 thicknesses of cheesecloth in a large colander, overhanging a bit on both sides. Place the colander over a large bowl or clean sink. Pour the curds and whey into the cheesecloth and let drain at room temperature for 15 minutes. With clean hands, gather the cheesecloth up around the curds and rinse the cheese (and the cloth) under cold water to eliminate more whey. Return the cheese to the colander and continue draining for another 45 minutes to 1 hour. Turn the cheese out into a bowl. Stir in the salt and as much of the cream as you wish. Chill, covered, then serve. The preserves or herbs can be mixed into the cottage cheese or sprinkled over the top if desired. The refrigerated cheese will keep for about a week.

QUESO DE CABRA

The Pilgrims made fresh goat cheese, and they may have served it at the first Thanksgiving. Around the same time Spanish settlers also brought the tradition to northern New Mexico, where it thrived in home kitchens into the middle of the twentieth century. Cooks saved liquid rennet from the stomachs of butchered goats and added it to goat milk to form curds, producing a soft, uncured *queso fresco*. We use store-bought rennet today and like to serve the cheese with flour tortillas and apple butter or a little honey, sorghum, or molasses.

MAKES APPROXIMATELY ¾ POUND

½ gallon goat's milk
(not ultrapasteurized)
(see Ingredient Tip)

4 junket rennet tablets (available
in the baking section of
supermarkets)

Make sure your utensils, surfaces, and hands are scrupulously clean. Warm the milk in a large saucepan to 110°F. If the milk gets too hot, let it cool back down to the proper temperature.

While the milk is heating, crush the rennet tablets with the back of a spoon and dissolve them in 1 tablespoon water.

When the milk reaches the proper temperature, remove it from the heat, add the rennet, and stir quickly. Then leave the pan undisturbed for 10 to 20 minutes, until the milk sets into a custardlike curd.

Line a large colander or sieve with 2 thicknesses of cheesecloth big enough to hang over the colander's edge by several inches. Set the colander over a large shallow bowl or tray—to catch the draining whey—where it can remain undisturbed for at least 4 hours and up to overnight. (The colander can be placed instead in a scrupulously clean sink for the whey to drain, but we like to keep the protein-rich liquid for use in soups and other dishes.)

Stir the now-stiff curd mixture, to break it up thoroughly, then pour or spoon it into the colander. After at least 4 hours, the cheese can be patted into a round. Wrap with the damp cheesecloth, overwrap with foil, and refrigerate. Remove about 30 minutes before you plan to serve the cheese. It will keep for several days, but plan to finish it by then.

INGREDIENT TIP

As in the recipe for homemade butter, we suggest using a dairy product that has not been ultrapasteurized, a process that heats the milk or cream to extremely high temperatures. That makes for better long-term storage, but it diminishes flavor and kills beneficial bacteria along with potentially harmful ones. Look for goat's milk that has been pasteurized, but not ultrapasteurized, in natural foods stores.

SELECTIONS FROM THE BREAKFAST MENU AT THE HESPERUS HOTEL IN MAGNOLIA, MASSACHUSETTS, 1902

Fried Deer-Foot Farm Sausage

Calves' Liver and Bacon

Baked Potatoes

Doughnuts with American Cheese

Always to make good butter or cheese shows great care and excellent judgment in the farmer's wife.

Sarah Josepha Hale, *Mrs. Hale's New Cook Book* (1857)

QUESO DE CABRA WITH DRIED APRICOTS OR MANGOES

For breakfast eating, the cheese is particularly nice with little nuggets of dried fruit embedded in it. Use ¾ to 1 cup packed dried fruit, such as apricots or mangoes, finely chopped. If the fruit is leathery, soak it for a few minutes in water or nectar. Stir it into softened cheese, then refrigerate for at least an hour for the flavor to develop.

HERBED QUESO DE CABRA

After you have patted the cheese into a round, roll it in minced fresh herbs. Dill is our favorite, but mint, oregano, and lovage are all tasty too.

HOMEMADE BUTTER

TECHNIQUE TIPS

We personally favor butter with the slight tang of lactic acid, which gives it a traditional, old-fashioned taste. Usually called *cultured butter* today, it is made in the accompanying variation with active buttermilk or yogurt cultures (acidophilus) to sour the cream. In home dairies of the past, families accumulated cream until they had enough for churning. While sitting out, the cream would sour slightly (distinctly different from spoiling) and develop more character.

Some small commercial dairies still produce butter in this style, which you can find in natural or gourmet supermarkets or can mail-order and freeze for up to six months. Vermont Butter & Cheese Company (800-884-6287 or www.vtbutterandcheeseco.com) sells luscious cultured butter.

We prefer a mixer for making whipped cream, but when we want to turn the cream into butter by design rather than accident, we use a food processor. It beats less air into the butter, leaving you less to squeeze out later.

On small family farms in the past, the women of the household usually assumed total responsibility for the vital but arduous work involved in dairy production. After milking the cows, they allowed the proverbial cream to rise to the top, separated it from the milk, and then churned it into butter, cream's highest destiny. Despite the drudgery of the labor, the ladies took enormous pride in the result. The process is much easier today with contemporary kitchen gadgets, but it still offers a satisfying sense of reward and yields a better butter than you can often buy. A couple of bites of this give real authority to the expression "crème de la crème."

MAKES ABOUT ½ POUND (1 CUP)

2 cups heavy (whipping) cream
(not ultrapasteurized)
(see Ingredient Tip, page 54)

Make sure your utensils, surfaces, and hands are scrupulously clean. Arrange a thickness of cheesecloth in a large colander, overhanging a bit on both sides. Place the colander over a bowl or plate.

Pour the cream into a food processor and process until butter forms and separates from the watery liquid (which is buttermilk), about 3 minutes. (You can drink the buttermilk or use it in baked goods or marinades.)

Scrape the butter out into the cheesecloth, then gather the cloth up at the top. Squeeze lightly, enough to release liquid from the butter, but taking care to avoid pushing the butter through the cheesecloth. Briefly rinse the cheesecloth mass under cold water, then drain and squeeze lightly again. It should release at least several more tablespoons of buttermilk. (This step is important because liquid left in the butter causes it to spoil more readily.) Use a spatula or large spoon to form the butter into a compacted mass. Refrigerate it briefly, if you wish, so that it holds its shape better. Then pack it into a crock, or mold it with a small bowl. Use the butter immediately or refrigerate tightly wrapped in foil for later use. The butter, properly worked to eliminate excess moisture, should keep for at least 5 days, or can be frozen for up to several months.

CULTURED BUTTER

You can start cultured butter from homemade crème fraîche or what Mexicans call *crema*. Stir together in a bowl the cream and 2 tablespoons buttermilk or plain natural yogurt with "active cultures." Let the mixture stand uncovered at room temperature for several hours, until it has developed a skin on the surface and perceptively thickened a bit. When tasted with a clean spoon (no fingers here!) it will have a faint hint of sourness. (It can be covered and refrigerated for a day or two, if you wish, before proceeding.) Then process as the Homemade Butter recipe directs.

HERB BUTTER

Mince ¼ cup of a single herb or a compatible combination of two or more. Good choices include parsley, cilantro, tarragon, chives, dill, sage, or lovage. Mix with ¼ pound of your own homemade butter or other softened unsalted butter and a bit of salt. Try this on Cheddar-Onion Fried Cornmeal Mush (page 256), Fresh Corn Fritters (page 99), or a simply prepared steak or chop. As with the following flavored butters, use within a few days or freeze for up to 2 months.

MUSTARD-LEMON BUTTER

Mix ¼ pound of your own homemade butter or other softened unsalted butter with 1 teaspoon Dijon mustard and ½ teaspoon dry mustard. Add a couple of teaspoons of minced lemon zest and 1 teaspoon lemon juice, or a little more to taste, along with a pinch of salt if you like. This is good with hot-smoked salmon or as a topping for Hashed Crab (page 194) or Smoked Trout Hash (page 197).

CHILE BUTTER

Mix ¼ pound of your own homemade butter or other softened unsalted butter with 1 to 2 minced fresh or pickled jalapeños or serranos or 1 tablespoon or more ground dried mild red chile along with a bit of salt. A tablespoon of minced cilantro can enhance the jalapeños, and ¼ teaspoon ground coriander adds complexity to the dried chile. Use this to top Migas (page 20), Heavenly Hash Browns (page 305), or warm tortillas.

CITRUS BUTTER

Mix ¼ pound of your own homemade butter or other softened unsalted butter with 1 tablespoon minced orange zest, 2 teaspoons orange juice or thawed frozen orange juice concentrate (undiluted), a squeeze of lemon juice, and about 1½ teaspoons sugar. Use on biscuits or buttermilk pancakes or slather on toasted Cranberry-Nut Bread (page 356).

SPICED HONEY OR MAPLE BUTTER

Mix ¼ pound of your own homemade butter or other softened unsalted butter with 3 tablespoons honey or maple syrup. Add ¼ teaspoon freshly grated nutmeg, anise, cinnamon, or a combination, and a pinch of cloves or allspice. Serve with Sweet Potato Pancakes (page 89) or Anadama Bread (page 362).

GINGER BUTTER

Mix ¼ pound of your own homemade butter or other softened unsalted butter with 3 tablespoons minced crystallized ginger and ¼ teaspoon ground ginger. It's scrumptious on English Muffins (page 366) or, if you're a real ginger fan, as a topping for Ginger Cream Scones (page 338).

STRAWBERRY BUTTER

Halve ½ pint strawberries and cut out the cottony white cores. Chop them roughly. Cook the strawberries and about 1 tablespoon sugar in a small saucepan over medium heat for approximately 5 minutes to eliminate water and concentrate the flavor. Then mix with ¼ pound of your own homemade butter or other softened unsalted butter. A couple of pinches of cardamom are great with this. Serve with Raised Waffles (page 108), Sourdough Flannel Cakes (page 90), or Flaky Buttermilk Biscuits (page 336).

CHOCOLATE OR VANILLA BUTTER

Mix ¼ pound of your own homemade butter or other softened unsalted butter with 2 tablespoons unsweetened cocoa powder, 2½ to 3 teaspoons sugar, and ¼ teaspoon pure vanilla extract. For vanilla butter, mix the same amount of butter with at least 1 teaspoon each of vanilla and sugar. The chocolate version defines decadence when paired with Chocolate Chip Pancakes (page 96), and the vanilla enhances both New Orleans Pain Perdu (page 116) and Buttermilk Breakfast Corn Bread (page 343).

BELOVED BUTTER

In Wisconsin, the land of butter, political leaders did everything they could to protect the dairy product from the encroaching popularity of margarine. Shortly after margarine's debut in the late nineteenth century, U.S. Senator Robert LaFollette called it "a monstrous product of greed and hypocrisy" and urged Congress to tax it so heavily that it would melt away. The state legislature took a stand in 1895, passing a law that stipulated fines and even jail terms for grocers and restaurateurs caught selling the substitute as the genuine article. Even as late as 1979, statutes prohibited the serving of margarine "to students, patients, or inmates of any state institution as a substitute for table butter unless ordered by a doctor."

CREAMY VANILLA BREAKFAST SPREAD

A BREAKFAST MENU
SUGGESTION USING
CREAM FROM YOUR OWN
JERSEY COW (NAMED
DORA IN THIS CASE)

Orange Juice

Very Small Crisp-Fried Orange
Lake Bream

Grits

Cornmeal Muffins

Kumquat Marmalade

Strong Coffee

Dora's Cream

Marjorie Kinnan Rawlings,
Cross Creek Cookery (1942)

You don't have to make your own butter and cheese to create something more special than standard supermarket dairy products. Grainy and soft textured, this quick spread feels like you're eating a cloud. We drop dollops over berries, top it with granola or toasted nuts, or use it in other ways as a substitute for vanilla yogurt or a creamy cheese. If you leave out the sugar, it can be drizzled generously at the table with honey, maple syrup, molasses, or cane syrup and scooped onto bread or fruit.

SERVES 4

1½ cups plain yogurt
(whole or skim milk)

1 cup ricotta cheese
(whole or skim milk)

1 teaspoon pure vanilla extract

1 to 2 teaspoons sugar or honey,
optional

Stir the ingredients together in a small bowl. Serve immediately or cover and refrigerate for up to a week.

THE GOLDEN COW

Many a sculptor can carve a cow with some authority, but no one does it quite like Duffy Lyon. Since 1960 the Iowa dairy farmer has crafted a larger-than-life-size cow out of frozen butter for the annual state fair in Des Moines. Lifelike in exquisite detail, her creations awe the million or so people attending the fair, one of the biggest and best shows of its kind in the country. Given the prominence of the dairy industry in the state, you would expect exhibits on pertinent products, of course, but few first-time visitors come prepared for something so udderly artful.

NOT-SO-PLAIN YOGURT

Like cheese, yogurt is a centuries-old method for preserving milk. It became an American counterculture favorite in the 1960s and then gained broad national acceptance in the following two decades in heavily sugared forms. The earthy tang of yogurt is a fine match for sweet seasonal fruit or good preserves, but most commercial products lack balance. We prefer to start with a fresh, unflavored version, easily made at home, and then add other elements to taste. Natural foods stores often carry packaged yogurt cultures, but the quickest and simplest way to start is with a good, basic yogurt labeled "with active cultures." The approach is similar in principle to the way cooks use sourdough starter, saved from previous dough, to make bread. Each batch develops distinctly more character. The recipe doubles easily. **MAKES APPROXIMATELY 2 CUPS**

2 cups whole milk, for best flavor, or low-fat or skim milk	¼ cup plain natural yogurt with active cultures

Make sure your utensils, surfaces, and hands are scrupulously clean. Warm the milk in a medium saucepan, bringing it just to a boil. (A full boil will likely run over the sides of the pan, so keep an eye on it.) Remove the pan from the heat and let the milk cool to about 115° F.

Meanwhile, pour very hot water into a Thermos large enough to hold at least 2 cups and let it warm briefly. Discard the water.

When the milk reaches the proper temperature, stir or whisk the yogurt into it and pour the mixture into the Thermos and cover it. Set the Thermos in a warm spot and leave it undisturbed for about 8 hours. Stir the mixture to check its consistency. If it isn't yet thick and yogurtlike, let it sit for several more hours. When ready, spoon into a bowl, cover, and refrigerate for up to a week. If you would like to make yogurt again, refrigerate ¼ cup to use within a week as the starter for the next batch.

FRUIT YOGURT

Many fruits will do, just stirred in as you wish. We're particularly fond of fig preserves, with a little fresh mint, or apricot preserves or jam. Try mixing a couple of fruits, such as the classic Melba combination of raspberries and peaches. Depending on the season, we might use both fresh, one in jam form and the other fresh, or both as cooked-down preserves.

VANILLA, ALMOND, OR MAPLE YOGURT

For vanilla or almond yogurt, add a teaspoon or a few drops, respectively, of pure vanilla or almond extract. Mix in, if you wish, a little granulated or brown sugar. Maple yogurt is simple too, with maple syrup or maple sugar combined with the yogurt to taste. Spoon the yogurt on top of pancakes and waffles, alongside maple syrup, as a foil for the richness of the syrup and cakes.

SAVORY CHIVE YOGURT

We like savory yogurts with dishes that aren't inherently sweet, such as corn cakes. You can vary proportions, but for a full herb flavor use ¼ cup minced chives to 1 cup yogurt. Other herbs can be added to complement specific dishes. For example, we might add a tablespoon of dill to top smoked or poached salmon, and thyme substitutes well with chicken or turkey hash.

YOGURT CHEESE

In the mid-1980s we came across an unfamiliar funnel contraption at the Kitchen Arts & Letters bookstore in New York. Proprietor Nach Waxman told us it was used for draining yogurt to convert it to cheese and that we would love the result. After our funnel gave out, we discovered that cheesecloth in a strainer works well. Technically, yogurt cheese is not considered a "made" cheese. Its preparation requires no heat, no rennet, and no curds for separating, which makes it no sweat as well.   **MAKES ABOUT 1 CUP**

2 cups Not-So-Plain Yogurt
(page 60) or other plain natural
yogurt with active cultures

Make sure your utensils, surfaces, and hands are scrupulously clean. Layer several thicknesses of cheesecloth in a large strainer. Place the strainer over a bowl or sink. Spoon the yogurt into the cheesecloth and let it sit at room temperature for at least 6 hours and up to overnight. When the consistency is like cream cheese, it is ready. Squeeze the cheesecloth once or twice to remove additional moisture. Use immediately or wrap and refrigerate. The cheese keeps for a week or longer.

HERBED YOGURT CHEESE

Mix savory herbs, fresh or dried, into yogurt cheese to add another dimension of zest. Flavor to taste with sage, lovage, dill, chives, or lemon thyme, for example. Among dried blends, we like zatar, a mixture of crumbled sumac leaves and other herbs and spices, which can be found in Middle Eastern markets. Serve herbed yogurt cheese with crisp baguette slices or warm pita wedges.

OLD-STYLE CREAM CHEESE

You can make a great cream cheese with the same technique, starting with sour cream rather than yogurt. Choose a sour cream made without lots of thickeners, stabilizers, and other goop you don't need. Daisy is a decent brand with national distribution.

CHUNKY VEGGIE CREAM CHEESE

Mix in ½ to 1 cup mixed vegetables to the Old-Style Cream Cheese variation. We suggest a good bit of peeled, seeded, and chopped cucumber and then other additions. Good options include grated carrot, minced celery or mild radishes, a chopped small tomato (halved and squeezed to eliminate seeds and water before chopping), and a bit of minced fresh parsley, dill, or chives. Add a little salt and either pepper or a bit of Tabasco sauce if you like. The cheese is great on a bagel or English muffin or spooned over a plain rolled omelet.

PEACHES AND CREAM CHEESE

Mix 1 to 2 pureed peaches—fresh is best, but even canned will work—into the yogurt cheese or Old-Style Cream Cheese variation. Serve alone or as a spread on thick slices of toast.

MORNING GLORIOUS YOGURT PARFAIT

Natural foods proponents have been combining yogurt with granola and fruit for half a century, but the mixture didn't win a wide audience until more recently. By the 1980s it became ubiquitous on hotel restaurant menus, where it usually lost any claim to distinction. Made with care, and the season's juiciest fruit, it offers an appealing mix of textures, flavors, and colors.

SERVES 4

2 heaping cups raspberries, blueberries, sliced bananas, sliced peaches, sliced strawberries, or a combination of 2 or 3 soft-textured bite-size fruits

1 cup plain, vanilla, or fruit-flavored yogurt

1 cup Crunchy Granola (page 263) or other granola

Minced fresh mint or mint sprigs, optional

Set aside 8 of the nicest-looking berries or fruit slices to decorate the top of each parfait.

Layer the ingredients into 4 parfait glasses or oversize wine goblets starting with the yogurt, then adding granola and berries. The specific amounts will vary a bit by the shape and size of your glasses. Make each layer thick enough that it will show through the glass attractively, but thin enough that you will be able to get at least 2 layers of each ingredient into each glass.

Top with the reserved fruit. Garnish with mint, if you like, and serve.

FRESH FRUIT SMOOTHIE

On-the-go eaters love smoothies. In addition to offering convenience and speed, they provide a painless way to get a healthy quantity of fruit into your daily diet. Choose fruit by season, but also don't hesitate to use frozen fruit in a smoothie; its icy tingle can be a plus in the drink.

SERVES 2

1½ generous cups chopped mangoes, peaches, plums, strawberries, raspberries, blueberries, watermelon, cantaloupe, or honeydew melon

1 small banana, cut into chunks

½ cup plain or fruit-flavored yogurt

½ cup skim or low-fat milk

6 ice cubes

Sugar, optional

Fresh fruit chunks and fresh mint sprigs, optional

In a blender, combine the chopped fruit, banana, yogurt, milk, and ice cubes. Puree until smooth. Add a little sugar if the drink is not as sweet as you like. Pour into tall glasses and drink up. On a leisurely morning, garnish the smoothie, if you wish, with fruit chunks on toothpicks and sprigs of mint for each glass.

MANGO LASSI

Similar to a fruit smoothie, though East Indian in origin and seasoning, mango lassi makes a superb breakfast drink, as we learned from an Indian-American child in Albuquerque. In a blender, combine 1 cup chopped ripe mango (about 1 mango), ½ cup plain yogurt, and 4 to 6 ice cubes. Puree until smooth. Check the flavor and add sugar and ground cardamom to taste. If practical, refrigerate the lassi for an hour or longer before serving. Pour into tall glasses and sprinkle with chopped pistachios if you wish.

MELON LASSI

A variation of Mango Lassi, this is made by using 1 cup chopped cantaloupe, watermelon, or honeydew in place of the mango. All are lovely in color as well as in taste. Top with chopped pistachios or a few slivered almonds.

SAVORY VEGETABLE SMOOTHIE

A smoothie doesn't have to be sweet. Start with 1 cup plain yogurt, 6 ice cubes, and a peeled, seeded, and roughly chopped cucumber to provide some of the body bananas do in a fruit version. Add a small tomato, a chopped celery stalk, a few spinach or romaine leaves, even a tablespoon or so of minced onion, as you wish, and salt and pepper to taste. Blend, garnish with a cucumber round, and enjoy.

ICY MEXICAN CHOCOLATE SMOOTHIE

INGREDIENT TIP

If you have easy access to a premier Mexican chocolate blend, such as one made by Ibarra or Mayordomo, you can substitute it for the cocoa and spices, simply combining it with the milk and yogurt. The result will be a bit grainier in texture but delightfully tasty.

This smoothie lacks some of the health appeals of its fruitier cousins, but it's just as quick and really wows chocolate fans. **SERVES 2**

1 cup milk

1 cup plain yogurt

2 tablespoons unsweetened cocoa powder (see Ingredient Tip)

1 to 2 tablespoons packed brown sugar

¼ to ½ teaspoon almond extract

¼ teaspoon pure vanilla extract, optional

¼ teaspoon ground cinnamon

1 small banana, cut into chunks

Orange slices, cinnamon sticks, or both, optional

In a blender, combine the milk, yogurt, cocoa, 1 tablespoon brown sugar, ¼ teaspoon almond extract, the vanilla if desired, and cinnamon and puree until smooth. Add the banana and blend again until well combined, adding more brown sugar and almond extract if you like. Pour into tall glasses. If you wish, garnish with orange slices, cinnamon sticks, or both.

MOCHA SMOOTHIE

Add a teaspoon or more espresso powder or up to ½ cup brewed coffee to the blend. For leisurely weekends, a splash of brandy or Kahlúa can add a special note to the smoothie.

MALTED SMOOTHIE

For a toned-down variation, perhaps more suitable for children, just blend together 1¼ cups milk, 1 large ripe banana, ¼ cup malted-milk powder, about 1 tablespoon either light or dark brown sugar, and several ice cubes.

BANANA-DATE SMOOTHIE SHAKE

A BREAKFAST MENU
SUGGESTION FOR A
SOUTHERN MORNING
PARTY

Creamed Chicken in Timbales or
on Toast

Asparagus with Butter Sauce

Olives or Pickles

Tomato Stuffed with Cucumber
and Celery on Lettuce Leaf with
Mayonnaise

Hot Rolls or Biscuits, Buttered

Iced Tea

Ice Cream   Cake

Mrs. S. R. Dull, *Southern
Cooking* (1928)

The date shake, a hallmark of southern California's desert date country, is probably America's premier milk shake. The honeyed dates, fresh or dried, mixed with ice cream, make for a splendid snack or lunch treat. Here we adapt the concept as a breakfast smoothie, still thick and rich but not nearly as heavy.

SERVES 2 TO 4

1 cup chopped pitted dates, preferably Medjool

1 cup milk

1 small banana, cut into chunks

3 cups vanilla frozen yogurt

Combine the dates and the milk in a blender. Puree until smooth but with flecks of date throughout. Add the banana and yogurt, and puree again until smooth. Pour into tall glasses and serve with iced-tea spoons.

CHERRY-VANILLA SMOOTHIE SHAKE

Substitute dried cherries (no need to chop) for the dates and add ½ teaspoon pure vanilla extract. If the cherries are particularly tangy, you may want to blend in a tablespoon of sugar or more to taste.

BUTTERMILK WITH CRUMBLIN'S

Milk, being a complete food, is not a beverage, and should not be used as such . . . Milk is not easy of digestion unless sipped slowly or masticated, as it were. When poured down the throat like a glass of water it enters the stomach in a mass, is coagulated by the ferment, *rennin.* It is then separated into curds and whey by the muscular action or churning of the stomach. It is finally rolled into a hard ball, which is difficult of digestion from its very density.

Sarah Tyson Rorer, *Mrs. Rorer's New Cook Book* (1902)

A frosty glass of buttermilk, laced with crumbled buttermilk corn bread, is a southern classic, enjoyed in both the morning and the evening. No longer a by-product of butter churning, today's commercial buttermilk is a cultured skim or low-fat milk, but it remains thick, tangy, and refreshing. Our colleague John T. Edge, director of the Southern Foodways Alliance in Oxford, Mississippi, has a Yankee friend who christened this a "hillbilly smoothie." We like a slice of cantaloupe on the side.   SERVES 1

About 1½ cups buttermilk, well chilled

1 fist-size square of corn bread, preferably buttermilk corn bread such as Buttermilk Breakfast Corn Bread (page 343)

Pour the buttermilk into an oversize tumbler. Crumble the corn bread into the glass and stir with a long-handled iced-tea spoon. Sip, spoon, and swoon.

CHEESE BLINTZES WITH BERRY SAUCE

Blintzes and other dairy dishes such as cheesecakes are traditionally served at the Jewish Shavuot, a late spring harvest festival that celebrates the giving of the Torah at Mount Sinai. Today every Jewish-American mother and grandmother seems to have a slightly different way of making the thin crepelike pancakes with a creamy filling. Originally stuffed in Russia and Poland with simple farmer, pot, or hoop cheese, blintzes began to get richer and more extravagant as immigrants prospered in the United States. Unfortunately—as with the bagel—the quality of the dish suffered as it gained mainstream popularity, particularly in the frozen versions now featured at breakfast buffets across the country. Made from scratch, however, with a combination of good cheeses and a luscious fruit sauce, blintzes remain delicately sublime. The egg in the blintz filling may not cook through entirely in the recipe's brief sautéing time. If this is of concern, you may want to prepare the baked Cheese Blintz Casserole instead (page 70). **SERVES 6**

FILLING

Two 8-ounce packages farmer or pot cheese

½ pound ricotta cheese (preferably whole milk)

½ pound cream cheese, softened, or sour cream

3 tablespoons sugar

2 large eggs

¼ teaspoon pure vanilla extract

¼ teaspoon salt

BERRY SAUCE

3 cups blueberries, raspberries, blackberries, sliced strawberries, or other berries

½ cup fresh or reconstituted frozen orange juice

2 to 4 tablespoons sugar

½ teaspoon pure vanilla extract, optional

BLINTZ BATTER

1 cup unbleached all-purpose flour

2 tablespoons sugar

Pinch of salt

3 large eggs

1 cup milk

4 tablespoons (½ stick) unsalted butter, melted

¾ teaspoon pure vanilla extract

Unsalted butter for panfrying

TECHNIQUE TIP

While a selection of good cheeses is much more readily available today than in the past, even in small-town supermarkets, we think it continues to be important to stay in touch with a premier cheese shop. Some of our favorite mail-order sources—all worth a visit when you're in the vicinity— include Zingerman's in Ann Arbor, Michigan (734-332-4946), Formaggio Kitchen in Boston (617-354-4750), Murray's (212-243-3289) and Balducci's (212-673-2600) in New York, and the small but remarkable Artisan Cheese in San Francisco (415-929-8610).

Prepare the filling, the day before if you wish, stirring the ingredients together in a large bowl. Cover and refrigerate if not using shortly.

Prepare the berry sauce, also the day before if you wish. In a small saucepan, combine half the berries with ½ cup water, the orange juice, 2 tablespoons sugar, and the vanilla if desired. Simmer over medium heat briefly, until the berries dissolve into the sauce. Add the remaining berries and heat through. Taste and add more sugar if you wish. Keep warm if using shortly, or cool, cover, and refrigerate for later use, reheating before serving.

Prepare the batter, first combining the flour, sugar, and salt in a food processor. Process, then add the remaining batter ingredients and process again until smooth.

Heat an 8-inch skillet or omelet or crepe pan, preferably nonstick, until a drop of water bounces and sizzles briefly before evaporating. Add about 1 teaspoon butter and swirl it around to coat the skillet. Quickly add 2 tablespoons batter and swirl it around until the skillet is coated. Cook until the batter dries on the surface, about 30 seconds. Then flip the blintz and cook the other side for about 15 seconds, until faintly golden. (Blintzes should not brown.) Repeat for the remaining blintzes, adding more butter as needed to prevent sticking. We stack them on a plate with paper towels or wax paper between them, to separate them more easily, though many people don't bother with this step.

When all of the blintz batter is cooked, spoon 2 to 3 tablespoons filling on the lower third of the first blintz. Fold up the bottom, turn in the sides, and then fold over snugly but not tightly. Repeat with the remaining blintzes.

Melt 2 tablespoons butter in a skillet over medium-low heat. Arrange several blintzes at a time in the skillet, starting seam side down, and sauté until faintly brown and a bit crisp on both sides, about 5 minutes total. Repeat with the remaining blintzes and serve with the fruit sauce.

OLD-FASHIONED BLINTZES

For the filling, eliminate the ricotta and cream cheeses. Use a full 2 pounds farmer, pot, or hoop cheese or drained cottage cheese. For complete authenticity, make the blintzes with your homemade Creamy Cottage Cheese (page 53).

EMBELLISHED BLINTZ BATTER

Add up to ½ teaspoon ground cinnamon or ¼ teaspoon freshly grated nutmeg to the batter. Some cooks use up to twice as much melted butter in the batter as we do.

APPLE-TOPPED BLINTZES

Sautéed apples are our favorite alternative to a fruit sauce on blintzes. Slice 3 to 4 cooking apples, such as Rome Beauty, McIntosh, or Jonagold, and cook them over medium heat until just soft in 4 tablespoons (½ stick) butter, then add 3 to 4 tablespoons granulated or brown sugar and continue cooking until very soft and golden. Add a dusting of cinnamon if you wish. In Oregon, we've seen a handful of cranberries added to the apples for a beautiful crimson-studded fall topping.

CHEESE BLINTZ CASSEROLE

As scrumptious as blintzes can be, they do take a little time to prepare in traditional ways. Contemporary Jewish cooks have developed quicker casserole alternatives, such as this version modeled on one from Gloria Kaufer Greene, author of *The New Jewish Holiday Cookbook* (1999). Rather than start from frozen packaged blintzes, as many recipes suggest, she tweaks the batter and cooking process. You'll use the preceding filling and can crown the casserole with the berry sauce or with fresh strawberries or applesauce. To make the blintz batter, combine in a food processor 1⅓ cups flour, 2 tablespoons sugar, 1¼ teaspoons baking powder, and ¼ teaspoon salt. Process, then add 4 large eggs, 1¼ cups milk, 4 tablespoons (½ stick) unsalted butter, 2 tablespoons sour cream, and 1 teaspoon pure vanilla extract and process again until smooth. Measure out 1½ cups batter and pour it into a buttered 9 x 13-inch baking dish. Bake at 350°F for 9 to 11 minutes, until just set. Remove from the oven, spoon the filling over it in large dollops, and smooth the surface. Give the remaining batter a quick stir, then pour it evenly over the filling. Return it to the oven and bake for 35 to 40 minutes longer, until the top is puffed and lightly colored in spots. It may crack in a few areas. Cool for at least 10 minutes (it will deflate), then serve with large spoonfuls of sour cream and the berry sauce. Leftovers will keep for a couple of days, but we prefer them chilled rather than reheated.

LBJ'S CHEESE BLINTZES

Lyndon Johnson's culinary tastes generally ran toward Texas barbecue and chili, but he also loved cheese blintzes, especially those made by Secretary of Defense Robert McNamara's wife. Since food intended for a president has to go through official channels, McNamara usually gave the blintzes to Liz Carpenter, Lady Bird's spunky aide who never met a rule worth abiding. In a hurry one day, the secretary simply dropped off the dish with a Secret Service agent, who had it destroyed per regulations. A furious Johnson cursed the agent and promptly ordered the Secret Service to leave his food alone.

CHARLESTON CHEESE PUDDING

Sarah Rutledge featured a similar French-inspired cheese soufflé in *The Carolina Housewife* (1847), a seminal nineteenth-century cookbook. The dish evolved in later Charleston cookbooks into a heftier strata, with bread rather than egg whites providing volume, but we prefer the earlier, more ethereal version. To balance the richness, add a side of something tangy, such as Fried Green Tomatoes (page 319) or Green Tomato–Mint Chutney (page 414).

SERVES 4 TO 6

5 tablespoons unsalted butter	4 large eggs, separated
1/3 cup dried bread crumbs	1/2 pound sharp Cheddar cheese, grated (about 2 cups)
1/4 cup unbleached all-purpose flour	
	1/2 teaspoon salt or more to taste
1 cup whole milk	1/4 teaspoon dried thyme
1/2 cup half-and-half	Pinch or two of cayenne pepper

Preheat the oven to 375°F. Butter a 1½-quart soufflé dish or other baking dish with relatively straight and high sides.

Melt 1 tablespoon of the butter in a small skillet over medium heat. Stir in the bread crumbs and sauté them until golden and crisp, about 5 minutes. Scatter the crumbs around the bottom and sides of the soufflé dish, then shake out any crumbs that don't stick and discard them.

Melt the remaining butter in a medium saucepan over medium heat. Whisk in the flour, combining well, then slowly pour in the milk and half-and-half. When combined, whisk several tablespoons of the warm milk mixture into the egg yolks, then pour the egg yolks into the milk mixture. Continue whisking occasionally, allowing the mixture to thicken. Mix in the cheese, salt, thyme, and cayenne pepper and remove from the heat. Stir until the cheese is nearly melted. The mixture should be rather stiff and assertively seasoned.

Quickly beat the egg whites until just stiff but not dry and then fold them into the cheese mixture. Spoon the mixture into the prepared dish. Bake for 30 to 35 minutes, until well risen, medium-brown, a bit dry looking on the surface, and set, with just a touch of remaining jiggle. Serve immediately.

CHARLESTON CHEESE PUDDING WITH EMERALD SAUCE

The vivid green of this pestolike sauce contrasts smartly with the golden soufflé. Chop 1 cup parsley leaves and ½ cup arugula leaves in a food processor with 2 tablespoons pine nuts, 1 garlic clove, and about ¼ teaspoon salt. With the motor running, slowly pour in ½ cup olive oil, processing until a thick sauce forms. Use the sauce within a few hours for the brightest taste and color.

Light, airy soufflés can be showstoppers, puffed up and a bit dry on the surface, silky and moist underneath. With attention to a few guidelines, they're not as challenging as their reputation suggests.

- Cook it in a proper dish, either one made for soufflés or a baking dish of similar size with straight sides.
- Always flavor the base mixture well, because the egg whites will dilute the intensity.
- Beat the egg whites until stiff peaks form, but only until that moment. They should remain creamy looking, not dry.
- A soufflé is most fragile during the first half of the baking, when the egg white structure is still setting. Avoid opening the oven during that time. You can peek in near the end of the cooking to check progress, but avoid jostling the dish or slamming the oven door.
- Make sure your oven racks have enough clearance for a soufflé to rise at least a couple of inches above the rim of the baking dish. If needed, remove an upper rack before beginning.
- Remove a soufflé from the oven when it still jiggles the slightest bit at the center, then serve immediately. It will deflate as it cools, losing visual appeal but retaining most of the texture.

BISHOP HILL COTTAGE CHEESE PUDDING

Mildly sweet and profoundly soothing, this is something of a cross in texture and flavor between rice pudding and cheesecake. In dairy-rich Sweden, cooks make the dessert dish *ost kaka* with a fresh cheese curd from milk mixed with flour and enriched with eggs. Immigrants to the Bishop Hill area of western Illinois streamlined the preparation over time with commercially available cottage cheese and began eating it at breakfast as well as other meals. The pudding is often accompanied by a berry sauce or a fruit jam, but as with a great cheesecake, the fruit is an embellishment, not a requirement. It halves well for a smaller group, or leftovers can be refrigerated and served chilled later.   **SERVES 8**

3 cups cottage cheese, not nonfat

¼ cup unbleached all-purpose flour

¼ cup half-and-half

¼ teaspoon salt

¼ teaspoon pure almond extract

¼ teaspoon ground cardamom

4 large eggs

¾ cup sugar

Ground cinnamon

Preheat the oven to 375°F. Butter a 9- to 10-inch round baking dish.

Mix the cottage cheese, flour, half-and-half, salt, almond extract, and cardamom in a medium bowl. Beat the eggs in a mixing bowl until foamy, then add the sugar and beat until thick ribbons form. Spoon the cheese mixture into the eggs and beat just to combine. Spoon into the prepared dish, smooth the surface, and sprinkle cinnamon lightly over the top. Place the dish in a larger dish of warm water. Bake for 20 minutes, reduce the oven temperature to 300°F, and continue baking until lightly set and golden brown, and a knife inserted in the center comes out clean, about 40 minutes longer. Serve warm, spooned from the baking dish, with an additional dusting of cinnamon if you wish.

AN AMERICAN ORIGINAL

The first American cookbook to cover breakfast extensively as a meal on its own appeared at the time of the Civil War. In *Breakfast, Dinner, and Tea: Viewed Classically, Poetically, and Practically* (1865), Julie Andrews took an erudite but hearty approach to morning food. Her eight chapters on the subject ranged from "Bread" to "Butter" and "Coffee, Cocoa, and Chocolate" to "Meat, Fish, and Omelettes." Between the recipes she interspersed verse, history, quotations, and notes on famous people and foreign dishes.

CREAMY SILVER DOLLAR CHEESE CAKES

INGREDIENT TIP

Quark, a cheese that originated in Germany, is made from uncooked cow's milk curds with yogurt and buttermilk cultures. That, coupled with the quirky name, might sound unpromising to some people, but to our tastes it's a winning combination of sour cream, cream cheese, and yogurt flavors. In texture it reminds us of a cross between sour cream and ricotta, a little like cottage cheese without the accompanying milky liquid. You can find Quark at natural foods stores or other stores with extensive cheese sections.

Closer to a pancake in appearance than a New York cheesecake, these delicate and diminutive cakes pop up regularly in dairy-rich states from Vermont to California. Chock full of dairy products loosely bound by just enough flour to hold them together, they are lightly crispy on the surface and meltingly creamy inside. We accompany the cakes with applesauce, avoiding heavy flavorings such as maple syrup or blintz sauce that compromise the subtlety of the cakes' flavor.

SERVES 4

1 cup cottage cheese, drained

⅔ cup Quark, sour cream, or Yogurt Cheese (page 62)(see Ingredient Tip)

2 large eggs

1 tablespoon unsalted butter, melted

3 tablespoons unbleached all-purpose flour

Pinch of salt

Vegetable oil for panfrying

Boiled Cider Applesauce (page 276) or other applesauce, warmed

Whisk the cottage cheese, Quark, and eggs together in a medium bowl. Add the butter, flour, and salt and stir until well combined.

Warm a griddle or a large heavy skillet over medium heat. Pour a thin film of oil on the griddle. Spoon the batter, 1 generous tablespoon at a time, onto the hot griddle, where it should sizzle just a bit. If it splatters and pops, the surface is too hot and the cakes will disintegrate. Make as many cakes at a time as you can fit without crowding. Cook the cakes for about 2 minutes, until golden on the bottom and lightly firm. (If a cake begins to pull apart when moved, it hasn't cooked quite long enough. Give it another 30 seconds and try again.) Turn gently. Cook for 1 to 2 minutes on the second side, until golden.

Lay the little cakes side by side on plates, rather than stacked, to keep the surfaces crisp. Serve hot, with applesauce on the side.

STACKED REDS SUNNY SIDE UP

Like many hearty morning dishes, cheese enchiladas probably reached the breakfast table originally as leftovers from the night before. Cooks simply placed a fried egg on top and called it breakfast food. The result is so good that many southwesterners now make their enchiladas fresh for the morning. Drenched in a red chile sauce, this rendition features stacked rather than rolled tortillas, which speeds up the preparation. You can make the chile sauce up to a week ahead to serve at least six and then multiply the rest of the recipe by the number of diners.

SERVES 1 HEARTILY

SELECTIONS FROM THE BREAKFAST MENU ON THE SS *GEORGE WASHINGTON,* 1921

Rice or Oatmeal with Milk

Scrambled Eggs with Asparagus Tips

Hamburg Beef Steak with Onions

Dutch Cheese

RED CHILE SAUCE (MAKES 4½ CUPS)

2 tablespoons vegetable oil

1 medium onion, minced

3 garlic cloves, minced

¾ cup ground dried mild red chile, such as New Mexican, ancho, or guajillo

1 quart water, chicken stock, or beef stock

1 teaspoon dried oregano, preferably Mexican

1 teaspoon salt

ENCHILADA

Vegetable oil for panfrying

3 corn tortillas, blue if available

2 teaspoons minced onion

¾ cup Red Chile Sauce, warmed

¼ pound mild Cheddar or Monterey Jack cheese or a combination, grated (about 1 cup)

1 large egg, fried sunny side up or over easy

Prepare the sauce, first warming the oil in a heavy saucepan over medium heat. Add the onion and garlic and sauté until the onion is limp. Stir in the chile and then the water, a cup at a time. Add the oregano and salt and bring the sauce just to a boil. Reduce the heat to a bare simmer and cook for 20 to 25 minutes. The completed sauce should coat a spoon thickly but still drop away from it easily. Use warm, refrigerate covered for up to a week, or freeze for later use.

Prepare the enchilada, first preheating the broiler. Warm ½ to 1 inch of oil in a small skillet until the oil ripples. With tongs, dunk a tortilla in the oil long enough for it to turn limp, a matter of seconds. Don't let the tortilla crisp. Repeat with the remaining tortillas and drain them.

On an ovenproof plate, layer the first tortilla with half of the onion and one third of the chile sauce and cheese. Repeat for the second layer. Top with the third tortilla, then add the remaining chile sauce and sprinkle the rest of the cheese over all.

Broil the enchilada until the cheese melts. Arrange the egg on top of the enchilada. Serve hot.

STACKED GREEN CHILE–CHICKEN ENCHILADAS SUNNY SIDE UP

Add ½ cup cooked shredded chicken to the filling, layering it on top of the first and second tortillas, before you sprinkle on the onion. Replace the Red Chile Sauce with Mesilla Valley Green Chile Sauce (page 40).

Breakfast should be the most cheerful event of the day. The dining room should be in order. If used as a sitting room through the evening, ask the family to pick up the games, newspapers, ash trays, etc., before retiring. . . . Use gaily embroidered linen, a checked gingham breakfast cloth and napkins, or possibly decorated oilcloth doilies, which give a cheerful note.

Ida Bailey Allen, *Mrs. Allen's Modern Cook Book* (1935)

WARM PANELA CHEESE WITH DIABLO BREAKFAST SALSA

We discovered the model for this dish at a cheery Mexican café in Los Angeles, Guelaguetza, an outpost of Oaxacan coking in the middle of Koreatown. Like a handful of other cheeses prized for their refusal to melt, mild Mexican panela retains its shape and solidity when heated. As a breakfast specialty, Guelaguetza serves a local variation of this cheese topped with a warm, spicy chile sauce. Among our personal favorites in the book, this is a dish for people who want to leap into the day with gusto. Accompany it perhaps with black beans.

SERVES 4

DIABLO BREAKFAST SALSA

3 to 4 small to medium tomatoes, preferably Roma or plum

6 plump garlic cloves, dry-roasted in a skillet until soft

2 tablespoons dried ground mild red chile, such as ancho, New Mexican, or guajillo

1 to 2 teaspoons ground pasilla de Oaxaca chile or 1 to 2 canned chipotle chiles

½ teaspoon dried oregano, preferably Mexican

½ teaspoon minced fresh epazote or ¼ teaspoon dried, optional

2 whole allspice or ¼ teaspoon ground

2 cups chicken or vegetable stock

¼ cup vegetable oil

Salt to taste

Vegetable oil for panfrying

1 medium onion cut from end to end into thin wedges

1 pound panela cheese, cut into 8 equal rectangles, preferably about ¼ to ½ inch thick, at room temperature (see Ingredient Tip)

Minced fresh cilantro, optional

Prepare the salsa up to a couple of days before you plan to serve the cheese. Preheat the broiler. Place the tomatoes on a small baking sheet, covered with foil for easier cleaning. Broil the tomatoes for 15 to 18 minutes, turning them occasionally, until they are soft and the skins split and turn dark in spots.

Puree the tomatoes (skins, cores, and all) with the garlic, both kinds of chile, oregano, epazote, allspice, and stock in a blender. In a heavy skillet or large saucepan, warm the oil over high heat. Pour in the sauce, being careful to avoid splatters as the liquid hits the hot oil. When the mixture stops its most insistent sputtering, reduce the heat to medium-low and simmer for about 15 minutes, until the sauce thickens but still spoons easily. Salt the sauce, then reserve it or cool, cover, and refrigerate for later use, warming again before serving.

A BREAKFAST MENU

SUGGESTION FROM

FANNIE FARMER

Raspberries

Shredded Wheat Biscuit

Dried Smoked Beef in Cream

Hashed Brown Potatoes

Baking-Powder Biscuit

Coffee

Fannie Merritt Farmer, *The Boston Cooking-School Cook Book* (1896)

Coat a heavy skillet, large enough to hold the cheese in a single layer, with a thin film of oil. (If you lack a large enough skillet, cook the onion and half the cheese together, then keep warm while you add a bit more oil to the skillet and cook the remaining cheese.) Warm over medium heat and add the onion wedges, sautéing until soft, about 5 minutes. Push the onion to one side, add the cheese, and cook for about 2 minutes per side, until golden and a bit crusted in spots.

Spoon a pool of sauce onto each plate, then top with equal portions of hot cheese, onion, and, if you wish, a sprinkling of cilantro. Serve immediately.

BREAKFAST QUESO RANCHERO

In south Texas you sometimes find a closely related dish made with a melted cheese—"skillet-fried" mozzarella or asadero—topped with a simpler roasted tomato–based salsa. Leave the epazote and allspice out of the salsa. Cut the cheese into similar-size blocks and fry the same way, though the result will be a creamy melting mass. Add a hefty spoonful of creamy long-cooked pinto beans, if you like, and serve scooped onto big flour tortillas.

SWEET FRIED RICOTTA

**A BREAKFAST MENU
SUGGESTION FROM AN
ARAB-AMERICAN CHARITY**

Variety of Cheese

Olives

Baladi Bread

Coffee or Tea

NAJDA, *Arabic Cook Book*
(1961)

South Carolina food authority Hoppin' John Taylor came across this idea while living in Italy but adapted it to a southern style reminiscent of hushpuppies. In addition to a breakfast treat, the crispy nuggets make a great late-afternoon snack with a glass of Marsala.   **SERVES 4 OR MORE**

2 cups ricotta cheese, preferably whole milk

2 tablespoons superfine or granulated sugar

1 generous teaspoon grated lemon zest

1 teaspoon pure vanilla extract

1 teaspoon ground cinnamon

3 tablespoons self-rising flour or 3 tablespoons unbleached all-purpose flour mixed with ¼ teaspoon baking powder and a pinch of salt

Peanut oil or other vegetable oil for deep-frying

Confectioners' sugar or honey

Mix the ricotta, sugar, lemon zest, vanilla, and cinnamon in a medium bowl. Add the flour, a few teaspoons at a time, stirring to make a stiff dough.

Pour 2 inches of oil into a heavy high-sided skillet or Dutch oven. Heat to 365°F. Line a baking sheet with paper towels and place it near the stove.

Form the dough into tablespoon-size nuggets and fry them, a handful at a time, until golden brown, about 4 minutes. Remove with tongs or a slotted spoon and drain on the paper towels. Dust the hot fritters with confectioners' sugar or drizzle honey over them and serve immediately.

SWEET FRIED MIXED-CHEESE FRITTERS

Replace ¾ cup of the ricotta with store-bought creamy fresh goat cheese or your own Queso de Cabra (page 54). The goat cheese should be very soft and crumbled or mashed before you begin to mix it with the ricotta and other ingredients.

RINKTUM TIDDY

When British rarebit jumped the Atlantic to our eastern seaboard, New World tomatoes generally replaced Old World ale as the liquid in the Cheddar-based dish. The name changed too, becoming alternatively Rum Tum Tiddy, Ring Tum Ditty, and Blushing Bunny, the latter based on the "rabbit" misspelling of "rarebit." This doesn't keep well, but the recipe halves easily. Accompany it with crisp bacon or ham slices or, in late summer, with fresh tomato slices.

SERVES 4

3 tablespoons unsalted butter

1 tablespoon unbleached all-purpose flour

1 teaspoon dry mustard

One 14- to 15-ounce can diced or chopped tomatoes, pureed, or 1½ cups tomato juice

2 teaspoons Worcestershire sauce

Pinch of sugar, optional

2½ heaping cups grated sharp Cheddar cheese (about 12 ounces)

Salt and freshly milled black pepper to taste

4 slices toast made from good white bread, cut in half on the diagonal

Minced fresh chives or thinly sliced scallion greens, optional

Melt the butter in a heavy saucepan over medium-low heat. Stir in the flour and mustard and cook for 2 minutes, stirring occasionally. Whisk in the tomatoes, Worcestershire sauce, and the sugar if you feel the tomatoes could use a little perking up. Heat the mixture through, cooking for a couple of minutes longer. Whisk in the cheese, a handful at a time, until completely melted. Divide the toast among the plates, then spoon the cheese sauce over each. Sprinkle with chives if you wish and serve immediately.

TOMATO TOAST

Simply leave out the cheese and you have another classic. Tomato toast in this quantity will serve two, so eliminate two of the toast slices. This is the Yankee equivalent of southern Tomato Gravy (page 317).

4

Pancakes, Waffles, and Special Toasts

SOMETIMES LOVE is in a name. That's the case with flapjacks, slapjacks, flannel cakes, feather cakes, flatcars, and heavenly hots, just a few of the admiring American tags for the unpretentious pancake.

We certainly didn't invent the dish, which is at least as old as the Roman Empire, but we invested it with the power of poetry and gave it an unprecedented place at the center of our breakfast table.

Like waffles and French toast, also Old World creations, pancakes found favor in Europe originally as lunch, supper, or special-occasion foods. They became associated particularly with Shrove Tuesday, the last day before Lent, when they represented the culinary delights to be denied over the following forty days. Fully aware of this custom, early American colonists regarded pancakes and waffles as something of a treat, a perspective that may have helped to spark our love affair initially. After we heightened the pleasure with sweet local syrups and added a side of salty pork for contrast, we had a meal worthy of daily indulgence. Anything that good Americans turn into breakfast fare.

BUTTERMILK PANCAKES WITH BLUEBERRY SAUCE

TECHNIQUE TIP

In making any pancakes, we find the following guidelines helpful:

- When you use baking powder or soda for leavening, avoid mixing the batter too thoroughly. Slight streaks of dry ingredients should remain visible. If you will be adding beaten egg whites to the mixture, begin that process when there are still large streaks of uncombined flour. By the time you fold in the whites, the mixture will be perfect.
- Cook pancakes on a griddle, preferably, or in a large heavy skillet. A sturdy nonstick surface or well-seasoned cast iron works best.
- Cook in the thinnest film of oil and replenish it between batches. Pancakes should sizzle and hiss when they hit the griddle or skillet. For a pretest, flick a few drops of water over the hot cooking surface, adjusting the temperature until they sizzle and evaporate instantly.
- Butter and syrup served with pancakes should be at room temperature or, in the case of syrup, heated in advance.
- Pancake batters can usually do double duty as waffle batters. We like to add a couple of extra tablespoons of melted butter to the batter to ensure a crisp crust.

The favorite of many contemporary cooks, this pancake uses buttermilk for its light tang and browning abilities. We like to add a little cornmeal for crunch as well, an approach Mary Cornelius suggested as far back as 1856 in *The Young Housekeeper's Friend*. Blueberries make a natural mate for the cake, but instead of introducing them in a customary filling, we intensify their flavor contribution in a robust fruit sauce. For the sauce we love to use tiny lowbush blueberries, midsummer jewels from Maine and other parts of New England, but start with any good berries available to you.   **SERVES 4 OR MORE**

FRUIT SAUCE

3 cups blueberries or huckleberries, fresh or frozen

2 to 4 tablespoons sugar

Fresh lemon juice to taste

PANCAKES

1½ cups unbleached all-purpose flour

¼ cup stone-ground cornmeal

1 teaspoon baking soda

½ teaspoon salt

2 tablespoons unsalted butter, melted

1 large egg, separated

1¾ to 2 cups buttermilk

Vegetable oil for panfrying

1 to 2 teaspoons bacon drippings, optional

Unsalted butter, softened

Prepare the sauce, combining the blueberries, 2 tablespoons of the sugar, and ¼ cup water in a medium saucepan. Bring the mixture to a simmer over medium-high heat. Cook until the sugar melts into a syrup and the fruit is soft, 5 to 10 minutes. Taste the sauce. Add 1 to 2 tablespoons more sugar if needed to fortify the fruit flavor, dissolving the sugar into the sauce before removing the pan from the heat. Stir in a few drops of lemon juice, just enough to balance and brighten the fruitiness. Keep the sauce warm.

Prepare the pancakes, stirring the flour, cornmeal, baking soda, and salt together in a medium bowl, preferably one with a spout for pouring. Scrape in the melted butter and stir the mixture until the butter disappears into the dry ingredients.

Beat the egg white until soft peaks form and reserve it.

In another bowl, whisk together the egg yolk with 1¾ cups of the buttermilk until frothy. Pour this into the dry ingredients and mix until well combined. If the batter doesn't seem easily pourable, add up to the remaining ¼ cup of buttermilk. Fold the egg white into the batter.

Warm a griddle or a large heavy skillet over medium heat. Pour a thin film of oil onto the griddle. If you wish, add ¼ to ½ teaspoon of bacon drippings to the oil for a heartier flavor. Pour or spoon out the batter onto the hot griddle, where it should sizzle and hiss. A generous 3 tablespoons of batter will make a 4-inch pancake. Make as many cakes at a time as you can fit without crowding.

Cook the pancakes until their top surface is covered with tiny bubbles but before all the bubbles pop, 1 to 2 minutes. Flip the pancakes and cook until the second side is golden brown, 1 to 2 minutes longer. Repeat with the remaining batter, adding to the griddle as needed a bit more oil and bacon drippings if desired.

Serve immediately with butter and the fruit sauce.

EXTRA-TENDER BUTTERMILK PANCAKES

Replace ¼ cup wheat flour with an equal amount of rice flour. Since it has no gluten, it makes for even more tender cakes. Make them a bit smaller in size for easiest handling.

DOUBLE-BLUEBERRY BUTTERMILK PANCAKES

If they're in season, and you're buried in berries, add about 1 cup berries to the pancakes themselves. Don't mix them into the batter, but instead sprinkle a tablespoon or so over each pancake as it begins to cook. That way you prevent all the batter from turning blue.

SILVER DOLLAR PANCAKES

Small pancakes seem to fascinate children. Just reduce the size by using only 1 tablespoon batter per cake. Cook them a bit more briefly but in big batches.

PIGS IN BLANKETS

For this staple of pancake houses, wrap warm buttermilk cakes around fried link sausages, serving two or three of the burritolike rolls to each diner. Applesauce or sautéed apples taste better on the side than a blueberry sauce.

CITRUS BUTTERMILKS

For extra tang, add 2 teaspoons grated lemon zest and 2 tablespoons of lemon juice to the pancake batter. Orange also works well, using 1 tablespoon grated zest and 3 tablespoons juice. Eliminate the same quantity of buttermilk as you add in juice.

BANANA-NUT BUTTERMILKS

This is a good fruit-pancake alternative when berries are not available. To get the best distribution of bananas and nuts, we add them as the pancakes begin to cook on the griddle. Slice 1 to 2 medium bananas in rounds thin enough so that they won't be higher than the pancake when cooked and flipped. Pour the pancake batter onto the griddle, then quickly arrange the slices evenly on each pancake and sprinkle chopped macadamia nuts, pecans, or walnuts around the bananas.

NEW ENGLAND BROWN-BREAD GRIDDLE CAKES

New England's cherished brown bread features a mixture of corn, rye, and wheat flours. Our Rum-Raisin Syrup is really wonderful here.

SERVES 4

¾ cup unbleached all-purpose flour

½ cup whole wheat flour

½ cup rye flour

½ cup stone-ground cornmeal

2 tablespoons packed dark brown sugar

2 teaspoons baking powder

½ teaspoon salt

3 tablespoons unsalted butter, melted

2 large eggs, separated

1½ cups milk

Vegetable oil for panfrying

Bacon or sausage drippings, optional

Unsalted butter, softened

Rum-Raisin Syrup (page 416) or real maple syrup, warmed

Stir together the flours, cornmeal, brown sugar, baking powder, and salt in a medium bowl, preferably one with a spout for pouring. Scrape in the melted butter and stir the mixture until the butter disappears into the dry ingredients.

Beat the egg whites until soft peaks form and reserve them.

In another medium bowl, whisk together the egg yolks with the milk until frothy. Pour this mixture into the dry ingredients and mix until well combined. Fold the egg whites into the batter.

Warm a griddle or a large heavy skillet over medium heat. Pour a thin film of oil onto the griddle. If you wish, add ¼ to ½ teaspoon drippings to the oil for a heartier flavor. Pour or spoon out the batter onto the hot griddle, where it should sizzle and hiss. A generous 3 tablespoons of batter will make a 4-inch pancake. Make as many cakes as you can fit without crowding.

Cook the pancakes until their top surface is covered with tiny bubbles but before all the bubbles pop, 1 to 2 minutes. Flip the pancakes and cook until the second side is golden brown, 1 to 2 minutes longer. Repeat with the remaining batter, adding to the griddle as needed a bit more oil and bacon drippings if desired.

Serve immediately with butter and syrup.

BUCKWHEATS

INGREDIENT TIP

You can find buckwheat flour at a natural foods store if it's not available at your supermarket. Coarser, grittier, and grayer than wheat flour, it is often sold in bulk.

The most popular of all pancakes throughout much of our history, buckwheats provided the warmth and earthy grit that sustained Americans during many a winter month. Dutch and German settlers popularized them originally, but they became a breakfast staple almost everywhere by the late nineteenth century. After that period they gradually faded from favor in the increasing pursuit of quick convenience. Though they're simple to make, good buckwheats require an overnight fermentation of the batter, a step that's more than amply rewarded in nutty, tangy flavor.

SERVES 4

OVERNIGHT BATTER

1¼ cups milk, warm (not hot)

1 teaspoon active dry yeast (about ½ envelope)

1 cup buckwheat flour (see Ingredient Tip)

½ cup unbleached all-purpose flour

2 tablespoons cornmeal, preferably stone-ground

2 teaspoons dark brown sugar, optional

½ teaspoon salt

1 large egg, separated

½ teaspoon baking soda

1 tablespoon unsalted butter, melted

Vegetable oil for panfrying

Bacon drippings, optional

Unsalted butter, softened

Real maple syrup, warmed

Start the batter the night before you plan to serve the buckwheats. Pour the milk into a medium bowl, preferably one with a spout for pouring. Stir in the yeast and set it aside briefly until it begins to bubble. Stir in both flours, the cornmeal, brown sugar, and salt. Cover the bowl with a towel and refrigerate it overnight.

In the morning, let the bowl sit at room temperature as you proceed with the remaining ingredients. Beat the egg white until soft peaks form and reserve it. Mix into the batter the egg yolk, baking soda, and enough water to make the batter pourable, about ¼ cup. Scrape in the melted butter and stir the mixture until the butter disappears into the dry ingredients. Fold the egg white into the batter.

Warm a griddle or a large heavy skillet over medium heat. Pour a thin film of oil onto the griddle. If you wish, add ¼ to ½ teaspoon of bacon drippings to the oil for a heartier flavor. Pour or spoon out the batter onto the hot griddle, where it should sizzle and hiss. A generous 3 tablespoons of batter will make a 4-inch pancake. Make as many cakes at a time as you can fit without crowding.

Cook the pancakes until their top surface is covered with bubbles but before all of the bubbles pop, 1 to 2 minutes. (The bubbles will be fewer and larger for buckwheats than for wheat-flour pancakes.) Flip the pancakes and cook until the second side is golden brown, 1 to 2 minutes longer. Repeat with the remaining batter, adding to the griddle as needed a bit more oil and drippings if desired. Serve immediately with butter and syrup.

PUMPKIN PANCAKES

Few lumber camps serve a noon meal, it generally being eaten in the woods. But what breakfasts and what suppers! In the morning the clamor of the gut hammer, steel striking against steel . . . brings men boiling from the doors of the bunkhouses. In front of each plate is a dish of fruit, usually canned prunes. These are generally ignored by the loggers and pushed aside. But in no time at all huge platters of fried bacon, eggs, potatoes, toast or biscuits, and hot cakes are on the table within easy reach of the jacks. From then on, it's every man for himself and no talk.

Whistleberries, Stirabout, & Depression Cake (written for the Federal Writers' Project, 1936–1942)

Instead of fruit, consider winter squash as a flapjack filling. We use pumpkin here, which produces a moist, scrumptious cake that makes most comparable pies pale in contrast. Thicker and denser than most pancakes, this rendition highlights the pumpkin flavor by going light on spicing.

SERVES 4 OR MORE

1¾ cups unbleached all-purpose flour

3 tablespoons packed light brown sugar

1 teaspoon baking powder

¾ teaspoon salt

½ teaspoon baking soda

¼ teaspoon ground cinnamon

¼ teaspoon ground cloves

¼ teaspoon ground ginger

2 large eggs

1½ cups buttermilk

½ teaspoon pure vanilla extract

One 15-ounce can pumpkin purée

Vegetable oil for panfrying

Unsalted butter, softened

Sorghum syrup or real maple syrup, warmed

Mix the dry ingredients together in a large bowl.

In a medium bowl, whisk the eggs with the buttermilk and vanilla until frothy. Whisk in the pumpkin until combined. Pour this mixture into the dry ingredients and mix until combined, with a few streaks remaining. The batter will be fairly thick. Add tablespoons of water as necessary to make it spoonable but short of runny.

Warm a griddle or a large heavy skillet over medium heat. Pour a thin film of oil onto the griddle. Pour or spoon out the batter onto the hot griddle, where it should sizzle and hiss. A generous ¼ cup of batter will make a 4-inch pancake. Make as many cakes as you can fit without crowding.

Cook the pancakes until their top surface is pocked with little bubbles but before all the bubbles pop, 1½ to 2 minutes. This batter forms fewer bubbles than many pancakes, so also watch for the edges to look just a bit firm and dry before turning.) Flip the pancakes and cook until the second side is golden brown, 1½ to 2 minutes longer. Repeat with the remaining batter, adding a bit more oil to the griddle as needed.

Serve immediately with butter and syrup.

SPICEBOX PUMPKIN PANCAKES

For sweeter, spicier cakes, increase the cinnamon and ginger to ½ teaspoon each, the vanilla to ¾ teaspoon, and maybe add ¼ teaspoon allspice too.

SWEET POTATO PANCAKES

In this southern specialty, use an equal amount of mashed baked sweet potato in place of the pumpkin. The baking time for the potato will vary depending on size and thickness, but plan for about 1 hour in a 350°F oven. Peel and mash it while warm, though you can hold it then for a day or two before proceeding. Increase the buttermilk by 2 tablespoons. Use the spices listed in the main recipe or the ones in the Spicebox version.

A RACE THAT TAKES THE CAKE

One of the most unusual customs associated with pancakes and Shrove Tuesday comes from Olney, England, where women race through town on the day before Lent, flipping pancakes in a skillet. Local legend claims the tradition began in 1445, when a cook making pancakes realized that she was late for church and ran to the service carrying her laden skillet. Pancake fans in Liberal, Kansas, learned about the event around the time of World War II and in 1950 began challenging Olney to an annual race. Teams of women from the two towns face off in Liberal every year, merrily flipping their cakes down the streets.

SOURDOUGH FLANNEL CAKES

TECHNIQUE TIP

It takes a few days to make a sourdough starter with natural wild yeast, but the process is fun and yields a homey, tasty treasure you can enjoy and "refresh" for years. You always replace what you have used and return it to the refrigerator to keep the starter alive and active.

Begin at least a week before you plan to cook your first pancakes. That may be more time than necessary, but you don't want to rush it. Watch the starter develop like a plant you're growing from seed.

Use a glass, ceramic, or plastic bowl, because sourdough can corrode metal. Mix together 1 cup flour with about ½ cup warm water to form a simple cohesive dough. (If you overdo the water, just add a bit more flour.) Add 2 or 3 unwashed organic grapes or a couple teaspoons of honey—their natural sugars will encourage the yeast. Cover the bowl with a clean damp dish towel or damp cheesecloth. Set the starter in a warm (not hot), out-of-the-way spot and dampen the cloth once or twice each day as needed. By the third or fourth day, the starter should have gotten larger, become somewhat bubbly, and developed a mild but not unpleasant sour aroma. If you used grapes in the starter, remove their solid remnants now and also scrape off or pull off any hard crust. Sprinkle over the starter 1 more cup of flour and another ½ cup of lukewarm

Under such names as "a stack o' hots" and "a string o' flats," a tall pile of golden pancakes has always been a popular way to start the day in the mountain West. These straightforward, high-rising yeast cakes are based on an old Wyoming range recipe, but they would have found equal favor in early mining and logging camps. Western pioneers continued using sourdough for leavening longer than most Americans, because of the scarcity of commercial products, and the region has retained a strong attachment to the distinctive tangy flavor to this day. This version of the pancakes relies on a relatively fast and easy sourdough technique, but the accompanying tip describes how to make a more complex, natural starter similar to what chuck-wagon cooks prized in the past.

SERVES 4

QUICK SOURDOUGH STARTER
1½ teaspoons active dry yeast (about ¾ envelope)

1 cup unbleached all-purpose flour

PANCAKES
1½ cups unbleached all-purpose flour

¼ cup sugar

2 teaspoons baking soda

1 teaspoon salt

½ recipe Quick Sourdough Starter

2 large eggs

1½ cups milk

¼ cup vegetable oil

Bacon drippings, sausage drippings, vegetable oil, or a combination for panfrying

Unsalted butter, softened

Blackberry or raspberry jam or preserves or real maple syrup

Prepare the starter, mixing the yeast in a bowl with 1 cup lukewarm water. When dissolved, stir in the flour and mix until well combined. Cover the mixture, place in a warm spot, and let sit overnight or for up to 12 hours. (Longer is fine—the starter will just develop more tang. Knead in more water if the mixture is not easily pliable.) It will look like sticky, bubbly goo. Divide and place half in a glass or ceramic jar (it corrodes metal) for later use. The other half is ready to be used for your pancakes.

Prepare the pancakes, first mixing together the flour, sugar, baking soda, and salt in a medium bowl. Dump in the sourdough starter, eggs, milk, and vegetable oil and mix just until combined. The dough should remain somewhat lumpy, though you should eliminate any lumps that are substantially larger than others.

water. Work the starter and new ingredients together into a soft, cohesive dough, adding a few more tablespoons of water if dry. Cover as before and leave it for another day or two, until it looks softer and puffier. Keep the cloth damp, and if you live in a particularly dry climate, wipe the surface of the starter with just a bit of water to make sure it stays moist.

Divide the starter in half at this point and put one portion in a lidded container to refrigerate for future use. Prepare sourdough pancakes, bread, or biscuits with the other half. Whenever you make something with the refrigerated starter, return ½ to 1 cup of dough to the jar before proceeding, to have it ready for the next time. Remember, the starter is alive and needs to be fed and exercised every couple of weeks if you haven't used it. Take it from the refrigerator, add a tablespoon or two of flour and warm water, stir, and let it sit out at room temperature overnight. Scoop it out and knead it a bit before returning it to the refrigerator. Every few times you exercise it, replace half of the starter with a similar amount of flour and water to give it plenty of nourishment.

Warm a griddle or a large heavy skillet over medium heat. Melt a thin film of drippings on the griddle. Pour or spoon out the batter onto the hot griddle, where it should sizzle and hiss. Three tablespoons of batter will make a 3- to 4-inch pancake. The batter can be used to make larger plate-size cakes if you wish. Make as many cakes as you can fit without crowding.

Cook the pancakes until their top surface is covered with bubbles but before all of the bubbles pop, 1 to 2 minutes. Flip the pancakes and cook until the second side is golden brown, 1 to 2 minutes longer. Repeat with the remaining batter, adding a bit more drippings to the griddle as needed.

Serve immediately with butter and syrup.

PAPER-THIN APRICOT PANCAKES

TECHNIQUE TIP

The pancakes can be made a day ahead or even several weeks in advance and frozen. In either case, place wax paper between them and wrap them tightly. The entire stack of pancakes can be assembled up to the night before, covered, and left to stand at room temperature. Warm, covered, in a 300°F oven for about 10 minutes. Then scatter with the almonds, garnish with the mint, and serve.

Many people today think of crepes in America as a 1970s brunch entree, but British and colonial cooks made similarly thin cakes centuries ago. Recipes often called them a "Quire of Paper Pancakes"—a quire being twenty-four sheets of paper folded in half—and instructed readers to serve them in a stack with a dusting of sugar between layers. This is our contemporary version of the idea, flavored with apricot jam and a little brandy. We like it best served as "dessert" for a company breakfast, following a savory dish. It's dedicated to our daughter Heather, who bravely tackled apricot crepes the first time she made breakfast for us.

SERVES 4 TO 6

FILLING
½ cup apricot jam
2 tablespoons unsalted butter
2 tablespoons brandy

CREPE-STYLE PANCAKES
1 cup unbleached all-purpose flour
2 tablespoons sugar
¼ teaspoon salt

¾ cup plus 2 tablespoons milk
3 large eggs
3 tablespoons unsalted butter, melted
¼ teaspoon pure vanilla extract

Unsalted butter for panfrying
Toasted slivered almonds
Fresh mint sprigs

Prepare the filling, combining the jam, butter, and brandy in a small saucepan. Warm it over medium heat, stirring in a teaspoon or more water if the mixture is too thick to spread easily.

Prepare the pancakes, first combining in a blender or a food processor the flour, sugar, and salt. Process, then add the remaining pancake ingredients and process again until smooth.

Cook the batter over medium heat in a hot 8-inch skillet, omelet pan, or crepe pan, preferably nonstick. When a drop of water bounces and sizzles briefly before evaporating, add about 1 teaspoon butter to the skillet, then swirl it around to coat the skillet. Quickly add 2 tablespoons batter and swirl it around until the skillet is coated. Cook until the batter dries on the surface, 30 to 45 seconds. Then flip the pancake and cook the other side for 15 to 30 seconds, until faintly golden. (Avoid getting them darker than this.) Repeat for the remaining pancakes, adding more butter as needed to prevent sticking. We stack them on a plate with paper towels or wax paper between them to simplify their separation later. You should end up with 16 to 18 pancakes.

When all of the pancakes are cooked, set aside the most attractive one for the top. Lay a pancake on a platter, then brush it with 1 to 2 teaspoons of the apricot filling. Repeat with the remaining pancakes and filling, building a 2- to 3-inch-tall stack topped with the most attractive pancake. Brush the remaining filling over the top, sprinkle with the almonds, and tuck mint sprigs in around the edges. Present at the table whole and then cut into wedges to serve.

PAPER-THIN APRICOT-RICOTTA PANCAKES

Eliminate the brandy from the filling and reduce the apricot jam to ¼ cup. Warm the jam and butter together until combined, then remove from the heat and stir in ¼ cup ricotta cheese. Use it as you would the regular filling. When you assemble the pancake stack, though, brush the top with an extra tablespoon of plain apricot jam, then sprinkle with the almonds.

CORNMEAL CREPE TRIANGLES WITH APRICOT FILLING

In the batter, replace 3 tablespoons flour with stone-ground cornmeal. Cook as instructed. The crepes will be folded rather than stacked. When it comes time to assemble them, spread a couple teaspoons of filling over each crepe, then fold in half and in half again, into a loose triangle. Repeat with the remaining crepes and filling, allowing 3 to 4 overlapping crepes per person. Sprinkle with sugar and almonds and add a spoonful of sour cream or créme fraîche to each serving if you wish.

SWEDISH PANCAKES

Swedish-American cooks introduced another type of thin pancake that became a big hit throughout areas where they settled, particularly the Midwest. Our version comes from several provided to us by Joyce Swedlund, whose immigrant parents moved to west-central Illinois in the early twentieth century. Because they are small as well as skinny, plan on serving plenty of the pancakes to each diner.

SERVES 4

3 large eggs

1 cup milk

1 cup half-and-half

1¼ to 1½ cups unbleached all-purpose flour (see Ingredient Tip)

1 tablespoon sugar

¾ teaspoon salt

¾ teaspoon ground cardamom

Vegetable oil and unsalted butter for panfrying

Unsalted butter, softened

Lingonberry preserves, Spiced Fresh Blueberries (page 273), or fresh blueberries, huckleberries, or blackberries

Whisk the eggs with the milk and half-and-half until frothy. Whisk in the flour, starting a few tablespoons at a time to prevent lumps, then whisk in the sugar, salt, and cardamom.

Warm a griddle or a large heavy skillet over medium heat. Pour a thin film of oil onto the griddle and add a teaspoon or two of butter. Pour or spoon out the batter onto the hot griddle, where it should sizzle and hiss. A scant 2 tablespoons of batter will make a 3-inch pancake, about as large as you'll want to go with this batter. Because they spread so much, pour the batter out quickly, in one motion, then pause long enough for the previous pancake to firm, so that the cakes don't run into each other. Make as many cakes as you can fit without crowding. (Stir the batter up from the bottom each time you make a cake.)

Cook the pancakes for about 1 minute, until their top surface is covered with tiny bubbles, like most American pancakes, or the batter has lost its gloss and turned a couple of shades darker near the outside edges, depending on whether you've used more or less flour, respectively. Flip the pancakes with a thin-bladed spatula and cook until the second side is golden brown, a minute or two longer. Repeat with the remaining batter, adding a bit more oil and butter to the griddle as needed. Serve immediately with butter and preserves or fruit.

SEARS'S FINEST

A San Francisco institution, Sears' Fine Food has long boasted about its "World Famous 18 Swedish Pancakes." Former circus clown Ben Sears and his Swedish wife, Hilbur, opened the coffee shop in 1938, and from the first they featured a family recipe for their airy coaster-size cakes, which they served eighteen to a plate. The Boyajian family now runs the café, but little has changed, including the menu and the lines outside on Powell Street. The restaurant sells its pancake mix by mail order at 415-986-1160, but getting through on the phone can be tougher than getting through the door.

ETHEREAL CLOUD CAKES

As plump as the previous pancakes are thin, but also as light as a cloud, these beauties offer a slightly crisp surface and a tender, moist center. You cook them a bit lower and slower than most griddle cakes, and because they are fragile, it's best to keep them on the small side.   **SERVES 4 OR MORE**

¾ cup cake flour, soft-wheat biscuit flour, or unbleached all-purpose flour

1 teaspoon baking soda

¼ teaspoon baking powder

½ teaspoon salt

2 large eggs, separated

1 cup ricotta cheese, preferably whole milk

⅓ cup sour cream

¾ cup whole milk

Vegetable oil for panfrying

Unsalted butter, softened

Real maple syrup, warmed

Stir together the flour, baking soda, baking powder, and salt in a medium bowl, preferably one with a spout for pouring.

In another bowl, whisk the egg yolks, ricotta, sour cream, and milk. Pour the wet ingredients into the dry ingredients.

Beat the egg whites until soft peaks form and fold them into the batter.

Warm a griddle or a large heavy skillet over medium heat. Pour a thin film of oil onto the griddle. Pour or spoon out the batter onto the hot griddle, where it should sizzle and hiss. Adjust the temperature so that it is just below medium. A generous 2 tablespoons of batter will make a 3-inch pancake. Make as many cakes at a time as you can fit without crowding.

Cook the pancakes until their top surface is covered with tiny bubbles but before all the bubbles pop, about 2 minutes. Flip the pancakes and cook until the second side is golden brown, about 2 minutes longer. Repeat with the remaining batter, adding a bit more oil to the griddle as needed. (Any leftover batter can be saved and used the following day. The pancakes won't rise as high but will taste every bit as good.)

Serve immediately with a modicum of butter and maple syrup.

CHOCOLATE CHIP PANCAKES

More friends mentioned these as a childhood favorite than any other pancake except the classics. Scatter a scant tablespoon of chocolate chips over each 3-inch pancake just after you pour the batter out on the griddle. The slower frying of the cloud cakes allows the chocolate to melt nicely while the batter cooks. Serve with Chocolate Butter (page 58) for a double wallop.

WHOLE GRAIN PANCAKES WITH PEACH SAUCE

In recent decades and the past as well, many of the American advocates for whole-grain foods put such a priority on nutrition that they neglected flavor. Our friend Lois Stouffer didn't make that mistake in creating these pancakes during her self-described "granola days." She's fine-tuned the cakes so well over the years, in fact, that you might forget they're meant to be healthy.

SERVES 3 TO 4

PEACH SAUCE

4 cups (5 to 6 medium) sliced peeled fresh or frozen peaches

1 medium to large orange, zest grated, pith and membranes removed, and pulp chopped

4 tablespoons (½ stick) unsalted butter

½ teaspoon ground mace or freshly grated nutmeg

¼ teaspoon ground cinnamon

2 to 3 tablespoons dark rum, such as Myers's

PANCAKES

½ cup whole wheat flour

¼ cup unbleached all-purpose flour

¼ cup wheat germ, preferably raw (see Ingredient Tip)

2 tablespoons wheat bran (see Ingredient Tip)

1½ teaspoons baking soda

1 teaspoon salt

1 large egg

¾ cup buttermilk

¾ cup plain yogurt

2 tablespoons vegetable oil

Vegetable oil for panfrying

Plain or vanilla yogurt, optional

Prepare the sauce, combining the ingredients in a small saucepan with ½ cup water. Bring to a simmer over medium heat, then reduce and cook briefly until the fruit is soft and begins to dissolve into the liquid. Mash the fruit a bit as it cooks to release more juice, but leave some recognizable peach chunks. (The sauce can be made a day ahead and refrigerated, covered. Reheat it before proceeding.)

Prepare the pancakes, first stirring together the flours, wheat germ, wheat bran, baking soda, and salt in a large bowl. In a smaller bowl, whisk the egg together with the buttermilk, and yogurt, and oil. Pour the wet ingredients into the dry ingredients and stir just to combine. The batter will be somewhat thick, better for spooning than for pouring.

Warm a griddle or a large heavy skillet over medium heat. Pour a thin film of oil onto the griddle. Spoon out the batter onto the hot griddle, where it should sizzle and hiss. A generous ¼ cup of batter will make a thick 4-inch pancake. Make as many cakes as you can fit without crowding.

Cook the pancakes until their top surface is dotted with tiny bubbles but before all of the bubbles pop, 1 to 2 minutes. Flip the pancakes and cook until the second side is golden brown, 1 to 2 minutes longer. Repeat with the remaining batter, adding a bit more oil to the griddle as needed.

Serve immediately with the peach sauce and, if you wish, yogurt.

FRESH CORN FRITTERS

INGREDIENT TIP

If you live where soft-wheat biscuit flour is readily available, try it instead of all-purpose flour for an even more tender cake.

TECHNIQUE TIP

One of the old secrets to success with this and other fresh corn dishes comes from the way you carve the kernels from the cob. With an ear of corn standing upright, slide a medium knife down the ear, slicing off the top half of the kernels. Rotate the ear and repeat the motion until you've given the entire ear a trim. Turn the knife over on its dull top side and scrape down the ear again, pressing against the cob to release the thick, custardy milk. Use everything in the recipe except the scalped cob.

Despite the confusing but traditional name, these "corn fritters" are actually flour pancakes. Unlike many cakes, which tend to be associated with cold weather, they are a summer treat, at their peak in flavor when made with corn right out of the garden. As Marion Harland said about an earlier version in *Common Sense in the Household* (1871), "Eaten at dinner or breakfast, these always meet with a cordial welcome." At either meal, we like them with a side of another late-summer favorite, slices of red-ripe tomatoes.

SERVES 4 OR MORE

Kernels and scrapings from 3 ears fresh sweet corn (about 2 cups) (see Technique Tip)

2 large eggs

2 tablespoons milk or half-and-half

1½ tablespoons unsalted butter, melted

3 tablespoons unbleached all-purpose flour (see Ingredient Tip)

1 scant tablespoon sugar

¾ teaspoon salt

½ teaspoon baking powder

Vegetable oil, bacon drippings, or a combination for panfrying

Unsalted butter, softened

Mix the corn kernels and scrapings with the eggs, milk, and melted butter in a medium bowl. Sprinkle in the flour, sugar, salt, and baking powder and mix just until combined.

Warm a griddle or a large heavy skillet over medium heat. Pour a thin film of oil onto the griddle. If you wish, add ¼ to ½ teaspoon bacon drippings to the oil for a heartier flavor. Pour or spoon out the batter onto the hot griddle, where it should sizzle and hiss. About 2 tablespoons of batter will make a 3-inch cake. (Anything much larger tends to tear.) Make as many cakes as you can fit without crowding.

Cook the pancakes until their top surface is covered with tiny bubbles but before all the bubbles pop, about 2 minutes. Flip the pancakes and cook until the second side is golden brown, 1 to 2 minutes longer. Repeat with the remaining batter, adding to the griddle as needed a bit more oil and bacon drippings if desired. Serve immediately with softened butter.

CORN CAKES WITH BACON AND CHEDDAR

Add 3 to 4 slices crumbled crisp bacon and ¼ pound grated sharp Cheddar (about 1 cup) to the batter with the corn kernels. Serve with Chile Butter (page 57) or Spiced Honey Butter (page 57) with a little minced fresh sage added if you wish.

CORNMEAL HOECAKES

A BREAKFAST MENU
SUGGESTION FOR A
SPECIAL DAY

Fresh Pineapple

Thin Yellow Cornmeal Pancakes

Salsa Verde

Mexican Chocolate

Marion Cunningham, *The Breakfast Book* (1987)

Long before Dutch settlers introduced their wheat-flour *pannekoeken* to the Mid-Atlantic colonies, native Americans in many parts of the country made a similar cake with cornmeal. The early European settlers adopted the notion readily, using their hearth fires to cook the cakes like an Old World unleavened bread. They sometimes smeared the batter on the blade of a clean and buttered hoe and then held it over the flame until done, giving rise to the descriptive hoecake name. Now generally griddle cooked, the cakes vary enormously in style, with people differing vociferously about the color of the cornmeal, the type and amount of liquid in the batter, and the addition of superfluous ingredients that alter the original nature of the dish, such as flour, eggs, and baking powder. Forthright in taste and texture, a true hoecake is one of life's simple pleasures. Often overlooked today, except in pockets of the South and New England, they deserve a return to prominence on American tables.

SERVES 4

1½ cups stone-ground cornmeal, white if you live south of the Mason-Dixon Line, yellow if north

1 teaspoon salt

1 cup boiling water

2 tablespoons milk

Bacon drippings, sausage drippings, vegetable oil, or a combination for panfrying

Unsalted butter, softened

Cane syrup or real maple syrup, warmed, or jam, optional

Preheat the oven to 325°F.

Pour the cornmeal into a heatproof medium bowl, preferably one with a spout for pouring. Stir in the salt. Place the bowl in the oven for 5 to 8 minutes to warm the meal through and toast it lightly. Remove it from the oven as soon as it begins to deepen in color.

Pour the boiling water into the warm cornmeal, about ½ cup at a time, being cautious of the hot bowl. Stir vigorously, eliminating any lumps, then mix in the milk. The batter will resemble a thick gruel at this point.

Warm a griddle or a large heavy skillet over medium heat. Add just enough drippings to the griddle to coat the surface with a thin film. Spoon the batter by tablespoonfuls onto the griddle, leaving several inches between the dollops. With the back of the spatula, squash the batter down into cakes about 3 inches in diameter. (The batter should bubble merrily. If it splatters menacingly instead, the griddle is too hot. Reduce the heat before continuing.) Make as many cakes as you can fit without crowding. Cook the cakes until the batter appears quite firm, 3 to 4 minutes. (These take a little longer than traditional wheat-flour pancakes.) Turn carefully and cook the cakes on the other side until medium brown and crispy, about 3 minutes longer. Repeat with the remaining batter, adding a bit more water to the batter if it thickens and more fat to the griddle as necessary. (While the cakes are best right from the griddle, you can keep them warm in a low oven on baking sheets while you finish making the entire batch of cakes. Don't stack the cakes until serving time.)

Serve the hoecakes stacked on warm plates, topped with plenty of butter. Pass syrup separately to drizzle lightly over the cakes, if desired, but be careful not to mask the subtle corn flavor.

RHODE ISLAND JONNYCAKES

In Rhode Island cooks care passionately about the local corncakes known as "jonnycakes." They get riled about spelling errors—don't dare add an *h* to *jonny*—and absolutely adamant about the use of the local White Cap flint cornmeal. Make a thinner batter, adding ½ cup more boiling water and 2 more tablespoons of milk.

BAKED CUSTARD JOHNNYCAKE

This is a vintage Florida version of the baked batter style, resembling corn bread with a custardy layer on top. Butter a 9-inch square pan or an 8- to 9-inch ovenproof skillet and preheat the oven to 350°F. Stir together in a mixing bowl 1 cup cornmeal, ½ cup flour, 1 to 2 tablespoons sugar, 1 teaspoon baking soda, and ¾ teaspoon salt. Whisk in 1 cup buttermilk, followed by 2 eggs and then 1 cup of whole milk. Pour into the prepared pan and bake for 30 to 33 minutes, until lightly browned and puffed.

BLUE CORN–PIÑON PANCAKES WITH APRICOT-PIÑON COMPOTE

Buckwheat griddle-cakes, with fried steaks, ham, or sausages, or cold meat or hash, are a popular breakfast for winter. With many families, buckwheat cakes are the constant breakfast, with some little varieties of meat, and tea or coffee, during the winter. It will be found more healthful to vary occasionally, with corn griddle-cakes, or muffins, or some other hot cakes.

Mrs. T. J. Crowen, *The American Lady's System of Cookery* (1852)

Native Americans in the Southwest used blue cornmeal well before the Spanish arrived in the region, but it didn't move much beyond the borders of Arizona and New Mexico until the 1980s, when southwestern foods became popular across the country. In these tender raised cakes, the nuttiness of the corn gains additional heft from piñon or pine nuts which grow in the same area of the country. The Spanish planted apricot trees nearby, close to the Rio Grande and other sources of water, and they produce so abundantly that local cooks use them any way they can, including in a compote.   **SERVES 4**

APRICOT-PIÑON COMPOTE

1 tablespoon unsalted butter

⅓ cup pine nuts (see Ingredient Tip)

1 cup chopped fresh or dried apricots

1 to 2 tablespoons light corn syrup

¼ teaspoon ground Mexican cinnamon (*canela*) or other ground cinnamon

1 drop pure almond extract

PANCAKES

1¼ cups pine nuts (see Ingredient Tip)

¾ cup unbleached all-purpose flour

½ cup blue or other cornmeal

1 tablespoon sugar

¾ teaspoon baking powder

¾ teaspoon salt

2 tablespoons unsalted butter, melted

2 large eggs

1¼ cups milk

2 drops pure almond extract

Vegetable oil for panfrying

Prepare the compote, warming the butter in a small skillet over medium heat. Stir in the pine nuts and sauté until lightly toasted, about 2 minutes. Watch the nuts carefully; they will continue cooking off of the heat and can burn easily. In a saucepan, combine the apricots, corn syrup, cinnamon, and almond extract with 1 cup of water. Bring to a simmer over medium heat, reduce the heat to low, and cook until the sauce is fairly thick and spoonable, about 10 minutes. Stir in the pine nuts. Keep the compote warm or let it cool to room temperature.

Start the pancake batter, placing ¾ cup of the nuts in a food processor and pulsing briefly until ground. Avoid processing the nuts so long that they turn to butter. Add the flour, cornmeal, sugar, baking powder, and salt and pulse to combine just until a coarse meal forms. Spoon the mixture into a large bowl and stir in the butter until it disappears. Add the eggs, milk, almond extract, and remaining nuts.

Warm a griddle or a large heavy skillet over medium heat. Pour a thin film of oil onto the griddle. Pour or spoon out the batter onto the hot griddle, where it should sizzle and hiss. A generous 3 tablespoons of batter will make a 4-inch pancake. Make as many cakes as you can fit without crowding.

Cook the pancakes until their top surface is covered with tiny bubbles but before all the bubbles pop, 1 to 2 minutes. Flip the pancakes and cook until the second side is golden brown, 1 to 2 minutes longer. Repeat with the remaining batter, adding a bit more oil to the griddle as needed.

Serve the pancakes immediately, accompanied by the warm compote.

PUFFY PANCAKE WITH CARAMELIZED QUINCE

After the buckwheat crop was harvested, my father, never a patient man, could hardly wait for the pancake season to open. My mother did not like to begin too early, for, like other habits, once started it was difficult to break, and the routine lasted until spring, without respite. . . .

I remember once when, after [my father] had repeatedly raised the pancake question without effect, he attempted to take

Not as stratospheric as the Dutch baby or as flat as a common pancake, the puffy or souffléed pancake is lofted gently by whisked egg whites. Our version owes its genesis to California artist Amanda Haas, who served us superb pancakes one fall morning topped with sautéed quinces right off the tree. If quinces are out of season or otherwise unavailable, substitute apples or pears, reducing the cooking time for the fruit by half.   **SERVES 2 OR MORE**

QUINCE TOPPING

1 large quince (14 to 16 ounces) or 2 medium quinces (see Ingredient Tip)

4 tablespoons (½ stick) unsalted butter

1½ tablespoons granulated sugar

1½ tablespoons packed light brown sugar

PUFFY PANCAKE

3 large eggs, separated

½ cup half-and-half

1 teaspoon sugar

½ teaspoon salt

¼ teaspoon pure vanilla extract

1 tablespoon unsalted butter, melted

¼ cup unbleached all-purpose flour

Lemon or orange wedges

Prepare the quince, first peeling, coring, and slicing it like an apple into top-to-bottom slices about ¼ inch thick. Cut the slices into thirds, more or less. Melt the butter in a heavy 8- to 10-inch skillet over medium heat, add the quince, and sauté briefly, stirring until coated with butter. Cover the skillet and cook the quince for 15 minutes, by which time it should have begun to color and to develop a few light brown edges. If not, cover and continue cooking for 2 to 3 minutes longer. Uncover, stir in the sugars and continue cooking for 5 to 8 minutes longer, until the fruit is uniformly golden and very tender. (The mixture can be made a day ahead if you wish, covered, and refrigerated. Reheat just long enough to warm the fruit before proceeding.)

Preheat the broiler, setting the baking rack 5 to 6 inches from the heat source.

Prepare the pancake batter, first whisking the egg yolks with the half-and-half until uniformly yellow. Whisk in the sugar, salt, vanilla, and butter, then the flour by sprinkling it around the edge of the bowl about 1 tablespoon at a time and whisking until smooth. Beat the egg whites until they form soft droopy peaks, then fold them into the egg yolks. Pour the batter evenly over the quince. Return to medium heat on the stove top for 3 minutes, until the mixture is lightly set around the edges. Transfer the pancake to the oven and broil for 1½ to 2 minutes, until medium-brown on the top and beginning to pull away from the sides of the skillet. Run a knife around the inside edge of the skillet to loosen, then flip the pancake onto a platter. (Expect it to lose a bit of altitude through flipping.) Cut and serve immediately, with lemon wedges on the side for each diner to squeeze over the top.

matters into his own hands. . . . I rushed in to find the whole top of the stove covered with a grayish, foaming mass which had gushed from the mouth of the batter pitcher to overflow upon the floor in rivulets, pools, friths, firths, lagoons, narrows, guts, and whatever other forms a seething liquid may take. . . . My mother burst into gales of laughter that fairly rocked the now-empty batter pitcher standing on the stove. "He must have put in a dozen yeast cakes," she gasped.

Della Lutes, *The Country Kitchen* (1936)

DUTCH BABY

For return on taste relative to effort, few breakfast dishes match Dutch babies, a poofy oven-baked blend of pancake, omelet, and popover. Variations on the theme reached a national audience through major twentieth-century cookbooks with a central European heritage, including Irma Rombauer's early editions of *Joy of Cooking*. They are also known as German pancakes, a name that's more appropriate perhaps but a lot less cuddly.   **SERVES 2 TO 4**

¾ cup unbleached all-purpose flour

1 tablespoon sugar, optional

½ teaspoon salt

4 large eggs

⅔ cup whole milk

2 tablespoons unsalted butter, melted

Confectioners' sugar

Lemon wedges

Fruit preserves or jam, optional

Preheat the oven to 450°F. Generously butter a 10-inch skillet.

Whisk the flour, sugar if desired, and salt together in a medium bowl. Add the eggs and milk and whisk until well combined. Add the butter and whisk until it disappears into the batter.

Pour into the prepared skillet and bake for 15 to 18 minutes, until puffed and golden. Serve the Dutch baby immediately, cutting with a knife or spoon into 4 wedges. (They will deflate as they cool.) Dust each portion with confectioners' sugar and garnish with lemons for squeezing over the top. Add a spoonful of preserves to the baby if you wish.

GALE GAND'S BIG APPLE PANCAKE

Talented pastry chef Gale Gand grew up eating Sunday breakfast at Walker Brothers' Pancake House in Chicago, which features a German apple pancake. She offers her own wonderful twist on it in *Butter Sugar Flour Eggs* (1999). Gale first melts 2 tablespoons butter in the skillet, then adds ¼-inch-thick slices of 2 peeled apples and sautés them until tender, about 10 minutes. She then stirs in 2 tablespoons packed light brown sugar until melted. The pancake batter is poured directly over the apples and cooked in the standard fashion, though Gale takes the pancake out of the oven just after it has puffed, sprinkles it with cinnamon and brown sugar, and then returns it to the oven to finish baking.

GRITS AND BITS WAFFLES

TECHNIQUE TIP

Because different models of waffle irons hold differing amounts of batter, the number of waffles you can make from a recipe will vary a little depending on your iron. We've tested our recipes with a Villaware waffler with a large American "four-square" grid that cuts apart into four small waffles. The batter typically fills this iron about four times. If you have extra batter, resist the urge to add it to the last waffle, trying to enlarge it, or you'll end up with a goopy mess. We just make a smaller waffle using only a portion of the iron, freezing it for later if it's a leftover.

Southern cooks have long excelled with waffles, which they often eat plain in the morning and later in the day as a base for savory creamed dishes. This is a personal favorite from the region, a treat at any meal.   **SERVES 4 TO 6**

2 cups unbleached all-purpose flour

2 tablespoons sugar

1¼ teaspoons baking powder

1 teaspoon salt

¾ cup stone-ground grits, not instant

12 tablespoons (1½ sticks) unsalted butter, melted

4 large eggs, separated

1¼ cups milk

6 to 8 slices crisp cooked bacon, crumbled

Unsalted butter, softened

Cane syrup or maple syrup, warmed

Stir the flour, sugar, and baking powder together in a small bowl until well combined. Reserve.

Bring 1 quart water to a boil in a medium saucepan over high heat. Stir in the salt and then the grits, whisking constantly until the water comes back to a boil. Reduce the heat to low and continue cooking, stirring occasionally, until very thick and creamy, about 30 minutes. Stir in the melted butter and scrape the grits into a large bowl.

Stir in the egg yolks, one at a time, mixing well after each addition. Add the flour mixture, stirring only until combined, followed by the milk. The batter should be thin. In another bowl, beat the egg whites with a mixer until stiff but still glossy.

Heat a greased waffle iron. Stir the bacon into the batter and fold in the egg whites. Cook the waffles one at a time, following the directions from the waffle-iron manufacturer. They should be crisp and brown when done.

Serve the waffles individually as they are ready or hold them briefly in a warm oven until all are finished. Offer them with softened butter and syrup.

CHEESE GRITS WAFFLES

Reduce the butter by 2 tablespoons and mix 6 ounces of grated sharp Cheddar or other mild melting cheese (about 1½ cups) into the grits before proceeding. You can leave out the bacon if you wish, but we keep the bits ourselves.

COUNTRY HAM AND GRITS WAFFLES

Instead of bacon, stir in about ¾ cup tiny bits of smoky, savory country ham. If the meat is especially long-aged and salty, reduce the salt in the batter by half.

RAISED WAFFLES

Great waffles boast a crisp honeycombed surface and a tender, moist interior. One of the best ways to get there is with a yeast batter, an idea popularized by Fannie Farmer in her original 1896 cookbook and closely associated today with the delightful Marion Cunningham, who now updates Farmer's book. Many cooks shy away from yeast batters and doughs, but they are worth a little extra time for the complexity they add to taste. As with our buckwheat pancakes, you start the evening before with a couple of quick steps. The yeast does the real work overnight, producing a fine, ready-to-use batter by the morning. The classic accompaniments of butter and maple syrup are always welcome, but try these on a spring morning with big spoonfuls of Strawberry Butter (page 57) instead. **SERVES 4 OR MORE**

2 cups unbleached all-purpose flour

1 tablespoon sugar

1 teaspoon instant fast-acting dry yeast

¾ teaspoon salt

8 tablespoons (1 stick) unsalted butter, melted

2 cups milk, warmed (not hot)

1 teaspoon pure vanilla extract

2 large eggs, separated

Unsalted butter, softened

Real maple syrup, warmed

At least 6 hours and up to the evening before you plan to serve the waffles, stir the flour, sugar, yeast, and salt together in a large bowl. Pour in the melted butter and stir until it disappears. Stir in the milk and vanilla. Cover with plastic wrap and set aside in a warm place overnight.

Just before you plan to prepare the waffles, stir the egg yolks into the batter. Beat the egg whites with a mixer until stiff but still glossy.

Heat a greased waffle iron. Fold the egg whites into the batter. Cook the waffles one at a time, following the directions from the waffle-iron manufacturer. They should be crisp and brown when done. Serve the waffles individually as they are ready or hold them briefly in a warm oven until all are finished. Accompany them with butter and syrup.

RAISED WAFFLES WITH SAUSAGE

Bruce Aidells, the creative force behind the sausage company that bears his name, makes a similar waffle trading out 1 cup of flour for cornmeal and lacing the batter with ½ pound chopped cooked sausage. Any well-flavored sausage will do, but Aidells recommends one of his smoked poultry and fruit varieties.

ZESTY RAISED WAFFLES WITH CITRUS BUTTER

Stir in the minced zest of 1 large orange and 1 large lemon after you add the egg yolks. Serve with warm Citrus Butter (page 57).

LAFCADIO HEARN'S NICE CHEAP WAFFLE

Lafcadio Hearn, author of *La Cuisine Créole* (1885), loved the food of New Orleans but also tried to protect his pennies when eating. About the time he wrote his cookbook, one of the first on the local Creole food, he opened a restaurant dedicated to five-cent dishes. It failed after his partner took off with the cash and the cook, but Hearn remained devoted to the cause. He called his recipe for a yeast waffle the "Economical Way." "Take two eggs," he said, "a cup of sweet milk, one cup of water and three cups of flour, with two tablespoonfuls of yeast powder mixed in it before sifting; add a tablespoonful of melted lard or butter, and a teaspoonful of sugar. Mix all well, and bake in waffle irons. This is a nice cheap waffle."

SPICED APPLE BUTTERMILK WAFFLES

TECHNIQUE TIP

When preparing these or other waffles, consider making extras to freeze for another day. To serve later, simply unwrap them from their freezer bag, preheat your oven or toaster oven to 375°F, and warm the waffles for about 3 minutes. They come out much better than frozen supermarket versions.

You don't need to plan ahead and start overnight to make terrific waffles. This expeditious version relies on buttermilk for tang and grated apple for enhanced taste and texture.

SERVES 4 OR MORE

2 cups unbleached all-purpose flour

1½ teaspoons baking soda

½ teaspoon salt

1 teaspoon ground cinnamon

1 teaspoon ground ginger

½ teaspoon ground allspice, ground cloves, or freshly grated nutmeg

6 tablespoons unsalted butter, melted

1¾ cups buttermilk

2 large eggs, separated

2 tablespoons molasses

1 teaspoon pure vanilla extract

1 medium apple, preferably a somewhat tart variety such as Granny Smith or Jonagold, peeled if you wish and grated (about ⅔ cup)

Unsalted butter, softened

Real maple syrup, warmed

Stir together the flour, baking soda, salt, and spices in a large bowl. Pour in the melted butter and stir until it disappears. Stir in the buttermilk, egg yolks, molasses, vanilla, and apple.

Just before you plan to prepare the waffles, beat the egg whites with a mixer until stiff but still glossy.

Heat a greased waffle iron. Fold the egg whites into the batter. Cook the waffles one at a time, following the directions from the waffle-iron manufacturer. They should be crisp and brown when done. Serve the waffles individually as they are ready or hold them briefly in a warm oven until all are finished. Accompany them with softened butter and syrup.

BASIC BUTTERMILK WAFFLES

Leave out the apples, cinnamon, and ginger. Replace the molasses with 1 tablespoon sugar and, if you plan to serve the waffles with a savory topping such as Creamed Chicken with Ham (page 151), eliminate the vanilla extract too. With the vanilla, these can take a multitude of fruit accompaniments, but for something unexpected try Ahwahnee Creamed Bananas (page 281) or your holiday cranberry sauce, warmed.

If a forkful of hot cake dripping butter and maple syrup now brings me back to my childhood kitchen, with all the anticipatory bustle of a pancake morning, I'm reminded that its evocative force was just as keen when I was still a child. Then, my little Log Cabin syrup tin linked me directly to the exciting world of the winter forest, where lumberjack camp cooks flipped their flapjacks high into the air and smoke belched from the stovepipes of maple sugar shacks, sending the sweet smell of boiling sap floating over the deep drifts of snow.

John Thorne, *Simple Cooking* newsletter (January–February 1996)

SAVORY CHEESE WAFFLES

Starting with the Basic Buttermilk Waffles variation, eliminate the sugar and the vanilla. Stir ¼ pound of grated mild cheese, such as Gouda or Cheddar (about 1 cup), into the batter before spooning it up for the individual waffles. These make a great base for a thick winter vegetable stew.

EXTRA-CRUNCHY WAFFLES

In another twist on the Basic Buttermilks, we like the texture provided by several tablespoons of granola or chopped nuts. Pecans, walnuts, hickory nuts, or hazelnuts are especially good—sprinkled over the batter in the iron just as you begin cooking. Cover the entire surface evenly. What you sacrifice in moistness you gain in toothsome crunch.

SWEET POTATO WAFFLES WITH SORGHUM SYRUP

INGREDIENT TIP

Much of the sorghum syrup on the market today, like maple syrup, has little of the real thing in it. Look for a 100% sorghum syrup, sometimes called *sorghum molasses,* such as the one made by Arrowhead Mills and sold widely in natural foods stores. For a mail-order source, Lee Brothers Boiled Peanuts Catalog (803-720-8890) carries a top-of-the-line syrup made in small batches in Benton County, Tennessee.

Another southern waffle, this enjoys a venerable heritage that can be traced back at least as far as 1847, when Sarah Rutledge included a version in *The Carolina Housewife.* Our rendition is a bit more elaborate than hers, dressed up with sour cream and the South's yummy sorghum syrup, which tastes similar to molasses but is more flinty. We like chilled or hot cider as an accompaniment.

SERVES 4

1⅓ cups unbleached all-purpose flour

1 teaspoon baking powder

½ teaspoon baking soda

¾ teaspoon salt

½ teaspoon ground cinnamon

½ teaspoon ground allspice

1½ cups mashed cooked sweet potato (about 2 small to medium potatoes)

1 cup sour cream

3 large eggs, separated

8 tablespoons (1 stick) unsalted butter, melted

3 tablespoons sorghum syrup or molasses (see Ingredient Tip)

Unsalted butter, softened

Sorghum syrup, or molasses, warmed (see Ingredient Tip)

Sour cream, yogurt, or crème fraîche, optional

Stir the flour, baking powder, baking soda, salt, cinnamon, and allspice together in a large bowl. In another bowl, stir together the sweet potato, sour cream, egg yolks, butter, and sorghum. Pour the wet ingredients into the dry and mix just to combine. The batter should be thick but still spoonable.

Just before you plan to prepare the waffles, beat the egg whites with a mixer until stiff but still glossy.

Heat a greased waffle iron. Fold the egg whites into the batter. Cook the waffles one at a time, following the directions from the waffle-iron manufacturer. They should be crisp and brown when done. Serve the waffles individually as they are ready or hold them briefly in a warm oven until all are finished. Accompany with butter, sorghum, and sour cream.

GINGERED SWEET POTATO WAFFLES WITH SORGHUM SYRUP

Eliminate the cinnamon. Add 1 teaspoon ground ginger and ¼ teaspoon freshly milled white pepper with the dry ingredients and 1 tablespoon grated or minced fresh ginger with the wet ingredients.

CREAM WEDDING WAFFLES

INGREDIENT TIP

Before vanilla extract became common, cooks often scented baked dishes with fragrant distillations of rose and orange blossoms. Look for orange-flower water in large grocery stores and at Middle Eastern or Asian markets. Here, it gives the waffles a lighter, more flowery complexity than vanilla.

Early Dutch immigrants commonly gave new brides long-handled fireplace waffle irons engraved with their initials and the wedding date. Future generations of Americans continued giving cooking equipment as wedding gifts, and they also often passed along recipes similar to this. The double leavening from baking powder and beaten egg whites assures an airy waffle, the kind of outcome that might elude a bride just learning to cook. Novice or not, you'll love the graceful payoff, both fluffy and creamy. **SERVES 4 OR MORE**

1½ cups unbleached all-purpose flour

1 tablespoon sugar

1 tablespoon baking powder

½ teaspoon salt

3 large eggs, separated

1½ cups plus 2 tablespoons heavy (whipping) cream

1 tablespoon orange-flower water (see Ingredient Tip)

1 tablespoon minced orange zest

Softly whipped cream

Blueberries, raspberries, halved strawberries, or sliced peaches, nectarines, or apricots

Stir the flour, sugar, baking powder, and salt together in a large bowl. Whisk the egg yolks with the cream and orange-flower water, then stir in the orange zest. Pour the mixture into the dry ingredients and mix just until combined.

Just before you plan to prepare the waffles, beat the egg whites with a mixer until stiff but still glossy.

Heat a greased waffle iron. Fold the egg whites into the batter. Cook the waffles one at a time, following the directions from the waffle-iron manu-facturer. They should be crisp and golden brown when done. (These are a bit lighter in color when ready than most good waffles.) Serve the waffles individually as they are ready or hold them briefly in a warm oven until all are finished. Offer them with whipped cream and berries.

THE BELGIAN WAFFLE

Some people call any waffle with large, deep pockets "Belgian." The version that spread the fame of the dish in this country, however, also included a voluptuous crown of whipped cream and strawberries. The Vermesch family, who had operated an American snack bar for the International Exposition in Brussels, reversed the tables at the 1964 New York World's Fair and served their Belgian specialty to an eager audience. Mariepaule Vermesch, sixteen years old at the time, added the topping to waffles cooked by her brother while her mother waited on customers. She still makes the dish at Mariepaule's Café in Albuquerque.

PECAN WAFFLES WITH BOURBON-PEACH PRESERVES

A BREAKFAST MENU

SUGGESTION FROM

FANNIE FARMER

Sliced Oranges

Wheat Germ with Sugar and
Cream

Warmed over Lamb

French Fried Potatoes

Raised Biscuits

Buckwheat Cakes with Maple
Syrup

Coffee

Fannie Merritt Farmer, *The
Boston Cooking-School Cook
Book* (1896)

The Camellia Grill in New Orleans makes the country's most famous pecan waffle, enjoyed at all hours of the day by everyone from construction crews to Garden District debutantes. We developed our own version to keep us content at home when we can't get to Louisiana. If you're averse to a little bourbon in the topping, substitute plain peach preserves, fresh peaches in season, crème fraîche, or a drizzle of cane syrup or honey.   **SERVES 4**

BOURBON-PEACH PRESERVES

1½ cups peach preserves

¼ cup bourbon or other American whiskey

WAFFLES

1 cup pecan pieces, toasted in a dry skillet until fragrant

1 cup unbleached all-purpose flour

¾ cup cornmeal, preferably stone-ground

2 tablespoons sugar

2 teaspoons baking powder

½ teaspoon salt

3 large eggs, separated

1½ cups milk

6 tablespoons unsalted butter, melted

Unsalted butter, softened

Prepare the preserves, warming the ingredients together in a small saucepan over medium heat.

Prepare the waffles, first chopping ¾ cup of the pecans in a food processor until they are uniformly fine. Add the flour, cornmeal, sugar, baking powder, and salt and continue processing until the mixture forms a fine meal. Transfer to a bowl and whisk in the egg yolks one at a time, followed by the milk and melted butter. In another bowl, beat the egg whites with a mixer until stiff but still glossy.

Heat a greased waffle iron. Fold the egg whites into the batter. Cook the waffles one at a time, following the directions from the waffle-iron manufacturer. They should be crisp and brown when done.

Serve the waffles individually as they are ready or hold them briefly in a warm oven until all are finished. Sprinkle each with a portion of the remaining pecans and accompany them with softened butter and warm Bourbon-Peach Preserves.

WILD RICE WAFFLES

**A BREAKFAST MENU
SUGGESTION FROM AUNT
JEMIMA FOR "A HE-MAN
BREAKFAST"**

Puffed Wheat and Bananas

Poached Egg on Buckwheat
Cakes

Coffee   Milk

*Tempting New Aunt Jemima
Pancake 'n Waffle Recipes,* an
undated promotional pamphlet

The nutty flavor and toothsome texture of wild rice make it a splendid ingredient for waffles, especially ones eaten with savory toppings such as Creamed Mushrooms (page 327) or Creamed Chicken with Ham (page 151). **SERVES 4**

WILD RICE

2 tablespoons unsalted butter or olive oil

2 heaping teaspoons minced onion

2 heaping teaspoons minced celery

1 cup uncooked wild rice

1½ cups chicken stock

1½ teaspoons salt or more to taste

WAFFLES

1 cup unbleached all-purpose flour

¼ cup whole wheat flour or additional unbleached all-purpose flour

1 teaspoon baking powder

½ teaspoon baking soda

¾ teaspoon salt

2 large eggs

¾ cup buttermilk

½ cup chicken stock

4 tablespoons (½ stick) unsalted butter, melted

Herb Butter (page 57)

Prepare the wild rice, first warming the butter in a saucepan over medium heat. Add the onion and celery and sauté until the onion is soft and translucent, about 5 minutes. Stir in the wild rice and sauté briefly until the grains glisten with fat and look lightly toasted. Add the stock, 1½ cups water, and the salt and bring to a boil. Cover, reduce the heat to medium-low, and cook until tender, with most of the kernels split open to reveal their white centers, about 55 minutes. (Check the rice toward the end of cooking, adding some hot water if the rice appears to be dry before it becomes tender.)

Remove the wild rice from the heat and let it steam, covered, for about 10 minutes, draining off any remaining liquid. (The wild rice can be made a day or two ahead, covered, and refrigerated. It does not have to be reheated before proceeding, but remove it from the refrigerator 15 to 30 minutes before you plan to use it to take off some of the chill.)

Prepare the waffles, first stirring the flours, baking powder, baking soda, and salt together in a large bowl. In a smaller bowl, whisk the eggs, buttermilk, and chicken stock together, then combine with the dry ingredients. Add the butter and the cooked wild rice and stir just until they are combined. The batter will be a bit thick and lumpy.

Heat a greased waffle iron. Cook the waffles one at a time, following the directions from the waffle-iron manufacturer. Spread the batter with a spatula if needed. When done, the waffles should be crisp and brown.

Serve the waffles individually as they are ready or hold them briefly in a warm oven until all are finished. Accompany them with Herb Butter.

NEW ORLEANS PAIN PERDU

INGREDIENT TIP

Maple syrup comes in multiple grades, as we explain in detail on page 416. We've discovered over the years that we prefer a lighter maple syrup, such as Vermont Grade A Medium Amber, with French toast. Its more delicate flavor seems to balance best with the egg-custard coating that distinguishes French toast.

No French cook would lay claim to what we call French toast, though there is something of a link in New Orleans *pain perdu* (literally "lost bread"). In Europe and elsewhere, people have long rescued stale bread by coating it in a flavored liquid and then cooking it. Americans turned the idea upside down by starting with fresh bread and then serving the toast as breakfast food rather than as a dessert or light supper. The New Orleans slant on the dish comes from the use of French bread and a heady, rich custard for the soaking sauce. We usually serve this and other similar toasts with smoky bacon or sausage links and maybe a glass of fresh-squeezed orange juice.

SERVES 4

4 large eggs

¾ cup whole milk

½ cup heavy (whipping) cream or half-and-half

2 tablespoons Irish whiskey, cognac, brandy, or bourbon

2 tablespoons sugar

2 teaspoons pure vanilla extract

½ teaspoon salt

8 French bread slices, cut about 1 inch thick on the diagonal

Unsalted butter

Vegetable oil

Confectioners' sugar

Sliced strawberries, other berries, or orange or tangerine slices

Real maple syrup, optional (see Ingredient Tip)

Preheat the oven to 300°F. Butter a baking sheet.

Whisk the eggs, milk, cream, whiskey, sugar, vanilla, and salt together in a shallow dish.

Dunk the bread slices into the egg mixture and soak them for at least 10 minutes, turning if needed to coat evenly, until saturated but short of falling apart.

Warm 1 tablespoon butter and 1 tablespoon oil together on a griddle or in a large heavy skillet over medium heat. Briefly cook the French toast in batches until golden brown and lightly crisp, turning once. Place the first slices on the baking sheet and keep them warm in the oven. Continue cooking the remaining slices, adding more butter and oil as needed. When all of the French toast is ready, dust with confectioners' sugar sprinkled through a strainer. Serve immediately with berries and maple syrup if desired.

NEW ORLEANS PRALINE PAIN PERDU

Instead of fruit and maple syrup for the topping, use softly whipped cream sweetened with chopped or crumbled praline candies. We add a few toasted pecan halves for good measure.

POPPYSEED FRENCH TOAST

In parts of the northern Midwest settled by Poles and Bohemians, beloved poppyseeds may pop up in nearly anything, including French toast. Stir 2 tablespoons of the seeds into the custard mixture before dipping the bread into it. Use brandy as the liquor.

EGGNOG FRENCH TOAST

Use 1½ cups eggnog to replace the milk and cream and use only 3 eggs in the custard. This variation seems festive at Christmas with a grating of fresh nutmeg.

ICE CREAM FRENCH TOAST

As long as you're getting carried away with the custard, go ahead and substitute melted vanilla or rum-raisin ice cream. You'll want 1¼ cups to replace the milk and cream in the recipe. We breakfast. guarantee your kids won't skip breakfast.

A CONTINENT OF TOAST

Americans generally call it French toast today, but our ancestors had a world of names for closely related dishes. In New Orleans itself it was sometimes known as "Spanish toast." In other various regions of the country, we've seen it referred to as "German toast," "Dutch toast," and "Mennonite toast." Many nineteenth-century Americans called it "Queen Esther's bread," and earlier British cooks knew it under such terms as "cream toast" and "poor knights."

BAKED CRÈME BRÛLÉE
FRENCH TOAST

TECHNIQUE TIP

Sharon Watkins uses the French toast as a dessert for special meals. She cuts the French toast into fingers, which she then either bakes or dusts with flour and flash-fries. Serve with raspberry sauce, chocolate sauce, or both.

———

SELECTIONS FROM

THE BREAKFAST MENU

AT PERHAR'S VIENNA

RESTAURANT IN

NEW YORK CITY, 1912

French Toast   Milk Toast

Cream Toast   Buckwheat
Cakes—Maple Syrup

French Pancake

German Pancake

———

We've always liked the idea of a baked French toast, the kind put together the night before and then slipped into the oven shortly before serving. We never found a tasty version, however, until we tried this stellar creation at a delightful Austin restaurant, Chez Zee. Chef-owner Patrick Dixson, who apprenticed in some of the finest restaurant kitchens in New Orleans, wanted a dish that was different and memorable but also ready to make with ingredients always on hand. When Patrick came up with this idea, his wife and restaurant co-owner Sharon Watkins says she almost licked the plate clean. The initial preparation can be done up to several days ahead of the final quick baking and serving, a handy feature for home and professional cooks alike. A true luxury, this is worth every last calorie.

SERVES 8

1 quart heavy (whipping) cream

1 vanilla bean

8 large egg yolks

¾ cup sugar

1¾ to 2 pounds (about 1 extra-large loaf) challah or other soft-textured egg bread, cut into 1-inch-thick slices

3 to 4 tablespoons unsalted butter, melted

Real maple syrup, warmed

Sliced fresh strawberries or other seasonal fruit

Softly whipped cream

Butter a 10-inch springform pan. Wrap the bottom and sides with foil, making the pieces long enough to fold up and over the top of the pan while baking. A criss-cross pattern of two or more long pieces of foil works best.

Combine the cream and vanilla bean in a medium saucepan over medium heat just long enough to warm the cream, about 5 minutes. Remove from the heat and let the mixture steep until cool, about 15 minutes. Pour the cream into a mixing bowl, straining out the vanilla bean. Cut the bean open lengthwise and scrape out all the fragrant little black seeds. (The remaining vanilla pod can be dried and then added to sugar to use for the next batch of French toast or other dishes.) Stir the vanilla seeds back into the cream.

Add the egg yolks and sugar to the cream, then whisk the custard mixture until well combined and uniformly light yellow. Make a layer of bread slices, cutting or tearing slices as needed to fit evenly. Pour about a quarter of the custard mixture evenly over the bread. Repeat with 3 more layers of bread and custard. The bread may rise a bit above the rim of the pan on the last layer. Pour the remaining custard over it slowly so that you get minimal runoff over the pan's edge. Fold the foil up over the top. Arrange a plate over the foil and weight it down with a can of beans or other heavy can from the pantry. Refrigerate for about 1 hour so that the custard soaks through the bread thoroughly. Remove the can and the plate.

Shortly before the mixture is finished soaking, preheat the oven to 325°F. Place the springform pan in a water bath that comes about halfway up the pan's side. Bake for about 1½ hours, until firm at the center. Open the foil top and cool the French toast. Fold the foil back over and chill until ready to use. (If you need your springform pan for something else, the French toast can be unmolded after several hours, when it is chilled thoroughly. Run a knife around the inside of the pan, then release the spring on the pan's side. Wrap the French toast tightly in plastic for longer storage).

When you are ready to serve the French toast, preheat the oven to 350°F. Cut the French toast into 8 wedges, or more or fewer as you wish. Arrange the wedges on a baking sheet, then brush each wedge lightly with melted butter. Bake for about 10 minutes, until warm in the center and lightly toasted and crisp on the surface. (You don't actually have the caramel topping of crème brûlée, but you get its familiar creamy custard and contrasting crunchy surface.) Arrange each wedge on a plate, surround with a pool of maple syrup, and garnish with fruit and whipped cream. Indulge yourself.

CALIFORNIA TOAST

The early Spanish settlers in California made a form of French toast that they called *fritada*. Cooks split day-old *bolillos,* small Mexican white-bread rolls, and dunked the pieces in the typical egg-milk mixture. Then they fried the bread in olive oil, made from the fruit of trees they introduced to the area. For a topping, they might use a wine-and-sugar syrup, which made a good alternative to maple syrup in the California clime.

CRANBERRY–CREAM CHEESE–STUFFED FRENCH TOAST

As a palatable method of disposing of stale bread, as well as to furnish a variety of agreeable dishes, toast is an important factor in the culinary economy of the home. As a dish for invalids it is indispensable.

Marion Harland, *Breakfast, Dinner and Supper* (1889)

Fresh fruit or cooked compotes make a good topping for French toast, but they work even better as a filling. With a stuffing of cranberries in this case, or other fruits suggested in the following variations, you can start with lofty slices of bread but maintain a moist center through the cooking process.   **SERVES 4**

One 1- to 1¼-pound loaf of white bread or brioche, unsliced

FILLING

¼ pound cream cheese, softened

1 to 2 tablespoons sugar

¼ teaspoon almond extract, optional

One 14- to 15-ounce can jellied whole cranberry sauce

1¼ cups whole milk

3 large eggs

1 tablespoon sugar

1 teaspoon pure vanilla extract

Pinch of salt

Unsalted butter

Vegetable oil

Confectioners' sugar

Real maple syrup, warmed

Preheat the oven to 300°F. Butter a baking sheet. Cut the bread into 8 equal slices about 1 inch thick.

Prepare the filling. Mash the cream cheese with 1 tablespoon sugar and, if you wish, the almond extract in a medium bowl. Stir in the cranberries and add more sugar if the flavor is too tart. The mixture should be thick and chunky.

In a shallow dish or bowl, whisk together the milk, eggs, 1 tablespoon sugar, vanilla, and salt.

With a serrated knife, cut a pocket into the side of each piece of bread, carefully slicing into but not through the bread. Spoon equal portions of the filling into each slice. Dunk the stuffed bread slices into the egg mixture and soak them for several minutes, turning if needed to coat evenly, until saturated but short of falling apart.

Warm 1 tablespoon butter and 1 tablespoon oil together on a griddle or in a large heavy skillet over medium heat. Briefly cook the French toast in batches until golden brown and lightly crisp, turning once. Place the first slices on the baking sheet and keep them warm in the oven. Continue cooking the remaining slices, adding more butter and oil as needed. When all of the French toast is ready, dust it with confectioners' sugar, sprinkling it through a strainer. Serve immediately with maple syrup.

CRAN-ORANGE FRENCH TOAST

Add 1 to 2 tablespoons Grand Marnier or Triple Sec to the egg mixture. Reduce the cranberry sauce in the filling by one half and add ¾ cup orange marmalade. If you'd like a switch from maple syrup, top it with Citrus Syrup (page 417).

CHERRY-STUFFED FRENCH TOAST

In place of the cranberries in the filling mixture, use 1½ cups pitted and lightly mashed tart cherries, fresh, frozen, or canned, and opt for the larger amount of sugar suggested. We like to use the tangy Montmorency cherries that grow on both sides of Lake Michigan. Try at least once with the vanilla-scented syrup used in Starfruit with Spiced Syrup (page 415).

BLACKBERRY-STUFFED FRENCH TOAST

Replace the cranberry sauce in the filling with 2 cups blackberry preserves or jam and eliminate the sugar. Garnish with a few plump, juicy fresh blackberries if available.

CREAMED BANANA FRENCH TOAST

Replace the cranberry filling with Ahwahnee Creamed Bananas (page 281). Sprinkle perhaps with thick shreds of toasted fresh coconut.

CHOCOLATE-STUFFED FRENCH TOAST

Mix together the cream cheese, sugar, and almond extract for the filling. Spoon it into the bread as directed, then slide a 1- to 1½-ounce portion of bittersweet or semisweet chocolate bar into each bread portion. Cook as directed. Serve with Chocolate or Vanilla Butter (page 58).

APRICOT-SAUSAGE FRENCH TOAST

Here's a variation that's as savory as it is sweet. Sauté ½ pound bulk breakfast sausage or smoky breakfast links sliced into thin half-moons. When brown, add ½ pound quartered fresh apricots and 2 teaspoons brown sugar and cook briefly until the fruit is soft and a bit juicy. Eliminate the sugar, almond extract, and cranberry sauce from the filling, just adding the apricot-sausage mixture to the cream cheese instead. We skip the confectioners' sugar on top.

SAVORY FRENCH TOAST WITH FRESH TOMATO RELISH

SELECTIONS FROM THE BREAKFAST MENU ON THE SS *GEORGE WASHINGTON*, 1921

Scrambled Eggs with Peas, Ham, Kippered, or Natural

Griddle and Buckwheat Cakes with Maple Syrup

Plain and Apple Pancakes

Buttered, Cinnamon, and Milk Toast

French toast doesn't need to be sweet. Many people, including Bill, prefer it in a savory form like this with meat and cheese. The simple relish of diced tomatoes, onion, parsley, and salad oil offsets the heft of the dish. **SERVES 4**

FRESH TOMATO RELISH

2 cups halved tiny tomatoes, such as cherry, pear, or Sweet 100s, preferably a combination of red and yellow or other colors

2 to 3 teaspoons vegetable oil

2 tablespoons minced red onion

2 tablespoons minced fresh parsley

Salt and freshly milled black pepper to taste

SAVORY FRENCH TOAST

4 large eggs

½ cup whole milk

1 teaspoon brown, Dijon, or yellow mustard

¼ teaspoon salt

¼ teaspoon freshly milled black pepper

8 large but thin slices rye or sourdough bread, or even sturdy split corn bread squares

¼ pound plain, chive, or scallion cream cheese, softened

8 thin slices smoked turkey, ham, mortadella, or corned beef, at room temperature

Unsalted butter

Vegetable oil

Preheat the oven to 300°F. Butter a baking sheet.

Prepare the relish, combining the ingredients in a small bowl. Reserve at room temperature.

Prepare the French toast, first whisking together the eggs, milk, mustard, salt, and pepper in a shallow dish.

Spread one side of each slice of bread with 1 tablespoon of the cream cheese. Top the first piece of bread with 2 meat slices, and top each with another slice of bread. Skewer each with a couple of toothpicks. Repeat to make 4 double-decker French toasts. Dunk the stuffed bread slices into the egg mixture and soak them briefly, turning to coat evenly, until saturated but short of falling apart.

Warm 1 tablespoon butter and 1 tablespoon oil together on a griddle or in a large heavy skillet over medium heat. Cook the French toast in batches, about 3 minutes per side, turning once, until golden brown and lightly crisp, with melted cheese. Place the first slices on the baking sheet and keep them warm in the oven. Continue cooking the remaining slices, adding more butter and oil as needed. When all the French toast is cooked, transfer it to plates. Spoon equal portions of the relish over each.

TORTILLA FRENCH TOAST

We found this simpler, lighter savory toast in El Paso years ago. Skip the meat and cream cheese. Dunk 8 flour tortillas in the egg batter and griddle-fry them for a minute or two on each side. Serve topped with the tomato relish or a chunky salsa, grated Cheddar cheese, and diced avocado. To eat this by hand, roll the cooked tortilla around the toppings while still very warm and then cut it into slices on the diagonal.

TAKING A BREAK FROM STEAKS AND CAKES

In 1866 a *Harper's Weekly* column addressed the subject of what to have for breakfast. The magazine suggested that people were tired of a constant morning diet of steaks, chops, eggs, and pancakes. For variety the writer recommended boiled hominy with syrup or cream, "German Fritters," and leftover cold chicken, turkey, veal, or lamb minced, warmed in gravy, and served on toast.

CRUNCHY FRENCH TOAST

The only time we buy boxed cornflakes is to make this toast. In the days of elegant railroad dining, the Atcheson, Topeka, & Santa Fe line served a version of this as a swank breakfast dish, and it has remained on fancy restaurant menus in the decades since at places such as New York's Plaza Hotel. James Beard popularized it among home cooks, demonstrating that you can create a lot of showy effect with very little effort.

SERVES 4

4 large eggs

1 cup whole milk

1 teaspoon pure vanilla extract

¼ teaspoon salt

Eight ¾- to 1-inch-thick slices challah or good white bread

2 heaping cups cornflakes, crumbled to about half their original size

Unsalted butter for panfrying

2 to 3 tablespoons sugar, optional

Real maple syrup, warmed

Preheat the oven to 325°F. Butter a baking sheet.

Whisk the eggs, milk, vanilla, and salt in a shallow dish or bowl. Dunk the bread slices into the egg mixture and soak them for a few minutes on each side, turning as needed to coat evenly but not fully saturated. Place the cornflakes on a plate or in another shallow dish. Press each slice of bread lightly into the cornflakes, coating both sides.

Warm about 2 tablespoons butter on a griddle or in a large heavy skillet over medium heat. Briefly cook the French toast in batches until golden brown and lightly crisp, turning once. If you wish, sprinkle each slice with sugar. Place the first slices on the baking sheet and keep them warm in the oven. Continue cooking the remaining slices, adding more butter as needed. When all the French toast is ready, serve with maple syrup on the side.

QUICK MAPLE TOAST

Preparing an egg batter for French toast isn't challenging or time-consuming, but some people bypass even that effort in the search for shortcuts on rushed mornings. Instead of relying on bland packaged products, good cooks in a hurry may make maple toast. They simply pour a tablespoon or two of maple syrup over a couple of slices of white bread, let it sit for a minute, repeat the process on the other side, and then give the bread time to absorb the syrup while they make coffee or shower. They cook the toast in butter on a griddle or in a skillet for a couple of minutes per side, until golden brown and crisp, and eat it perhaps with additional butter.

5

Morning Meats

STEAKS, SWEETBREADS, broiled kidneys, smoked liver, stewed tripe, fried chicken, veal cutlets, lamb chops, pork and squirrel brains—Americans used to feast on them all in the morning, along with the still-traditional bacon, sausage, and ham. We've cut back on meat today at all meals, but it remains the signature feature of an American breakfast.

No other people in history have come close to rivaling us as morning carnivores, and even now in these temperate times we continue to insist more than any other society on some kind of meat at a special breakfast.

Where we've lost our stride in recent decades is in variety. It may make sense to eat less meat overall, but our current predilection to restrict our breakfast options to a few basic cuts of pork betrays all reason. We deal here with those favorites, of course, but we also champion other choices that make a morning shine. For the breadth of breakfast possibilities once common in the country, and the promise they offer for arousing aromas and flavors, nothing to this day beats meat.

PAN-SEARED IOWA BREAKFAST CHOPS

In the pantheon of all-time American breakfast favorites, chops and steaks stand at the top of the class. We ate more bacon, more eggs, and maybe even more potatoes, but when we wanted something special to welcome the day, we sought a good cut of pork or beef. The tradition remains the strongest in the rural Midwest, where people know their chops. In this hearty morning version, we keep the meat moist and succulent through a quick pan-searing followed by covered stovetop cooking. Iowa cooks might favor home fries on the side, but we also like fried green tomatoes.

SERVES 4

2 thick slices smoky bacon, chopped	1 medium onion, halved and thinly sliced
4 loin pork chops, preferably bone in, about ½ pound each	½ cup chicken stock
	2 teaspoons Worcestershire sauce
Salt and freshly milled black pepper to taste	½ teaspoon dried marjoram or sage

Fry the bacon in a large heavy skillet over medium heat. Remove it with a slotted spoon, drain it, and reserve.

Salt and pepper the chops. Brown the chops on both sides in the bacon drippings. Cover the chops with the onion, then add the stock, Worcestershire, and marjoram. Cover, reduce the heat to medium-low, and cook for about 20 minutes, until the chops are cooked through, with the barest hint of pink at the center. Transfer them to a platter and raise the heat to high under the skillet. Cook briefly until the onion and stock have reduced to a sauce. Spoon over the chops, sprinkle with bacon, and serve.

SMOKED BREAKFAST CHOPS

Particularly popular in the Midwest, smoked pork loin chops make a distinctly different substitute for the regular chops in this preparation. Since they come precooked, just heat them through for about 10 minutes. A pat of Mustard-Lemon Butter (page 57) on each chop is a nice touch.

SOUTHERN PAN-SEARED PORK CHOPS WITH SWEET POTATO GRAVY

In a region where breakfast gravies are sometimes made with tomatoes and even chocolate, a sweet potato is no big deal. Eliminate the marjoram from the chops and add instead a pinch or two of cayenne. After you remove the chops from the pan, stir in about 1½ cups mashed cooked sweet potato (1 small sweet potato) and an extra ½ cup chicken stock, along with the other pan sauce flavorings. Simmer just until thick and gravylike.

LACQUERED BACON

INGREDIENT TIP

In *The Great American Meat Book* (1996), Merle Ellis grumbled, "If our pioneering forefathers had to rely on the supermarket bacon of today as the staple of the long trek westward, they wouldn't have made it much past Pittsburgh." Or maybe even the Hudson River. Most supermarket bacon is not truly cured and smoked in the way that produces authentic bacon. Most commercial producers simulate those processes in artificial ways that result in bland meat thinner than your napkin and too wet to fry properly. A pound of one of these bacons can easily end up losing two thirds of its weight to a pool of water and grease.

Treat yourself to the real thing. Generally, the shorter the ingredient list on the package, the better the bacon. The essentials are pork belly and salt, which to our minds rules out anything called "low-sodium bacon." We feel the same way about sodium nitrite, without which bacon tastes like roast pork. Both dry cures and brines can be used for curing the meat, and brown sugar, maple syrup, or molasses can provide solid flavor if the sweet and salty are properly balanced. Pepper, cayenne, cinnamon, or other spices may work as enhancements, but not always. Avoid bacon labeled "smoke flavor added" or any that doesn't indicate genuine smokehouse processing, always touted when

Although it's the quintessential breakfast meat, bacon doesn't always get the respect it deserves. We've eaten it so commonly for so long that we tend to be blasé about bacon, too easily accepting inferior versions that offer little of the potent blend of salt, smoke, and sweet. Start this glazed preparation—somewhat akin to smoked ribs basted in barbecue sauce—with real smokehouse bacon. It'll immediately spark your memory of the sunniest mornings of your life.

SERVES 4 OR MORE

⅓ cup mango chutney, any large chunks chopped

¼ cup apple juice or 3 tablespoons water with 1 tablespoon light or dark brown sugar

2 tablespoons yellow or brown mustard

1 tablespoon white or cider vinegar

12 thick slices (about ¾ pound) bacon (see Ingredient Tip)

Preheat the oven to 375°F.

Stir the chutney, juice, mustard, and vinegar together in a small bowl.

Arrange the bacon in a single layer on a baking sheet. Bake the bacon until it begins to look opaque and the fat begins to render, 10 to 12 minutes. Pour off any accumulated drippings.

Turn over the bacon and brush about one half of the glaze on each slice. Return the bacon to the oven and cook for 3 to 4 minutes longer. Remove the bacon from the oven and turn it over again. Brush it with the remaining glaze and return it to the oven for 3 to 5 minutes, until well browned and firm. (With the glaze coating, the bacon gets chewy and crunchy but stays short of crisp.) If you want to drain the bacon, do it on a rack rather than on paper towels to avoid wiping off the glaze. Serve warm.

CHILE-GLAZED BACON

Substitute a red-chile honey or chile jelly for the mango chutney and a tablespoon of pickling liquid from a jar of pickled jalapeños for the vinegar.

MAPLE-GLAZED CANADIAN BACON

Something of a cross between bacon and ham in taste and texture, smoked, ready-cooked Canadian bacon comes from the pork loin and offers a leaner and more subtle-tasting alternative to the two other popular breakfast meats. We like to glaze the meat with real maple syrup, first mixing a tablespoon of it with ½ teaspoon Dijon mustard. Coat a large skillet with just enough oil to create a thin film. Fry a dozen ⅓-inch-thick Canadian bacon slices until lightly browned on the first side, about 2 minutes. Turn and coat that side of the slices very lightly with the syrup mixture. When the bacon has cooked for about 2 minutes on the second side, turn and coat again with the remaining syrup mixture. Fry for another minute per side after coating with the glaze and serve warm.

it has been done. Serious bacon producers also cut their bacon thick, in meaty ⅛- to ¼-inch slices, which gives buyers the tastiest combination of crispy fat and chewy lean after cooking.

Our model for great bacon is Nueske's, a brand from a northern Wisconsin family business that's nearly seventy years old. Like any real smokehouse bacon, it costs more than the ordinary stuff but yields three quarters of its weight in meat after cooking. The meat is magnificent too, with full-bodied pork flavor, a fine salty tang from the curing, and smoky applewood sweetness. Nueske's distributes its bacon nationally in select supermarkets and meat markets and also sells directly by mail order (800-382-2266, www.nueske. com).

TECHNIQUE TIP

For cooking bacon plain without a glaze, set your sights on crispness and even browning. If you have a griddle, use it. Fry it over heat no hotter than medium. Turn each slice at least three times, first when the fat begins to turn soft and translucent. To avoid what aficionados call "pig-tails," the curling up of the bacon slices, press down on the bacon with a spatula frequently in the early stages of cooking. Drain on paper towels. Skip the microwave methods of cooking, which actually involve more fuss than frying.

HAM STEAK WITH REDEYE GRAVY

INGREDIENT TIP

When we want a whole country ham, we look locally for a Smithfield version or mail-order from S. Wallace Edwards & Sons (800-222-4267) in Surry, Virginia. If we just want some slices, we check Asian markets or call Kentucky's Gatton Farms (502-525-3437). Good city hams are more widely available, but be sure to get one that's been smoked properly instead of injected with liquid smoke. Burgers' Smokehouse in the Missouri Ozarks (800-624-5426) sells a good mail-order product.

This classic combo can be made with either dry-cured country ham, the old southern specialty, or milder, moister "city" ham, the kind most common in other parts of the country. Just heat the ham slices, to crisp their surface, and make a quick gravy with a spare cup of coffee. You'll be at the table in less time than it takes to order a fast-food breakfast.

SERVES 4

4 slices well-flavored ham, ¼ to ⅓ inch thick for country ham or ⅓ to ½ inch thick for city ham (see Ingredient Tip)

1 tablespoon bacon drippings or unsalted butter, optional

2 teaspoons unbleached all-purpose flour

1 cup fresh hot coffee

Pinch of brown sugar

Pinch of cayenne pepper

Salt and freshly milled black pepper to taste, optional

If the ham has a thick layer of surface fat, cut it off down to about ¼ inch. Then place the fat in a large heavy skillet and cook over medium heat to render it, about 5 minutes. Remove any fat that remains whole and discard it. Add the bacon drippings to the skillet unless enough fat was rendered to cover it with a thick film. Raise the heat to medium-high. Fry the ham steaks in batches until lightly browned in spots and a bit crispy on the edges, about 2 to 3 minutes per side. Arrange the steaks on a platter as they are done.

To make the gravy, reduce the heat to medium, then whisk the flour into the pan drippings. Pour in the coffee and scrape up the pan drippings from the bottom of the skillet. Add at least ¼ cup hot water, more for a milder coffee jolt. Season with brown sugar and cayenne. Taste the gravy and add salt and pepper as needed. Serve the gravy immediately over the ham slices.

BUTTERMILK BISCUITS WITH REDEYE GRAVY

With or without the ham, Flaky Buttermilk Biscuits (page 336) make a perfect mate for redeye gravy. Use your imagination with other breads as well. New Orleans chef Paul Prudhomme says in *Seasoned America* (1991) that he likes to pour redeye gravy over doughnuts.

"CO-COLA" REDEYE GRAVY

In some homes, even breakfast goes better with Coke. Substitute it for all or part of the coffee for a sweeter breakfast sop.

HAM STEAKS WITH MARYLAND CREAM GRAVY

In many areas cream gravy is the most traditional and popular topping for ham steaks. Jane Howard gives her recipe in *50 Years in a Maryland Kitchen* (1888). She says to dust the ham with flour before frying. When it's done, add to the pan drippings ½ cup each milk and whipping cream, with about 1 tablespoon butter, 1 teaspoon mustard, and a pinch of cayenne pepper. Bring to a boil and thicken lightly. We add salt and pepper to taste. These are especially good with fried green tomatoes, cooked in the skillet after the ham and before the gravy, then covered with the cream gravy too.

NEW DIRECTIONS

Antebellum American cookbooks seldom treated breakfast as a subject separate from other meals, simply assuming that many foods might be eaten at any time of the day. Dishes that became breakfast specialties—such as fried eggs, omelets, ham, hashes, pancakes, and waffles—appeared frequently, but usually in general chapters on meat, bread, or miscellaneous recipes. Eliza Leslie, in *Directions for Cookery* (1837), probably came closer than anyone to giving these dishes special treatment, devoting individual chapters to "Eggs, Etc.," "Directions for Curing Ham or Bacon," and "Warm Cakes for Breakfast and Tea."

COUNTRY HAM
WITH SAUTÉED HOMINY

SELECTIONS FROM THE

BREAKFAST MENU ON THE

SS *GEORGE WASHINGTON*,

1921

To Order from the Grill, 15 to 20
minutes:

Small Sirloin Steak

Lamb Chops

Beechnut Bacon

Virginia Ham

Deerfoot Sausages

———

Breakfast in America
always fascinates me. It
is a unique repast that
seems to have come
into being naturally,
born of the pioneer
dishes and the
indigenous foods. I can
find no close
resemblance to this
morning meal in the
European countries
from which the settlers
came; you couldn't say
there was anything
Dutch or German or
Swedish or French or
even English about it. I
am not talking here
about the convenience

When country ham isn't keeping company with redeye gravy—and sometimes when it is—it often comes with a side of grits in the South. As the progenitor of grits, hominy tastes just as good on the plate and offers more of a texture foil for the dense ham. If you need anything else to brace yourself for the day, we would opt for Sweet Potato Home Fries (page 307).   **SERVES 4**

4 tablespoons (½ stick) unsalted butter

4 slices smoky country-style ham, about ⅓ inch thick (see Ingredient Tip on page 130)

½ cup chicken stock or water

Two 15-ounce cans hominy (one yellow and one white corn, if available), drained

Pinch of cayenne pepper

Salt and freshly milled black pepper to taste, optional

Melt 1 tablespoon of the butter in a large heavy skillet over medium-high heat. Fry the ham slices in batches until lightly browned in spots and a bit crispy on the edges, about 2 to 3 minutes per side. Set the ham aside and keep it warm. Reduce the heat to medium, then add the remaining butter to the pan drippings. Pour in the stock and scrape up the pan drippings from the bottom of the skillet. Stir in the hominy and heat through, seasoning with cayenne, salt, and plenty of pepper. Spoon the hominy and juices onto a rimmed platter, top with the ham, and serve.

BAKED HAM AND APPLE ROLL

Many American preparations combine apples and pork, a hearty duo. This is a midwestern take on the theme that we encountered first in a slightly more elaborate form in Edward Harris Heth's *Wisconsin Country Cookbook and Journal* (1956). He in turn got the dish from a neighbor, Rosalie Barker. Heth enjoyed it in the morning with pancakes or waffles or at lunch with candied sweet potatoes and a salad. You can assemble the ham roll the evening before you plan to bake and serve it.

SERVES 4 AS A BREAKFAST SIDE DISH, 2 AS A MAIN DISH

2 tart apples, such as Granny Smith, peeled and grated

1 large ham steak, 1 to 1¼ pounds, about 7 or 8 inches by 9 or 10 inches

2 teaspoons Dijon mustard

2 teaspoons unsalted butter

¼ cup chopped onion

¼ teaspoon dried sage, optional

1 tablespoon light or dark brown sugar

Preheat the oven to 350°F. Butter a medium baking dish. Over the baking dish, squeeze the grated apples with your hands to release the excess juice. Reserve both the apples and juice.

Cut the bone out of the ham steak and trim away any pockets of fat and fat from the edges. Pound the ham lightly to ¼- to ⅓-inch thickness, arranging it so as to fill the hole left by the bone. Coat the top side of the steak with half of the mustard. Scatter the apples over the steak.

Warm the butter in a small skillet over medium heat. Add the onion and sauté until softened, about 3 minutes. Stir in the sage if desired. Spoon the onion evenly over the apples. Roll the steak up from one of its long sides. Secure the roll with toothpicks or tie with kitchen twine.

Place the steak in the baking dish and spoon some of the apple juice over it. Brush with the remaining mustard and sprinkle the brown sugar over the top. Bake until lightly glazed and tender, 25 to 30 minutes. With a sharp thin knife, cut into 1-inch-thick pinwheel slices and serve with some of the pan juices.

PHILADELPHIA SCRAPPLE

Scrapple has plenty of fans and probably even more foes. We sat staunchly in the camp of the latter until we happened on a couple of good restaurant versions and decided to experiment with the dish at home. We learned right away that it requires proper cooking to crisp the surface and leave the center moist, and that standard cuts of pork work as well as or better than the scraps of innards used originally in colonial Pennsylvania. Most cooks serve it as a sausagelike side dish, dressed sometimes with butter and maple syrup or accompanied by applesauce.

SERVES 8 OR MORE

A BREAKFAST MENU
SUGGESTION FOR THE
"SIMPLE LIFE"
Scrapple   Grape-nuts
Bread   Butter   Syrup
Grain-o
The Inglenook Cook Book (1911)

One 3-pound bone-in pork butt

One 1¼-pound smoked ham hock

½ large onion

1 tablespoon salt

2 to 3 teaspoons freshly cracked black pepper

1 teaspoon crumbled dried sage

¼ to ½ teaspoon cayenne pepper

½ teaspoon freshly milled white pepper

2 cups stone-ground cornmeal, preferably yellow

Vegetable oil or bacon or sausage drippings for panfrying

Cut the pork butt into several large chunks, leaving the bone in one. Place the pork butt and ham hock in a large stockpot or Dutch oven and cover with cold water by about 2 inches. Add the onion, salt, cracked pepper, sage, cayenne, and white pepper and bring to a boil. Skim off any foam, reduce the heat to medium-low, and simmer, uncovered, until the meat nearly falls apart, 3 to 3½ hours.

Strain and measure the stock. If you have more than 5 cups, return it to the pan and boil over high heat until reduced to approximately that amount. If you have less than 5 cups, add water as necessary and return it to the pot. When the meat is cool enough to handle, pull it into shreds, discarding surface fat and bone. Using a food processor, chop the meat into fine but toothsome bits with a little texture remaining. Add the cornmeal to the pot, a few handfuls at a time, breaking up any lumps, and then add the meat. Cook, frequently stirring up from the bottom until very thick and no longer tasting of raw corn, 20 to 25 minutes. Adjust the seasoning, if you wish. Pour the scrapple into 2 loaf pans and let cool briefly. Cover and refrigerate for at least 8 hours.

When ready to serve, unmold one or both "loaves" and cut as much as you wish to use into ½-inch to ¾-inch-thick slices. Warm ⅛ inch of oil in a large heavy skillet over medium-high heat. Fry the scrapple slices until golden and crusty, 2 to 3 minutes per side. Don't overcook, because scrapple should remain creamy at the center. Serve warm.

BUCKWHEAT SCRAPPLE

In Germany, where scrapple originated, cooks made it with buckwheat flour instead of the unknown-to-them New World cornmeal. The Pennsylvania Dutch, who were actually German, often used a mixture of the two grains. For buckwheat flavor, which many consider essential to scrapple, substitute the flour for up to half of the cornmeal.

SAUSAGE SCRAPPLE

If it's hard to come by a ham hock, you can use sausage instead. Add ½ pound crumbled cooked breakfast sausage to the drained stock along with pork butt, cornmeal, and spices.

MEAT AND GRAIN

Contemporary cooks may think that scrapple involves a strange and perhaps unharmonious combination of ingredients. Earlier Americans looked at the mixture differently, as an opportune pairing of meat and grain to stretch the former and fortify the latter. Many variations on the theme popped up in different areas. Cincinnati goetta and Minnesota gritswurst mate oatmeal and pork. In North Carolina, liver mush (aka liver pudding) brings together the namesake meat and cornmeal. We've read of a Montana "scrapple" made with pork and ground hominy and seasoned liberally with onion and cayenne and of a Kennebec "scrapple" from Maine that adds flaked salmon to cornmeal mush.

SAGE FARM SAUSAGE

TECHNIQUE TIP

If you want to make this into link sausage, stuff the meat into hog casings, which will produce links about an inch thick. Available at any good meat market, the casings usually come packed in brine and need to be soaked before use.

British in derivation, this became America's favorite breakfast sausage. Supermarkets sell many varieties, including some worthy ones, but we like to make it ourselves to ensure the quality of the meat, to fine-tune the seasonings to our tastes, and to control the level of fat, which should be generous if you're going to bother with the sausage at all. It's simple to put together, especially if you just make bulk sausage to form into patties instead of links. We season our sausage assertively and love it redolent of sage. You can start with smaller quantities of any or all of the flavorings, adding more if you wish after frying a bit to taste-test. Regardless of which direction you go, this puts a glorious country shine on any morn.

MAKES ABOUT 2½ POUNDS

2 pounds pork Boston butt (shoulder), plus ½ to ¾ pound pork fat (fatback), ground once or twice by your butcher or with a meat grinder at home

1 tablespoon crumbled dried sage

1 teaspoon salt

1 teaspoon freshly milled black pepper

½ teaspoon dried marjoram

⅛ to ¼ teaspoon cayenne pepper

Combine the ingredients in a large mixing bowl. This will probably be easier with your clean fingers.

Fry a small amount of the sausage in a small skillet, taste, and adjust the seasonings. Refrigerate the uncooked sausage, covered, for at least a few hours and up to several days, or freeze for up to 2 months. When ready to serve, form into thin patties and fry the sausage over medium-low heat until richly browned on both sides, 12 to 15 minutes total.

PEPPERED FARM SAUSAGE

Reduce the sage to 1 teaspoon and eliminate the cayenne. Reduce the ground black pepper to ½ teaspoon, but add 1½ teaspoons cracked black peppercorns and ¼ teaspoon freshly milled white pepper.

VENISON BREAKFAST SAUSAGE

Substitute 1 pound ground venison for 1 pound of the pork (the venison is too lean on its own to make good sausage). Add a couple of tablespoons of liquid to the mixture too, either brandy, stock, or dry red wine.

APPALACHIAN SAWMILL GRAVY

Farm sausage in cream, this is guaranteed to get you running on a sleepy winter morning. Crumble 1 pound sage or other farm sausage and fry it in a large heavy skillet over medium heat until well browned. Remove the sausage with a slotted spoon and drain it. Stir 2 teaspoons cornstarch together with 2 tablespoons water until smooth. Pour the cornstarch mixture into the pan drippings, then add 2 cups whole milk, a pinch of cayenne if you like, and salt and pepper to taste. Continue cooking until the gravy has thickened lightly, then spoon the sausage back into it and serve over biscuits.

Sausage was a frequent accompaniment of buckwheat cakes. Its odor and flavor still haunt me, proof that some mysterious ingredient in its making has been lost to mankind. As I pondered this culinary conundrum, the answer suddenly came to me. It was the *sage.* The whole secret lay in the sage. We grew our own in a neat little row along the garden's edge, picked and dried it, and crumbled it— aromatic, fresh, and pungent—into the meat.

Della Lutes, *The Country Kitchen* (1936)

PASQUAL'S CHORIZO

INGREDIENT TIP

A softer and more fragrant cinnamon than the cassia kind commonly available, *canela* is often found today in supermarkets. Check the Mexican or Hispanic foods section or just go to a Mexican or Hispanic market. For mail order, contact the Santa Fe School of Cooking (800-982-4688 or www. santafeschoolofcooking.com).

TECHNIQUE TIP

If the ancho chiles are recently dried, they will be somewhat leathery and not easily crumbled or cut with a knife. Use scissors to trim them into small squares before pulverizing.

Brimming with chile, garlic, and other seasonings, Mexican chorizo is one of the world's most vibrant sausages. Not long ago you had to hunt for it even in the Southwest, but it has swept the country since then, often in tamed versions that lack appropriate authority. For full flavor, make your own, an easy process, even with a few extra minutes for toasting and grinding your own spices. This version comes from Café Pasqual's, a bustling Santa Fe restaurant that serves joyously flavored breakfasts throughout the daylight hours. The chorizo is the natural mate to Breakfast Polenta Southwest Style (page 324).

MAKES 2 TO 2½ POUNDS

3 to 4 Mexican cinnamon (*canela*) sticks, each 2 inches long (see Ingredient Tip), or 1½ teaspoons ground regular cinnamon (cassia)

20 black peppercorns

10 cloves

1½ teaspoons cumin seeds

6 dried ancho chiles, stemmed, seeded, and finely chopped or crumbled

2 tablespoons ground dried mild New Mexican red chile, preferably Chimayó chile

2 tablespoons ground dried medium-hot New Mexican red chile, preferably *molido*

8 plump garlic cloves, minced

1 teaspoon kosher or other coarse salt

¼ cup red wine vinegar

2 pounds pork Boston butt (shoulder), plus ½ to ¾ pound pork fat (fatback), ground once or twice by your butcher or with a meat grinder at home

In a small heavy skillet over medium heat, combine the cinnamon, peppercorns, cloves, and cumin. Toast until fragrant, shaking the pan frequently, about 2 minutes. Cool briefly, then grind in a spice mill, mini–food processor, or coffee grinder (clean well afterward). Alternatively, grind with a mortar and pestle.

Transfer the spice mixture to a food processor and add the 3 chiles, garlic, and salt. With the motor running, pour in the vinegar so that a paste forms. If the mixture is too dry to hold together, add water 1 teaspoon at a time until it becomes cohesive.

Combine the pork and spice paste in a mixing bowl, mixing thoroughly. This will probably be easiest with your clean fingers. Cover and refrigerate for at least a few hours and up to a couple of days or freeze for up to 2 months.

Fry the chorizo in patties or crumbled in a heavy skillet over medium heat, in batches if necessary, until richly brown and crisp in spots, 8 to 10 minutes. Serve *pronto*.

CHORIZO AND EGGS

Whisk 8 eggs with 2 tablespoons water and salt and pepper to taste in a medium bowl. Crumble 4 to 6 ounces chorizo and fry it in a large heavy skillet over medium heat until brown around the edges. Add a few tablespoons of minced onion, if you wish, and sauté until limp. Pour in the eggs and cook to the desired doneness, stirring them up from the bottom as they cook.

CHORIZO-TOPPED BISCUITS WITH CREAM GRAVY

The Melrose Hotel in Dallas serves one of our favorite chorizo breakfasts, a bit more elegant and labor-intensive than most but absolutely scrumptious. To emulate the dish, fry chorizo in patties, make cream gravy from the pan drippings as on page 157 (substituting sausage for steak), and serve between steaming halved Flaky Buttermilk Biscuits (page 336) with the gravy spooned around. Sprinkle generously with thinly sliced scallion rings and freshly cracked peppercorns. The restaurant adds a shower of smoked corn kernels, but we skip that at home.

DELICIOUS BREAKFAST DISH

Take some hog meat prepared for sausages. Chop up some well boiled pig's feet, mix with it, and wrap up in a lace. Fry it, and serve hot.

Celestine Eustis, *Cooking in Old Créole Days* (1903)

SPICED LAMB SAUSAGE

A BREAKFAST MENU SUGGESTION FROM THE NATIONAL LIVE STOCK AND MEAT BOARD

Chilled Melon

Lamb Chop and Pineapple Grill

Corn-meal Muffins   Jelly

Coffee

"Meat Recipes and Menus," a 1931 promotional pamphlet

Americans used to enjoy lamb at all meals, not just dinner. At breakfast, home cooks served it in patties or hash, and refined restaurants offered lamb chops Mirabeau, with tomato and béarnaise sauces. The meat seems to be making a comeback as morning fare, now mainly in the form of sausage. Our favorite version boasts a heady, fragrant blend of sweet and savory spices that came originally from North Africa but is now found frequently in North America. The sausage brings out the best in a simple omelet or fried potatoes.

MAKES ABOUT 2 POUNDS

2 pounds lamb shoulder, loin, or various trimmings, ground by your butcher (see Ingredient Tip)

¼ cup minced fresh cilantro

4½ teaspoons olive oil, plus additional for panfrying

1½ tablespoons paprika

1 tablespoon minced garlic

2 teaspoons salt or more to taste

2 teaspoons freshly cracked black pepper

1 teaspoon ground cumin

1 to 1½ teaspoons harissa (Moroccan chile paste sold in small jars or tubes) or cayenne pepper or more to taste

½ teaspoon ground cinnamon

¼ teaspoon freshly grated nutmeg

Combine the ingredients in a large mixing bowl, starting with the smaller quantities of salt, and harissa. This will probably be easiest with your clean fingers.

Fry a small amount of the sausage in a small skillet, taste, and adjust the seasonings. Refrigerate, covered, for at least a few hours and up to several days or freeze for up to 2 months. When ready to serve, form into thin patties and fry the sausage over medium-low heat until richly browned on both sides, 12 to 15 minutes total.

GRILLED SPICED LAMB SAUSAGE

Grilling adds intensity to this sausage. Instead of forming the sausage into patties, make oblong meatballs and skewer them together. Brush them with oil before grilling briefly over medium heat until brown and crisp but still juicy.

LAMB SAUSAGE WITH ROSEMARY AND GARLIC

Sauté 2 tablespoons minced garlic and 2 teaspoons crumbled rosemary leaves in 2 tablespoons olive oil just until fragrant and the garlic only lightly colored. Mix with the 2 pounds lamb, 2 teaspoons salt, 1 teaspoon pepper, and, if you wish, 1 teaspoon hot red pepper flakes. Prepare as directed.

SAUSAGE-APPLE LOAF

INGREDIENT TIP

The best sausage for this loaf is Sage Farm Sausage (page 136) or a similar homemade sausage. It adds complexity to the dish that is difficult to achieve with mass-market products.

———

Probably the English pig—which is called a "bacon-type pig" in the United States—is now being taken too far toward leanness, at any rate for the finer points of *charcuterie*. He has become too much a factory animal; we neglect his ears, his tail, his trotters, his insides, his beautiful fat, and his flavor (pig's ears by the hundred thousand are fed to mink, from one of the Wiltshire bacon factories, which is a bit like feeding caviar to canaries).

Jane Grigson, *The Art of Charcuterie* (1967)

A breakfast meat loaf from the heartland, this is as richly soothing on a winter morning as a mug of hot chocolate.

SERVES 6

1 tablespoon unsalted butter	⅔ cup dried bread crumbs
1 small onion, minced	2 large eggs, lightly beaten
2 tablespoons real maple syrup	¼ cup milk
1½ pounds well-seasoned bulk breakfast sausage (see Ingredient Tip)	¾ teaspoon freshly milled black pepper
	½ teaspoon salt
1 cup grated apple	⅛ teaspoon cayenne pepper

Preheat the oven to 350°F.

Warm the butter in a small skillet over medium heat. Add the onion and sauté until very soft, about 5 minutes. Scrape the onion into a large mixing bowl and let it cool briefly. Add 1 tablespoon of the maple syrup and the remaining ingredients. Mix well.

Pack the mixture into a loaf pan, mounding it a bit in the center. Brush the remaining maple syrup over it.

Bake until the loaf is well browned with an internal temperature of 165°F to 170°F at the center, about 1 hour. Pour off the accumulated grease and let the loaf sit for about 10 minutes before cutting into slices and serving.

ROSALEA MURPHY'S GRAPE SAUSAGE

The founder and grande dame of the popular Pink Adobe restaurant in Santa Fe for almost fifty years, the late Rosalea Murphy used to make a very simple but tasty fruit sausage. She would start with about a pound of farm sausage, mix it with an egg and about ⅓ cup fresh bread crumbs to bind it, then stir in about a cup of seedless grape halves. She shaped the meat into patties and fried them over medium heat until richly brown.

PRIME-TIME BREAKFAST T-BONE

Throughout much of our history, nothing made a morning as special as a succulent steak. Americans still eat them occasionally, but usually minor cuts in puny portions compared to the past. Mark Twain wrote lovingly about a thick porterhouse served with buckwheat cakes and a mound of hot biscuits. Oliver Wendell Holmes favored filet mignon. Diamond Jim Brady, the man with the biggest appetite of all, ate almost any prime steak, usually saving it for the climax of the meal after already consuming a full gallon of orange juice, eggs, pancakes, and fried potatoes. Our sizzling breakfast T-bone harks back to those days in the quality of the cut and the heartiness of the enjoyment, though we trim the portion size to today's tastes. After cooking the steak, add a little butter to the pan and fry some eggs and tomatoes to go on the side.

SERVES 4 OR EVEN MORE

Two 1-pound T-bone steaks, 1 inch thick, at least choice grade and preferably prime

Salt and freshly cracked black pepper to taste

3 tablespoons unsalted butter, softened

2 teaspoons Worcestershire sauce or more to taste

Sprinkle the steaks with salt and pepper. Let them sit at room temperature for about 20 minutes.

Mix the butter with the Worcestershire sauce in a small bowl.

Warm a large cast-iron skillet over high heat. When the skillet is very hot, place the steaks in it, with the smaller, more tender section of the steaks angled to the outside of the pan, where they will get a bit less heat. Cook the steaks to the desired doneness, about 4 minutes per side for medium-rare. If juices begin to pool on the top of the steaks at any time, turn them, but keep the overall cooking time to around 8 minutes. Plate the sizzling steaks and immediately spoon Worcestershire butter over each, so that the melting butter can mingle enticingly with the meat juices. Serve without hesitation.

PRIME-TIME T-BONE WITH SAGE BUTTER

When seasoning the steaks with the salt and pepper, rub each with ½ to 1 teaspoon dried sage. Add to the butter 2 tablespoons minced fresh sage and reduce the Worcestershire sauce to 1 teaspoon.

AN OLD-FASHIONED FAST-FOOD BREAKFAST

The Pennsylvania Dutch, long renowned for their robust home cooking, used to feast in the morning on steak, fried oysters, cold chicken, scrapple, crumb cakes, fruit pies, and fried mush, usually digested with hot pepper vinegar or a shot of schnapps. Originally from Germany, where beef was uncommon in the past, they became steak lovers through the influence of British colonists and adopted the meat as a breakfast treat because of its short cooking time.

COUNTRY-FRIED STEAK AND ONIONS

Throughout the South and Southwest, crunchy country-fried and chicken-fried steaks are a menu standby at restaurants that feature a big breakfast. We personally prefer the dish in the morning, rather than later in the day, served with breakfast biscuits covered in the same cream gravy as the steak. Add a side of hash browns or grits and you won't have to eat until tomorrow. Don't knock the time-honored favorite if you haven't tried it.   **SERVES 4**

SELECTIONS FROM THE
BREAKFAST MENU AT THE
FIFTH AVENUE HOTEL IN
NEW YORK CITY, 1878

FRIED

Pig's Feet Breaded   Oysters with
Crumbs   Pickled Tripe

Calf's Liver   Sausages   Clams

Pork Chops

1 pound round steak, sliced ½ inch thick and twice-tenderized by the butcher

1 cup unbleached all-purpose flour

1 teaspoon baking powder

½ teaspoon baking soda

½ teaspoon freshly milled black pepper

½ teaspoon salt

¾ cup buttermilk

1 teaspoon Tabasco or other hot pepper sauce

1 medium to large egg

Vegetable shortening or vegetable oil

1 large or 2 medium onions, sliced into thin wedges

CREAM GRAVY

3 tablespoons unbleached all-purpose flour

2 cups heavy (whipping) cream or evaporated milk

¾ cup beef or chicken stock

Several drops of Tabasco or other hot pepper sauce

½ teaspoon freshly milled black pepper or more to taste

Salt to taste

Cut the steak into 4 equal portions and then pound the meat until it's about ¼ inch thick. Sprinkle the 1 cup flour on a plate. In a large shallow bowl, stir together the baking powder, baking soda, ½ teaspoon pepper, and ½ teaspoon salt and mix in the buttermilk, 1 teaspoon Tabasco, and egg. The mixture will be thin.

Melt enough shortening in a large heavy skillet over medium heat to measure ½ inch deep.

Dredge each steak first in flour and then in the batter. Dunk the steaks back into the flour, patting in the flour until the surface of the meat is dry.

Fry the steaks, turning once, until deep golden brown, about 4 minutes per side. You may have to press the steaks down from time to time so that they cook evenly. Drain the steaks, transfer them to a platter, and keep them warm.

Add the onion to the skillet and fry over medium heat until soft and translucent, about 5 minutes. Remove the onion from the skillet with a slotted spoon.

Prepare the gravy. You want about ¼ cup of pan drippings in the bottom of the skillet. Pour off any extra through a strainer, returning any browned cracklings or onion bits from the strainer to the skillet.

Warm the drippings over medium heat. Sprinkle in the 3 tablespoons flour, stirring to prevent lumps. Pour in the cream, stock, and several drops of Tabasco. Simmer until the liquid is thickened and the raw flour taste is gone, about 3 minutes. Frequently stir the gravy up from the bottom, scraping up the browned bits. Add the pepper and salt. This makes a lot of gravy, enough to pour over the steaks, onions, *and* the biscuits that you just have to eat with this. Serve immediately.

COUNTRY-FRIED STEAK WITH BROWN GRAVY

Some folks scorn "canned cow" in their gravy, or even dairy-fresh cream, preferring a beefier brew. When making a brown gravy, eliminate the whipping cream in the recipe and substitute 2 additional cups of beef stock for the evaporated milk.

MACHACA SCRAMBLE

TECHNIQUE TIP

Personal taste dictates the moistness of *machaca,* which varies from soupy with broth, dry as we prefer in our recipe, or *medio.* Customize to your liking by adding more beef stock for the skillet cooking and removing the meat from the stove while there's still plenty of liquid.

Well-seasoned beef that's slow simmered and then shredded, *machaca* is a legacy of Mexican ranchers and cowboys in southern Arizona and Texas. The preparation requires multiple steps, but ones that are simple to execute, can be done a day or more ahead, and reward you handsomely in the end. The meat reheats well, and leftovers make magnificent burritos or tacos for any meal of the day. **SERVES 6 OR MORE**

One 3-pound boneless shoulder chuck roast

Salt to taste

¼ cup bacon drippings or vegetable oil

1 cup beef stock

2 tablespoons ground dried mild red chile, such as ancho, New Mexican, or guajillo

1 bay leaf

1 Mexican cinnamon (*canela*) or other cinnamon stick

1½ medium onions, chopped

2 garlic cloves, minced

3 small tomatoes, preferably Roma or plum, chopped

1 tablespoon fresh lime juice

3 large eggs

Thin flour tortillas, warmed

Rub the roast thoroughly with a generous amount of salt.

Warm 2 tablespoons of the bacon drippings in a heavy lidded skillet or Dutch oven over medium-high heat. Brown the meat on all sides. Reduce the heat to low. Pour the stock over the meat and add the chile, bay leaf, cinnamon, 1 onion, and 1 garlic clove to the pan. Cover and simmer until the meat is very tender, 1 to 1¼ hours. Let the meat cool in the cooking liquid. When cool enough to handle, strain the liquid and reserve it. Shred the meat with your fingers on in a food processor in several small batches. (If your food processor has a plastic blade for dough, use it for the shredding.)

Rinse and dry the skillet. Warm the remaining bacon drippings in it over medium heat. Add the remaining onion and garlic and sauté until the onion softens, about 3 minutes. Stir in the meat and continue sautéing for 10 to 12 minutes. Scrape the meat up from the bottom every few minutes, cooking until it is well browned and crusty in spots but not burned. Stir in the reserved cooking liquid, tomatoes, and lime juice. Reduce the heat to low and cook until most of the liquid evaporates but the meat remains a little moist, about 25 minutes. Season with additional salt if needed. (The *machaca* may be made to this point up to several days ahead. Cover and refrigerate, warming the meat before proceeding.)

Whisk the eggs until combined. Mix them with the *machaca* and continue cooking until they are done. Spoon the mixture onto a platter or individual plates. The *machaca* can be spooned into the tortillas or eaten alongside them.

TUCSON BREAKFAST BURRO

Arizona burritos are never small, as the suffix *ito* implies, so they are known locally as burros. For a version that's served at breakfast and other meals, eliminate the egg from the *machaca* scramble, wrap the meat in thin flour tortillas, and arrange the burro on plates seam side down. Spoon Salsa Frontera (page 422) or other robust salsa over it, sprinkle perhaps with grated asadero or Monterey Jack cheese, and serve immediately.

TEXAS MACHACA

In west Texas, *machaca* is usually made from the beloved beef brisket, slow-simmered in beef broth for a couple of hours, shredded, and peppered with bits of tomato, onion, and 1 or 2 minced jalapeño or serrano chiles. Add eggs for a scramble or serve the meat by itself. Many people eat the *machaca* inside a soft breakfast taco.

NO BEEF WITH THIS

Food rationing during World War I didn't quell the American interest in a hearty breakfast. In an age when railroad dining still set a stylish tone across the country, one line developed a special morning menu for "Meatless Tuesdays" that included fruit, cereal, oysters, grilled whitefish, broiled mackerel, crabmeat au gratin, shredded chicken on toast, broiled squab, and plenty of egg options.

CREAMED CHIPPED BEEF ON TOAST

The first cooks to make *machaca* started with dried beef, which continues to be the core of this venerable dish from the opposite end of the country. In both the Southwest and the Northeast, the original settlers dried meat for preservation and then rehydrated it with locally flavored cooking liquids. In this case, cooks relied on a cream sauce, always popular among dairy-loving British colonists. The idea began losing favor after refrigeration eliminated the need for home-dried beef and the careful crafting that went into it. Poor commercial imitations of the meat and bad cafeteria and mess-hall preparations of the dish ruined its reputation. With good dried beef now available again, it's time to give the old favorite another try. Made well, it remains a brawny breakfast.

SERVES 4 TO 6

3 tablespoons unsalted butter

½ pound paper-thin dried beef slices, shredded (see Ingredient Tip)

3 tablespoons unbleached all-purpose flour

2 cups whole milk

1 cup half-and-half

⅛ teaspoon freshly milled white pepper

1 tablespoon minced fresh chives

Pinch of freshly grated nutmeg

4 to 6 slices toast

1 tablespoon minced fresh parsley

Melt the butter in a large skillet over medium heat. Stir in the dried beef and sauté until it develops a few crisp edges, about 5 minutes. Stir in the flour and cook until it just begins to color. Slowly whisk in the milk and half-and-half, then add the pepper, chives, and nutmeg. Continue cooking, stirring constantly, until thickened and creamy but still pourable, about 5 minutes longer. Ladle over toast, scatter with parsley, and serve immediately.

CREAMED LEBANON BOLOGNA ON TOAST

Nothing like the baloney all of us ate as school kids, the Pennsylvania Dutch's Lebanon bologna is beefy smoked summer sausage, fragrant with black pepper and a touch of sugar. It can be found commonly throughout the Mid-Atlantic states. Substitute ½ pound of it, or another good peppery summer sausage, sliced as thin as you can get it, for the chipped beef.

LUCIUS BEEBE'S BEEF

One of the most renowned gastronomes of his day, Lucius Beebe called himself a "professional consumer" rather than a cook. When Philip and Helen Evans Brown helped write *The Virginia City Cook Book* (1953), Beebe told them that he prepared only one dish, chipped beef drenched in "the heaviest cream obtainable." He loved beef in all forms for breakfast, once remarking "I think the most wonderful thing in the world, bar none, is to take the *Gold Coast* [his opulent private railroad car] aboard the night train out of Reno and roll down from the Comstock as the old bearded silver kings used to do, take the Oakland ferry across the Bay, and have breakfast of champagne and grilled beef bones at The Palace. It's a way of life that has no peer in the American record and makes even the plantation civilization of the Deep South look shabby."

MENUDO

The well-recognized "breakfast of champions" in the Southwest, this bold tripe stew easily trounces boxed cereal for the title. Cooks typically make it on weekends, partly because of the long preparation time and partly because of its fame as a hangover cure. Our version is *blanco*, a style in which red chile is added to taste at the table instead of cooked with the meat. Accompany the menudo with flour tortillas and maybe a short glass of whatever started your head thumping.   **SERVES 6 TO 8**

INGREDIENT TIP

Look for honeycomb tripe, the most tender variety, for menudo. If you're living in the right area, or just lucky, it will already be cleaned and maybe even cut for the stew. If not, you must clean the tripe right away because it perishes quickly otherwise. Start a day in advance of the cooking. Mix together 1 cup coarse kosher salt, an abrasive, and 1 cup inexpensive vinegar. Pour about one third of the mixture into a large bowl and add the tripe. With a clean brush, scrub the meat vigorously for about 5 minutes. Rinse the tripe under cold running water and repeat the process two more times. Transfer the tripe to a bowl and cover it with cold water. Chill, covered, for at least 8 hours and up to 24 hours, changing the water every 8 hours or so.

———

Head-cheese, with rolls and coffee, make a nice breakfast; also fried sausages; or meat or cod-fish cakes. A shoulder of lamb may be boned and broiled; or a breast may be nicely and thoroughly broiled; or lamb or chickens stewed.

Mrs. T. J. Crowen, *The American Lady's System of Cookery* (1852)

2 pounds honeycomb tripe, cleaned (see Ingredient Tip)

2 tablespoons vegetable oil

2 large onions, chopped

8 garlic cloves, minced

1 bay leaf

6 cups chicken stock

1 ham hock or ¾ pound oxtails

One 15- to 16-ounce can hominy, preferably white

1 tablespoon dried oregano, preferably Mexican

½ teaspoon ground cumin

Salt to taste

Chopped radish and minced fresh cilantro, optional

Chopped onion, hot red pepper flakes, and lime wedges

Cut the cleaned tripe thinly into bite-size pieces. Place the tripe in a stockpot or large, heavy saucepan, cover it with cold water, and bring it to a rapid boil over high heat. Boil the meat for 30 minutes, then drain and discard the water and reserve the tripe.

Rinse and dry the stockpot, return it to the stove, and add the oil. Warm the oil over medium heat and add the onions, garlic, and bay leaf. Sauté until soft, about 3 to 5 minutes. Add the stock, reserved tripe, and ham hock. Reduce the heat to a very low simmer, cover, and cook the meat for 3 hours. Remove the ham hock, discarding any bone and fat, shred it, and reserve. Add the hominy, oregano, cumin, and salt. Simmer for another ½ to 1 hour, until the stew is cooked down and the tripe is tender. Expect it to remain a little chewy. Add the reserved ham and heat it through.

Serve steaming in large bowls. Offer garnishes of radish and cilantro if you wish, but definitely provide onion, hot pepper flakes, and lime wedges so that the menudo can be customized by each diner. Leftovers will keep for several days.

MAPLE-GLAZED HAM, CHEESE,
AND LEEK SANDWICH

page 240

BAGEL WITH SMOKED SALMON
page 243

CRANBERRY–CREAM CHEESE
STUFFED–FRENCH TOAST

page 120

BLUEBERRY TURNOVERS

page 396

SATURDAY SUMMER STRATA
page 206

**CHUNKY RANCH-STYLE
HOME FRIES**

page 306

MANGO LASSI

page 64

OREGON SALMON HASH

page 196

RASPBERRY–CREAM
CHEESE COFFEE CAKE

page 374

GORGEOUS FRUIT SALAD
page 268

BASQUE PIPERRADA

page 49

**EGG CUP WITH
LACQUERED BACON**

page 128

**CHARLESTON SHRIMP
AND GRITS**

page 179

BUTTERMILK BREAKFAST
CORN BREAD WITH BUTTER
AND MARGARITA
MARMALADE AND
PARADISE PRESERVES

pages 343, 408, 410

TROPICAL FRUIT PARFAIT

page 294

STACK OF SILVER
DOLLAR PANCAKES

page 84

CREAMED CHICKEN WITH HAM

Southerners in particular eat cold leftover fried chicken for breakfast, but if you finished that off the night before, try this creamy cooked dish. As in the South, we like to serve it on waffles, perhaps our Wild Rice Waffles (page 115) or Basic Buttermilk Waffles (page 110). The chicken keeps well for a day or more if you want to make it ahead or just create some deliberate leftovers for another meal.   **SERVES 4 TO 6**

A BREAKFAST MENU
SUGGESTION FOR A
SPRING MORNING

Flannel Cakes   Coffee

Fried Chicken, Cream Sauce

Scalloped Potatoes

Salad with French Dressing

Sarah Tyson Rorer,
Philadelphia Cook Book (1886)

1¼ to 1½ pounds boneless, skinless chicken breasts, cut into bite-size cubes

Salt and freshly milled black pepper to taste

3 tablespoons unbleached all-purpose flour

6 tablespoons unsalted butter

2 large shallots, chopped

6 ounces small tender wild mushrooms such as chicken-of-the-woods or oyster, preferably, or portobello or button mushrooms, thinly sliced

3 to 4 ounces country ham or other smoky ham, cut into small dice

¼ cup dry sherry

1 cup chicken stock

1 cup half-and-half

1 teaspoon minced fresh chervil, thyme, or summer savory or ½ teaspoon dried

Pinch of freshly grated nutmeg

Fresh chervil, thyme, or summer savory sprigs, optional

Sprinkle the chicken with salt and pepper, then dust lightly with flour.

Melt the butter in a large heavy skillet over medium heat. Add the chicken and sauté until golden brown on all sides and partially cooked through, about 5 minutes. Sprinkle the shallots, mushrooms, and ham around the chicken and cook for about 2 minutes longer. Pour in the sherry and let it reduce for a couple of minutes. Pour in the stock and half-and-half and sprinkle with the chervil and nutmeg. Reduce the heat to a bare simmer, cover, and continue cooking for 15 to 20 additional minutes until the chicken is quite tender. If the sauce still seems thin, continue cooking, uncovered, for a couple of minutes longer. Garnish with herb sprigs, if you wish, and serve.

FRIED QUAIL AND FARM SAUSAGE

One of the most popular American cookbooks of all time, *Buckeye Cookery and Practical Housekeeping* (1877) promoted quail as the centerpiece of a special fall Sunday breakfast. The editors broiled their birds and served them on buttered bread, but we fry them and plate them with breakfast sausage. Farm-raised quail are becoming more widely available and compare favorably with ones from the wild.

SERVES 4

1 cup unbleached all-purpose flour

3 tablespoons stone-ground cornmeal

2 teaspoons paprika

2 teaspoons chili powder

¾ teaspoon salt

½ teaspoon crumbled dried sage

8 quail, split or semiboned, about 6 to 7 ounces each

Vegetable oil for panfrying

½ pound Sage Farm Sausage (page 136) or other well-seasoned bulk sausage

2 shallots, minced

2½ to 3 cups chicken stock

Combine the flour, cornmeal, paprika, chili powder, salt, and sage in a shallow dish. Reserve ¼ cup of the seasoned flour and dredge the quail in the rest of it.

Pour ½ inch of oil into a large heavy skillet and heat the oil to 350°F. Fry the quail until golden and crisp, about 4 minutes per side. Transfer the quail to a rimmed platter or shallow serving dish and keep them warm.

Pour off all but about 2 tablespoons of the cooking oil through a strainer, returning any cracklings from the strainer to the skillet. Add the sausage to the skillet and brown it, breaking it apart into bite-size bits as it cooks. Remove the sausage with a slotted spoon and spoon it around the quail. Warm the remaining pan drippings over medium heat. Stir in the shallots and cook until beginning to soften, just a minute or two. Sprinkle in the reserved seasoned flour, stirring well to prevent lumps. Gradually pour in the stock, continuing to stir. Simmer the mixture until it has thickened into a rich tan gravy, about 3 minutes. Adjust the seasoning if needed. Pour the gravy around the quail and sausage and serve immediately.

FRIED QUAIL AND ANDOUILLE SAUSAGE BAYOU STYLE

Eliminate the paprika and chili powder. Replace the farm sausage with 6 ounces chopped andouille. Add 2 to 3 tablespoons brandy or sherry and cook down briefly before adding the stock. Serve over thick slices of toasted French bread.

6

On the Waterfront

ALTHOUGH MANY PEOPLE love smoked salmon in the morning, other fish and shellfish seldom surface at breakfast today. Some cooks maintain a traditional attachment to local and regional specialties—such as the fried trout of the mountain West, the cod cakes of New England, and Charleston's magnificent shrimp and grits—but these dishes never traveled broadly and seem to be sinking slowly even on their home turf.

Companies can't box this kind of breakfast food, so no one pushes it through mass advertising. Before marketing pros began telling us what to eat, we woke up eagerly in the morning to anything edible from our rivers, lakes, and seas. American cooks need to recall those vibrant tastes, rejoice in them again, and do our own kind of advertising on the plate.

BACON-FRIED TROUT

When Americans cook fresh fish in the morning, they usually do it in the frying pan. At various times and places we've fried halibut from coastal waters, crappie and croakers straight from the stream, all manner of creatures in cakes and hashes, and even in the depths of Idaho and Utah winters, tiny Bonneville ciscos caught with dip nets in the freezing waters of local lakes. Of all the choices, none surpass trout coated with a little cornmeal and skillet-cooked in bacon drippings. Try them with Fresh Corn Fritters (page 99).   **SERVES 4**

8 thick slices bacon

Unsalted butter

1 cup stone-ground cornmeal

½ teaspoon dried sage

Pinch of cayenne pepper

Salt and freshly milled black pepper to taste

4 trout, about ¾ pound each, gutted but heads intact

Fry the bacon in a large heavy skillet over medium heat until brown and crisp. Drain the bacon and reserve it. Add butter as necessary to the drippings in the skillet to measure a generous ¼ inch of cooking fat.

On a large plate, stir together the cornmeal, sage, cayenne, salt, and pepper. Cut 2 moderately deep diagonal slashes into the sides of each fish. Roll the fish in the cornmeal mixture, coating it thoroughly, including in the cavities and slashes. Warm the bacon drippings over medium heat. Fry the fish until lightly browned on both sides and flaky throughout, turning it once, 10 to 12 minutes. Serve the trout with the bacon on the side.

PECAN-CRUSTED TROUT

Substitute ¾ cup finely ground pecans for an equal amount of the cornmeal.

MARION CUNNINGHAM'S OATMEAL-DREDGED TROUT

America's most famous breakfast cook dips trout into milk (about ½ cup should suffice for 4 fish), then dunks it in rolled oats (about ⅔ cup total) and seasons to taste with salt and pepper. If the oats seem too bulky for your taste, they can be ground more finely in a food processor.

CRUNCHY BUTTERMILK-DIPPED CATFISH

Both of us landlubbers, raised far inland, grew up thinking that catfish was the only fish anyone ate. We still enjoy it frequently, including at breakfast. Today's farm-raised catfish are milder than their wild cousins, so we dunk them in tangy buttermilk and dredge them in well-seasoned cornmeal before frying.

SERVES 4

⅔ cup buttermilk

Minced zest of 1 lemon

1 cup stone-ground cornmeal

6 tablespoons extra-fine stone-ground cornmeal (corn "flour") or unbleached all-purpose flour

1½ teaspoons seasoned salt, such as Lawry's

1 teaspoon onion powder (if it's been sitting in your pantry for years, go buy some new or just leave it out)

1 teaspoon freshly milled black pepper

¾ teaspoon paprika

½ teaspoon cayenne pepper

Peanut or other vegetable oil for deep-frying

1½ pounds catfish fillets, cut into 3-ounce sections

Lemon wedges

Stir the buttermilk and lemon zest together in a shallow dish. On a plate or in another shallow dish, combine the cornmeals, salt, onion powder, pepper, paprika, and cayenne.

Pour several inches of oil into a deep heavy skillet and heat it to 350°F. Dunk the catfish in the buttermilk mixture, pausing briefly to let the liquid drip back into the dish. Dredge the catfish in the cornmeal mixture, coating it thoroughly.

Deep-fry the catfish in batches until golden brown and crusty outside with flaky interiors, 6 to 8 minutes. Garnish the catfish with lemon wedges and serve immediately.

CRUNCHY CATFISH WITH CARIBBEAN HOT SAUCE

Caribbean hot sauces served in the islands with fried flying fish and grouper also spike up the flavor of farm-raised catfish. Add splashes of store-bought sauce judiciously to the buttermilk mixture, then serve more at the table.

CRUNCHY CATFISH WITH TOMATO GRAVY

To dress the catfish for a special breakfast, serve the fillets atop pools of Tomato Gravy (page 317).

PAN-SEARED CREOLE FISH

If you're avoiding fried foods, or just want a change of pace, pan-sear your breakfast fish instead. This is a gulf-inspired preparation, featuring a lively red-bean vinaigrette with sturdy, mild-flavored white fish fillets. Accompany the dish with rice or Heavenly Hash Browns (page 305). It's fine to start with canned beans for this recipe, but use water instead of the liquid from the can, which doesn't work well in the sauce.

Serves 4

SAUCE

1 cup warm cooked red, black, or pinto beans with ¼ cup cooking liquid

¼ cup vegetable oil

1 to 2 tablespoons white wine vinegar

Dash or two of Crystal, Tabasco, or other hot pepper sauce

2 tablespoons unbleached all-purpose flour

½ teaspoon salt

Pinch of cayenne pepper

Four 6-ounce snapper, grouper, mahimahi, or other somewhat firm white fish fillets, no thicker than ½ inch

Vegetable oil and unsalted butter

1 avocado, preferably Hass, cut into bite-size chunks

Prepare the sauce, placing the beans, oil, 1 tablespoon vinegar, and hot sauce in a food processor. Pulse the mixture several times to combine loosely. It should have a slightly coarse texture. Taste and add a bit more vinegar or hot sauce if needed to add pizzazz.

Stir together the flour, salt, and cayenne in a small bowl. Pat the mixture lightly on the fish fillets. Warm enough oil and butter in equal amounts over medium-high heat to measure about ¼ inch deep in a large heavy skillet. When very hot, but short of smoking, add the fillets to the pan and sear them quickly, about 1½ minutes per side until lightly crisp and rich golden brown. Drain the fish fillets.

Divide the sauce among the plates, spooning a small pool onto each. Top with a fish fillet, then a sprinkle of avocado chunks. Serve warm, passing additional hot sauce on the side.

SMOKED FISH PLATTER WITH HOME-SMOKED WHITEFISH

INGREDIENT TIP

Nova has become a marketing term for almost any cold-smoked salmon, but it properly applies to wild fish caught in the waters off Nova Scotia, a type that's still superior in flavor. It's milder and less salty than lox, which derives its name from *lachs,* the German word for salmon. Sturgeon, a connoisseur's delight, is smoked only lightly to allow the flavor of the fish to shine. Smoked sablefish (wild black cod) has an old reputation as a poor man's sturgeon, but good versions are opulently tasty.

**A BREAKFAST MENU
SUGGESTION FOR A NEW
YORK BANQUET FOR 8 TO
10 LUCKY GUESTS**

1 Pound Nova or other Smoked
Salmon

½ Pound Smoked Sturgeon

3 Smoked Chubs

3 Herring Fillets, either in Wine
Sauce or German-style Rollmops

1 Pound of Cream Cheese

8 to 12 Bagels or Bialys

Sliced Tomatoes and Onions

1 Pound of Rugelach Cookies
(if your idea of breakfast
includes dessert)

Undated Russ & Daughters
Catalog

Most of the smoked fish Americans eat for breakfast is cold-smoked in a process best left to professionals. The main exception is whitefish from the chilly waters of the Great Lakes, which local home cooks have hot-smoked for generations. It contrasts smartly with lox, nova, and other cold-smoked fish, offering a distinctly different texture and flavor. Many delis and markets today sell whitefish already cooked, but smoking it yourself adds another dimension to the kind of special-occasion meal appropriate for this grand platter. Get some serious bagels and a chunk of cream cheese and enjoy a banquet to boast about.

SERVES 6 OR MORE

WHITEFISH BRINE

½ cup kosher salt

¼ cup packed light or dark brown sugar

4 teaspoons minced fresh dill or 2 teaspoons dried

1 tablespoon freshly cracked black pepper

One 1½-pound chunk whitefish, sablefish, sea bass, or pike

½ pound lox or nova (see Ingredient Tip), sliced paper-thin

½ pound smoked sturgeon or sablefish or a combination (see Ingredient Tip) or additional lox or nova, or other cold-smoked fish, sliced paper-thin

Lemon wedges

1 medium onion, thinly sliced

Prepare the brine, stirring together the ingredients in a medium bowl and dissolving them in 1½ cups water. Place the whitefish in a zipper-lock plastic bag and pour the brine over the fish. Refrigerate for at least 2 hours and up to 8 hours, noting that the fish gets saltier and sweeter the longer it marinates.

Drain the fish and let it sit at room temperature to air-dry for about 30 minutes.

Fire up a smoker or covered grill to 225°F to 250°F, following the manufacturer's instructions for smoking. Oil the cooking grate well. Place the fish on the grate as far from the fire as possible.

Smoke, covered, until the fish flakes throughout, 30 to 40 minutes. Open the smoker only when necessary and cover as quickly as possible to minimize the loss of heat and smoke.

When the fish is cool enough to handle, separate it into small chunks, discarding the skin and most of the bones. (The fish can be wrapped tightly and refrigerated for up to several days.) Serve the whitefish warm or chilled.

Arrange the whitefish on a platter, surrounded by the other fish. Garnish with lemons and onion and serve.

REALLY APPETIZING FISH

Nearly a century ago, Joel Russ began selling smoked and pickled fish from a pushcart on New York's Lower East Side. The enterprise evolved into the Russ & Daughters appetizing store, a distinct type of Jewish business in that era that focused on fish and dairy products. Mark Russ Federman, Joel's grandson, maintains the style and quality of the original operation today, selling some of the finest lox, nova, sturgeon, and herring on earth. If you're going to be in New York, make a pilgrimage to the shop, located at 179 East Houston, between Orchard and Allen Streets. The expert staff can explain every nuance in the flavor of the various fish, and they slice and package it all to order. It's an experience you won't forget, but if you can't make it there in person, you can at least order the fish for an extraordinary breakfast platter from 800-RUSS-229 or www.russanddaughters.com.

SMOKED SABLE AND SALMON ROLLS

INGREDIENT TIP

You can save money at some shops by requesting trimmings from smoked salmon fillets or salmon cut from the wing rather than the belly. These less-than-perfect pieces work fine in any dish like this where you're going to chop them and add a bit of seasoning anyway.

If you want to do something different with the presentation of smoked fish, try these lovely, silky pinwheels. We like to prepare them the night before we're serving them.

SERVES 4

½ pound smoked salmon, coarsely chopped (see Ingredient Tip)

1½ tablespoons extra virgin olive oil

1 heaping tablespoon minced fresh chives

1 tablespoon fresh lemon juice

⅛ teaspoon freshly milled white pepper

6 to 8 ounces smoked sablefish, sliced about ⅛ inch thick

Whole chives and lemon slices or capers

Mix the salmon, oil, chives, lemon juice, and pepper in a bowl.

Place a piece of plastic wrap over a cookie sheet. You are going to lay the sablefish out in a rectangle about 8 × 12 inches on the plastic wrap. Arrange the sable with the pieces just—but completely—overlapping. It's OK to end up with a bit different surface area than we suggest; just make sure there are no holes. Spoon the salmon mixture evenly over the sable, gently patting it into place. Starting from one of the rectangle's long sides, roll the mixture into a snug cylinder, using the plastic wrap to help support and shape it. Wrap the plastic somewhat tightly around the completed cylinder and refrigerate for at least 1 hour and up to overnight.

Take the roll from the refrigerator and unwrap carefully. With a sharp, thin-bladed knife, cut the roll into ½- to 1-inch slices. Let sit at room temperature just briefly to take the chill off. Then garnish with chives and lemon slices and serve.

SMOKED SALMON MOUSSE AND SABLE ROLLS

Use ½ pound store-bought salmon mousse to fill the sablefish roll. The mousse will be easier to work with if it's very cold.

BOILED SALMON

In the past Americans didn't eat smoked salmon for breakfast in the way we do today, partly because it was usually salted heavily for preservation. An early home recipe for smoked salmon as a breakfast dish, from 1880, says the fish should be "soaked three or four hours in plenty of water, then dried in a towel, and boiled until hot through; butter and serve very hot."

SMOKED-SALMON CUPS WITH SMOKED-SALMON SAUCE

SELECTIONS FROM THE BREAKFAST MENU ON THE SS *MAINE*, 1902

Broiled Fresh Mackerel, Anchovy Butter

Fried Cod, Tartar Sauce

Fish Cakes

Veal Cutlets, Sauce Piquant

This is elegant looking and tasting but requires deceptively little effort. You make both parts of the chilled dish the day before serving, so all you have left to do is combine them, sit down, and enjoy breakfast.   **SERVES 6**

SMOKED-SALMON CUPS

6 ounces nova or lox

½ cup heavy (whipping) cream

2 large egg whites

2 tablespoons sour cream

½ teaspoon fresh lemon juice

Pinch of freshly milled white pepper

1 cup spinach leaves, sliced into thin ribbons

1 tablespoon minced fresh dill

SMOKED-SALMON SAUCE

½ cup sour cream

2 tablespoons half-and-half or milk

1 ounce nova or lox, finely chopped

1 teaspoon minced fresh dill

Pinch of freshly milled white pepper

⅓ cup spinach leaves, sliced into thin ribbons

Fresh dill sprigs

Preheat the oven to 325°F.

Butter 6 ramekins that will hold at least ¾ cup each. Cut parchment paper or wax paper circles the diameter of each ramekin and line each one.

In a food processor, combine the salmon, cream, and egg whites and process until they form a thick paste. Add the sour cream, lemon juice, and white pepper and combine until smooth. Add the spinach and dill and pulse once or twice, just enough to mix in the spinach but not to chop it further.

Pour the mixture into the ramekins, making sure the ingredients are distributed evenly. Arranged the ramekins in a larger baking dish and pour in enough warm water to come halfway up the sides of the cups. Cover the pan loosely with foil. Bake for 25 minutes, then uncover and continue baking for 5 to 10 minutes more, until the smoked salmon mixture is lightly firm to the touch and slightly golden. Cool to room temperature, cover, and refrigerate for at least 1 hour and up to overnight.

Prepare the sauce, mixing the ingredients together in a small bowl. Cover and refrigerate.

Shortly before serving, run a small knife around the sides of each cup to loosen the salmon. Invert onto plates. Stir the sauce a few times to loosen it, then spoon it equally around the smoked salmon cups. Garnish with the spinach ribbons and dill sprigs and serve.

SEATTLE SALMON KEDGEREE

INGREDIENT TIP

Good mail-order sources for Pacific salmon and other West Coast seafood include Newman's Fish Market in Portland (503-227-2700) and Seattle's Pike Place Fish (800-542-7732 or www.pikeplacefish.com).

Scottish settlers in the Pacific Northwest introduced coastal cities to kedgeree, a tasty jumble of odd but ultimately harmonious ingredients. The lentils, rice, and spice come from the dish's Indian colonial parentage, but the smoked fish and eggs were a British enhancement. Closely associated with the sea, it can still be found at waterfront cafés such as the Athenian Inn in Seattle's Pike Place Market. Our version features the region's fine hot-smoked salmon, a flakier and smokier version than the better-known cold-smoked lox and nova. We describe how to smoke the fish yourself, but you can skip that step if you prefer and begin with a store-bought version. Add bloody Marys and Classic Baked Apples (page 275) for a full breakfast feast. **SERVES 4 TO 6**

DRY RUB

2 teaspoons coarsely ground black pepper

1 teaspoon kosher or other coarse salt

¼ teaspoon freshly milled white pepper

¼ teaspoon cayenne pepper

One ¾-pound salmon fillet, preferably wild Pacific salmon, skin on (see Ingredient Tip)

3 tablespoons unsalted butter

½ medium onion, chopped

3 cups cooked white rice

1 cup cooked lentils

2 hard-boiled eggs, peeled and grated

¼ cup seafood or chicken stock

¼ cup half-and-half

¼ teaspoon curry powder

⅛ teaspoon freshly grated nutmeg

¼ cup minced fresh parsley, preferably flat-leaf

Salt to taste

Paprika

Prepare the dry rub, combining the ingredients in a small bowl. Rub the spice mixture over the fish, cover it, and let it sit at room temperature for 20 to 30 minutes.

Fire up a smoker or covered grill to 225°F to 250°F, following the manufacturer's instructions for smoking. Oil the cooking grate well. Place the fish on the grate as far from the fire as possible.

Smoke, covered, until the fish flakes throughout, for 30 to 40 minutes. Open the smoker only when necessary and cover as quickly as possible to minimize the loss of heat and smoke.

When cool enough to handle, flake the fish into a bowl, discarding the bones and skin. Break it into small, uniform pieces. (The fish can be smoked up to several days before you prepare the kedgeree. Keep it tightly covered and refrigerated until needed.)

Warm the butter in a large skillet over medium heat. Add the onion and sauté it briefly until soft. Stir in the rice, lentils, eggs, stock, half-and-half, curry powder, and nutmeg and heat through. Stir the fish into the kedgeree, warming it through if needed. Stir in the parsley and add salt. Transfer to a platter, sprinkle generously with paprika, and serve.

CLASSIC KEDGEREE

Kedgeree originally featured flaked finnan haddie—smoked haddock—instead of salmon. Once common in the Northeast and Northwest, it is harder to find today but makes a wonderful substitute. See the following recipe for Creamed Finnan Haddie for shopping suggestions.

A DIFFERENT KETTLE OF FISH

Outside the Pacific Northwest, American cooks have made kedgeree with a range of fish and shellfish other than smoked salmon and haddock. Sarah Josepha Hale suggests turbot as an option in *Mrs. Hale's New Cook Book* (1857), and Eleanor Roosevelt uses boiled whitefish in a recipe she submitted for the 1933 *Congressional Cook Book.* A Louisiana fish-camp version goes with freshly caught catfish. Local shrimp sometimes finds its way into the dish in South Carolina, where a dinner rendition might be garnished with coconut, chutney, and Jerusalem artichoke relish. The fishiest versions of all leave out fish entirely, stripping the seafaring favorite of its soul.

CREAMED FINNAN HADDIE

INGREDIENT TIP

It became difficult for a while to find real smoked haddock anywhere in the United States, but it's starting to show up again with greater frequency. Browne Trading (800-766-2402), a fish and caviar mail-order supplier in Portland, Maine, now smokes its own deeply flavored finnan haddie. On the other coast, Pike Place Fish in Seattle's Pike Place Market carries a quality finnan haddie from New Brunswick, Canada (800-542-7732, www.pikeplacefish.com). You can also substitute smoked cod, whitefish, and the hot-smoked salmon of the Pacific Northwest for a different dish in a similar vein.

It has been my long-held notion that [finnan haddie] is one of the consummate breakfast foods of the world. Give me a platter of choice finnan haddie, freshly cooked in its bath of water and milk, add melted butter, a slice or two of hot toast, a pot of steaming Darjeeling tea, and you may tell the butler to dispense with the caviar, truffles, and nightingales' tongues.

Craig Claiborne, *A Feast Made for Laughter* (1982)

This is a surefire sleeper: little known and unappealingly named, but outrageously good when prepared well with premier fish. Centuries ago, fishermen in the village of Findon, Scotland, developed a way of preserving their haddock catch by drying it and then hanging it to cold-smoke over a smoldering fire. New Englanders adopted the finnan haddie for their breakfast tables, often in a creamed version, but it plunged in popularity after the area's haddock supply fell dangerously low. The fish is back again now, and so is the dish. Serve it spooned over toast, Wild Rice Waffles (page 115), or, as we suggest here, warm Herbed Popovers. **SERVES 4**

1 pound finnan haddie (see Ingredient Tip)

1½ cups whole milk

½ cup heavy (whipping) cream

2 tablespoons unsalted butter

2 tablespoons unbleached all-purpose flour

Salt and freshly milled black pepper to taste

Herbed Popovers (page 342), freshly made and halved, optional

Minced fresh chives

Combine the finnan haddie in a saucepan with the milk and cream. You will probably need to cut the fish into 2 or 3 chunks to fit it in the pan. At this point the fish will be somewhat stiff, easily cut through but not easily bent. Warm over very low heat for 15 to 20 minutes to soften the fish and infuse the milk with its subtle smokiness. Remove from the heat and let the finnan haddie steep in the milk mixture while you prepare the sauce.

In another saucepan, warm the butter over medium-low heat. When the foam begins to subside, whisk in the flour. Cook, stirring frequently, until smooth and just a bit golden in color, 2 to 3 minutes. Slowly whisk in the milk mixture. Continue cooking the mixture for several minutes, until it coats a spoon somewhat thickly. Flake the now-supple finnan haddie into bite-size chunks (there aren't normally any bones, but it pays to be alert), discard the skin, and stir the fish into the sauce. Warm it through, then add salt and a generous amount of pepper. The fish juices should have thinned the sauce slightly, but if it is too thick for easy spooning and drizzling, add a little additional water or milk.

Keep the finnan haddie warm while preparing the popovers or another crispy bread accompaniment. Spoon the finnan haddie and sauce over the halved popovers. Sprinkle with chives. Serve immediately.

BROILED TANGERINE-TERIYAKI FISH FILLET

INGREDIENT TIP

Mirin is a syrupy Japanese rice wine that gives teriyaki its distinctive taste. Most of what is sold in American supermarkets and even Asian markets is a synthetic version, with corn syrup as the main ingredient. It's acceptable for an occasional batch of teriyaki, but real distilled mirin adds more flavor. Look for it in natural foods stores.

Japanese breakfasts frequently include soy-glazed fish, an idea that floated naturally into Hawaii and California households. Simple to make, the sauce produces a subtly flavored and richly lacquered dish that cooks quickly under the broiler. Serve it with sticky rice and tangerine sections.   **SERVES 4**

TANGERINE-TERIYAKI SAUCE

¼ cup mirin (see Ingredient Tip)

2 tablespoons sake or dry sherry

2 tablespoons soy sauce, preferably not low-sodium

2 tablespoons fresh tangerine juice or fresh or reconstituted frozen orange juice

1 tablespoon minced fresh ginger

1 teaspoon sugar

1½ pounds salmon, sablefish, or other meaty fish fillets, in 4 equal portions

Warm the mirin and sake in a small saucepan over medium-low heat for 5 minutes. Mix in the soy sauce and continue heating until reduced by about half, 5 to 8 minutes longer. Add the remaining ingredients, stirring until the sugar dissolves. (The sauce can be made up to a week ahead, covered, and refrigerated.)

Preheat the broiler. Arrange the salmon on an oiled baking sheet. Brush each piece thickly with teriyaki sauce, avoiding dipping the brush or spoon back into the sauce after you have touched the raw fish. Broil until just cooked through, about 4 minutes for ½-inch-thick fillets. Brush again with the remaining sauce before serving.

MISO-TERIYAKI FISH FILLET

Eliminate the tangerine juice from the sauce. Add 1 tablespoon white miso paste after the soy sauce.

FISH FILLET WITH YOUR SIGNATURE TERIYAKI SAUCE

The basics of teriyaki sauce are mirin, sake, and soy, usually bolstered by a little sugar. Use that as a starting point for building your own signature sauce for this fish and other dishes. Experiment with other fruit juices, Asian chile paste, scallions, garlic, or other aromatics. Your version is bound to be an improvement on the many one-dimensional commercial products on the market today. The sauce will typically keep for at least a week, so double or triple the recipe if you wish to use it other times on chicken, meat, or vegetables.

KEYS FISH STEAM WITH OLD SOUR

INGREDIENT TIP

Key limes, or the similar Mexican *limónes,* are increasingly available across the country, especially in midwinter. They can also be ordered from Frieda's by Mail (800-241-1771, 714-826-6100, or www.friedas.com).

Bahamians brought this fish stew to the Florida Keys generations ago. We make the "steam," also known as a "Nassau Breakfast," with grouper or snapper fillets and flavor it with a local condiment called "old sour," a preserved key lime juice used when the fruit was out of season. You can omit the seasoning and still have a fine breakfast, but it's definitely worth making and keeping for other fish and seafood preparations. Serve the stew over grits.   **SERVES 4**

OLD SOUR

2 cups fresh key lime juice or other lime juice (see Ingredient Tip)

1 tablespoon salt

1 or more small dried hot chiles, such as cayenne or datil, optional

1 large or 2 medium yellow onions, sliced into thin matchsticks

1 green, orange, yellow, or red bell pepper, sliced into thin matchsticks

1 large or 2 medium tomatoes, chopped, or 1 cup canned diced tomatoes, drained

1 teaspoon salt

½ teaspoon freshly milled black pepper

2 key limes or 1 larger lime, thinly sliced (see Ingredient Tip)

2 to 3 cups seafood stock or water

1½ pounds grouper or snapper fillets, cut into at least 4 pieces

4 tablespoon (½ stick) unsalted butter

2 to 3 cups hot Just Plain Grits (page 320) or other grits

Caribbean or other hot pepper sauce

Florida cooks normally make old sour 4 to 6 weeks in advance of using it. The aging definitely deepens the flavor, but the distinctive tang starts developing within a day if you can't wait. Simply mix together the ingredients and pour into a small-necked bottle. With a rubber band or string, secure a small square of double-thickness cheesecloth over the top and leave the bottle uncapped. Store in a cool dark cabinet until ready to use, then remove the cheesecloth and cap or cork the bottle. It keeps indefinitely at room temperature.

You'll need a deep skillet or Dutch oven at least 8 inches in diameter. Layer first the onion, then the bell pepper, followed by the tomato. Sprinkle with about half of the salt and pepper, then top the vegetables with the lime slices. Pour in enough stock to come up even with the limes. Cover and simmer over medium heat for 18 to 20 minutes, until the vegetable are soft and the stock is somewhat reduced. Uncover and arrange the fish on top of the mixture. Sprinkle with the remaining salt and pepper and arrange a tablespoon of butter on each piece of fish. Pour enough additional stock around the fish to come up even with it. Cover again, reduce the heat to medium-low, and continue cooking for 6 to 8 minutes, until the fish is cooked through and flakes.

Spoon hot grits into shallow bowls. Top with a piece of fish. Then ladle out the broth and vegetable mixture and spoon it over and around the fish equally. Pass the old sour and hot sauce at the table.

MAKING WAVES IN THE DELAWARE BAY

Captains of old pilot boats in the Delaware Bay often ate a robust and unusual breakfast according to *The Delaware Heritage Cookbook* (1988). The traditional fare consisted of chopped boiled potatoes topped with steamed or baked fillets of cod, striper, or weakfish, covered heavily with layers of crumbled bacon, hard-boiled eggs, a diced raw onion, and melted butter. That's a seaborne version of a "trucker's special" that could sink a ship.

SHAD ROE WITH BUTTER AND BACON

A BREAKFAST MENU SUGGESTION FROM OLD VIRGINIA

Iced Tomato Juice

Broiled Fresh Shad Roe with
Crisp Bacon

Southern Spoon Bread

Hot Coffee

Irene King, *Culinary Gems from
the Kitchens of Old Virginia*
(1952)

Every spring, shad migrate conveniently from the Atlantic into eastern coastal rivers and from there into the frying pan. The females of the breed, the largest member of the herring family, have huge egg sacs prized for their distinctive flavor. The roe deteriorates quickly, so purchase it as fresh as possible and cook it shortly afterward. To keep the grainy texture from becoming unpleasant, sauté the roe gently to crisp the surface while maintaining a rosy center.

SERVES 4

4 thick slices bacon, halved

2 tablespoons unsalted butter

2 pairs medium shad roe, 8 to 10 ounces per pair

Salt and freshly milled black pepper to taste

3 tablespoons Dijon mustard

Fry the bacon in a heavy skillet over medium heat until crisp. Remove, drain, and reserve it. Add the butter to the bacon drippings, warm through, and reduce the heat to medium-low.

Gently add the pairs of shad roe and sprinkle them in the pan with salt and pepper. Cook until lightly browned on the bottom, 2 to 3 minutes. Carefully turn each pair with a broad spatula and cook until lightly browned on the second side and *just* firm, about 2 minutes longer. You want them to remain very pink at the center.

Gently remove from the pan and separate the lobes for 4 servings by slicing the membrane attaching the 2 lobes of each pair. Arrange on plates or a serving platter.

Stir the mustard into the pan drippings and add about ¼ cup water, enough to make a light sauce. Spoon the sauce over the roe, garnish with bacon, and serve.

SHAD ROE WITH HOMINY

For southern panache, the late Bill Neal liked to warm a can of drained yellow or white hominy in the pan dripping sauce and serve it on the side with the roe.

SALMON CROQUETTES

The predecessor of today's chic crab and other seafood cakes, the croquette has a long and honorable history in American cooking. Nineteenth-century cookbooks proposed versions with lobster, oyster, shad roc, chicken, veal, potato, hominy, rice, salsify, and more. The canned salmon croquette outlasted them all and remains a solid breakfast favorite in many homes, particularly in the South. Our recipe doubles easily, and you can do everything except the final cooking in a few minutes the night before.   **SERVES 4**

2 tablespoons unsalted butter

½ small yellow onion, minced

¼ cup minced green bell pepper

One 14½- to 15½-ounce can salmon, drained, skin removed, and flaked

2 generous tablespoons mayonnaise

1 teaspoon fresh lemon juice

¾ cup saltine cracker crumbs or dried bread crumbs

Salt to taste

Vegetable oil for panfrying

Warm the butter in a medium skillet over medium heat. Add the onion and green pepper and sauté until soft, about 3 minutes. Scrape the mixture into a medium bowl and combine it with the salmon, mayonnaise, lemon juice, and ½ cup of the cracker crumbs. Add salt judiciously, depending on the saltiness of the crackers. Shape the mixture into eight ½-inch-thick patties. Sprinkle the remaining cracker crumbs over both sides of the patties, pressing them gently to stay in place. Cover and refrigerate for at least 15 minutes and up to the night before.

Rinse and dry the original skillet, then pour about ¼ inch of oil in, and warm over medium heat. Fry the croquettes in batches until golden brown and crisp, 2 to 3 minutes per side, turning once. Drain and serve.

SALMON CROQUETTES WITH MUSTARD-LEMON PAN SAUCE

After the croquettes are cooked, drain off all but 1 tablespoon of oil from the skillet. Add 2 tablespoons unsalted butter, 1 tablespoon Creole or spicy brown mustard, the juice of ½ lemon, and a little salt and pepper. Pour over the croquettes and serve.

Because shad was practically the only fish we ever ate and spring was the only time it was ever seen, we were always much too excited to wait for dinner, so we'd cook it for breakfast whenever it was caught. First we would eagerly search the head for pearls, always hoping to find one. I don't know how we came to expect pearls in the head of the shad except that it did have what looked like a pearl, the size of a large grain of corn and the same shape. We always served shad with scrambled eggs, bacon, steamed hominy, new-found honey, soft, rich batter bread, delicious cold milk, hot coffee, and a sip of dandelion wine. It was truly a meal to celebrate the coming of spring.

Edna Lewis, *The Taste of Country Cooking* (1977)

SALT-COD CAKES

A BREAKFAST MENU SUGGESTION FOR SUNDAY MORNING IN NEW ENGLAND

Fish Cakes   Baked Beans

Scrambled Eggs   Corncakes

Coffee

Ella Shannon Bowles and Dorothy S. Towle, *Secrets of New England Cooking* (1947)

Salt mackerel was one of my father's favorite dishes. It came in a "kit" or small wooden pail and smelled to heaven when it was opened. For breakfast a fish was washed, scraped on the inside, put in cold water the night before, and set on the back of the stove.... When everything else was ready to serve the

The "Sacred Cod," as the Massachusetts legislature once named the fish, fueled the New England economy in the colonial period and became one of the region's most common foods. Normally salted and dried at sea for preservation before arriving on shore, cod often served as the centerpiece of two consecutive meals. Cooks might make a boiled dinner of the salt cod one evening and then, the following morning, prepare cod balls or cakes from the leftovers. They bolstered the flavor of the cakes by frying them in pork fat, in the same way we use bacon drippings today. You must plan ahead to enjoy this breakfast, because the salt cod must soak for at least 8 hours and up to 24 hours before it will be ready to cook. If you want to dress these up for company, place each on a juicy tomato slice and drizzle with Hollandaise Sauce (page 32) or Mustard-Lemon Butter (page 57).

SERVES 4

½ pound salt cod (see Ingredient Tip)

1 heaping cup leftover mashed potatoes or one ½-pound russet or other baking potato, peeled, boiled, and mashed with 2 tablespoons unsalted butter

½ cup half-and-half

1 large egg

⅓ cup minced onion

¼ teaspoon Worcestershire sauce

Salt and freshly milled black pepper to taste

Flour, dried bread crumbs, or cracker crumbs for dredging

Vegetable oil and bacon drippings or butter for panfrying

Lemon wedges

Rinse the salt from the surface of the fish. Cover with cool water and soak for at least 8 hours and up to 24 hours, changing the water several times. Drain and place in a saucepan with fresh cool water to cover. Warm over medium heat, bringing the water just to a simmer, and adjust the heat as needed so that bubbles break only occasionally on the surface. Cook until soft and easily flaked, about 15 minutes, then drain again. When cool enough to handle, pull the cod into small shreds.

Combine the cod and potato in a medium bowl. Stir in the half-and-half, egg, onion, and Worcestershire sauce. Add salt with a light hand, since the cod will have retained some salinity, and pepper. The mixture should be quite moist but not soupy. Refrigerate it briefly if it's too wet to hold together. Form into 12 patties about ½ inch thick, then dredge each lightly in flour. Refrigerate, uncovered, for 10 to 20 minutes.

Warm a thick film of the oil and drippings in a large heavy skillet over medium heat. Fry the cod cakes in batches until medium-brown and crispy, 3 to 4 minutes per side. Serve the cakes immediately, garnished with lemon wedges.

CREOLE-STYLE SALT-COD CAKES

Substitute mashed cooked plantain for the potato and add a good pinch of ground ginger and a splash of Caribbean or other hot pepper sauce to the cod mixture.

FRESH COD CAKES

For a creamier result, substitute 1 pound cooked flaked cod for the salt cod, skipping its lengthy preparation steps. You'll need more salt, about ½ teaspoon or more to taste.

DARE COUNTY FISH CAKES

Cooks have made cakes out of any flaky fish they had in quantity, whether fresh or salted. Along North Carolina's Dare County coast, the fish of choice traditionally is the local drum. Commonly salted in the past, it's now more often available fresh. Substitute 1 pound flaked cooked drum for the salt cod. Eliminate the Worcestershire sauce and add instead 2 teaspoons minced fresh basil or 1 teaspoon dried and ½ teaspoon salt or more to taste.

CHESAPEAKE CATFISH-BACON CAKES

Skip the preparation steps for the salt cod. Replace the cod with 1 pound flaked cooked fresh catfish and add 3 or 4 slices crumbled crisp bacon to the mixture, along with a pinch or two of Old Bay seasoning, if you wish, and ½ teaspoon salt or more to taste. Fry in bacon drippings.

HOMINY FISH CAKES

Skip the preparation steps for the salt cod. Another southern coastal treat, these cakes replace the mashed potatoes in the recipe with an equal amount of cooked hominy, mashed with the butter as directed. The fish can be flaked cooked saltwater bass or grouper or freshwater catfish, among many possibilities.

---

water was drained off (we said "dreened" off) and the fish allowed to pan-broil for about ten minutes. Transferred to a platter and dotted with butter, it made a most palatable accompaniment to boiled potatoes. Nowadays it would not be considered acceptable unless the platter were cluttered up with a few sprigs of parsley, an embellishment that would have been lost upon my father, to whom "weeds" by way of garnishing were a matter for ribaldry.

Della Lutes, *The Country Kitchen* (1936)

SUNRISE CRAB CAKES

Culinary writer Edward Behr traced the introduction of crab cakes in American cookbooks to an 1897 Baltimore work, Marietta Hollyday's *Domestic Economy,* which called the cakes a "very nice" breakfast dish. They remain just that, though crab has jumped in price and may have a different effect on our domestic economies today. Hollyday spiced her cakes with red pepper and salt, but we favor the Old Bay seasoning that German-Jewish immigrant Gustav C. Brunn created in Baltimore a few decades later. For a special breakfast, serve the orange-scented crab cakes atop a thin slice of country ham and on the side offer Oven-Crisped Tabasco Cottage Potatoes (page 308) and Hollandaise Sauce (page 32) made with orange juice in place of lemon juice.   **SERVES 4**

1 pound lump crabmeat, preferably blue crab

¾ cup saltine cracker crumbs

1 medium or large egg

⅓ cup finely minced celery

2 tablespoons mayonnaise

1 tablespoon Dijon mustard

2 teaspoons minced fresh orange zest

½ teaspoon Old Bay seasoning or a splash or two of Tabasco or other hot pepper sauce and a generous pinch of salt

Vegetable oil for panfrying

Orange wedges

Spread the crab out in a large shallow bowl, being careful to avoid breaking up the lumps. Sprinkle the cracker crumbs over the crab.

Whisk the egg in a small bowl until just foamy. Stir in the celery, mayonnaise, mustard, orange zest, and Old Bay seasoning. When well combined, spoon over the crab and gently mix the ingredients together. The mixture should remain chunky. Let the mixture sit for several minutes before forming into cakes. Form the crab lightly into 8 plump patties, ¾ to 1 inch thick and about 2½ inches wide. Press each cake together firmly so that the ingredients adhere, but avoid packing it down any more than necessary to hold it together. Cover the cakes and refrigerate for at least 30 minutes before cooking. (The crab cakes can be formed the night ahead, then covered and refrigerated if you wish.)

Warm ½ inch of oil to 350°F in a large saucepan or deep skillet. Temperature precision is especially important here because higher heat may cause the cakes to disintegrate.

With a thin-bladed spatula, transfer the crab cakes one at a time to the oil, laying them into it gently. They may pop a bit just after they go into the oil. Fry until deep golden brown, about 2 minutes per side. Drain on a rack and repeat with the remaining cakes. Garnish with orange wedges and serve immediately.

CRAB AND SCALLOP CAKES

Substitute ½ pound chopped sea or bay scallops for ½ pound of the crab.

CRAB AND CORN CAKES

Replace ¼ pound crab with ¾ cup fresh or frozen (thawed) corn kernels. We like these with hollandaise, but a piquant tartar sauce is tasty too. To make the latter, mix ¾ cup mayonnaise with 1 to 2 tablespoons minced red onion, 1 tablespoon each chopped cornichons and minced parsley, 1 to 2 teaspoons minced pickled jalapeño, and a pinch of salt.

A MAINE MORNING

Writing in Harper's *New Monthly Magazine* in 1880, W. H. Bishop described a breakfast he had during a visit to the Maine islands. His host disappeared one evening with a hoe to dig for clams in nearby mud flats. He returned with "half a mess," which he served the next morning with biscuits, three kinds of cake, stewed peaches, and stewed prunes.

SELECTIONS FROM THE BREAKFAST MENU AT THE OAKLAND BEACH HOTEL IN WARWICK, RHODE ISLAND, 1880

FISH

Little Neck Clams fried in crumbs

Stewed Clams   Eels

Clam Fritters   Codfish, with cream

CAJUN CRAWFISH PATTIES

The Acadians of rural Louisiana have their own special way with seafood cakes, which they love to make with freshwater crawfish (aka crayfish, but never on Cajun turf). Serve with scrambled or fried eggs and toasted French bread or Croquignoles (page 350).

SERVES 4

1½ cups packed fresh bread crumbs

1 pound blanched peeled crawfish tails, chopped, plus any fat (see Ingredient Tip)

2 ounces tasso or other smoky ham, chopped (see Ingredient Tip)

3 tablespoons unsalted butter

¾ cup chopped onions

½ cup chopped celery

½ cup chopped green bell pepper

1 tablespoon fresh lemon juice

1 teaspoon Worcestershire sauce

1 teaspoon Crystal, Tabasco, or other hot pepper sauce

½ teaspoon salt

¼ teaspoon cayenne pepper

1 large egg, lightly beaten

1 cup saltine cracker crumbs

Vegetable oil for panfrying

Preheat the oven to 350°F. Scatter the bread crumbs on a baking sheet and bake until dry and golden, about 5 minutes. Dump the crumbs into a mixing bowl.

In a food processor, chop together the crawfish (fat too, if any) and tasso, using the pulse button just enough times to mince the mixture. Stop short of pureeing it. Add to the mixing bowl.

Melt the butter in a medium skillet over medium heat. Stir in the onions, celery, and bell pepper and sauté briefly until the vegetables are soft. Stir in the lemon juice, Worcestershire sauce, Tabasco, salt, and cayenne and remove from the heat. Scrape the mixture into the mixing bowl. Add the egg and combine. Form into 8 or 12 patties, no thicker than ½ inch. The mixture will be a bit fragile. Coat the patties with the cracker crumbs by holding each patty in your hand and sprinkling both sides with cracker crumbs. Refrigerate the patties for about 10 minutes. Warm ¼ inch of oil in a large heavy skillet over medium heat and fry the patties until golden brown and crisp, 2 to 3 minutes per side. Drain and serve hot.

SEAFOOD AND EGGS

Many cooks like to serve fish and seafood at breakfast folded into omelets. They are a popular brunch menu item at fancy restaurants today, but contemporary chefs didn't invent the idea. Even at the lowest point in American home cooking, during the 1950s, Narcissa Chamberlain championed an amazing array of seafood specialties in *The Omelette Book* (1955). A self-described "home-made" cook, she offered versions featuring everything from anchovies to whitebait. The options included seven omelets made with shrimp and eight enriched with lobster.

CLAM BELLY BROIL ON TOAST

The soft-shell "gaping" clams of New England, steamers are a summer treat whether steamed, fried, or, as we suggest here, broiled. Because of the brittle shell, often broken in shipping, some inland seafood merchants are reluctant to stock steamers. Beg.   **SERVES 4**

2 dozen freshly shucked soft-shell "steamer" or "mano" clams (see Ingredient Tip)

2 large eggs, lightly beaten

2 tablespoons milk

1 cup fine saltine cracker crumbs

½ teaspoon freshly milled black pepper

8 tablespoons (1 stick) unsalted butter, melted

4 slices good white or whole wheat toast

Minced fresh chervil or parsley

Lemon wedges

Cut away the beards or any hard parts left on the clams so that you are left with just the soft, scrumptious bellies. Whisk together the eggs and milk in a small bowl. Combine the cracker crumbs and pepper in a second small bowl and put half of the melted butter in another.

Preheat the boiler, arranging the baking rack at least 4 and preferably 6 inches away from the heat.

Dunk a clam in the egg mixture, then in the cracker crumbs, then in the butter. Place it on a baking sheet. Repeat with the remaining clams. Broil the clams, watching carefully, until just golden brown and crisp, about 3 minutes.

Arrange each toast slice on a plate and top with equal portions of the clams. Divide the remaining melted butter among them, spooning it over the top, then sprinkle each with chervil and garnish with a lemon wedge. Squeeze the lemon over the clams just before diving in.

OYSTER PAN ROAST

Americans used to eat oysters all day long, often opting for this classic preparation at breakfast. When we eat a pan roast later in the day, we load it up with wine, cream, and chili sauce, but for a breakfast dish we exercise a little more restraint with those ingredients. Serve the pan roast spooned over big fluffy cornmeal biscuits or whole wheat toast.   **SERVES 4**

2½ dozen freshly shucked medium oysters, with their liquor

Up to ½ cup bottled clam juice or seafood stock

8 tablespoons (1 stick) unsalted butter

3 tablespoons minced onion

2 tablespoons dry white wine

¼ cup heavy (whipping) cream

3 tablespoons chili sauce (the ketchup-style condiment)

2 teaspoons Worcestershire sauce or more to taste

1 teaspoon celery salt or more to taste

Cornmeal Biscuits (page 337) or whole wheat toast

Cayenne pepper or paprika

Strain the liquor from the oysters and measure it. Add clam juice to equal ½ cup.

Melt the butter in a medium skillet over medium heat. Add the onion and sauté until soft and translucent, about 5 minutes. Pour in the wine and simmer for 1 minute. Mix in the cream, chili sauce, Worcestershire sauce, and celery salt and heat through. Add the oysters and the oyster liquor mixture and simmer until the oysters are just plump and lightly firm, a few minutes more. Serve in broad shallow bowls over your bread of choice or with bread on the side. Dust with cayenne or paprika.

SOFT-SHELL CRABS ON TOAST

We eagerly await the short season each year for soft-shell crab, one of the marine world's consummate delicacies. We once ate it at all three meals in a single day, cooking it in different ways for the different times. This is a scrumptious breakfast (or lunch or supper) preparation.　　**SERVES 4**

¼ cup unbleached all-purpose flour

½ teaspoon freshly milled black pepper

¼ teaspoon salt

¼ cup milk

1 large egg

1 garlic clove, minced

¾ cup fine saltine cracker crumbs

Vegetable oil for panfrying

4 cleaned large fresh soft-shell crabs

2 tablespoons unsalted butter

Juice of ½ medium lemon

4 slices good white or whole wheat toast

4 thin slices smoky ham, warmed, optional

Minced fresh parsley

Lemon wedges

Stir together on a plate or in a shallow dish the flour, pepper, and a bit of salt. In a shallow dish, whisk together the milk, egg, and garlic. Arrange the cracker crumbs on another plate or shallow dish.

Warm a generous ¼ inch of oil in a large skillet over medium-high heat.

Dip each crab into the seasoned flour, then into the egg mixture, and then into the cracker crumbs. Gently shake to eliminate excess cracker. Fry the crabs in batches until golden brown, 3 to 4 minutes per side. Drain the crabs. Pour off any excess oil beyond 1 tablespoon. Stir in the butter and lemon juice and heat through. Working quickly, arrange toast on each plate and top each piece with a ham slice if you wish. Arrange each crab on top, then spoon equal portions of the pan sauce around. Sprinkle with parsley. Garnish with lemon wedges and serve. All the crab is edible.

CHARLESTON SHRIMP AND GRITS

If we had to choose one dish to have for breakfast every day for the rest of our lives, this South Carolina specialty would be it. In that case we might vary the style of dish on a regular basis, but as long as we're eating shrimp and grits only occasionally, we'll stick with our version of the traditional preparation, presented originally in our *American Home Cooking* (1999). Nothing else we serve at breakfast startles and satisfies friends so fully.

SERVES 4

1½ pounds medium shrimp, peeled, halved lengthwise, and deveined if you wish

Juice of 1 lemon

Tabasco or other hot pepper sauce

1½ teaspoons salt or more to taste

1½ cups stone-ground grits, not instant or quick-cooking (see Ingredient Tip, page 320)

6 thick slices bacon, chopped

1 small onion, finely chopped

¼ cup finely chopped green bell pepper

1 garlic clove, minced

½ cup thinly sliced scallions

2 tablespoons unbleached all-purpose flour

1 cup chicken stock

1 to 2 tablespoons unsalted butter

1 cup (about ¼ pound) grated medium to sharp Cheddar cheese

Tabasco or other hot pepper sauce

Combine the shrimp with the lemon juice and a couple of generous splashes of hot pepper sauce. Let sit while you begin the grits and gravy.

Make the grits in a large heavy saucepan, first bringing 6 cups of water and 1 teaspoon of the salt to a boil. Whisk in the grits a few handfuls at a time. (They will bubble up initially.) When you have added all the grits, reduce the heat to a very low simmer and cook over low heat for 35 to 40 minutes, stirring occasionally at first and more frequently toward the end.

While the grits simmer, get the gravy under way. Fry the bacon in a medium skillet over medium heat until brown but still limp. Stir in the onion, green pepper, and garlic and continue cooking until the onion and pepper are limp, about 5 minutes. Add the scallions, sprinkle the flour over the mixture, and continue sautéing for 5 minutes longer. Stir in the stock and remaining salt and cook for 5 minutes longer. Remove from the heat while you finish the grits.

When the grits are thick and creamy, stir in as much of the butter as you wish, followed by the cheese. Add a splash of hot pepper sauce and additional salt if you like. Cover the grits while you finish the gravy.

The truism that as a nation we are inordinate flesh-consumers is tattered by much wear. Since vegetarianism comes as a hard lesson to the mass of our race, and the exacting palate demands [at breakfast] more definite flavors than those of eggs in any form, resort to crustacean and finny delicacies should follow as a matter of course and of common sense.

Marion Harland, *Marion Harland's Complete Cook Book* (1906)

Return the gravy to medium heat and stir in the shrimp. Cook until the shrimp are opaque throughout, about 5 minutes. Serve immediately, mounding the grits in large shallow bowls or on plates and covering them with shrimp and gravy.

SLIGHTLY NORTH OF BROAD SHRIMP AND GRITS

A Charleston restaurant called Slightly North of Broad serves a tasty contemporary variation on the local theme. To simulate the preparation at home, substitute scallops for about half of the shrimp and replace the bacon drippings with the fat left by frying 6 ounces spicy Mexican chorizo. To the chorizo drippings, add a couple of tablespoons of butter and ¼ pound slivered country ham, sautéing the ham until it gets a bit crisp. Remove the ham with a slotted spoon, proceed with the recipe, and then add it back in at the same time as the shrimp and scallops.

BREAKFAST SHRIMP FERNANDINA STYLE

On the Florida coast around Fernandina Beach, rice replaces grits in a similar shrimp-and-gravy dish. You'll need 1 to 1½ cups of white rice cooked by your favorite method.

7

Heavenly Hashes

HASH DEVELOPED AS a lowly leftovers dish but became one of the glories of American home cooking. The name comes from the French *hacher,* meaning to chop or mince, but nothing in all of Gaul resembles a hearty American hash. Our country's rendition began, according to early recipes, as something of a gravy-thickened stew of meat, potatoes, and other scraps from previous meals.

These versions still exist and can be good, but hash transcended its origins when it hit a hot skillet and took on a crusty exterior that brings out the best in the basic ingredients.

Yankee cooks in particular perfected the idea and then carried it across the country to the many areas they settled in the nineteenth century. From the era of "hash houses," our original fast-food joints, to the present, professional cooks in restaurants have served tons of hash but never added much to the preparation. Hash evolved in home kitchens and reached its zenith in common family skillets. This is real American food in the most fundamental way, a treasure of our home cooking.

CORNED BEEF HASH

The most popular American hash, and a truly inspired creation when prepared properly, corned beef hash suffers many humiliations today. Some cooks, even in fine restaurants, confuse a canned version with the real thing, and other people who start from scratch think they have to dress it up with superfluous touches to make it an appealing dish. Simplicity thrives in this case, with nothing more required for success than good basic ingredients, an ardent hand in dicing the meat and potatoes, and diligence in turning and crusting the hash. Of all the varied toppings proffered these days, the best remains gently poached eggs.

SERVES 4 OR MORE

2 tablespoons vegetable oil

1 tablespoon unsalted butter

½ to 1 medium onion, finely diced

1½ pounds corned beef, chilled and finely diced

1 to 1¼ pounds waxy red potatoes, boiled and finely diced

1 cup corned beef cooking broth or beef stock

2 tablespoons heavy (whipping) cream or sour cream, optional

2 teaspoons yellow mustard

1 teaspoon freshly milled black pepper

Salt to taste

Poached Eggs (page 30), optional

Warm the oil and butter together in a large heavy skillet over medium heat. Add the onion and sauté until soft, about 5 minutes. Mix in the remaining ingredients, going easy on the salt at first, especially if using the corned beef's cooking broth. Simmer, covered, for about 10 minutes, stirring the mixture up from the bottom once after about 5 minutes and patting it back down.

Uncover and continue cooking until the liquid is absorbed, several more minutes. Scrape the mixture up from the bottom and pat it back down several more times, until the meat and vegetables have melded together and the mixture gets crusty in spots, about 10 minutes longer. Top each portion, if you wish, with one or two poached eggs and serve.

BEEF HASH

Replace the corned beef with a similar quantity of boiled or roasted beef. Add a finely diced carrot or two at the same time the onion goes into the skillet. Skip the prepared mustard, but feel free to add a pinch of dry mustard, a sprinkle of hot red pepper flakes, a shot of Worcestershire sauce, or a bit of minced fresh herbs, perhaps parsley, thyme, or sage.

RED FLANNEL HASH

This is the archetype of American hashes, made originally with leftovers from a traditional New England boiled dinner. Cooks in the past frequently prepared two hashes from the leftovers—one with the vegetables and the other with the corned beef—but this favorite brings them together. We describe in the following tip how to make the boiled dinner first, which gives you two great meals for the price of one, but you can skip that step and expedite the hash if you have access to cooked corned beef by the pound. Either way, you're in for a singular treat that soars splendidly above the sum of its humble parts. **SERVES 4 TO 6**

INGREDIENT TIP

Making a New England boiled dinner a night or two before you want the hash preps all the ingredients you need. Simmer, covered, a 3½- to 4-pound corned beef brisket section for about 3 hours, until very tender, in water flavored with a couple of bay leaves and a teaspoon each of mustard seeds and peppercorns. Set the meat aside and add to the cooking liquid 12 small waxy potatoes and 4 chunked carrots. Cook for 10 minutes and add 2 large onions, cut into 8 wedges each, and a large turnip and rutabaga, each cut into bite-size chunks; cook for 15 minutes longer. Cut a medium cabbage head into 8 wedges and add it to the vegetables, cooking until all are tender, 5 to 10 minutes longer. Meanwhile, simmer 6 medium beets in another pot of water until tender, about 25 minutes, then peel and slice them. Reserving the portions of everything you need for the hash, serve the rest, slicing the corned beef and surrounding it on a platter with the vegetables.

TECHNIQUE TIP

When making hash, don't become too attached to any particular recipe. The idea is a license to experiment with leftovers and scraps of food from the fridge and pantry. Just keep in mind a few general parameters:

6 tablespoons unsalted butter

½ to 1 cup cooked chopped onion

2 to 3 cups chopped cooked waxy red potatoes

½ to 1 cup chopped cooked beets

1 to 1½ cups chopped cooked mixed additional vegetables such as carrots, turnips, or cabbage

1½ pounds cooked corned beef, chilled and finely chopped

½ cup boiled dinner cooking liquid or salted beef stock (see Ingredient Tip)

2 teaspoons yellow mustard

Freshly milled black pepper to taste

Prepared or freshly grated horseradish, optional

Warm 4 tablespoons of the butter in a heavy skillet, preferably 10 to 12 inches in diameter, over medium-high heat. Add the onion and cook for a minute; then add the potatoes, beets, and other vegetables. Cook for 5 minutes, stirring the mixture around, warming it through, and allowing some of the steam from the vegetables to escape.

Pat the mixture down and let it cook for 6 to 8 minutes, until it begins to brown richly. Scrape it up again with a sturdy spatula, getting up any browned bits, and add the remaining butter, allowing it to melt down through the hash. Pat it back down evenly again, add the corned beef and the cooking liquid, and cook for 6 to 8 minutes longer. Stir in the mustard and pepper and, if you wish, the horseradish. Scrape the hash back up, again retrieving all the browned bits. You may need to adjust the temperature downward a little, but don't unless you're close to burning the mixture. You need enough heat to develop a rich brown crust. Cook until the hash is well browned and crisp and the vegetables and meat are still moist, 6 to 8 minutes longer. Serve immediately, with horseradish on the side for a real eye-opener.

BARBECUED BRISKET HASH

What Bostonians do with a boiled dinner barbecuers do with a smoked brisket dinner. To turn the meat into a magnificent hash, use about 4 cups shredded leftover brisket to 2 cups chopped cooked potatoes. In a little butter and oil, first sauté a large diced onion, a red or green bell pepper, and a minced fresh or pickled jalapeño. When the vegetables are soft, add the meat and potatoes along with about a cup of beef or other stock, a tablespoon of yellow mustard, and a tablespoon of salsa. Simmer, covered, for about 15 minutes, then uncover and let cook for a few minutes more, until crusty on the bottom. You can also start with baked or simmered brisket for this hash, but corned beef doesn't fit well in the mix.

BEEFING UP

Home cooks and chefs alike have roamed the cow in search of hash meat. Chicago food editor and steak lover William Rice favors leftover chuck steak combined with chopped celery (if it's in the fridge), onions, potatoes, and a good bit of paprika. For the uptown Mansion on Turtle Creek in Dallas, Dean Fearing developed a ranch-style fajita hash that uses fried corn tortillas in place of potatoes. Cooks in southern New Mexico mix the local green chile with corn and ground beef, while some Mexican-Americans start with their savory ground picadillo. Salsas frequently come on the side with southwestern hashes, but James Beard opted for Heinz Chili Sauce, a ketchup with a kick, for beef hashes.

- Red meat and potatoes make a potent combo, but neither is essential. Use your imagination on compatible ingredients that crisp evenly together while retaining individual character and internal succulence. Vegetables such as onions, bell peppers, and celery often add to the mix.
- Cut at least most of the ingredients into similar-size pieces.
- Stock or another liquid usually helps keep hashes moist. Wine works in many cases, as do leftover gravy, cream, tomato sauce, and more.
- Always cook in a sturdy pan—preferably cast iron—with plenty of surface area. As you cook, make a sport of slinging your hash, scraping it up and then patting it down until it's beautifully browned.

HAM AND SWEET POTATO HASH

INGREDIENT TIP

Dice the ham into smaller pieces according to the length of its aging. With a 6-month-old country ham, we make the cubes as small as ¼ to ⅓ inch. Cut the vegetables to a similar size.

SELECTIONS FROM THE BREAKFAST MENU AT THE TREMONT HOUSE IN NEW YORK CITY, 1859

BROILED	FRIED
Beef Steaks	Pig's Feet
Pork Steaks	Calf's Liver
Hashed Meat	

This combination of southern favorites makes a superlative hash. Select the appropriate quantity of ham based on its age and saltiness, reducing the amount as those elements climb the scale. Poached eggs on the side or the top admirably pull together the salty, smoky, and sweet flavors.   **SERVES 4**

2 tablespoons vegetable oil

2 tablespoons unsalted butter

1 large yellow onion, diced

1 small red bell pepper, diced

1 small green bell pepper, diced

One 1-pound sweet potato, boiled until just tender, peeled, and diced

¼ to ¾ pound cooked ham, diced (see Ingredient Tip)

¼ cup heavy (whipping) cream or half-and-half

Salt to taste

Warm the oil and butter together in a large heavy skillet over medium heat. Add the onion and peppers and sauté until soft, about 5 minutes. Mix in the remaining ingredients, going easy on the salt at first, especially if the ham is of the aged country style. Simmer, covered, for about 10 minutes, stirring the mixture up from the bottom once after about 5 minutes and patting it back down.

Uncover and continue cooking until the liquid is absorbed, the meat and vegetables have melded together, and the mixture gets nicely crusty on the bottom, 5 to 8 minutes longer. Serve hot.

HAM, SWEET POTATO, AND GREENS HASH

Substitute about 2 cups chopped spinach or chard for the green bell pepper.

HAM AND CORN BREAD HASH

We got this idea from the late Bert Greene, a much-loved food columnist and cooking teacher. In a large ovenproof skillet, sauté 2 cups diced corn bread in a few tablespoons of butter until crisp, then set the corn bread aside. Add another tablespoon of butter to the skillet and then sauté a chopped onion, ½ red bell pepper, chopped, and a garlic clove. When soft, stir in 2 diced red-ripe plum tomatoes or other small tomatoes, 1 cup corn kernels, a dash or two of Tabasco or other hot pepper sauce, and 2 cups diced ham. Cover and cook for about 5 minutes. Lightly stir in the corn bread cubes and transfer to a 375°F oven and bake 10 minutes, until heated through.

SPICY ITALIAN SAUSAGE HASH

Mother's hash doesn't taste of soap grease, rancid butter, spoiled cheese, raw flour, boarding-house skillets, hotel coffee, garden garlics, bologna sausage, or cayenne pepper; neither is it stewed and simmered and simmered and stewed, but is made so nicely, seasoned so delicately, and heated through so quickly, that the only trouble is, "there is never enough to go round." Cold meat of any kind will do, but corned beef is best.

Buckeye Cookery and Practical Housekeeping (1880)

Sausage and hash browns pair well on any breakfast plate, but they mate best of all perhaps in a hash.

SERVES 4

¾ pound Italian sausage links, cut into ½-inch chunks

2 teaspoons olive oil, optional

1 small green bell pepper, diced

2 plump garlic cloves, slivered

½ recipe Heavenly Hash Browns (page 305) or 1 to 1¼ pounds other hash brown potatoes

Fry the sausage chunks in a large skillet over medium heat, adding the olive oil if the sausage is especially lean. Cook until browned in spots, about 5 minutes. Stir in the bell pepper and garlic, and continue cooking until the vegetables soften, about 3 minutes more. Add the hash browns, pat the mixture down, and cook until heated through and nicely crusty on the bottom, 3 to 5 minutes more. Serve hot.

LAMB SAUSAGE HASH

Substitute Spiced Lamb Sausage (page 140) for Italian sausage. If stuffed into links, it will take about the same amount of cooking time. The bulk sausage should be seared a minute or two less in its initial cooking.

CAPITOLADE OF CHICKEN

Cooked chicken reheated in a mushroom sauce, capitolade is closer to the French sense of hash than most American versions. It indeed won the favor of many Francophiles in the early years of the republic, including Thomas Jefferson, who reportedly served it at Monticello with mushrooms gathered in the wild.

SERVES 4

BREAD CRUMBS

2 teaspoons unsalted butter

¾ cup packed fresh bread crumbs

4 tablespoons (½ stick) unsalted butter

2 large shallots, minced

6 ounces small tender wild mushrooms, such as chicken-of-the-woods or oyster, or portobello or button mushrooms, thinly sliced

2 tablespoons unbleached all-purpose flour

¼ cup dry white wine

1 cup chicken stock

½ cup half-and-half

½ teaspoon salt or more to taste

3 cups shredded or diced cooked chicken

1 tablespoon minced fresh parsley or 1 teaspoon minced fresh thyme, chervil, or summer savory

Fresh thyme, chervil, or summer savory sprigs, optional

Preheat the oven to 375°F. Butter a medium baking dish.

Prepare the bread crumbs, first melting the 2 teaspoons butter in a small skillet over medium heat. Stir in the bread crumbs and toast them until golden, stirring occasionally. Scrape the bread crumbs out of the skillet and reserve them.

Prepare the hash, first melting the 4 tablespoons butter in the same skillet over medium heat. Stir in the shallots and mushrooms and cook until the mushrooms are limp, about 5 minutes. Sprinkle in the flour and, when incorporated, pour in the wine and simmer briefly until reduced by half. Pour in the stock and the half-and-half, add salt, and cook for about 5 minutes longer, until lightly thickened. Stir in the chicken and heat through. Remove from the heat and add the parsley.

Spoon the capitolade into the prepared dish. Sprinkle with the bread crumbs and bake for 15 to 20 minutes, until the bread crumbs are nicely browned and the sauce is bubbly.

CHILDREN EXCEPTED

American restaurant menus in the nineteenth century often posted hours for meals served. Around the time of the Civil War, the Willard Hotel in Washington, D. C., advertised breakfast from 7:00 to 11:00 in the morning, dinner from 1:30 to 3:30 in the afternoon, and, in the evening, tea from 7:30 to 9:00 and supper from 9:30 to 11:00. The restaurant posted different hours for "children and servants," who were seated only at 7:00 for breakfast, 12:00 for dinner, and 6:00 for tea.

CHICKEN–WILD RICE HASH

Most notable hashes feature root vegetables and a crisp, skillet-seared surface. This is an exception in both respects. It uses wild rice for starchy heft and is baked for a moister finish. We assemble the hash the night before serving and just pop it in the oven in the morning.   **SERVES 4**

A BREAKFAST MENU SUGGESTION FOR A KANSAS BREAKFAST PARTY

1st Course.—Quail on toast. Currant jelly. Tea, coffee, or chocolate.

2nd Course.—Sweetbreads garnished with canned French peas. Roll or biscuit, cold.

3rd Course.—Lamb chops, tomatoes, fried potatoes.

4th Course.—Fried oysters. Muffins.

5th Course.—Fillets of prairie-chicken, potato balls.

6th Course.—Charlotte russe, canned strawberries.

Mrs. C. H. Cushing and Mrs. B. Gray, *Kansas Home Cook-book* (1886)

2 tablespoons unsalted butter

1 red bell pepper, chopped

¼ cup minced onion

⅓ cup chopped hickory nuts or pecans

2 cups cooked wild rice

2 cups chopped or shredded roast or smoked chicken

Salt to taste

SAGE WHITE SAUCE

2 tablespoons unsalted butter

2 tablespoons unbleached all-purpose flour

1½ cups whole milk

½ cup chicken stock or additional milk

1 teaspoon dried sage

⅛ teaspoon freshly milled white pepper

Salt to taste

Preheat the oven to 375°F.

Warm the butter in a large skillet over medium heat. Stir in the bell pepper and onion and sauté until soft, about 5 minutes. Stir in the hickory nuts, followed by the wild rice and chicken, and then season with salt.

Prepare the sauce, first melting the butter in a medium saucepan over medium heat. Whisk in the flour and cook for 1 minute, then slowly whisk in the milk and stock. Cook until the mixture comes to a boil and thickens, 3 to 5 minutes longer. Stir in the sage, white pepper, and salt.

Spoon half of the chicken–wild rice mixture into a buttered medium baking dish. Top with half of the sauce. Repeat with the remaining chicken–wild rice mixture and sauce. (The hash can be prepared to this point the night before, covered, and refrigerated. Let it sit at room temperature for 15 to 20 minutes before proceeding.) Bake the hash, covered, for about 20 minutes, then uncover and continue baking for about 10 minutes longer, until the sauce is bubbly and begins to color.

ROAST TURKEY–WILD RICE HASH

If you've got leftover turkey instead of chicken, liven the hash a bit with a Mornay sauce rather than simple white sauce. Add ½ cup grated Gruyère or Swiss cheese to the white sauce just before removing it from the heat.

SHRIMP AND PORK HASH

This hash owes its inspiration to one we enjoyed for breakfast at the Mauna Lani Bay hotel in Hawaii. A reflection of the state itself, as well as the local culinary style, it combines very Asian ingredients in a very American way.

SERVES 4

3 scallions, limp green tops removed, cut into several chunks

1 plump garlic clove

One 8-ounce can water chestnuts, drained

1 pound medium shrimp, peeled

¾ pound ground pork

2 tablespoons soy sauce

4½ teaspoons Asian sesame oil

1 teaspoon Asian chile paste or ½ teaspoon hot red pepper flakes or more to taste

One ½-pound sweet potato, boiled or baked until soft and peeled

3 tablespoons sesame seeds

Peanut oil or other vegetable oil for panfrying

4 or 8 Poached Eggs (page 30)

Hollandaise Sauce (page 32)

Asian chile paste, optional

Scallion rings

Prepare the hash mixture in a food processor. With the machine running, add the scallions and garlic. When minced, add the water chestnuts and pulse to chop until in even bits with some remaining texture. Then add the shrimp and process similarly. Add the pork, soy sauce, sesame oil, and chile paste and process briefly until well combined. Turn the mixture into a large bowl.

Without washing the processor's work bowl, change to the large shredding disk and grate the sweet potato. (Alternatively, grate the sweet potato on the large holes of a box grater.) Stir it and the sesame seeds into the mixture. It should be stiff. Form the hash into 8 patties no thicker than ½ inch. (The hash can be made to this point a day in advance, covered, and refrigerated. Add about a minute to the cooking time of each side of the patties.)

Warm a thin film of oil in a large skillet over medium heat. Fry the patties in batches until richly brown and crisp, turning them once, at least 3 minutes per side. Check to make sure the first patty is done at the center, cooking it a bit longer if needed. Arrange 2 hash patties on each plate, 1 or 2 poached eggs over or beside the hash, and spoon hollandaise over all. Place a dot of chile paste on each plate if you wish, so that guests can customize the heat level. Scatter scallions over and serve immediately.

DERBY DAY TURKEY HASH WITH CORN BATTY CAKES

A BREAKFAST MENU SUGGESTION FOR A KENTUCKY DERBY DAY BREAKFAST

Corn Meal Waffles Topped with Turkey Hash

Sausage Patties   Fried Apples

Endive, Artichoke Bottoms, Tomatoes, Cucumbers with French Dressing

(Maple Syrup on Waffles for Dessert)

Coffee

Marion Flexner, *Out of Kentucky Kitchens* (1949)

Lettice Bryan offered one of the first printed recipes for a turkey hash long ago in *The Kentucky Housewife* (1839). She said, "This is a breakfast dish, and thought by many people to be better than when the turkey is first cooked." Kentucky cooks continue to echo that sentiment, serving this version of turkey hash at many celebratory breakfasts, including one at the governor's mansion on the day of the Kentucky Derby. It often comes with crispy, lacy corn batty (or batter) cakes, which crossed over the Blue Ridge from Virginia well before the first Run for the Roses in 1875.

SERVES 4 TO 6

CORN BATTY CAKES

¾ cup stone-ground cornmeal, preferably white

½ teaspoon baking powder

¼ teaspoon baking soda

½ teaspoon salt

1 cup buttermilk

1 large egg

1 tablespoon unsalted butter, melted

TURKEY HASH

3 tablespoons unsalted butter

2 tablespoons bacon drippings or vegetable oil

2 cups chopped onions

¼ pound button mushrooms, thinly sliced

½ cup chopped green bell pepper

3 tablespoons unbleached all-purpose flour

2 cups turkey or chicken stock

3 tablespoons heavy (whipping) cream or half-and-half

1 tablespoon Worcestershire sauce

1 tablespoon tomato-based barbecue sauce

3½ to 4 cups finely diced roast or other cooked turkey

¼ cup minced fresh flat-leaf parsley

Salt and freshly milled black pepper to taste

Bacon drippings or vegetable oil

Minced fresh flat-leaf parsley

Begin the preparations for the corn cakes, stirring together the cornmeal, baking powder, baking soda, and salt in a medium bowl. Combine the buttermilk, egg, and melted butter in another bowl and whisk lightly. Reserve both.

Prepare the hash, first warming the butter and drippings in a large heavy skillet, preferably 10 to 12 inches in diameter, over medium-high heat. Add the onions and cook for a minute, then add the mushrooms and bell pepper.

Cook for 5 minutes, stirring the mixture around, warming it through, and allowing some of the steam from the vegetables to escape.

Pat the mixture down and let it cook until it begins to brown richly, 6 to 8 minutes. Scrape it up again with a sturdy spatula, getting up any browned bits. Sprinkle flour over it, stir the mixture until the flour is incorporated, then pour in the stock, cream, Worcestershire sauce, and barbecue sauce. Bring the mixture, which will look like gravy, to a boil. Cook it down for about 10 minutes, until so thick that when you pull a spatula through the mixture it leaves a trail. Scrape up from the bottom while the mixture cooks. Add the turkey, parsley, salt, and pepper. Scrape the hash back up again. Continue cooking and scraping until the liquid is cooked down and the hash mixture remains moist but has a few crisp edges, another 6 to 8 minutes. Don't turn the temperature down unless you're close to burning the mixture. You need enough heat to develop a rich brown crust. Keep the hash warm while you finish the batty cakes.

Warm a griddle, preferably, or a large heavy skillet over medium heat. A sturdy nonstick surface or well-seasoned cast iron works best. Add just enough bacon drippings to the griddle to coat the surface with a thin film. Pour the wet ingredients into the dry and mix just until combined. Spoon the batter by tablespoonfuls onto the griddle, leaving several inches between the dollops. The batter will spread immediately into thin cakes about 3 inches in diameter. (The batter should bubble merrily. If it splatters menacingly instead, the griddle is too hot. Reduce the heat before continuing.) Cook the cakes until the batter appears quite firm and loses its shine, about 2 to 3 minutes. Turn carefully and cook the cakes on the other side until medium brown and crispy, 2 to 3 minutes longer. Repeat with the remaining batter, adding more fat to the griddle as necessary.

Arrange 2 or 3 corn cakes on one side of each plate and mound the hash on the other side, overlapping a bit in the center. Serve hot, with sprinklings of parsley over the hash.

FRIDAY-AFTER-THANKSGIVING TURKEY HASH

If you've been celebrating Turkey Day rather than Derby Day, consider adding leftover mashed potatoes or dressing or both to the hash. You can substitute them for some of the turkey if you wish or just add up to a cup or so total, stirring in a little more stock or cream to keep the mixture moist. You can skip the corn cakes since you will have added a good bit of starch to the meal already.

CRUSTY CHICKEN HASH

For a chicken hash much crustier than capitolade, substitute roast or other cooked chicken for the turkey in this recipe. Keep the corn cakes or forgo them at your discretion.

HASHED CRAB

Like crab cakes, crab hash should show off the main ingredient and not overshadow it. When it's available, we like to use succulent Dungeness crab from Pacific waters in this hash, but blue crab or other crab also works fine. The dish's rich flavor begs for a cool and tangy accompaniment, such as Honeyed Oranges with Jalapeños (page 286) or a fruit compote. **SERVES UP TO 4**

(page 286)

**QUICK GARLIC MAYONNAISE
(MAKES ABOUT 1 CUP)**

1 cup store-bought mayonnaise

4½ teaspoons extra-virgin olive oil

1 teaspoon minced garlic

¼ teaspoon fresh lemon juice

2 to 4 drops of Tabasco or other hot pepper sauce

HASH

2 tablespoons unsalted butter

½ cup fresh bread crumbs

1 medium to large egg

3 tablespoons Quick Garlic Mayonnaise

1 tablespoon Dijon mustard

½ teaspoon celery seeds

¼ teaspoon salt or more to taste

Several splashes of Tabasco or other hot pepper sauce

1 pound lump crabmeat, preferably Dungeness

1 tablespoon vegetable oil for panfrying

Minced fresh parsley

Lemon wedges

Prepare the mayonnaise, whisking together the ingredients in a small bowl. Use immediately or refrigerate for up to a week.

Prepare the hash, first melting 1 tablespoon of the butter in a small skillet over medium heat. Stir in the bread crumbs and toast them until golden brown and quite crisp, stirring occasionally, about 5 minutes. Scrape the bread crumbs out of the skillet and reserve them.

Whisk the egg in a large bowl until just foamy. Stir in the mayonnaise and mustard, then add the celery seed, salt, and Tabasco. When well combined, add the crab and gently mix the ingredients together, being careful to avoid breaking up the lumps of crabmeat too much. The mixture should remain chunky.

Warm the oil with the remaining butter in a medium to large skillet over medium-high heat. Spoon in the crab mixture and pat it down. Cook it for about 3 minutes, until the bottom of the mixture is coloring in spots. Stir it up from the bottom with several broad strokes from the spatula, gently pat

Since childhood, "hash" has been for me one of the most evocative menu words in the English language. I think the pleasure hash brings is a combination of its comfort food consistency and the voyage of discovery as you eat it.

William Rice, *Steak Lover's Cookbook* (1997)

it back in place, and continue cooking until golden brown and crisp in spots, 3 to 5 minutes longer. Toss the bread crumbs with the mixture.

Spoon onto plates and scatter parsley over each. Top with dollops of garlic mayonnaise, garnish with lemon wedges, and serve without hesitation.

A HASH FOR ALL SEASONS

Culinary investigators Cora, Rose, and Bob Brown scouted the country in the 1930s for special hashes to include in their *America Cooks* (1940). They found most of the favorites we feature, but many others as well. In Illinois they enjoyed a haystack hash combining minced pork chops with mashed potatoes, bread crumbs, and ketchup, all mounded together into the namesake shape and then baked with an egg on top. The treat in Tennessee was hashed hog's head, flavored with onion, mace, red pepper, cloves, and walnut ketchup and served with a side of applesauce. The intrepid Browns also sampled a barbecue hash in Georgia that revolved around pork liver, beef, and lamb and a sour hash in Minnesota based on calf's heart.

OREGON SALMON HASH

Salmon hash often puts a shine on Pacific Northwest mornings. You find it in fancy hotel dining rooms, cheap cafés, and, in this simple but sublime form, on many home tables.   **SERVES 4**

2 tablespoons unsalted butter

2 tablespoons vegetable oil

1 pound Yukon Gold or waxy red potatoes, peeled if you wish and cut into ½-inch cubes

½ medium onion, preferably red or yellow, diced

3 tablespoons half-and-half

1 teaspoon Dijon mustard

Salt and freshly milled black pepper to taste

¾ to 1 pound hot-smoked salmon, *not* cold-smoked nova or lox, flaked

3 tablespoons minced fresh chives

2 teaspoons minced fresh dill or 1 teaspoon dried

Sour cream, optional

Capers or caperberries, optional

Warm the butter and oil in a large heavy skillet over medium-low heat. Add the potatoes, stirring them well to coat with the fat. Cover and cook the potatoes for 10 minutes, during which time you should hear only a faint cooking noise.

Uncover and turn the potatoes. Raise the heat to medium and cook for 5 minutes longer, until uniformly soft with some crisp brown spots. Add the onion and pat the mixture down. Cook until the onion is soft and the mixture begins to stick in a few spots and brown on the bottom, 5 minutes longer. Scrape up from the bottom, then add the half-and-half, mustard, salt, and a generous grinding of pepper. Raise the heat to medium-high. Continue cooking until the liquid evaporates and the mixture begins to crisp and brown again, 5 to 8 minutes longer. Scrape up from the bottom and pat back down another time or two. Add the salmon and herbs and cook for a couple minutes longer, until heated through. Serve hot, topped if you wish with a dollop of sour cream and a sprinkle of capers.

DOUBLE SALMON HASH

Double your pleasure with two salmon tastes and textures. Reduce the amount of smoked salmon to ½ pound. Broil or grill a ½-pound fresh salmon steak or fillet section until just cooked through, then flake it when cool enough to handle. Add it to the hash along with the smoked salmon.

Of all the great American dishes to suffer under the present-day tyranny of gastronomic pretension and snobbism, perhaps none has undergone a more lamentable demise in popularity than that wonderful creation known as hash.

James Villas, *American Taste* (1982)

SMOKED TROUT HASH

In place of the smoked salmon, use 2 smoked trout, about 1 pound total, flaked. Decrease the amount of chives by 1 tablespoon and increase the fresh dill by 1 teaspoon. A touch of horseradish can be good too, either mixed in or on the side.

MINNESOTA FISH HASH

In the "land of 10,000 lakes," cooks make a similar hash with local lake fish. Replace the salmon with a pound of poached or broiled whitefish or walleye, which is similar to sole in flavor. Increase the dill by 1 teaspoon.

PORTSMOUTH SALT-COD HASH

In New England fishing communities such as Portsmouth, New Hampshire, residents enjoy an abundance of fresh fish but have never forsaken the salt cod that's been popular since colonial days. We like this hash topped with garlicky mayonnaise, though many locals might vote against the notion, perhaps opting instead for a cruet of malt vinegar on the side. **SERVES 4**

½ pound salt cod (see Ingredient Tip, page 170)

4½ teaspoons olive oil

2 lightly packed heaping cups cubed French or country bread, crust removed (about ½-inch cubes)

3 thick slices bacon, chopped

2 plump garlic cloves, slivered

1 heaping cup leftover mashed potatoes or one ½-pound russet or other baking potato, peeled, boiled, and mashed with 2 to 3 tablespoons unsalted butter or olive oil

1 to 2 tablespoons heavy (whipping) cream

Freshly milled black pepper to taste

Pinch or two of cayenne pepper

Salt to taste, optional

2 to 3 tablespoons minced fresh parsley

Quick Garlic Mayonnaise (page 194), optional

Lemon wedges

Rinse the salt from the surface of the fish. Cover with cool water and soak for at least 8 hours and up to 24 hours, changing the water several times. Drain and place in a saucepan with fresh cool water to cover. Warm over medium heat, bringing the water just to a simmer, adjusting the heat as needed so that bubbles break only occasionally on the surface. Cook until soft and easily flaked, about 15 minutes, then drain again. When cool enough to handle, pull the cod into small flakes.

Warm the olive oil in a large skillet over medium-high heat. Add the bread cubes, stirring to coat them evenly with oil. Sauté the bread, stirring frequently, until lightly browned on all sides, crunchy in some spots, and chewy in others. Remove with a slotted spoon and transfer to a plate more or less in a single layer.

Add the bacon to the skillet and fry it over medium heat until brown and crisp. Remove the bacon with a slotted spoon and drain it.

Stir the garlic into the pan drippings and cook for 1 minute. Add the cod and potatoes to the skillet and combine with a spatula, mashing them together. Stir in 1 tablespoon of the cream, a few grinds of pepper, and cayenne. Add salt with a light hand, if at all, since the cod will have retained some salinity. Pat the mixture down and cook without disturbing until a golden-brown crust forms on the bottom, about 5 minutes. Scrape it up from the bottom with several broad strokes from the spatula, adding the remaining cream if it seems dry. Pat the hash back down again and continue cooking until golden-brown and crisp on the bottom, about 5 minutes longer. Add the parsley and the reserved bread cubes and bacon and heat through briefly.

Spoon the hash onto plates. Top with dollops of garlic mayonnaise, garnish with lemon wedges, and serve piping hot.

SNAPPER HASH WITH GARLIC-CILANTRO MAYONNAISE

Nearly any fresh flaky white fish will make a good hash in a similar style. Skip the soaking needed for dried salt cod, just poaching or otherwise cooking ¾ pound fresh fish. Pull it into flakes, discarding skin and bones. Fresh cod can be used, but we prefer a red or other snapper. Trade out the parsley in the hash for cilantro and add at least 1 tablespoon of it to the mayonnaise too.

LEFTOVERS RULE

Miss T. S. Shute's *The American Housewife Cook Book* (1880) was one of the earliest American cookbooks to include a full chapter on breakfast as a meal different from lunch, dinner, or supper. She recommended a number of meat dishes, usually made with leftovers from dinner, including hashes, ragouts, and fricassees. Shute also favored salt fish in balls or omelets, boiled or stewed white beans, hominy with cream and sugar, and eggs fried, poached, or scrambled.

NORTH WOODS CHANTERELLE HASH

Voluptuous chanterelle mushrooms pop up like stubby golden para-sols in many northern states during summers that follow damp springs. For such a luscious ingredient we keep the preparation simple and let the mushroom star. Foragers can easily double the quantity of this vegetable hash, but we make it here for two people because of the price of store-bought chanterelles. To prepare the dish out of season, or if chanterelles aren't available to you, substitute other wild mushrooms such as chunky orange lobster mushrooms (caps only), hen-of-the-woods, chicken-of-the-woods, or even cultivated mushrooms. **SERVES 2**

1½ tablespoons olive oil

1½ tablespoons unsalted butter

2 medium shallots, minced

¾ pound chanterelle mushrooms, trimmed and diced

¼ pound cremini or button mushrooms, diced

½ pound cooked Yukon Gold or Yellow Finn potatoes, finely diced

2 tablespoons heavy (whipping) cream, half-and-half, or milk

Salt and freshly milled black pepper to taste

Warm the oil and butter together in a medium heavy skillet over medium heat. Sauté the shallots for 1 to 2 minutes, then add the mushrooms, stir, cover, and sweat for about 5 minutes, until the mushrooms are limp. Add the potatoes, drizzle with cream, and sprinkle with salt and pepper. Scrape up from the bottom, stir, pat back down, and cook for about 2 minutes, until the potatoes begin to brown in spots. Raise the heat, scrape up again, pat back down, and continue cooking for 2 to 3 minutes more, until the liquid is evaporated and the potatoes a bit crusted. Serve immediately.

MUSHROOM–CELERY ROOT HASH

Eliminate the potatoes from the hash. Peel 1 smallish celery root (celeriac), about ¾ pound, and cut it into small dice. Bring it to a boil in salted water and cook until crisp-tender, about 5 minutes. Add to the recipe as you would the potatoes. We like the added texture of ½ teaspoon celery seeds stirred in at the same time, but they are not essential.

MUSHROOM-SALSIFY HASH

In an earlier age, salsify appeared in nearly every American cookbook. Enjoying something of a small renaissance today, it boasts a nutty root-vegetable flavor. Have ready a pot of hot water into which you have squeezed 1 lemon. Peel 1 pound salsify roots one at a time, quickly cutting them into bite-size chunks and then adding them to the pot. (They brown very quickly when cut.) Cook until crisp-tender, about 8 minutes. Use as directed for the potatoes.

MIXED VEGETABLE HASH

Inspired by a dish served at a small hotel in Galena, Illinois, on the bluffs of the Mississippi, we created our own rendition of what the innkeepers call hobo hash. For a vegetarian version, eliminate the bacon and simply add a couple of tablespoons of vegetable oil to the butter. As long as you don't overcook the broccoli, the color will remain vibrant and inviting, accented by bits of red pepper.

SERVES 4

4 thick slices bacon

2 tablespoons unsalted butter

2 medium leeks, white and light green parts, or 1 medium onion, sliced into thin half-moons

2 pounds russet potatoes, peeled, diced, and parboiled just until tender

¾ pound broccoli, chopped

½ raw or roasted red bell pepper, diced

¼ cup sour cream

½ teaspoon salt or more to taste

¼ teaspoon freshly milled white pepper

Several pinches of hot red pepper flakes

¼ pound Cheddar cheese, grated (about 1 cup)

Fry the bacon in a large heavy skillet over medium heat until brown and crisp. Remove the bacon with a slotted spoon and reserve it. Add the butter to the drippings and warm through. Stir in the leeks and sauté until they just begin to soften, a couple of minutes. Add the potatoes, broccoli, and red bell pepper and stir up from the bottom to combine. Cover and cook for 5 minutes, until the broccoli is somewhat tender. Uncover, add the sour cream, salt, white pepper, and hot pepper flakes and pat the mixture back down. Raise the heat to medium-high and cook without disturbing until a golden-brown crust forms on the bottom, about 3 additional minutes. Scrape up from the bottom, turn, pat back down again, and cook for about 3 minutes more, until crusty again. Stir the reserved bacon into the hash and serve, immediately sprinkling each portion with cheese.

TAMALE HASH

Seldom seen in cookbooks, this is a homey favorite in the Southwest after a tamale dinner, mentioned as often as any dish by area residents in reminiscences about favorite breakfast foods. Any kind of tamale works—pork or beef, corn and cheese, green chile and zucchini, or whatever is on hand.

Seldom seen in cookbooks, this is a homey favorite in the Southwest after a tamale dinner, mentioned as often as any dish by area residents in reminiscences about favorite breakfast foods. Any kind of tamale works—pork or beef, corn and cheese, green chile and zucchini, or whatever is on hand.

SERVES 2

2 tablespoons unsalted butter

1 tablespoon vegetable oil

½ medium onion, diced

½ cup fresh or frozen corn kernels, optional

3 to 4 cooked tamales, depending on size, husked and cut into bite-size chunks

Red Chile Sauce (page 74) or Mesilla Valley Green Chile Sauce (page 40)

Crème fraîche (crema) or sour cream

2 Bacon-Basted or Butter-Basted Fried Eggs (page 24)

Grated Cheddar or Monterey Jack cheese or crumbled *queso fresco* or *cotija* cheese

Warm the butter and oil in a medium skillet over medium heat. Add the onion and sauté until very soft, about 7 minutes. Mix in the corn if you wish. Add the tamale chunks and stir them in gently. It's fine for some of the pieces to disintegrate, but keep a good portion of them in toothsome chunks. If the mixture is dry, stir in a tablespoon or two of the chile sauce or crème fraîche. Cover for 2 to 3 minutes to heat through, then uncover and cook for an additional minute or two, letting a bit of crust form in spots.

Spoon onto plates and arrange eggs over or on the side. Add a generous ladling of sauce around, a dollop of crème fraîche, and a handful of cheese for each portion and serve immediately.

8

Stratas and Other Morning Casseroles

BAKED DISHES that generally combine eggs, cheese, and bread in balanced proportions, stratas began popping up in American cookbooks around the turn of the twentieth century. Precedents existed in European and early American cheese puddings, but the addition of bread or other starches made it a distinctly different dish.

Unfortunately for cooks today, the strata and similar casseroles acquired a reputation during the Depression and World War II as meatless economy preparations for hard times, and they never quite overcame that humble standing. Many people in fashionable food circles continue to ignore their potentials, but good versions boast a wealth of hearty flavors and appeal to almost any appetite.

On top of that, you can usually do everything except the baking the night before serving. Simply put the strata in the oven as you start the coffee and sit down to a bountiful one-dish breakfast in less than an hour. Starting off in such a simple and comforting way makes the rest of the day a snap.

CLASSIC CHEESE STRATA

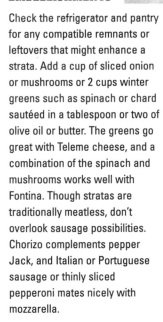

CLASSIC STRATA EMBELLISHMENTS

Check the refrigerator and pantry for any compatible remnants or leftovers that might enhance a strata. Add a cup of sliced onion or mushrooms or 2 cups winter greens such as spinach or chard sautéed in a tablespoon or two of olive oil or butter. The greens go great with Teleme cheese, and a combination of the spinach and mushrooms works well with Fontina. Though stratas are traditionally meatless, don't overlook sausage possibilities. Chorizo complements pepper Jack, and Italian or Portuguese sausage or thinly sliced pepperoni mates nicely with mozzarella.

The name *strata,* which is simply a fancy term for layering, was in print at least as early as the 1940s but became common only in the last couple of decades. Before then, Americans knew this dish by many labels, including *escalloped cheese, never-fail soufflé,* and *Christmas-morning lifesaver.* This classic version demonstrates the aptness of each name, old and new, and the simple appeal of a basic combination of cheese, eggs, and bread. **SERVES 6**

One 1- to 1¼-pound loaf country or sourdough bread, crusts removed if thick

1¼ cups (about 5 ounces) grated or crumbled medium to sharp Cheddar, smoked Cheddar, Monterey Jack, Muenster, Brie (rind removed), St. Andre (rind removed), or other good melting cheese

1½ cups small-curd cottage cheese or more of the cheese you chose above

3 tablespoons minced fresh chives or 2 teaspoons minced fresh thyme or rosemary or 1 teaspoon dried thyme or rosemary, optional

5 large eggs

1 cup milk or half-and-half

1 teaspoon dry mustard

½ teaspoon salt

Freshly milled black pepper

4 tablespoons (½ stick) unsalted butter, melted

Oil or butter a deep 9- to 10-inch baking dish.

Slice the bread about ½ inch thick. Arrange the bread, grated cheese, cottage cheese, and chives in 2 or 3 equal alternating layers in the baking dish. Cut or tear bread slices if needed to make snug layers.

Whisk the eggs with the milk, mustard, salt, and pepper. Pour the custard over the bread mixture. Drizzle with the melted butter. Cover and refrigerate the strata for at least 1 hour and up to overnight. Remove the strata from the refrigerator 20 to 30 minutes before you plan to bake it.

Preheat the oven to 350°F. Bake the strata for 50 to 55 minutes, until puffed, golden brown, and lightly set in the center. Serve hot.

SATURDAY SUMMER STRATA

TECHNIQUE TIP

The wealth of specialty breads available today encourages experimentation with stratas. Just pick a variety compatible with the cheese and any embellishments you are considering, removing the crust if it's thick. Egg-rich challah, brioche, and Italian panettone offer resonant alternatives. Cakey corn breads can turn to mush in a strata, but sturdier southern-style versions work well, particularly when toasted first to improve the texture. Even soft white bread makes a good strata, though we like to layer it with a darker whole grain bread to enhance the taste and appearance.

Sheila Lukins and Julee Rosso introduced us to stratas in their popular 1984 *Silver Palate Good Times Cookbook*. We've tinkered ever since then with our version of their Basil Breakfast Strata, which they presented as a front-porch summer brunch dish. This is our current rendition, a big favorite with the Glow Club, Cheryl's Saturday-morning women's running group.

SERVES 6 OR MORE

One 1- to 1¼-pound loaf country or sourdough bread, crusts removed if thick

½ pound cream cheese or St. Andre cheese (rind removed), cut into small cubes or bits

½ pound fresh or other mozzarella, cut into small pieces or grated

¾ cup prepared pesto

6 ounces thinly sliced prosciutto

1 pound (about 3 medium) red-ripe tomatoes, thinly sliced

5 large eggs

1½ cups milk or half-and-half

½ teaspoon salt

Freshly milled black pepper to taste

Oil or butter a deep 9- to 10-inch baking dish.

Slice the bread about ½ inch thick. Arrange 2 to 3 equal alternating layers of the bread, cheeses, pesto, prosciutto, and tomatoes in the baking dish. Cut or tear bread slices if needed to make snug layers.

Whisk the eggs with the milk, salt, and pepper. Pour the custard over the bread mixture. Cover and refrigerate the strata for at least 2 hours and up to overnight. Remove the strata from the refrigerator 20 to 30 minutes before you plan to bake it.

Preheat the oven to 350°F. Bake the strata for 50 to 55 minutes, until puffed, golden brown, and lightly set in the center. Serve hot.

AUTUMN STRATA

Eliminate the pesto and tomatoes. Sauté ½ pound sliced mushrooms, 1 or 2 minced garlic cloves, ¼ teaspoon hot red pepper flakes, and ¾ pound fresh spinach, chard, or escarole in 3 tablespoons olive oil until the mushrooms are tender and any liquid has evaporated. Arrange alternating layers of the bread, cheeses, prosciutto, and mushroom mixture and proceed as directed.

COMPANY BREAKFASTS

The formal breakfast— or perhaps it would be more accurate to say the company breakfast, for this meal is not as a rule very formal—is much in favor with people of the leisure class, and also with the artist and *littérateur,* who frequently have considerable time to kill.

Christine Terhune Herrick, ed., *Consolidated Library of Modern Cooking and Household Recipes* (1904)

As Lukins and Rosso suggest, stratas make a great dish for brunch, an American institution that derives partially from an older event usually known as a "company breakfast." Popular for a generation or so beginning around 1880, these meals provided an opportunity to entertain less expensively and more informally than at dinner. In *Miss Parloa's Kitchen Companion* (1887), a best-seller of the era, Maria Parloa noted that the "little breakfast-parties" were becoming more common each year and suggested several keys to success. She advised serving between nine o'clock and noon and keeping the meal simple, elaborate menus being "in as bad taste as if the guests came to breakfast in full dress." She illustrated the idea of simplicity in a suggested bill of fare that included cantaloupe, breaded fillet of bass, tenderloin steaks, baked eggs, hominy griddle cakes, fried sweet potatoes, and three kinds of homemade bread.

ARTICHOKE–GOAT CHEESE STRATA

A sunny combo of Californian-Italian flavors, this is a strata that shines year-round. We cube the bread in this case rather than slice it so that the pieces are closer in size to the artichoke hearts, and then we toast it too for extra flavor and texture. Good additions, if on hand, include a handful of slivered briny black olives or soaked sun-dried tomatoes. **SERVES 8 OR MORE**

One 1- to 1¼-pound loaf sourdough bread or black olive bread, crusts removed if thick

Three 6- to 6½-ounce jars marinated artichoke hearts, drained and 3 tablespoons of the marinade reserved

2 teaspoons minced fresh thyme or tarragon or 1 teaspoon dried

3 plump garlic cloves, roasted in a dry skillet until soft and smashed

¾ pound creamy fresh goat cheese, crumbled

¾ cup freshly grated Parmesan cheese

8 large eggs

2½ cups half-and-half or milk

1 teaspoon salt

¾ teaspoon freshly milled black pepper

3 tablespoons extra virgin olive oil

Preheat the oven to 400°F. Oil or butter a deep 9- to 10-inch baking dish.

Slice the bread into approximately 1-inch cubes. Transfer the bread to a baking sheet and toast for about 20 minutes, stirring once or twice, until golden brown and lightly crisp. Slice the artichoke hearts about ⅓ inch thick. Mix them with the thyme and garlic in a small bowl. Arrange 2 or 3 equal alternating layers of the bread, cheeses, and artichoke hearts in the baking dish.

Whisk the eggs with the half-and-half, salt, pepper, and reserved artichoke marinade. Pour the custard over the bread mixture. Drizzle the olive oil over the surface. Cover and refrigerate the strata for at least 2 hours and up to overnight. Remove the strata from the refrigerator 20 to 30 minutes before you plan to bake it.

Preheat the oven to 350°F. Bake the strata for 50 to 55 minutes, until puffed, golden brown, and lightly set in the center. Serve hot.

IDA BAILEY ALLEN

A successful cookbook author, food magazine editor, and radio-show hostess, Ida Bailey Allen enjoyed a long culinary career that stretched from World War I to the Vietnam War. From the beginning she emphasized meatless and economy dishes that helped cooks cope with the deprivations of war and depression. She stayed close to those homey themes up to her last book, *Best Loved Recipes of the American People* (1973), which included stratas called Cheese Custard with Olives and Escalloped Bread and Cheese. The latter is one of the earliest printed recipes we've found that touts the enhanced flavor benefits of assembling a strata in advance and letting it sit overnight before baking.

ALMOND–CINNAMON TOAST FEATHERBED

TECHNIQUE TIP

Advance preparation is a major advantage of breakfast stratas, but you don't have to put them together ahead of time. For a supper casserole, or one decided on at the last minute, just change a couple of steps in the assembly. Soak the bread in the milk or cream initially for 30 seconds or so. Then whisk together the milk that was not absorbed by the bread into the egg mixture. When building the layers of the strata, pour about one third of the egg custard over each layer as you build the dish rather than pouring it all over the top at the end.

———

SELECTIONS FROM THE BREAKFAST MENU AT THE NEW GRAND HOTEL IN NEW YORK CITY, 1905

SPECIALS FOR BREAKFAST

Swedish Fish Balls

Wurst mit Eier

Browned Pork and Beans

Little Neck Clams with Shirred Eggs

———

Among all the names nominated over time for stratas, *featherbed* is our favorite. It particularly suits this slightly sweet version, built on airy challah and creamy mascarpone and dotted with fragrant cinnamon, almonds, and almond paste.   **SERVES 6 OR MORE**

One 1- to 1¼-pound loaf challah, Portuguese sweet bread, raisin bread, soft white bread, or pannetone

4 tablespoons (½ stick) unsalted butter, softened

2 teaspoons ground cinnamon

¼ cup sugar

6 ounces almond paste, cut into small bits

½ pound mascarpone or ¼ pound mascarpone plus ¼ pound ricotta cheese

5 large eggs

1½ cups half-and-half or milk

¼ cup amaretto liqueur

1 teaspoon salt

3 tablespoons unsalted butter, melted

⅓ cup slivered almonds, optional

Butter a deep 9- to 10-inch baking dish.

Slice the bread approximately ½ inch thick. Toast the slices until crisp and golden. (If they are too thick for your toaster, this can be done on a dry griddle or on a baking sheet in a 400°F oven.) Stir together the butter, cinnamon, and sugar in a small bowl. Spread the mixture evenly over the toast.

Arrange 2 to 3 equal alternating layers of the bread, bits of almond paste, and mascarpone in the baking dish. Cut or tear the bread slices if needed to make snug layers.

Whisk the eggs with the half-and-half, amaretto, and salt. Pour the custard over the bread mixture. Drizzle the melted butter over the surface. Cover and refrigerate the strata for at least 2 hours and up to overnight. Remove the strata from the refrigerator 20 to 30 minutes before you plan to bake it.

Preheat the oven to 350°F. Plan on a total baking time of 55 to 60 minutes. Cover and bake for 40 minutes. Uncover and scatter the almonds over the top if you are using them. Continue baking, uncovered, until puffed, golden brown, and lightly set in the center, 15 to 20 minutes longer. Serve hot.

KENTUCKY HOT BROWN STRATA

Louisville's grand old Brown Hotel created a wonderful sandwich years ago called the Hot Brown, which combines turkey or chicken with bacon and a warm Cheddar sauce. The blend of ingredients works just as well, and maybe better, in a strata.

SERVES 6 OR MORE

One 1- to 1¼-pound loaf country or sourdough bread, crusts removed if thick

6 ounces chopped smoked or roast turkey

6 ounces bacon, finely chopped and cooked crisp

1 large tomato, chopped

¾ pound medium to sharp Cheddar cheese, grated (about 3 cups)

5 large eggs

2 cups milk or half-and-half

½ teaspoon dried sage, optional

½ teaspoon salt

⅛ teaspoon cayenne pepper

Oil or butter a deep 9- to 10-inch baking dish.

Slice the bread about ½ inch thick. Arrange 3 equal alternating layers of the bread, turkey, bacon, tomato, and cheese in the baking dish. Cut or tear the bread slices if needed to make snug layers.

Whisk the eggs with the milk, sage, if you wish, salt, and cayenne. Pour the custard over the bread mixture. Cover and refrigerate the strata for at least 2 hours or up to overnight. Remove the strata from the refrigerator 20 to 30 minutes before you plan to bake it.

Preheat the oven to 350°F. Bake the strata for 50 to 55 minutes, until puffed, golden brown, and lightly set in the center. Serve hot.

EMBELLISHMENTS FOR KENTUCKY HOT BROWN STRATA

Replace the turkey with smoked or roast chicken or the bacon with ¼ to ½ pound ham. A chopped roasted red bell pepper can be added with the tomato or can replace it. Use chicken or turkey stock in place of half of the milk. For extra zest in the cheese element, add about ⅓ cup freshly grated Parmesan to the egg-milk mixture.

TECHNIQUE TIP

Diminutive stratas can be made in individual portions using 1-cup ramekins or soufflé dishes. Be sure to cut any vegetables or meats into small pieces and arrange the ingredients in only a single layer each. You can also make a full-size strata in a springform pan, which facilitates cutting it into neat wedges for serving.

A BREAKFAST MENU SUGGESTION FOR A SOUTHERN WEDDING BREAKFAST

Cantaloupe

Broiled Chicken, with Mushroom Sauce on Toast, Garnished with Parsley

Buttered Hot Rolls

Tomato on Lettuce with Mayonnaise

Cheese Straws

Ice Cream in the shape of Waffles, with Chocolate Sauce

Black Coffee

Mrs. S. R. Dull, *Southern Cooking* (1928)

SAUSAGE AND CHEESE GRITS CASSEROLE

INGREDIENT TIP

You can speed up the recipe by at least 20 minutes if you use quick-cooking (not instant) grits. We normally take the time to make grits from the coarser stone-ground variety, but the mix of flavors and textures in this casserole doesn't suffer as much as many dishes when made with the faster version. Reduce the cooking water for the grits to the amount suggested on the package.

Come an' see what yo'
got
On yo' breakfast table:
Ram, ham, chick'n 'n
mutton,
Ef yo' don't come now
You won't get nuttin'.

Old lumberjack ditty quoted in Nelson Algren, *America Eats* (1992)

A common casserole on southern tables at breakfast and beyond, this is one of our favorite ways to greet the dawn. Our friend Ellen Stelling, a transplanted South Carolinian, first introduced us to this dish some twenty years ago. We like to use our Sage Farm Sausage in the dish, but you can substitute a similar commercial variety, perhaps enlivening it with a pinch or two of dried sage, thyme, or hot red pepper flakes.   **SERVES 6**

¾ teaspoon salt or more to taste

1 cup stone-ground grits (see Ingredient Tip)

1 pound Sage Farm Sausage (page 136) or other bulk breakfast sausage, fried until well browned

¼ pound mild or smoked Cheddar cheese, grated (1 cup)

3 tablespoons unsalted butter

¼ teaspoon Tabasco or Texas Pete, or other hot pepper sauce or more to taste

3 large eggs, lightly beaten

1 to 2 scallions

Preheat the oven to 350°F. Butter a medium baking dish.

Bring 1 quart water and ¾ teaspoon salt to a boil in a large heavy saucepan over high heat. Whisk in the grits, a handful at a time. Reduce the heat to a bare simmer and cook the grits until thick and soft, 30 to 40 minutes. Stir the grits occasionally as they cook, more frequently as they thicken, scraping them off the bottom to prevent scorching. If the grits become too stiff to stir easily, before they are cooked through, add a bit more hot water.

Remove the grits from the heat and stir in the sausage, cheese, butter, and hot pepper sauce. Check the seasoning, adding more salt and hot pepper sauce if you wish. Mix in the eggs, stirring briskly. Spoon into the prepared dish. (The casserole can be made to this point, covered, and refrigerated overnight. In the morning, let it sit at room temperature for 20 to 30 minutes before baking.)

Bake until puffed and lightly set, 35 to 40 minutes.

While the grits bake, slice the scallions, both white and green portions, into sections about 2 inches long. Cut each section into long, thin strips and reserve.

When the casserole is ready, spoon it onto plates immediately or let it cool for about 10 minutes and then cut into soft-textured squares. Garnish each portion with a little shower of scallion strips and serve.

SAUSAGE AND CHEESE GRITS CASSEROLE WITH TENNESSEE TRUFFLES

In springtime, an Appalachian cook's thoughts turn to ramps, the odiferous member of the extended onion family that local wags call "Tennessee truffles." Becoming more common in well-stocked supermarkets during their brief season, they are a heady addition to casseroles such as this. Parboil a couple of ounces of chopped ramps, both white and green parts, until very limp. Drain and stir into the grits when adding the sausage.

CHEESE GRITS

Eliminate the sausage and add at least 2 more ounces (½ cup) of grated Cheddar to the grits. Reduce the number of eggs to 2.

CORNMEAL-MUSHROOM CASSEROLE

As with the preceding grits dish, buttery cornmeal mush or polenta offers boundless variety as the base for casserole dishes. In this case the mush is made ahead and chilled, then griddled to crusty perfection before being layered with mushrooms, blue cheese, and other ingredients. We prefer yellow cornmeal for the sunnier cast it lends to the dish, but white and blue cornmeal also work fine. You can do all the assembly, or part of it as you wish, the night before.

SERVES 6

A BREAKFAST MENU SUGGESTION FOR A MORNING PARTY BEFORE THE MASTERS GOLF TOURNAMENT

Bloody Mary   Cheese Straws

Brunch Casserole

Mushroom Soufflé

Fresh Fruit Salad with Poppy Seed Dressing or Hot Curried Fruit

Honey Orange Braids

Chocolate Peppermint Sticks

Junior League of Augusta, *Tea-Time at the Masters* (1977)

CORNMEAL MUSH

1 teaspoon salt

1½ cups coarsely ground cornmeal

2 ounces cream cheese, in several chunks, softened

2 tablespoons unsalted butter

FILLING

3 thick slices bacon, chopped

2 tablespoons unsalted butter

2 large shallots, minced

1 pound button or cremini mushrooms, thinly sliced

3 ounces blue cheese, crumbled, or, for a milder flavor, cream cheese, in several chunks, softened

Salt to taste, optional

1 to 2 tablespoons unbleached all-purpose flour

Several tablespoons vegetable oil

Oil a baking sheet.

Heat 6 cups water and the salt in a large heavy saucepan over high heat. When the water reaches a rolling boil, scatter in the cornmeal a handful at a time, stirring constantly. When you have added all the cornmeal, reduce the heat to a bare simmer. Cook the cornmeal until creamy and very thick, almost stiff, about 25 to 35 minutes, depending on its coarseness. Remove from the heat and stir in the cream cheese and butter. Pour the mush onto the baking sheet and set aside to cool to room temperature. Cover the pan and refrigerate for at least 4 hours and up to 2 days.

Prepare the filling, first frying the bacon in a medium skillet over medium heat. When brown and crisp, remove the bacon with a slotted spoon and reserve it. Add the butter to the skillet and, when melted, mix in the shallots and cook until they begin to soften, about 1 minute. Stir in the mushrooms, cover, and let them sweat for 5 to 7 minutes, until limp but still glistening with liquid. Mix in the blue cheese, add salt if you wish, and remove from the heat. (The filling can be made the night before, covered, and refrigerated.)

Preheat the oven to 350°F. Butter a large shallow baking dish. You want to use something that has about half the surface area of the baking sheet.

Turn the mush out of the pan and cut it into neat slices about 3 inches square. Dust the slices lightly with flour.

Warm a griddle or large heavy skillet over medium-high heat. Fry the mush slices in batches in a thin film of oil, avoiding crowding, until golden brown and crusty on both sides, about 5 to 8 minutes total. Arrange a layer of mush in the prepared dish, cutting slices if needed to cover the dish. Spoon the mushroom filling evenly over the mush, then top with another layer of mush. Bake until the top is golden brown and crisp, about 25 minutes. Serve immediately.

CORNMEAL CASSEROLE WITH CALICO VEGETABLES

Change out the mushroom filling mixture for a bright vegetable combo. Warm 2 tablespoons olive oil in a large skillet over medium heat. Stir in 1 chopped medium yellow onion, 1½ cups corn kernels, and ¾ cup diced bell pepper, preferably a combination of green and red, and cook until the vegetables are very soft, about 7 minutes. The mixture should remain moist, so add a tablespoon or two of water if the mixture begins to brown. Stir in ⅓ cup chopped pimiento-stuffed green olives and ¼ cup of dry Jack, Parmesan, manchego, or Asiago cheese. Add salt and pepper to taste. After layering the filling between the cornmeal, sprinkle 1 to 2 tablespoons of cheese over the casserole before baking.

SPINACH BREAD PUDDING

A BREAKFAST MENU

SUGGESTION FROM

IRMA ROMBAUER

Broiled Grapefruit

Omelet with Crabmeat and
Bacon or Scrambled Eggs and
Calf Brains

Broiled Tomatoes

Biscuits   Honey

Coffee

Irma Rombauer, *Joy of Cooking*
(1943)

Distinctions become difficult in the world of breakfast casseroles, but we call this a bread pudding instead of a strata because the ingredients are mixed rather than layered, baked in a shallower dish, and usually assembled on the day of serving rather than the night before. It's not the kind of difference you take to the copyright office.

SERVES 6

6 tablespoons unsalted butter

1 cup thinly sliced leeks (both white and green parts) or 1 large onion, diced

One 10-ounce package frozen chopped spinach, thawed

¾ cup finely diced Canadian bacon

3 cups herb-seasoned poultry-stuffing bread crumbs

1¼ cups small-curd cottage cheese

3 large eggs, lightly beaten

½ teaspoon baking powder

Salt and freshly milled black pepper to taste

1¼ to 1½ cups chicken stock

Halved cherry or small red teardrop tomatoes, halved, optional

Preheat the oven to 350°F. Butter a shallow medium baking dish.

Warm the butter in a large skillet over medium heat. Stir in the leeks and the spinach and sauté until the leeks are very soft, about 7 minutes. Add the Canadian bacon and continue cooking the mixture briefly. Transfer to a large bowl. Add the remaining ingredients, using the smaller amount of stock and stir to combine. The mixture should be very moist but not soupy. Add some or all of the remaining stock if needed. Spoon into the prepared dish.

Bake the pudding for about 45 minutes, until it's slightly puffed and golden brown with a few crunchy spots on top. Serve hot, garnished if you wish with tomato halves.

THE JOY OF STRATAS

In early editions of the *Joy of Cooking*, Irma Rombauer featured a strata that she called simply Cheese, Bread and Egg Dish. It appeared with eggs and other breakfast foods in a long chapter called "Luncheon and Supper Dishes." Rombauer started her version with slices of white bread and flavored it with paprika, cayenne, and optional mustard. She also featured a bread-crumb and curry variation that she called alternatively a *fondue* or *monkey,* both names associated in the United States with early stratalike preparations.

ORCAS ISLAND CRAB AND EGG CASSEROLE

SELECTIONS FROM THE BREAKFAST MENU ON THE SS *NEW YORK & PUERTO RICO*, 1905

Devilled Kidney   Jamboli

Fried Calf's Brains   Lamb Stew

Peaches with Cream

Tea, Coffee and Broma

Susan Fletcher created this luscious casserole to showcase the local Dungeness crab on Orcas Island, in Washington's lovely San Juan chain, where she and her husband run the Turtleback Farm Inn. Something of a crustless pie, it's easy to toss together the night before the baking despite a moderately long list of ingredients, all of which combine magnificently to bolster the crab flavor. You can halve the casserole successfully for a smaller group, but reduce the cooking time by about 15 minutes.

SERVES 8

1 pound cooked crabmeat, preferably Dungeness lump crabmeat, picked over for shells and cartilage (see Ingredient Tip)

2 heaping tablespoons minced onion

1¾ cups grated Swiss or raw-milk Cheddar cheese

¼ cup freshly grated Parmesan cheese

1 tablespoon unbleached all-purpose flour

1½ to 2 teaspoons Old Bay seasoning

½ teaspoon baking powder

½ teaspoon salt

½ teaspoon freshly milled black pepper

½ cup mayonnaise

6 large eggs

1½ cups milk

2 teaspoons Dijon mustard

1 teaspoon Worcestershire sauce, the white wine variety if available

Sour cream, optional

Whole chives with blossoms, in season, or minced fresh chives

Capers

Preheat the oven to 375°F. Butter a 9-inch deep-dish pie plate or similar-size baking dish. Layer the crab, onion, and cheeses in the dish.

Stir the flour, Old Bay seasoning, baking powder, salt, and pepper together in a medium bowl. Whisk in the mayonnaise and eggs, combining just until uniformly yellow, then add the milk, mustard, and Worcestershire sauce. Pour over the crab mixture. (The casserole can be made to this point, covered, and refrigerated overnight. In the morning, let it sit at room temperature for 20 to 30 minutes before baking.)

Bake the casserole until puffed and golden brown, 45 to 50 minutes. Cool for 10 minutes, then slice into wedges or squares. Serve warm, garnished if you wish with sour cream, chives, and capers.

BACON AND EGG PIE WITH BLACK PEPPER CRUST

INGREDIENT TIP

Because the filling of the pie is subtly seasoned, this is a place where the quality of the bacon makes a huge difference in the final result. If you lack a source for truly excellent bacon, see page 128.

In the past, Americans often ate pies at breakfast, both savory and sweet versions. Shaker cooks usually get the credit for this elementary savory rendition that we modified for our own tastes.

SERVES 6

SINGLE FLAKY BLACK PEPPER PIE CRUST

1¼ cups unbleached all-purpose flour

1 to 1½ teaspoons freshly cracked black pepper

¾ teaspoon salt

2 tablespoons unsalted butter, cut into small cubes, well chilled

4 tablespoons lard, well chilled

2 tablespoons vegetable shortening, well chilled

3 to 4 tablespoons ice water

FILLING

6 thick slices bacon, chopped and cooked crisp (see Ingredient Tip)

4 large eggs, lightly beaten

1½ cups heavy (whipping) cream or half-and-half

1 teaspoon Dijon mustard

¾ teaspoon salt

½ teaspoon freshly milled black pepper

One or two pinches of freshly grated nutmeg

Grease a 9-inch pie pan.

Prepare the pie crust. In a food processor, pulse together the flour, pepper, and salt, then scatter the butter over it and quickly pulse several times just to submerge the butter in the flour. Scoop the lard and shortening into small spoonfuls and scatter them over the flour-butter mixture; pulse again quickly several more times until they disappear into the flour too. Sprinkle in 2 tablespoons of the ice water and pulse again quickly, just until the water disappears.

Dump the mixture into a large bowl or onto a pastry board. Lightly rub the dough with your fingers, adding more water a tablespoon at a time. When the dough holds together if compacted with your fingers, it's ready. Pat the dough into a fat disk. Wrap the dough in plastic and refrigerate for at least 30 minutes.

Roll out the dough on a floured board into a thin round an inch or two larger than the pie pan. Arrange the crust in the pie pan, avoiding stretching it. Crimp the edge decoratively, then refrigerate it for at least 15 minutes longer.

Preheat the oven to 425°F. Partially bake the crust until just beginning to color, 6 to 8 minutes. Cool briefly. (The pie shell can be prepared to this point a day ahead.) Reduce the oven temperature to 375°F.

Scatter the bacon over the pie shell. Whisk together the eggs, cream, mustard, salt, pepper, and nutmeg until completely combined and pour into the pie shell.

Bake for 25 to 28 minutes, until puffed and lightly browned and a small thin knife inserted in the center comes out clean. Let sit for at least 10 minutes to firm a bit before slicing. Cut into wedges and serve.

RED CHILAQUILES

**If to eat a hearty
breakfast meant
getting up at six
o'clock, or even before,
we got up, and ate with
the family, and went
out sustained by both
good cheer and good
food.**

Della Lutes, *The Country
Kitchen* (1936)

Mexico's most common breakfast dish, chilaquiles migrated years ago across the border and took on a distinctive southwestern tang. Cooks in this country generally intensify the chile sauce base, relying often on the stout flavor of the dried ancho chile, as we do here. We also substitute commercial corn chips for the fried day-old tortillas used in Mexico as a way of cleaning out the bread-basket. The dish doesn't keep, so halve the recipe for a pair of diners. Serve with refried beans or whole pintos or black beans.   **SERVES 4**

ANCHO SAUCE

1 tablespoon vegetable oil

½ medium white onion,
minced

1 plump garlic clove, minced

¼ cup ground dried ancho chile or
commercial chili powder

2 tablespoons ground dried New
Mexican red chile or other ground
dried mild red chile

2 cups water or chicken stock

½ teaspoon dried oregano,
preferably Mexican

½ teaspoon salt

8 heaping cups tortilla chips

About ¼ pound cooked crumbled
Pasqual's Chorizo (page 138) or
other chorizo, optional

1½ cups grated asadero, Monterey
Jack, or Chihuahua cheese (about
6 ounces), at room temperature

6 tablespoons crumbled *queso
fresco* or grated *cotija* or Parmesan
cheese, at room temperature

¾ to 1 cup crème fraîche (crema)
or sour cream thinned with
1 tablespoon milk, at room
temperature

About ¼ cup fresh cilantro leaves

Prepare the sauce, first warming the oil in a small saucepan over medium heat. Add the onion and garlic and sauté until the onion is limp, about 3 minutes. Stir in the chile and then the water, 1 cup at a time. Add the oregano and salt and bring the sauce just to a boil. Reduce the heat to a simmer and cook for 15 to 20 minutes. The completed sauce should coat a spoon thickly but still drop off easily. (The sauce can be made up to a week ahead, covered, and refrigerated. Reheat before proceeding.)

Immediately before you plan to serve the chilaquiles, and not a minute earlier, scatter the chips into and over the warm sauce, stirring them gently to coat with sauce. Immediately spoon the chips and sauce onto a rimmed serving platter. Scatter over them the chorizo if desired, both cheeses, dollops of crème fraîche, and then the cilantro. Serve and enjoy.

GREEN CHILAQUILES

Replace the red sauce with a tangier sauce of tomatillos and green chiles. Broil 1 pound husked whole tomatillos on a baking sheet for 15 to 18 minutes, turning occasionally. They are ready when soft and dark in spots. When cool enough to handle, finely chop them. Warm 1 tablespoon olive oil in a skillet over medium heat. Add ½ cup finely chopped onion and 1 minced garlic clove and sauté until soft and translucent, about 5 minutes. Add 1 cup chopped roasted mild green chile, such as New Mexican or Anaheim (fresh or frozen), 1 cup chicken stock, and 1 teaspoon salt and bring to a boil. Reduce the heat to a simmer and cook for 5 minutes. Stir in the tomatillos and heat through. Add ¼ cup chopped cilantro and the sauce is ready to use.

CALABACITAS TORTILLA CASSEROLE

A southwestern strata with less cheese than most versions, this casserole features the summer vegetables found in the squash-and-corn dish known as *calabacitas*. Because it uses flour tortillas for the starch instead of a thicker bread, it doesn't benefit much from an overnight soak, but it can be assembled a day ahead of baking if you wish. **SERVES 4 TO 6**

1 tablespoon vegetable oil

1 cup grated zucchini

1 small onion, diced

1 plump garlic clove, minced

One 14½- to 15-ounce can diced tomatoes with green chiles with any juice or 1 large tomato, diced, with ½ cup chopped roasted mild green chile, preferably New Mexican or poblano, fresh or frozen

1 cup fresh or frozen corn kernels

4 large eggs

½ cup half-and-half or milk

½ teaspoon salt or more to taste

¼ teaspoon ground cumin

4 flour tortillas, preferably thick ones 6 to 7 inches in diameter

¼ cup grated mild Cheddar, Monterey Jack, or asadero cheese or crumbled *queso fresco* (about 1 ounce)

Preheat the oven to 350°F. Grease a medium baking dish. A 1½-quart soufflé dish or other deep round dish works perfectly for this.

Warm the oil in a large skillet over medium heat. Stir in the zucchini, onion, and garlic and sauté until the vegetable have begun to soften, about 5 minutes. Add the tomatoes and green chiles along with the corn. Raise the heat to medium-high and cook until most of the liquid has evaporated but the vegetables are still moist, 5 to 8 minutes longer. Cool the mixture briefly.

Whisk the eggs, half-and-half, salt, and cumin together in a medium bowl. Arrange a tortilla in the bottom of the baking dish. Top with one third of the vegetable mixture and one third of the egg mixture. Repeat. Spoon on the remaining vegetable mixture, top with the last tortilla, and then pour the remaining egg mixture over it all. Top with the cheese. (The dish can be made up to this point the night before if you wish. Cover and refrigerate. Remove from the refrigerator 20 to 30 minutes before you plan to bake it.)

Bake for 30 minutes, until puffed, golden brown, and lightly set at the center. Allow the casserole to sit for about 10 minutes before slicing into wedges and serving.

TORTILLA CASSEROLE WITH CHICKEN

Chicken makes a tasty addition to this casserole. Use about 1 cup sautéed or poached chicken to supplement the vegetable mixture.

EVERYDAY FOOD

The *Good Housekeeping Everyday Cook Book* of 1903 boasts in its introduction about several new features contained in the work, including a blank "memoranda" page after each recipe for cooks to add notes of their own about a dish. Several years ago we found a used copy of the book that was well annotated by the original owner. Linked to an early strata recipe named Escalloped Cheese, she penned a version of her own that she called Cheese Pudding. It resembled the book's strata but substituted mustard for paprika in the seasoning. Interestingly, she also spelled out the ingredient portions with greater precision than *Good Housekeeping*'s editors.

CHAURICE AUX POMMES DE TERRE

SELECTIONS FROM THE BREAKFAST MENU AT THE WALDORF-ASTORIA IN NEW YORK CITY, 1899

Consommé en tasse

Mousse de Volaille, Vénitienne

Côtelettes d'Agneau

Glaces Assorties

Petits Fours

This is our take on an old New Orleans breakfast dish that's a close cousin of shepherd's pie. Mashed potatoes provide a starch base for the highly seasoned chaurice, a Creole sausage readily made at home.   **SERVES 4 OR MORE**

CHAURICE

1 pound boneless pork Boston butt (shoulder) or country-style ribs, ground once or twice with all of the fat, by your butcher or with a meat grinder at home

¼ cup minced onion

1 garlic clove, minced

2 tablespoons minced fresh parsley

1 teaspoon minced fresh thyme or ½ teaspoon dried

2 teaspoons pure ground dried mild red chiles, such as New Mexican or ancho

¾ teaspoon salt or more to taste

¼ teaspoon cayenne pepper or more to taste

¼ teaspoon freshly cracked black pepper

¼ teaspoon ground allspice

BREAD CRUMBS

1 tablespoon unsalted butter

1 cup packed fresh bread crumbs

2 to 2½ cups mashed potatoes, warm or chilled

⅓ cup sliced scallion greens

¼ cup to ½ cup milk or half-and-half

1 large egg

Prepare the sausage, mixing together all the ingredients in a large bowl. Cover and refrigerate for at least a few hours. (It keeps, uncooked and refrigerated, for up to a week and freezes well for up to 2 months.)

Shortly before you plan to serve the dish, prepare the bread crumbs, first melting the butter in a small skillet over medium heat. Stir in the bread crumbs and toast them until golden, stirring occasionally, about 4 minutes. Scrape the bread crumbs out of the skillet and reserve them.

Preheat the oven to 350°F.

Fry the chaurice in a large skillet over medium heat until richly browned and a bit crusty, about 8 minutes. Drain the chaurice, if you wish, then spoon it into a medium baking dish. Mix the mashed potatoes with the scallion tops and enough milk to thin enough to spread easily. Spoon the mashed potatoes over the sausage and smooth it evenly. Whisk the egg with 1 tablespoon milk and brush it over the potatoes. Scatter the bread crumbs over the egg.

Bake for about 30 minutes, until the bread crumbs are brown and the potatoes bubbly. Serve hot.

CHAURICE AUX POMMES DE TERRE WITH VEGETABLE TRINITY

In Louisiana, the common use of green bell pepper, celery, and onion as a base for local dishes is so revered that it's called *the trinity*. To serve more people, or just add a little more in the way of vegetables to the dish, sauté a mixture of the three. We like ¾ cup of each, diced, cooked in 2 tablespoons oil or butter over medium heat until soft, about 5 minutes. Adjust the proportions to your desires and refrigerator contents. Mix with the cooked chaurice in the bottom of the baking dish or spoon it over the sausage. Either way, top with the potatoes as directed.

SWEET POTATO AND SAUSAGE CASSEROLE

For another dimension of flavor, substitute mashed sweet potatoes for the regular potatoes, mixing in a few tablespoons each of butter and milk or cream.

HASH-BROWN PIE

This evolved from a dish served by Crescent Dragonwagon at the Dairy Hollow House in Eureka Springs, Arkansas, before she converted her bed-and-breakfast inn into a nonprofit retreat for writers. We call it a pie because of the chewy-crunchy potato crust, a key element of the dish.　　**SERVES 6**

¼ cup vegetable oil or 2 tablespoons vegetable oil plus 2 tablespoons bacon or sausage drippings

2 pounds (about 3 large) russet potatoes, peeled and grated

1 small to medium onion, finely diced

¾ teaspoon salt or more to taste

¾ teaspoon freshly milled black pepper or more to taste

1 cup crème fraîche

½ cup half-and-half

3 large eggs

1 to 2 tablespoons minced fresh chives

¼ teaspoon dry mustard

1 cup grated pepper Jack, butterkäse, or sharp Cheddar cheese (about ¼ pound)

Paprika

Preheat the oven to 375°F.

Warm the oil in a heavy ovenproof 8- to 9-inch skillet over medium heat. Add the potatoes and onion, stir to coat with the oil, sprinkle in at least ½ teaspoon each salt and pepper, and pat the mixture down. Parcook the potatoes, scraping up and patting back down several times, until golden, somewhat sticky, crispy in spots, and reduced in volume by about half, about 15 minutes. Remove from the heat. Press the potato mixture down around the bottom and up the edge of the skillet to form a crust about 1½ inches high. A spoon helps in shaping it evenly.

Whisk together the crème fraîche, half-and-half, eggs, chives, dry mustard, and ¼ teaspoon each of salt and pepper.

Sprinkle the cheese into the potato crust, then pour the crème fraîche mixture over the cheese. Dust with paprika.

Bake for 25 to 30 minutes, until puffed and lightly browned and a small thin knife inserted in the center comes out clean. Let sit for at least 10 minutes to firm a bit before slicing. Cut into wedges and serve.

9

Breakfast Sandwiches

ACCORDING TO a colorful and lovable legend, the Earl of Sandwich invented his namesake chow during a pokerlike game in eighteenth-century England, when he asked a servant to put some meat between bread so he could eat at the card table without missing any of the action.

We happen to know enough contemporary poker players to understand the plausibility of the idea and also to realize that any of them or their peers in past millennia would have been similarly inspired in such a situation. Whatever the debut, and to whomever we owe the debt, the sandwich began appearing in the United States by the early nineteenth century, often as a traveler's snack.

That usage zoomed with the coming of the automobile age, which transformed the sandwich into America's preeminent road food. In that role it reached a broad audience as a breakfast concoction through the efforts of McDonald's and other chains to extend their reach into the morning hours. They were pioneers much like the earl, however, popularizing a natural notion. Some American restaurants offered breakfast sandwiches more than a century ago, and certainly many home cooks must have put fried eggs and pork between bread well before any mass-production kitchen slapped together a version. Given the status of the sandwich in the United States as our overall favorite food, an icon of our diet, it's long been bound for the breakfast table and at least in our land is just as appropriate there as at the card table.

A GROWN-UP'S JELLY SANDWICH

Most of us probably ate an occasional jelly or jam sandwich for breakfast when we were children. For both of us, it didn't get much more adventuresome than Welch's grape jelly or Smucker's strawberry jam on Sunbeam or Wonder bread. We still indulge once in a while, but with upgraded ingredients. We call our current version grown-up and prefer to think of ourselves that way, though we're aware that in this predilection we could be just overgrown kids.

SERVES 2

¼ cup fig preserves

4 slices challah, brioche, or soft white sandwich bread

¼ pound mascarpone or cream cheese, softened

¼ cup apricot preserves or orange marmalade

Spread half of the fig preserves on each of 2 slices of bread. Divide the mascarpone between the 2 sandwiches, spreading it over the preserves. Spread half of the apricot preserves on each of the two remaining slices of bread. Top each sandwich with one of these slices, preserves side down. Slice on the diagonal and serve.

The enlightened housewife, or whoever assumes culinary responsibility in the home, will seek to encourage in children their rather primitive expressions of appreciation for whatever pleases their palate. Insistence on good manners should always be compatible with the little ones' thorough enjoyment of the food. They will grow old soon enough; and with age they will make the easy adjustment, wherever necessary, to the stupid ways of their elders.

Angelo Pellegrini, *The Unprejudiced Palate* (1948)

FRIED EGG SANDWICH WITH CARAMELIZED ONIONS

A good fried egg sandwich always seems to rise well above our expectations for it. The idea, the ingredients, and the preparation define simplicity, but the resulting combination of crunchy toast and silken egg tastes almost elegant. We like to add well-cooked onions to the mix and sometimes other items that jump out at us from the pantry or fridge, including ones mentioned in the following variations. Make one once and you'll never be stymied again about what to serve for breakfast, lunch, or supper.

SERVES 2 GENEROUSLY

2 tablespoons unsalted butter

½ medium to large onion, thinly sliced

1 teaspoon fresh tarragon or ½ teaspoon dried, optional

4 large slices firm sandwich bread—white, whole wheat, multigrain, sourdough, pumpernickel, or other favorite

2 to 3 tablespoons unsalted butter, softened

FRIED EGGS

4 large eggs

Additional unsalted butter or bacon drippings

Salt and freshly milled black pepper to taste

Warm the butter in a skillet over medium-low heat. Add the onion and sauté until the slices are beginning to brown and crisp in a few spots, 8 to 10 minutes. Stir in the tarragon if you wish. Keep the onion warm.

Generously butter both sides of each slice of bread with the softened butter. Cook the bread on a griddle over medium heat until lightly brown and crisp on both sides, about 8 minutes total. Keep the bread warm.

Crack each egg into a cup or saucer. Warm 1 to 2 tablespoons of butter or bacon drippings on the griddle over medium heat. Nudge the eggs one by one gently onto the griddle, side by side. Salt and generously pepper the eggs immediately. Cook the eggs for 1 minute, sprinkling them with salt and pepper while they fry. Gently turn the eggs, puncturing the yolks so that they run a bit as they finish cooking "over hard," another 1 to 2 minutes.

Arrange a slice of bread on each of 2 plates. Divide the onion mixture between them, then top each nest of onion with a pair of eggs and another toast slice. Serve immediately.

BACON AND EGG SANDWICH

Add 2 or 3 slices crispy bacon over the eggs for extra crunch and another complementary flavor.

A GOOD BET

Our best BET is a bacon, egg, and tomato combo. Skip the caramelized onion and tarragon and use a couple of red-ripe tomato slices.

CHEESE AND EGG SANDWICH

Toast the bread on a griddle with thinly sliced Colby, mild Cheddar, Teleme, or another good melting cheese. When the bread is browned and the cheese soft, combine with the eggs and, if you wish, the onions.

EGG AND CANADIAN BACON SANDWICH

McDonald's basic concept for a morning sandwich is sound. With high-quality ingredients and prompt eating, a homemade version shines. Stack together a single fried egg, a seared thin slice of Canadian bacon, and sliced mild Cheddar between toasted halves of an English muffin.

MARIE MATARAZA'S PEPPER AND EGG SANDWICH

SELECTIONS FROM THE
BREAKFAST MENU AT
SHANLEY'S RESTAURANT
IN NEW YORK CITY, 1905

Sandwiches:

Chicken   Roast Beef

Tongue   Club

Ham   Sardine

Popular food writer Marie Simmons gave us this idea in *The Good Egg* (2000), where she fondly remembers her mother's Italian take on a scrambled egg sandwich. Marie Mataraza made the treat often for her family, particularly as road food for a trip in the days before fast-food egg sandwiches became ubiquitous. She simply wrapped the to-go version in wax paper. Both Maries say that if the wax paper didn't get fall-apart soggy, they didn't use enough oil for frying the peppers. If that raises any health hackles, consider the fact that the elder Marie is still making the sandwiches regularly as she approaches ninety.   **SERVES 2**

3 tablespoons olive oil or more to taste

1 garlic clove, bruised

3 long Italian frying peppers, stemmed, seeded, and cut into long thin strips

3 large eggs

Salt and freshly milled black pepper to taste

2 large kaiser or hard rolls, split

Warm the olive oil and garlic clove in a medium skillet over medium heat. When the garlic begins to brown, remove and discard it. Add the peppers, cover, and sweat until very limp, 8 to 10 minutes. Uncover and sauté until brown in spots, 3 to 5 minutes longer.

Whisk the eggs, 2 tablespoons water, salt, and pepper together just until combined in a small bowl. Turn the heat under the skillet down to medium-low, then pour in the eggs. Cook, frequently stirring up from the bottom with a spatula, until the eggs have formed curds but still look a little runny, about 3 to 4 minutes. Do not overcook. Remove from the heat and stir through an additional time or two before piling onto the rolls. Eat immediately or wrap in wax paper for a breakfast picnic.

PEPPER AND EGG SANDWICH EMBELLISHMENTS

Mrs. Mataraza occasionally elaborates her sandwich mixture by frying along with the peppers up to a whole sliced onion or 6 ounces crumbled Italian sausage.

DENVER SANDWICH

Some people call this a *western sandwich*, but we prefer the alternative *Denver* tag because it's a mile-high in flavor. The core is a well-seasoned omelet from frontier days that doesn't need to be pretty or perfectly cooked. Some cafés in the West serve the omelet alone in the morning, but it's better on bread because of the preparation style.   **SERVES 2**

2 large slices sourdough bread

1 to 2 tablespoons unsalted butter, softened

FILLING

3 large eggs

Salt and freshly milled black pepper to taste

Tabasco or other hot pepper sauce, optional

1½ tablespoons unsalted butter

¼ cup minced ham

1 small tomato, preferably plum, finely chopped

½ medium onion, chopped

¼ cup chopped green bell pepper

Romaine leaves or other crisp lettuce, optional

Generously butter both sides of each slice of bread with the softened butter. Cook the bread on a griddle over medium heat until lightly brown and crisp on both sides, about 8 minutes total. Keep the bread warm.

Briefly whisk the eggs, salt, and pepper together in a bowl with 1½ tablespoons water. Whisk just enough to combine the yolks and whites. Add a dash of Tabasco if you wish.

Warm the butter for the filling in a 7- to 8-inch omelet pan or skillet, preferably nonstick, over medium heat. Swirl the butter to coat the surface of the pan thoroughly. Stir in the ham, tomato, onion, and bell pepper and sauté until the vegetables are softened and the tomato liquid has mostly evaporated, about 5 minutes.

Raise the heat to high. Add the egg mixture and swirl it to coat the surface of the entire pan. Let the pan sit directly over the heat for a few seconds, until the eggs just begin to set in the bottom of the pan. Tilt the pan so that uncooked egg can flow to the bottom of the pan. The eggs should cook just a little longer than a traditional omelet, remaining moist but not wet at the center and golden on the outside. Pull the pan sharply toward you several times and then tilt the pan and use a spatula to fold the front half of the omelet over the back. Tip the omelet out onto one of the grilled bread slices, shaping it with the spatula if needed. Cover each with lettuce if you wish. Top with the other slice of grilled bread and halve. Serve promptly.

SUNRISE QUESADILLAS

Unlike the grilled cheese sandwich, a close cousin, the quesadilla appears commonly on breakfast menus throughout the Southwest. Some people eat them plain, but others embellish them with scrambled eggs, bacon, chile, and more, as we do here.

SERVES 2 TO 4

2 thick slices bacon, halved

1 large egg

Salt to taste

1¼ cups grated Cheddar, Monterey Jack, Muenster, or asadero cheese (about 5 ounces)

Vegetable oil for panfrying

4 flour tortillas, preferably about 5 inches in diameter (see Ingredient Tip)

1 cup Mesilla Valley Green Chile Sauce (page 40), Salsa Frontera (page 422), or other favorite salsa

1 cup Heavenly Hash Browns (page 305) or other hash brown potatoes, optional

Diced tomato or avocado, optional

Fry the bacon in a medium skillet over medium heat until brown and crisp. Drain the bacon, reserving the drippings. Whisk the egg with the salt just until combined. Pour the egg into the skillet and reduce the heat to medium-low. Cook, frequently stirring up from the bottom with a spatula, until the egg has formed curds but still looks a little runny, about 3 to 4 minutes. Stir about 2 tablespoons of the cheese into the egg. Remove from the heat and stir through an additional time or two.

If you have a large griddle, you will be able to cook the 2 quesadillas simultaneously. If not, cook the quesadillas in a heavy skillet one at a time, placing the first one in a low oven while you cook the second.

On a griddle or in a skillet, warm a thin film of oil over medium heat. Place 2 tortillas side by side on the griddle and cover each with about ¼ cup of the cheese. Cook briefly until the cheese begins to melt and the tortilla turns golden and lightly crisp, 2 to 3 minutes. Working quickly, spoon half of the egg onto each tortilla, covering the cheese, followed by about 2 tablespoons of the chile sauce, 2 bacon halves, and the hash browns if you wish. Spoon on 2 more tablespoons of the chile sauce and another ¼ cup of cheese. Top with another tortilla, then flip quickly and carefully with a broad spatula. (The flipping gets easier with practice. If you lose a little of the filling when turning, simply scoop it back into place.) Cook the quesadilla's second side until golden and crisp and the remaining cheese is melted. If cooking in a skillet, repeat with the remaining tortillas and filling.

Transfer to a cutting board and slice each quesadilla into quarters. Reassemble on each plate, with the remaining cheese scattered over the top. If you wish, scatter tomato or avocado over the cheese and serve with the remaining chile sauce on the side. Remind your guests, if necessary, to eat the quesadilla by hand like a sandwich.

CLASSIC QUESADILLAS

A quesadilla, whether for morning or for night, can be as simple as cheese and a tortilla or two. Because of the brawn of the filling in the Sunrise Quesadilla, they need the heft of flour tortillas to support them, but a more restrained cheese version can be made with corn tortillas as well. Use at least 1½ cups grated cheese with 5-inch flour tortillas, proportionately more with larger flour tortillas or a little less with the corn variety. If you wish, add a bit of minced fresh or pickled serrano or jalapeño, a few cilantro leaves, or minced scallion tops. Serve sliced into wedges with salsa or a good bottled Mexican hot pepper sauce such as Cholula, Valentina, or Búfalo.

EMBELLISHMENTS FOR CLASSIC QUESADILLAS

Simple cheese quesadillas make a great canvas for almost anything in the fridge or pantry. We like sliced mushrooms sautéed with a little chipotle chile, but sauté any veggie you would prefer cooked rather than raw, such as onions, zucchini or other squash, squash blossoms, or corn. Roasted and peeled strips of fresh green or red chiles, called *rajas* in the Southwest, offer a festive note. Diced tomato or halved tiny tomatoes, black or green olives, or avocado or guacamole can go in or over. Leftover beans or black-eyed peas, steak, or chicken makes more substantial fare. If you have a bunch of things to use, make several different kinds of quesadillas rather than loading them up with competing flavors. Quesadillas can be served flat, folded, or double-deckered.

A BREAKFAST MENU SUGGESTION FOR BREAKFAST IN BED

Ham and Farm Cheese Butter-Fried Sandwich

Baked Apple

Marion Cunningham, *The Breakfast Book* (1987)

Only the egg seems to have it all figured out, riding the waves of exile and repatriation. It was cast out by the cholesterol faction and then reclaimed by the high-protein diet. It can be divided. It can be an egg-white *omelette aux fines herbes* in West Hollywood, and it can be a scrambled-egg sandwich at the Busy-Bee Diner in Buffalo, Wyoming. I wish I were half as clever as an egg.

Ann Patchett, *Gourmet,* September 1999

SAUSAGE ON SWEET POTATO BISCUITS

A BREAKFAST MENU SUGGESTION FOR AN "ECONOMICAL" NEW ORLEANS BREAKFAST

Bananas

Grits and Milk

Meat Rissoles

Potato Croquettes

Biscuit

Rice Griddle Cakes

Louisiana Syrup

Café au Lait

The Daily Picayune

The Picayune's Creole Cook Book (1901)

Fast-food restaurants serve something in this vein, but the combo of sausage patties and biscuits goes back much further than drive-up windows. In areas where you find the pair together on breakfast sideboards and in sandwiches, such as the Carolinas, the bread is usually a buttermilk biscuit. A slightly sturdier sweet potato biscuit adds its own elusive flavor as well as architectural stability. A poached or fried egg makes a perfect accompaniment.

MAKES 6 BISCUIT SANDWICHES

1¼ pounds Sage Farm Sausage (page 136) or other well-seasoned breakfast sausage

BISCUITS

½ pound sweet potato, cooked, mashed, and chilled

6 tablespoons milk

1¼ cups low-gluten biscuit or pastry flour or unbleached all-purpose flour

2 teaspoons baking powder

1 teaspoon sugar

¾ teaspoon salt

¼ teaspoon freshly grated nutmeg

Pinch or two of cayenne pepper

3 tablespoons unsalted butter, well chilled

2 tablespoons lard or vegetable shortening, well chilled

12 thin slices medium to sharp Cheddar cheese at room temperature

Brown mustard

Form the sausage into 6 patties about 3 inches in diameter.

Preheat the oven to 450°F.

Prepare the biscuits, first pureeing the sweet potato with the milk in a food processor or blender.

Sift the flour, baking powder, sugar, salt, nutmeg, and cayenne into a large bowl, preferably shallow. Cut the butter and lard into small chunks and add them to the dry ingredients. Combine with a pastry blender just until a coarse meal forms. Make a well in the center and pour in the sweet potato mixture. With your fingers and a few swift strokes, combine the dough just until it's a sticky mess. Turn out onto a lightly floured board or, better, a pastry cloth. Clean, dry, and flour your hands. Gently pat out the dough and fold it back over itself about a half-dozen times, just until smooth. (A dough scraper helps greatly with this.) Pat out again into a circle or oval about ¾ inch thick. Cover the dough lightly and refrigerate it for about 20 minutes.

After removing the dough from the refrigerator, cut it with a biscuit cutter, trying to get as many biscuits as possible since the dough toughens if it's rerolled. You should be able to get at least six 3- to 3½-inch biscuits. Make your biscuits with a quick, clean, straight-down push on the cutter. If you twist the cutter, as seems to be a natural motion for many people, it twists the dough, resulting in an uneven biscuit. Transfer the biscuits to an ungreased baking sheet, spacing them an inch or two apart. Bake the biscuits in the center of the oven, turning the baking sheet around once halfway through the baking time. Bake 3-inch biscuits for 12 to 14 minutes total, until raised and lightly browned on the top edges. (These biscuits rise less than buttermilk biscuits.)

While the biscuits bake, fry the sausage patties in a heavy skillet over medium heat, in batches if necessary. Cook until richly brown on the surface and well done throughout, several minutes per side. Place 2 slices of cheese on top of each patty about a minute before you remove it from the heat. Keep warm while you wait for the biscuits.

When the biscuits are ready, immediately split them and add a dollop of mustard to each half. Slip a sausage patty with cheese into the biscuits and serve piping hot.

MOTHER'S KNOWS BEST

A New Orleans breakfast and lunch institution, Mother's serves the most incredible meat biscuits on earth. They come with either "debris," the shards of roast beef that fall into the gravy in the oven, or "black ham," the caramelized outer portion of a glazed baked ham. Every year the unpretentious, order-at-the-counter restaurant sells 200,000 of the biscuits. The first time we ate one of the sticky, crispy bundles of bliss, we wanted to beg Mother to adopt us.

HAM BISCUITS

Traditionally, the famed southern ham biscuit is a party hors d'oeuvre, but many people, including us, love them at breakfast as well. We prefer them the original way with one paper-thin slice of country ham, but if you're using a less-robust city ham, add a little more meat. We make them here with extra-rich cream biscuits, but you can also use the buttermilk variety (page 336).

MAKES 1 DOZEN HAM BISCUITS

page 336

CREAM BISCUITS

2 cups low-gluten biscuit or pastry flour or 1¾ cups unbleached all-purpose flour plus ¼ cup cake flour or, less desirably, 2 cups unbleached all-purpose flour

2½ teaspoons baking powder

¾ teaspoon salt

3 tablespoons unsalted butter, well chilled

2 tablespoons lard or vegetable shortening, well chilled

¾ cup plus 2 tablespoons heavy (whipping) cream, well chilled

Brown mustard, unsalted butter, or both

Thinly sliced country or city ham

Freshly grated or prepared horseradish, optional

Peach or mango chutney, optional

Preheat the oven to 450°F.

Prepare the biscuits, first sifting the flour, baking powder, and salt into a large bowl, preferably shallow. Cut the butter and lard into small chunks and add them to the dry ingredients. Combine with a pastry blender just until a coarse meal forms. Make a well in the center and pour in the cream. With your fingers and a few swift strokes, combine the dough just until it's a sticky mess. Turn out onto a lightly floured board or, better, a pastry cloth. Clean, dry, and flour your hands. Gently pat out the dough and fold it back over itself about a half-dozen times, just until smooth. (A dough scraper helps greatly with this.) Pat out again into a circle or oval about ½ inch thick. Cover the dough lightly and refrigerate it for about 20 minutes.

After removing the dough from the refrigerator, cut it with a biscuit cutter, trying to get as many biscuits as possible since the dough toughens if it's rerolled. You should be able to get about twelve 2-inch biscuits from the dough. Make your biscuits with a quick, clean, straight-down push on the cutter. If you twist the cutter, as seems to be a more natural motion for many people, it twists the dough, resulting in an uneven biscuit. Transfer the biscuits to an ungreased baking sheet, spacing them an inch or two apart. Bake the biscuits in the center of the oven, turning the baking sheet

Sometimes the very people who used to extol the virtues of a hearty breakfast (bacon, eggs, milk, coffee, cream, butter, hot breads) can be heard leading the assault on every one of those traditional foods— and doing so now, as before, in the name of good health. . . . For my part, I intend to take my chances with measured rations of the foods that have made

around once halfway through the baking time. Bake for 7 to 9 minutes, until raised and golden brown.

Split the biscuits. Slather the top and bottom with mustard, butter, or both. Arrange a slice or two of ham on each bottom half. Determine the quantity of ham based on its saltiness and flavor intensity, using less as it goes up the scale toward a long-aged country ham. Serve with chutney and horseradish on the side, if you wish, for guests to garnish their biscuits with either or both as desired.

AN OLD SANDWICK

Back in 1839, well before sandwiches hit the fast track in American eating habits, Lettice Bryan in *The Kentucky Housewife* suggested a "ham sandwick" as a "very fine" breakfast dish. Instead of putting the ham between bread, she seasoned it with pepper, nutmeg, and lemon, dredged it in a flour batter, and then fried it in lard until "yellowish brown." With the pan drippings, Bryan went on to make a cream gravy, which she served on top of the ham.

MAPLE-GLAZED HAM, CHEESE, AND LEEK SANDWICHES

A BREAKFAST MENU

SUGGESTION FOR THE

WEEK DAY

Cantaloupe

Milk Toast

Frankfurters

Stewed Potatoes

Postum

The Inglenook Cook Book (1911)

A bracing twist on the breakfast sandwich, this offers a scrumptious mix of sweet and savory. You can change the balance of the flavors through your selection of bread, increasing the sweetness with a choice of raisin bread, for example, or decreasing it with a rye alternative.   **SERVES 4**

4 tablespoons (½ stick) unsalted butter, softened

8 slices raisin, nut, rye, or whole wheat bread

1 large or 2 small to medium leeks (white and light green parts), halved lengthwise and sliced into thin half-moons

8 thin slices mild smoky ham, about the size of the bread slices

1 tablespoon real maple syrup

Four 1-ounce slices creamy cheese with character, such as St. Andre or Brie

Using a total of 2 tablespoons of butter, spread butter on one side of each bread slice. Warm the remaining 2 tablespoons butter in a large skillet over medium heat. Add the leeks to the skillet and sauté until soft, about 7 minutes. Remove with a slotted spoon and reserve. Lightly brush both sides of the ham slices with maple syrup. Add the ham slices to the skillet, in batches if necessary, and fry for about 1 minute per side, until heated through and a bit crusted in spots.

With the buttered side of 4 slices of bread down, arrange 2 ham slices over each. Spoon leeks evenly over the ham slices. Top each with a slice of cheese, then the remaining slices of bread; buttered-side up. If you want to use the same skillet for toasting the sandwiches, rinse it out well. Using the skillet or a griddle over medium heat, cook until the sandwiches are golden brown and crisp, 8 to 10 minutes, turning once.

CREATIVE IDEAS

Commercial cereals run a close second to canned soups as products touted for use in all kinds of cooking. Kellogg's test kitchen came up with two of the most peculiar ideas we've seen in print, both dishes developed to sell the company's cornflakes. For pasta lovers, the 1971 promotional pamphlet "Kay Kelloggs' Creative Cookery" suggested topping fettuccine with Parmesan cheese and crushed cornflakes, and for frankfurter fans, the marketers recommended Hot Doggities, skewered wieners dunked in ketchup and then cereal.

BREAKFAST TACOS

Texans put almost anything in a breakfast taco that has a faint morning connection, including scrambled eggs, refried beans, chorizo, potatoes, and the beef stew known as *carne guisada*. We particularly like this well-seasoned mixture of meat and potatoes, a variation on picadillo, another common filling. For an authentic breakfast taco, forget corn-tortilla shells, lettuce-and-tomato toppings, and other features you may associate with a taco. Morning versions usually feature soft flour tortillas and seldom come with any vegetable garnishes except a salsa. **SERVES 4 OR MORE**

2 tablespoons vegetable oil

1 medium onion, minced

3 to 4 plump garlic cloves, minced

1½ pounds chorizo or freshly ground chuck

1 tablespoon unbleached all-purpose flour

¾ teaspoon dried oregano, preferably Mexican, optional

¼ to ½ teaspoon cayenne pepper, chile de árbol, or other ground dried hot red chile, optional

1 medium baking potato, peeled, quartered, parboiled for 10 minutes, and finely diced

¾ cup beef or chicken stock or potato cooking water

½ teaspoon salt or more to taste

1 large egg, lightly whisked, optional

One dozen 6- to 7-inch flour tortillas, warmed

About 1 cup (¼ pound) grated mild Cheddar or Monterey Jack cheese

Salsa Frontera (page 422) or other favorite salsa

Warm the oil in a large skillet over medium heat. Stir in the onion and garlic and sauté until beginning to soften, about 5 minutes. Add the meat and cook until richly brown for chorizo, or until its has lost its raw color for ground beef. Stir in the flour. If you are using the beef, you will probably want to add the oregano and cayenne for additional seasoning. (The chorizo will likely have plenty of seasoning already.) Add the potato, stock, and salt and reduce the heat to low. Simmer the mixture for another 5 to 8 minutes, until the potatoes are tender and the mixture looks like a chunky gravy. It should remain moist but not watery. (The meat mixture can be made to this point a day or two ahead. Cover and chill. Reheat before proceeding.) If you are adding the egg, mix it in just before serving.

Spoon the filling equally into the tortillas, sprinkle with cheese, and fold them over, arranging up to 3 on each plate, partially overlapping to help the tortillas remain folded. Serve salsa on the side so that each diner can customize the tacos.

IRMA GALVAN'S BULGING BREAKFAST TACO

Our favorite Tex-Mex breakfast café, Irma's in downtown Houston, offers a taco stuffed with a tour-de-force mixture of chorizo, bacon, potato chunks, tomatoes, pasilla chiles, pinto beans, and cheese, all bound together with a little egg. Just use your sense of taste in blending the ingredients, as Irma did in creating it. Round out the feast with the restaurant's Breakfast Lemonade (page 435).

GOAT CHEESE AND AVOCADO TACO

Scoop several tablespoons of room-temperature creamy, fresh goat cheese into a tortilla and garnish with several thick avocado slices. A grating of Monterey Jack, some thinly sliced pickled jalapeños, or a large spoonful of Refried Beans (page 330) might increase the appeal.

HAND-HELD BREAKFAST BURRITO

A burrito variation on the taco is easier to eat on the run, particularly if you wrap the bottom third of the burrito in foil to keep it better contained. Use your choice of fillings, straining it of any liquid. Spoon several tablespoonfuls of the filling down the center of a warm thin flour tortilla. Sprinkle with cheese if you like. Fold up at least 1 inch at the bottom edge of the tortilla. Roll up into a snug tube.

BAGEL WITH SALMON SPREAD

Even airport snack bars now sell bagel sandwiches with flavored cream-cheese spreads. This is a much better version than most, chunky with smoked salmon and nicely seasoned. Less expensive trimmings of nova or lox, sometimes available in delis, work fine in the spread. We especially like onion bagels for the base. **SERVES 2 TO 4**

FILLING

6 ounces cream cheese, softened

6 ounces nova or lox, chopped

3 to 4 tablespoons finely diced red onion or minced fresh chives

2 to 4 tablespoons drained capers, minced if large

1 tablespoon snipped fresh dill or 1½ teaspoons dried

Squeeze or two of fresh lemon juice, optional

2 bagels, split

Combine the filling ingredients in a bowl. If you opted for a smaller amount of capers, the lemon juice will add a bit of tangy sparkle to the filling.

Toast the bagel halves. For 4 servings, spoon an equal amount of the mixture on each half, mounding it up in the middle. For 2 servings, divide the mixture in half and spoon onto the bagel bottoms, then top with the remaining bagel halves. Serve while the bagel is warm.

THE RISE OF THE DELI

In the original American delis of the nineteenth century, German immigrants introduced the country to wurst, ham, and other meats from their homeland, selling them as delicacies, the source of the word *delicatessen*. Jewish-Americans entered the business later, around the turn of the twentieth century, and changed the nature of the trade over time. Unlike old Jewish "appetizing stores" that specialized in fish and could therefore carry dairy products as well, kosher delis offered only meat. As Jews became assimilated and more affluent, many of their delis began serving cream with coffee and even branched out further into cheesecakes and Reuben sandwiches with Swiss cheese. Joan Nathan in *Jewish Cooking in America* (1994) calls the delicatessen "the Jewish eating experience in America," but it's also become a quintessential part of the eating experience of all Americans.

BREAKFAST BLT

Anytime we're stuck eating in a café with a boring breakfast menu, we turn on our smiles and ask deferentially if the kitchen could possibly make us a BLT. Virtually all restaurants have the ingredients on hand, and the cooks generally pay attention to what they're doing when it's a special order. Try it sometime, or even better, make your own version at home on a toasted English muffin.

SERVES 4

HERB MAYONNAISE

½ cup mayonnaise

¼ cup minced fresh chives, basil, or a combination

Splash of Tabasco or other hot pepper sauce, optional

4 English muffins

Leaf- or butter-lettuce leaves

12 thick slices bacon, halved and cooked crisp

4 thick slices red-ripe beefsteak tomato, preferably similar in size to the English muffins

Salt to taste

4 fried eggs, optional (using the cooking instructions for the Fried Egg Sandwich on page 230)

Prepare the mayonnaise, mixing together the ingredients.

Use a fork to split each English muffin into 2 halves. Toast the English muffins until golden brown. Spread each half with a liberal tablespoon of the mayonnaise. Arrange the lettuce on top of the mayonnaise on the 4 muffin bottoms, adding enough to show off a green fringe for each sandwich. Pile on equal portions of bacon and tomato for each sandwich, salting the tomatoes lightly. Top with fried eggs, if you wish, and crown with the remaining muffin slices.

BLGT WITH CHEESE

Replace red-ripe tomatoes with tangy green ones. Fry 4 cornmeal-coated green tomato slices as described on page 319. Add slices of Teleme, fresh mozzarella, or another mild melting cheese.

BACON AND TOMATO BISCUITS

In her delightful reminiscence *More than Moonshine* (1983), Sidney Saylor Farr recalls wonderful childhood breakfasts of ham biscuits, egg biscuits, and bacon and tomato biscuits. Skip the lettuce and replace the English muffins with 3-inch buttermilk biscuits, such as those on page 336. Use mayonnaise or not, as you wish.

THE BREAKFAST CLUB

For heartier eaters and a more towering presence, start these with 6 muffins for 4 eaters. Toast all the muffin halves, then use a half from each of the extra two to add a third layer for a double-decker sandwich. Double the number of tomato slices so that you can place one on each deck. Add several thin slices of cooked turkey or chicken to the top deck of each, and definitely put a fried egg somewhere in your tower. This is knife-and-fork food.

MISSISSIPPI BACON SANDWICH WITH MILKY TOMATO GRAVY

This inspired creation from the Mississippi Gulf Coast contains some of the same ingredients as a BLT, but it's entirely different in character. The ripe red tomatoes are fried, and it's served open-face with a luscious topping that's a twist on the popular southern tomato gravy. Oh, mercy. **SERVES 4**

I have a sneaking suspicion that Americans eat sandwiches for breakfast far more often than you might imagine. Think about it: how many mornings have you started out with a plain piece of toast, only to cover it with bits and pieces from the vast landscape of your kitchen cabinets and fridge: cranberry sauce, a piece of sharp Cheddar, a slab of cold broiled chicken? Or, in summer, mayo, bacon, and a juicy slab of tomato? . . . I know I do it all the time. It's fast, creative, and personal; I've never made a breakfast sandwich I didn't love.

Ken Haedrich, *Country Breakfasts* (1994)

4 large red-ripe but not mushy-soft tomatoes

½ cup unbleached all-purpose flour

½ teaspoon salt or more to taste

½ teaspoon freshly milled black pepper or more to taste

½ teaspoon onion or garlic powder, optional

⅛ teaspoon cayenne pepper or more to taste

8 to 12 thick slices bacon

Vegetable oil, optional

1¼ cups milk

¼ cup half-and-half or heavy (whipping) cream or additional milk

4 large slices white toast

Minced fresh parsley, basil, or thyme

You want 8 really nice slices out of the middle of the tomatoes, ⅓ to ½ inch thick. Once you have cut the slices, chop the remaining tomato pieces into bite-size bits. Reserve the tomato slices and the chopped tomatoes with their juice.

Stir the flour, salt, pepper, onion powder if desired, and cayenne together in a shallow bowl.

Fry the bacon in a large heavy skillet, preferably cast iron, over medium heat until brown and crisp. (Go for the greater number of slices if your guests are real bacon fans.) Remove the bacon and drain it. You will want about ¼ cup fat to fry the tomatoes and make the gravy. You can use just bacon drippings, pouring off any extra, or use a portion of the drippings and oil to equal the proper amount.

Dredge the tomato slices in the seasoned flour, reserving at least 1 table-spoon of the flour. Fry the tomatoes in the skillet over medium heat until the coating is golden brown and crisp, 2 to 3 minutes per side. Remove the tomatoes carefully with a spatula or slotted spoon. Keep them warm while you prepare the gravy.

Sprinkle 1 tablespoon of the seasoned flour into the pan drippings, stir-ring to prevent lumps. Pour in the milk and half-and-half slowly, frequently stirring up from the bottom, scraping up the browned bits. Stir in the chopped tomatoes and juice and continue cooking for 3 to 5 minutes, until thick and burnished red-brown in color. Adjust the seasoning.

Arrange a toast slice on each plate and top with 2 side-by-side fried tomato slices. Place the bacon over the tomatoes. Spoon a few tablespoons of gravy over the top of each open-face sandwich and sprinkle with parsley. Serve the remaining gravy on the side.

THE AMERICAN BRUNCH

Coined to describe a meal with features of both breakfast and lunch, the term *brunch* seems to date to the Victorian period but seldom saw print until the 1950s. In the following decades Americans made it a signature banquet of their own, though the basic idea goes back to the second breakfast common in many European countries for centuries. Even today, from Scandinavia to Spain, some people start the day with just a light bite and then eat something more substantial in the late morning. Americans broadened that notion into a special-occasion meal where we celebrate the bounty once typical of our breakfasts. However new and notable the phenomenon seems, brunch is basically just history reinventing itself.

AVOCADO MASH ON SOURDOUGH TOAST

This simple and versatile combination from California is open to many embellishments. Consider adding thinly sliced Monterey Jack or a light slather of cream cheese, a squeeze of lime, a grated hard-boiled egg, chopped tomato, green or black olive slices, or diced mild radishes, such as the French breakfast variety. Serve the sandwich open-face.

SERVES 2

1 large avocado

Cholula, Tabasco, or other hot pepper sauce to taste

Salt to taste

2 slices sourdough bread

Unsalted butter

Mash the avocado roughly with a fork, mixing in a dash or two of hot sauce and a couple of pinches of salt.

Toast the sourdough and butter it generously on one side. Mound equal portions of the avocado over the toast and serve. Eat with your fingers or a fork, depending on who's looking.

SHORT LIST OF OTHER (POSSIBLY) TEMPTING BREAKFAST SANDWICHES

- Peanut butter, mayonnaise, and bacon, on toasted whole wheat
- Baked beans, hot, on toasted Boston brown bread or Anadama Bread (page 362)
- Refried pinto or black beans, manchego cheese, and pickled jalapeños on a crusty roll
- Mozzarella and tomato with either a fresh basil leaf or pesto, hot or cold, on an English muffin or country bread
- Cream cheese with chopped pimiento-stuffed green olives, or Chunky Veggie Cream Cheese (page 62), cold on an English muffin or bagel
- Pears and blue cheese, hot or cold, on walnut bread
- Cream cheese with grated lemon zest, hot or cold, on Brown Sugar–Zucchini Bread (page 357)
- Cheddar slices, apple butter, and chopped hickory nuts or walnuts on whole wheat or raisin bread

10

Home-Crafted Cereals

FUTURE HISTORIANS may well remember twentieth-century America as the land of Coca-Cola and cold cereal. Both products are so characteristic of the country that they couldn't have been conceived elsewhere, and each became one of our most emblematic exports to the rest of the world.

We also consumed the two commodities in prodigious quantities, of course. The cereal boxes we open in one year, laid end to end, would extend to the moon and back to our kitchens, and the sugar contained in all the boxes would coat each of us with over three pounds of manufactured sweetness.

Other people ate cereal before us—at least as far back as ancient Greece and Rome—but they cooked it themselves from local grains and ate it warm at any meal. Some of the most eccentric dietetic reformers in American history took that old notion, moved the preparation into industrial plants, and gave us the "Snap, Crackle, and Pop" of cold breakfast cereal. In the decades after the turn of the last century, the new products zoomed in sales because of their convenience and one of the most innovative and successful marketing campaigns ever launched. Despite their continuing popularity, however, few if any of the commercial cereals compare to homemade varieties in flavor, nutrition, and overall satisfaction. When you get creative with cereal and tailor it from mass tastes to your own, you may find yourself rather than Tony the Tiger roaring that it's great.

SPICED OATMEAL WITH APPLES AND CIDER SYRUP

TECHNIQUE TIP

We suggest soaking the oats overnight to reduce the cooking time in the morning, but if you forget, simply increase the cooking liquid to 1 quart and the simmering time to 30 to 40 minutes.

___

A BREAKFAST MENU

SUGGESTION FROM

FANNIE FARMER

Quaker Rolled Oats with Baked Apples, Sugar and Cream

Creamed Fish   Baked Potatoes

Golden Corn Cake

Coffee

Fannie Merritt Farmer, *The Boston Cooking-School Cook Book* (1896)

___

From the colonial period to the advent of boxed cereals in the late nineteenth century, Americans bought oats in bulk and cooked them into a nourishing porridge suitable at any hour of the day. Scottish and Irish immigrants helped make oatmeal broadly popular as a breakfast food after the Civil War, when it became the country's leading cereal for a few decades. Even after cold manufactured cereal replaced it as the morning favorite, oatmeal retained a strong and devoted following for its hearty, earthy savor. You'll understand why when you try this deeply flavored version, loaded with true texture.

SERVES 4

1 cup steel-cut oats (see Ingredient Tip, page 252)

3¼ cups water, milk, or a combination

1 tablespoon real maple syrup

½ teaspoon salt

½ teaspoon ground allspice

½ teaspoon ground cinnamon

¼ teaspoon freshly grated nutmeg

¼ teaspoon ground ginger

2 to 2½ cups unsweetened apple cider or juice

1 large or 2 small to medium apples, chopped, or ¾ to 1 cup applesauce, such as Rum Roasted Applesauce (page 276)

Slivered almonds, optional

Toast the oats in a heavy saucepan over medium heat until they deepen just slightly in color and become fragrant, about 5 minutes. Pour enough water over the oats to cover by about 2 inches. Cover the pan and let it stand overnight.

In the morning, drain the oats, then add either fresh water or milk or a combination, as you like. Bring just to a boil, then reduce the heat to a bare simmer and cook until tender and creamy but not mushy, 15 to 20 minutes total. After about 10 minutes of cooking, add the salt, allspice, cinnamon, nutmeg, and ginger, stirring it in gently. When the oats are done, cover with a clean towel and the pan lid and let stand off the heat for 5 to 10 minutes.

While the oatmeal cooks, prepare the syrup. In a medium saucepan, boil the cider down over high heat until reduced by approximately half.

Stir the apple gently into the oatmeal. Spoon the oatmeal into bowls, then top each with a drizzle of syrup. Scatter each, if you wish, with a small handful of almonds. Serve hot with the remaining syrup passed on the side.

OATMEAL WITH BROWN SUGAR–PECAN CRUMBLE

INGREDIENT TIP

In the United States, steel-cut oats are often labeled *Scottish* or *Irish,* though the Scottish and the Irish would just call them oats. Unlike America's most popular style of oats, sold rolled into thin flakes, these are whole unsteamed oat kernels that have been chopped into granular nuggets. The most widely available national brand is McCann's. They have a very different texture from rolled oats, with nubbly kernels that give way with an amiable little pop when pressed against your tongue.

TECHNIQUE TIP

Cereal grains differ in many respects, but there are a few key techniques that apply to most preparations of them.

- Use a heavy pan to cook cereals.
- Oats, millet, rye, and wheat are just a few of the cereals that have more flavor if toasted before being cooked. In working with a small to moderate quantity, you may want to toast them dry in the pan you plan to cook in, simply toasting them over medium-low heat and stirring occasionally until they darken a shade in color and become fragrant. The time will depend on the size of the grain, but it will be minimal in any case. Add a bit of butter if you wish, about 1 tablespoon per 1½ cups grain. For a larger quantity, you can spread the cereal on a baking sheet and toast it in a 250°F

At its best, when made with steel-cut oats, oatmeal exudes all the warmth and coziness we expect from a quintessential comfort food. It needs no topping more complex than a pat of butter, a dollop of cream, or maybe a spoonful of maple syrup, molasses, or honey. It can also be dressed richly, however, for a festive morning, as we do here. Serve with colorful Quinces and Cranberries in Syrup (page 292) or Poached Dried Fruit Compote (page 290). **SERVES 4**

1 cup steel-cut oats (See Ingredient Tip)

¾ cup water or milk or a combination

½ teaspoon salt

TOPPING

6 tablespoons unsalted butter, softened

6 tablespoons packed dark or light brown sugar

6 tablespoons small pecan pieces

6 tablespoons dried cherries or cranberries or diced dried apricots, peaches, or mangoes

Toast the oats in a heavy saucepan over medium heat, stirring occasionally, until they deepen just slightly in color and become fragrant, about 5 minutes. Pour enough water over the oats to cover by about 2 inches. Cover the pan and let it stand overnight.

In the morning, drain the oats, then add either fresh water or milk or a combination, as you like. Bring just to a boil, then reduce the heat to a bare simmer and cook until tender and creamy but not mushy, 15 to 20 minutes. Add the salt after the oats have cooked for about 10 minutes, stirring it in gently. When the oats are done, cover with a clean towel and the pan lid and let stand off the heat for 5 to 10 minutes.

While the oatmeal cooks, combine the topping ingredients in a small bowl.

Spoon the oatmeal into bowls, then spoon about a tablespoon of topping over each. Serve the remaining topping on the side with the hot oatmeal.

QUICKER TOASTED OATMEAL

For a hurried weekday morning, you may want to replace steel-cut oats with the more familiar and faster-cooking rolled oats (the kind labeled *old-fashioned,* not *quick-cooking* or *instant*). To improve their flavor, toast them first, a step you can do a night or two ahead. Simply add the oats to a skillet or saucepan and warm them over medium heat, about 5 minutes, stirring occasionally, until fragrant and slightly colored. Then cook according to package directions and add the Brown Sugar–Pecan Crumble topping if you wish.

LORA BRODY'S SLOW-COOKER OATMEAL

Slowing down the oatmeal's preparation can speed up your morning. We use this technique perfected by our friend Lora Brody, who includes a version of it in *Lora Brody Plugged In* (1998). Stir together in your slow cooker 1 cup old-fashioned rolled oats, 2 tablespoons unsalted butter, 2 teaspoons salt, 1 quart water, and up to ½ cup packed light or dark brown sugar. Toss in ½ cup raisins or dried cherries too if you wish. Slow-cook overnight, at least 8 hours.

OATMEAL CRÈME BRÛLÉE

A chewy melted-sugar topping is probably the most popular upscale flourish today for a lowly bowl of oats. It's nice in individual ramekins but a real showstopper when brought to the table in one large dish surrounded by the season's best fruit. Eliminate other toppings and spoon the hot oatmeal into the buttered dish or dishes. Sprinkle 1 tablespoon brown sugar over each individual ramekin or, if you're using a larger heatproof dish, scatter enough brown sugar over the oatmeal to cover it entirely. Place under the broiler, near the heat source, for 1 to 2 minutes, just until the sugar caramelizes. Watch carefully.

OATS AND RELIGION

In the 1870s, when stores sold oats only in bulk for making hot cereal, the owners of an oatmeal mill in Ohio came up with the image of a Quaker gentleman to represent the high quality and honest value of their product. They patented the symbol as the first trademark for an American breakfast cereal but then went bankrupt and sold out to Henry Parsons Crowell, a masterful merchandiser. Crowell developed the still-familiar round canister to set his oats apart from others and capitalized on the Quaker icon in the first national advertising campaign for a cereal, displaying the friendly figure in various appealing ways, including alongside a comely bare-breasted woman. A fervently religious man, Crowell gave much of his earnings to evangelical Christian causes, but real Quakers in the Society of Friends denounced his commercial exploitation of their church and even petitioned Congress to ban such practices.

oven for 10 to 20 minutes, with the time again depending on the size of the cereal grain.

- When you add liquid and begin to cook the cereal, keep the heat low to moderate so that the kernels can absorb the liquid fully.

- Vary the cooking liquid. Water always works, but you can use milk, cream, or unsweetened apple or white grape juice. Canned coconut milk (not cream of coconut) is good with oatmeal in particular.

- Don't stir, at least until the last few minutes of cooking, or the cereal will become a gummy mass.

- Wait until near the end of the cooking time to add salt. It can interfere with the cooking if added too early, but if you wait until the very end, it doesn't have a chance to be absorbed by the cereal grains.

- Sweetness is an individual thing. We often add a bit of sugar, brown sugar, maple syrup, honey, molasses, or other sweetener to cereal while cooking to heighten the flavor and then serve more on the side. If using a sweet liquid in cooking, such as white grape juice, keep its sugar content in mind when adding more sweetness.

LANCASTER FARMHOUSE
BAKED OATMEAL

Most Southerners eat oatmeal as they do grits—with salt, pepper, and butter. When I discovered that some people eat cream and brown sugar on their oatmeal, it seemed almost heretical if not downright nauseating.

Sarah Belk, *Around the Southern Table* (1991)

Baking oatmeal, a technique associated with the Pennsylvania Dutch, produces a slightly crumbly, more toothsome texture perfect for a winter morning. The lovely cinnamon scent coming from the oven is a bonus. In Lancaster County, the dried fruit in the dish would be schnitz, locally dried apple rings, but other fruits work too. If you like, serve Fried Apples (page 280) on the side instead or additionally.

SERVES 4

1½ cups old-fashioned rolled oats

2 tablespoons unsalted butter

1½ cups milk

2 tablespoons light or dark brown sugar

1 teaspoon ground cinnamon

¼ teaspoon salt

¾ to 1 cup chopped dried apples, apricots, or mixed fruit

1 cup heavy (whipping) cream, half-and-half, or milk, warm or chilled

Ground cinnamon, optional

Preheat the oven to 350°F. Butter a medium baking dish.

Place the oats and butter in a heatproof mixing bowl. Pour 1½ cups boiling water over them and let stand for 5 minutes. Stir in the milk, brown sugar, cinnamon, and salt. When well combined, mix in the apples. Spoon into the prepared dish. Cover and bake for 35 minutes, then uncover and continue baking for 5 to 10 minutes longer, until thick and bubbly. Spoon into bowls (it will be stickier than boiled oatmeal) and serve hot, with cream drizzled around the cereal and a dusting of cinnamon if you wish.

CREAMY OATMEAL PUDDING WITH VANILLA SAUCE

TECHNIQUE TIP

To battle the "brown" of most cereals, serve them in colorful bowls or add a bright fruit garnish.

Everyone knows that rice makes a nice homespun pudding, but so do many other grains. This can be made the night before to reheat briefly in the morning in a pan of simmering water. A creamy vanilla sauce brings out the best of the flavor. Serve with Breakfast Ambrosia (page 284).   **SERVES 4**

2 cups old-fashioned rolled oats

2 cups whole milk

3 tablespoons light or dark brown sugar

1 teaspoon pure vanilla extract

½ teaspoon ground ginger

½ teaspoon salt

VANILLA SAUCE

1 cup heavy (whipping) cream

1 tablespoon granulated sugar

1 teaspoon pure vanilla extract

Freshly grated nutmeg, optional

Butter four 1-cup ramekins.

Toast the oats in a heavy saucepan over medium heat until they deepen just slightly in color and become fragrant, about 5 minutes. Pour in 1 cup water, then add the milk, brown sugar, vanilla, ginger, and salt. Bring to a boil, cover, reduce the heat to a bare simmer, and cook for 5 minutes, until soft and very thick. Divide the mixture equally among the ramekins. Cover them with a single piece of foil. Let them sit at room temperature for 10 to 15 minutes, for the pudding to firm in the ramekins.

While the oatmeal molds set, prepare the sauce. Combine the ingredients in a saucepan and cook over medium heat until reduced to about ¾ cup.

Run a knife around the inside of the first ramekin. Turn upside down over a small plate and give it a shake to release the pudding. Repeat with the remaining ramekins. Spoon the warm sauce over each, grate a bit of nutmeg over the tops if you wish, and serve.

CRAZY ABOUT STIRABOUT

Irish miners in Montana used to love stirabout, a sweet, semiliquid oatmeal mush thinned with milk. The popularity stimulated the Big Ship boardinghouse in Butte to install a big copper pot with a chute where every miner could serve himself by pulling a lever. The miners usually ate two or three bowls, which pleased the proprietor since it cut down on their appetites for more expensive hot cakes, ham, and eggs. The miners turned out to be so finicky about the flavor, however, that the owner had to hire a proper cook to get the preparation right.

CHEDDAR-ONION
FRIED CORNMEAL MUSH

Before Europeans brought their porridges to the colonies, Native Americans made a version of their own with New World cornmeal. The settlers adopted the idea, usually calling it *hasty pudding,* and ate it often as a simple supper. After leftovers congealed overnight into "mush," cooks fried it in the morning as a breakfast cake. The breakfast dish has always been much better than the old name suggests, but Ella's restaurant in San Francisco proved to us recently that there was still room for improvement. We follow Ella's lead in making the mush creamier and crustier with the addition of good Cheddar and slivers of scallion. Try it with Persimmon and Mixed Fall Fruit Medley (page 293)

SERVES 4 TO 6

MUSH

1 teaspoon salt

Several pinches of cayenne pepper

1½ cups coarsely ground cornmeal

2 tablespoons unsalted butter

1 to 1½ cups grated sharp Cheddar cheese (4 to 6 ounces)

2 scallions (both green and white parts), cut into 1-inch pieces and then slivered

Flour or additional cornmeal for dusting

Vegetable oil for panfrying

Unsalted butter or Chile Butter (page 57)

Oil a loaf pan.

Heat 6 cups water, the salt, and cayenne in a large heavy saucepan over high heat. When the water reaches a rolling boil, scatter in the cornmeal a handful at a time, stirring constantly. When you have added all the cornmeal, reduce the heat to a bare simmer. Cook the cornmeal until creamy and very thick, almost stiff, about 25 to 35 minutes, depending on its coarseness. Remove from the heat and stir in the butter, cheese, and scallions. Spoon the mush into the loaf pan and set aside to cool to room temperature. Cover the pan and refrigerate for at least 4 hours and up to 2 days.

Turn the mush out of the pan and cut it into neat slices about ½ inch thick. Dust them with flour.

Warm a lightly oiled griddle or large heavy skillet over medium heat. Fry the mush slices in batches, avoiding crowding, until golden brown and crusty on both sides, about 8 to 10 minutes total. Add more oil to the griddle if the slices show any sign of sticking.

Serve the slices of mush hot with butter.

CLASSIC FRIED CORNMEAL MUSH

Leave out the cheese, cayenne, and scallion. Serve with maple syrup or Spiced Maple Butter (page 57).

FRIED CORNMEAL MUSH WITH MINT SAUCE

Cooks in the nineteenth-century Shaker village of Hancock, Massachusetts, made a mint syrup for the classic fried mush variation. Use ¾ cup each of mint and currant jelly and warm the jellies together with several tablespoons of whipping cream until you have a good pouring consistency. Add several tablespoons of minced fresh mint to the sauce just before serving.

FLAKES AND NUTS

Americans owe much of their devotion to cold cereal to Dr. John Harvey Kellogg, the director for decades of a Seventh-Day Adventist health retreat in Battle Creek, Michigan. He believed the key to human happiness lay in the freedom of the bowels, reasoning that constipation caused material to putrefy in the intestines and poison our bodies. Like his mentor, Sylvester Graham, who thought any pleasure in eating was immoral, Kellogg advocated a grain-based diet to maintain health and purity. That inspired his creation of an easily digestible cereal flake, which he made first of wheat and then of corn. Kellogg's regime failed to cure Charles W. Post, a patient the doctor considered all but dead, but Post prospered after dropping out of the program and returning to standard foods. He quickly repaid the doctor by developing a rival breakfast product that he called "Grape-Nuts," which he promoted as a stimulant of the brain rather than the bowels. The cereal industry has been looking up ever since, at some of the highest bottom lines in American business history.

TOASTED WHEAT WITH CARAMELIZED BANANAS

Many a mom on a winter morning has sent her kids off to school warmed and fortified by boxed cream of wheat. If you have fond memories of that cereal, you'll love this nuttier, more toothsome variation that's enlivened with a creamy banana topping.

SERVES 4

2 tablespoons unsalted butter

1 cup bulgur (precooked cracked wheat) (see Ingredient Tip)

1 teaspoon salt or more to taste

TOPPING

4 tablespoons (½ stick) unsalted butter

2 tablespoons light or dark brown sugar

2 medium bananas, peeled and halved lengthwise, then cut into 1- to 2-inch pieces

1 to 2 tablespoons half-and-half, optional

Warm the butter in a medium saucepan over medium-low heat. Add the bulgur and sauté it briefly, until fragrant and a bit more deeply colored, about 5 minutes. Pour in 3 cups hot water and the salt and bring to a bare simmer. Cover and cook for about 10 minutes. Let stand for 10 minutes longer off the heat. Pour the mixture into a colander or large strainer, covering the top with a towel to help keep it warm while it drains, about 10 minutes.

Prepare the topping, warming the butter and brown sugar in a small skillet over medium heat. When melted, add the bananas and stir to coat. Sauté until the bananas are soft, about 3 minutes. Add half-and-half for a richer, more pourable sauce.

Spoon the cereal into bowls, divide the topping equally among them, and serve.

CREAM OF WHEAT WITH CARAMELIZED BANANAS

If you prefer a creamy rather than a nutty texture, or just want a change from the bulgur, use wheat farina or cream of wheat cereal. Cook according to the package instructions, then top with the prepared bananas.

INGREDIENT TIP

A cracked wheat that's precooked, bulgur takes less time to prepare than most grains. It comes in several different grinds, but the medium grind is multipurpose and most widely available. Almost every supermarker sells bulgur today, either boxed or in the bulk section.

John Spratt will eat not fat,

Nor will he touch the lean;

He scorns to eat of any meat,

He lives upon Foodine.

But Mrs. Spratt will none of that,

Foodine she cannot eat;

Her special wish is for a dish

Of Expurgated Wheat . . .

Corrected Wheat for little Pete;

Flaked Pine for Dot; while "Bub"

The infant Spratt is waxing fat

On Battle Creek Near-Grub.

Bert Leston Taylor, "The Breakfast Food Family," quoted in Evan Jones, *A Food Lover's Companion* (1979)

WILD RICE PORRIDGE

"Jumping Christopher!"
I heard my father say.
"What do you mean by
setting pap down in
front of me? Where's
breakfast?"

I do not remember
what it was that
provoked this outburst,
but it must have been
some experimental
item of the menu, a
faintly suggestive
forerunner, perhaps, of
the orange juice, cereal,
toast, and coffee which
have now become the
standard American
breakfast.

Della Lutes, *The Country
Kitchen* (1936)

The deep, almost smoky flavor of wild rice and its remarkable crunch make it as appetizing in the morning as at later meals. The familiar combination with brown rice in a pilaf also works in a breakfast cereal, with the milder-flavored grain bringing out the nuttiness of the wild rice. Serve with a big, bright bowl of fresh cherries on the stem. **SERVES 4**

2 tablespoons unsalted butter	½ cup dried currants, cherries, cranberries, or golden raisins
1 cup wild rice	
1 cup brown rice	Half-and-half, milk, or heavy (whipping) cream
Real maple syrup	
½ teaspoon salt	

Warm the butter in a large saucepan over medium heat. Stir in the wild rice and brown rice and sauté briefly until they glisten with fat and look lightly toasted. Add 6 cups water, 1 tablespoon maple syrup, and the salt and bring to a boil. Cover, reduce the heat to medium-low, and cook for about 55 minutes, until most of the wild rice kernels split open and both it and the brown rice are tender. After about 45 minutes of cooking, uncover and scatter the dried fruit over the mixture. Quickly cover the pan again, without stirring. When done, remove from the heat and let steam, covered, for about 10 minutes.

Stir to combine, then spoon into bowls and serve, accompanied by more maple syrup and half-and-half.

WILD RICE AND OATMEAL PORRIDGE

We featured this variation on a wild-rice porridge in our *American Home Cooking* (1999). Eliminate the brown rice, but cook the wild rice in the same way with half as much butter, water, and salt. Cook 1 cup old-fashioned rolled oats with 2 cups water and a couple of pinches of salt until tender, then combine with the rice and enough milk to make it creamy. This reheats remarkably well if you want to prepare it ahead or make deliberate leftovers for another day.

CREAMY BREAKFAST RICE WITH DATES AND HONEY

The most common foods to be found on the breakfast tables in the mountains were eggs, bacon, side meat or ham, hot biscuits, cream gravy, jelly and preserves. Sometimes there would be a side dish of oatmeal or boiled, sweetened rice. We never ate dry cereals for breakfast, or sat down only to a dish of oatmeal and toast.

In 1960 my first husband and I moved to Indianapolis so he could get a better paying job. . . . I decided we would live like city people. The first morning I served a bowl of dry cereal and toast for breakfast Leon demanded how I thought a man could live on a breakfast like that. . . . Gradually we learned to adjust, but never completely.

Sidney Saylor Farr, *More than Moonshine* (1983)

Much of the world eats rice in the morning, often in the form of Chinese congee. Americans used to enjoy it a lot as well, fried in cakes like mush, cooked as a porridge, and just as reheated leftovers served in a cereal bowl with milk and sugar. Of all the varied possibilities, we like this creamy version, made with the Arborio rice used in risotto.

SERVES 4

One 15-ounce can coconut milk (not cream of coconut)

3 tablespoons unsalted butter

1 cup Arborio rice

Salt to taste

2 teaspoons pure vanilla extract

½ cup chopped fresh or dried dates

1 to 2 tablespoons honey or sugar, optional

Warm the coconut milk in a medium saucepan with 2 cups water over medium-low heat.

Warm 2 tablespoons of the butter in another medium saucepan over medium heat. Stir in the rice to coat it with the butter, sprinkle with salt, and cook for about 1 minute. Begin adding the warm coconut milk mixture about ½ cup at a time, stirring up from the bottom after each addition and then every minute or two. Add more liquid as soon as the previous addition has been nearly absorbed by the rice. When the rice is tender but still a bit toothsome, after 30 to 40 minutes, stir in the remaining butter, vanilla, dates, and honey if desired. (The amount of liquid needed fluctuates a bit with the rice and the heat. You may not need it all. If you happen to run out of liquid before the rice is ready, just heat additional water as needed.) Spoon into bowls and serve immediately, with honey on the table if you wish.

RICE CROQUETTES

Chill any leftover rice and form it into 2- to 3-inch ovals. Dunk in an egg wash (about 1 tablespoon milk whisked with 1 egg) and then in dried bread crumbs. Fry briefly in butter or oil or a combination, until golden and crisp on both sides. Serve plain or with additional honey.

SWEET COUSCOUS WITH FIGS

Some older American cookbooks recommend macaroni as a breakfast cereal, cooked in milk and sometimes sprinkled with raisins. This is a better pasta option in our book, made with tiny granular couscous. For year-round eating, we call for dried figs in the recipe, cooked with the semolina pasta, but in season we use fresh figs simply quartered and laid over the cereal right before serving.   **SERVES 4**

Scant 2 cups milk

2 tablespoons unsalted butter

½ cup chopped dried figs

½ to 1 tablespoon turbinado or light brown sugar

Pinch of salt

1 cup plain couscous

Additional turbinado or light brown sugar

Additional milk, optional

Warm the milk with the butter, figs, sugar, and salt in a medium saucepan over medium heat until small bubbles form at the rim and it just begins to approach a boil. Stir in the couscous, cover, and remove from the heat. Let the couscous stand for about 5 minutes. Spoon into bowls and pass additional sugar at the table, along with milk if you wish.

GRAINS AND GUNS

Biochemist Alexander P. Anderson perfected his quest for a "digestible" puffed cereal in the first years of the twentieth century. After trying various dangerous methods of production, and finally teaming up with an engineer who blew out the floor of his workshop, he and his partner eventually found success using an old cannon left over from the Spanish-American War. The cereal Shot from Guns made a literal debut at the World's Fair in 1904, when army surplus cannons exploded Quaker Puffed Rice over the heads of a huge crowd.

BUTTERY BARLEY WITH WALNUTS

Many people think of barley only as a soup ingredient, but the chewy grain also makes a soothing breakfast cereal. It pairs especially well with nuts and raisins, which perk up its subtle flavor without overwhelming it. The pearl barley called for in the recipe has been polished in processing so that it cooks a bit faster than the whole kernel. Try this with Butterscotch Baked Pears (page 299) when you're up for a big breakfast.   **SERVES 4**

1½ cups pearl barley	½ cup golden or dark raisins
3 tablespoons unsalted butter	1 teaspoon salt or more to taste
½ cup walnut pieces	Dark brown sugar, optional

Toast the barley in a dry heavy saucepan over medium heat for about 5 minutes, until lightly colored and fragrant. Pour in 3 cups water, reduce the heat to a bare simmer, cover, and cook for 20 minutes.

While the barley cooks, melt the butter in a small skillet over medium heat. Stir in the walnuts and sauté for a couple of minutes, until fragrant.

Mix the walnuts, raisins, and salt into the barley, gently stirring up from the bottom once. Cover again and cook for about 5 minutes longer. The barley is ready when the individual pearls are tender and plump and the cereal is thick but still spoonable. For best texture, cover with a clean towel, replace the lid, and let stand for 5 to 10 minutes. Ladle into bowls and serve hot, with brown sugar sprinkled on top if you wish.

BARLEY FLAKES WITH WALNUTS

For a quicker cereal with a softer texture, seek out barley flakes, common in natural foods stores today. Steamed and rolled before drying, they cook in the time it takes to read the first page of the newspaper. Combine 2 cups barley flakes with 2 cups water. Bring just to a boil, then reduce the heat to a bare simmer, cover, and cook 5 minutes. Stir in the walnut-butter mixture, raisins, and salt, cover with a clean towel, replace the lid, and let stand for 5 minutes before serving.

CRUNCHY GRANOLA

One of the original American health foods, granola went mainstream in the 1970s and too often became a one-dimensional cereal awash in sugar and fat. The only sure way to avoid mediocre versions is to make your own, a simple process. Use this basic but bountiful blend as a starting point for creating a signature granola.

MAKES ABOUT 6 CUPS

3 cups old-fashioned rolled oats

½ cup sliced almonds

½ cup wheat germ

¼ cup whole wheat flour

¼ cup oat bran

3 to 4 tablespoons packed light or dark brown sugar

2 teaspoons ground cinnamon

½ teaspoon salt

¼ teaspoon freshly grated nutmeg

¼ teaspoon ground ginger

½ cup unsweetened apple juice or cider

3 to 4 tablespoons honey, warmed

1 tablespoon pure vanilla extract

2 tablespoons unsalted butter, melted, almond oil, or vegetable oil

Preheat the oven to 300°F. Butter or oil a baking sheet.

Stir the oats, almonds, wheat germ, whole wheat flour, oat bran, brown sugar, cinnamon, salt, nutmeg, and ginger together in a large bowl. Whisk the apple juice, honey, vanilla, and butter together in a small bowl. Pour the wet ingredients over the dry, then toss well to mix.

Spread the granola on the prepared baking sheet. Bake for approximately 45 minutes, stirring the granola well every 15 minutes, until it's a shade browner than it started and dry to the touch. (It will become crisper as it cools.) Cool on the baking sheet, break up any large pieces, then store in an airtight container until ready to serve.

FRUITED GRANOLA

Mix your choice of dried fruit into the granola after it comes from the oven. Raisins, currants, and dried cranberries can be stirred in whole. Cut larger fruit into small bits. A favorite of ours is dried mango, found in natural foods stores and Asian groceries.

GRANOLA EMBELLISHMENTS

In creating your own special granola blend, consider adding ½ cup unsweetened shredded coconut, ¼ to ½ cup sesame seeds, ¼ to ½ cup sunflower seed kernels, several tablespoons of orange or tangerine juice, or other favorite flavors. Dry ingredients go in at the same time as the other dry ingredients, and wet ones are added with the rest of the liquid mixture.

MUESLI

Amish and Mennonite settlers from Switzerland brought muesli to the United States years before it emerged along with granola as a popular natural food. On first bite a newcomer may be startled by the unusual mix of uncooked oats, fruit, nuts, cream, and yogurt or milk, but it seldom takes many spoonfuls to convince the wary. We like to use a combination of fresh and dried fruit, but feel free to use one or the other in your version, depending on the season.

SERVES 2 TO 4

½ cup old-fashioned rolled oats

½ cup slivered almonds

1 tablespoon wheat germ or toasted wheat germ

½ cup milk, half-and-half, heavy (whipping) cream, or plain yogurt

1 tablespoon sugar or more to taste

1 small apple, peeled and finely chopped or grated

½ cup finely diced dried apricots or 1 small peach or very ripe pear, peeled and finely chopped or grated

¼ cup golden raisins, dried cranberries or cherries, fresh raspberries, or sliced fresh strawberries

Toast the oats in a small skillet or saucepan over medium heat until fragrant and a shade more golden, about 5 minutes. Transfer the oats to a mixing bowl and pour 1 cup hot water over them. Let them stand for at least 5 minutes or longer if you'd like them even softer.

While the oats soak, use the same skillet to toast the almonds over medium heat until fragrant and just lightly colored, about 3 minutes. Stir in the wheat germ and toast for 1 minute longer, then remove from the heat.

Pour the water off from the oats. Mix in the milk and sugar. When well combined, stir in the almond–wheat germ mixture, apple, apricots, and raisins. Alternatively, just scatter the apricots and raisins over the top. Spoon into shallow bowls and serve.

KELLOGG'S TRAVEL TIPS

"The Housewife's Almanac," a Kellogg's promotional pamphlet from 1938, touted the wonders of automobile travel across the country. The authors ranked the Kellogg plant in Battle Creek, Michigan, as one of the top sights, right alongside the Grand Canyon and the Alamo. In addition to a tour, visitors reaching the Michigan Mecca received a folder on how to equip the kitchen of a travel trailer, together with suggested daily on-the-road menus using "Kellogg's triple-tested recipes."

TOASTED CORN, OAT, AND WHEAT FLAKES

SELECTIONS FROM THE BREAKFAST MENU AT THE RESTAURANT AND QUICK LUNCH IN NEW YORK CITY, 1905

Quick Combination Breakfast

Including Fruit, Coffee and Rolls 25¢

Grape Nuts, Minced Chicken on Toast

Oatmeal, Liver and Bacon and Potatoes

Cracked Wheat, Fish Cakes with 1 Egg and Bacon

Rolled Oats, Fried Honeycomb Tripe and Potatoes

Some of the more appetizing store-bought processed cereals can be enhanced easily with a little oven toasting, which adds extra crunch and a suggestion of freshness. We think the idea works particularly well with a mix of flaked cereals. Serve warm or cold with milk in the customary fashion. Accompany with a juicy melon slice topped with a handful of berries.

MAKES ABOUT 12 CUPS

4 heaping cups cornflakes

4 heaping cups oat flakes

4 heaping cups wheat or bran flakes or raisin bran cereal

1 cup pecan, butternut, or hickory nut pieces

3 tablespoons nut oil, such as walnut, almond, or pecan

2 tablespoons sugar

Preheat the oven to 300°F.

Pour the cereals onto a baking sheet, top with nuts, and stir to combine. In a small bowl, stir together the oil and sugar until syrupy. Drizzle the mixture over the cereals, then stir again.

Bake for about 20 minutes, stirring once after 10 minutes. When done, the mixture will have a slightly deeper color and will be dry and somewhat crisp. Let the cereal cool on the baking sheet, where it will become even crisper. Serve or store in an airtight canister, zipper-lock bags, or the original boxes.

11

Fruitful Beginnings

FRUIT MAY BE the perfect breakfast food, but few people take full advantage of its potentials. We drink our juice, of course, cut bits of banana into our cereal, and nibble at the melon garnishes that restaurants regard as *de rigueur* in the morning, but we don't generally put fruit at the center of the plate.

In cases where we include it in any role at all, we tend to limit ourselves to a narrow range of options in both choosing and preparing fruit, sticking with the same kinds eaten in the same manner day after day.

Our outlook is particularly puzzling since fruit meets all of the touted American requirements for haste, health, and handiness. Most ways of enjoying it require less time than stopping for fast food en route to work, and all are likely to be more nutritious than anything you can pick up at a drive-up window or convenience store. More important, there's the big bonus of natural, truly arousing flavor. It's time for us to start thinking more fruitfully about our breakfasts.

Simply Delicious, No-Recipe Fresh Fruit

Anyone can enjoy fresh fruit regularly and add immeasurable pleasure to morning meals whether or not he or she cooks regularly or has time for a leisurely breakfast, whether the meal is for just one or a family. The only culinary skill required is savvy shopping. Because freshness and natural ripeness make a critical difference in flavor with most fruits, focus on what grows locally and buy seasonally at farmers' markets, produce stands, or grocery stores that know and care about quality. When you want something from another region of the country that isn't available in your area in a premier form, order it directly from small-scale growers who consider their work a craft. We've listed a few good suppliers we've used for particular fruits. One source for a broad range of special produce is Frieda's by Mail (800-241-1771, 714-826-6100, www.friedas.com). If you do your shopping well, any of the following fresh fruits make a magnificent but simple and quick breakfast.

APRICOTS

We were blasé about apricots until we finally tasted a good fresh one. When you have any choice, look for the Blenheim variety, which even in apricot regions is found more frequently at farmers' markets or produce stands than in supermarkets. Eat them out of hand or halved, pitted, and mixed with mint and a little apricot nectar. Mail-order from Eden Gardens in Tracy, California (209-832-5891 or edngrdn@ix.netcom.com).

BLACKBERRIES, RASPBERRIES, AND THEIR COUSINS

Few fruits rival ripe, juicy berries, but, unfortunately, they start to deteriorate as soon as they are picked. Shop for them as close to the source as possible and eat them within a day. As soon as you return home, gently remove them from the container and discard any that are moldy or disintegrating. Store them in a single layer on a baking sheet or shallow tray or dish, covered loosely with plastic wrap. Do not wash them until you're ready to eat them. Between late May and late June, Lagier Ranches in California's Central Valley harvests blackberries and several equally good varietal crosses back to back and ships them anywhere in the country. Call 888-353-5618, fax 209-982-9056, or go to www.LagierRanches.com. Blackberries are great with a splash of cream. For peak flavor, red raspberries should be deeply red in color, almost burgundy, and unbruised. They are so perishable that we have yet to find a grower willing to ship them.

CANTALOUPES, HONEYDEWS, AND OTHER MELONS

Truly ripe melons are highly fragrant with an earthy, musky scent. Look for ones with a smooth and slightly soft stem end. Cantaloupes and muskmelons should have no tinge of green under the netting. Unlike most fruits, they taste as good cold as at room temperature, but do not refrigerate them until close to serving time, if at all. Eat melon wedges plain, with a slight dusting of powdered sugar and ground ginger, a shower of shredded mint or lemon verbena leaves, or topped with a handful of blueberries, raspberries, or sliced strawberries.

CHERRIES

Contact Lagier Ranches, listed under "Blackberries, Raspberries, and Their Cousins," for organically grown cherries in their early summer season. For breakfast, we prefer them on the stem, perhaps dunked in sour cream sweetened with brown sugar or fortified with kirsch, a cherry brandy.

CHERIMOYA

Now being grown commercially in California, the cherimoya is like a divine fruit pudding in a shell. Serve it chilled on the half-shell, maybe with a light dusting of nutmeg. Eat around the watermelonlike seeds. A cherimoya cousin, the custardy atemoya, is also tasty.

DATES

Our favorite way to eat fresh or dried dates in the morning is with creamy goat cheese, which balances the fruit's sensuous honeyed richness. You can also put them on a bowl of warm oatmeal, mix them into granola, add them to winter fruit compotes, or cook them wrapped in bacon. The Deglet Noor variety is the most widely available across the country, but no other date matches the intense flavor of the regal and pricey Medjool. We buy these and other varieties directly from Robert Lower's Flying Disc Ranch in Thermal, California (706-399-5313). They can be purchased fresh in late fall and winter.

FIGS

Fresh figs reach their peak in the late summer and can often be found into the early autumn. Like dates, figs taste great fresh or dried alongside mild goat cheese or other creamy cheese. We especially like them halved and topped with spoonfuls of ricotta or mascarpone and a sprinkling of chopped pistachios or hazelnuts. Try them too with paper-thin slices of country ham or a drizzle of honey.

GRAPEFRUIT

The best-known grapefruits come from the Indian River area of eastern Florida, but we mail-order ours from Valley Fruit (800-255-1486 or 210-787-3241) in the Rio Grande valley of south Texas, which specializes in the vibrantly flavored red variety known as Rio Stars. Grapefruits ripen no further after picking, but they hold their juiciness and sweetness longer than most fruits. They store fine at room temperature for at least a week or refrigerated for several weeks.

GRAPES

At times when few fresh fruits are available, you can always find grapes. From tiny champagne grapes to hefty Red Globes, they put a little pop into a breakfast. In their late summer season, we're always on the lookout for Concords and scuppernongs, particularly tasty varieties that don't get a lot of national distribution.

LYCHEES

We've never forgotten our first experience with fresh lychees, picked from a majestic tree at a friend's Honolulu home one June morning. We savored them straight from the russet red shells, simply cracking the brittle exterior to get to the lusciously juicy white orb. That's still the way we like them best. The flavor is incomparable, almost floral, reminding us of roses and strawberries. Revered in China, they can be found most reliably during summer months in Asian groceries or farmers' markets with a strong Asian clientele.

MANGOES

Look for slightly soft, heavy mangoes with a full aroma, or let firmer ones mellow at room temperature for a few days. While an occasional mango can taste chalky, on the whole there are few more fabulously lush fruits. Score the skin into quarters, peel it back, impale the mango on a fork, and devour it like a taffy apple. We prefer the varieties available in late spring and summer, generally shipped less distance.

ORANGES, TANGERINES, AND CLEMENTINES

So common as breakfast juice, oranges also deserve respect as a table fruit. They and smaller cousins such as tangerines, mandarins, and clementines store for weeks and are at their best during the winter months, when many other fruits are unavailable. You can cut juice oranges such as Valencia into wedges, but navel oranges are best for sectioning. Serve with a steaming cup of mint tea.

PAPAYAS

Papayas should yield softly to pressure when ripe and can be refrigerated at that point to keep for a couple of days. We generally slice them vertically into quarters, then scoop out most (but not all) of the edible black seeds and sprinkle the fruit with lime juice.

PAPAWS

Uncommon in stores but available by mail order from Chris Chmeil's Ohio Valley–based Integration Acres (740-698-2124, www.integrationacres.com), the papaw is the largest native American fruit, common from the Appalachians west through the prairie states. Order it fresh from mid-August to early October or get frozen puree throughout the year. It tastes almost tropical, with a texture that's similar to a ripe banana in consistency. The pulp can be cooked into pudding or pie, but for breakfast eating, blend it into a smoothie or lassi or simply pull back the skin and enjoy, steering clear of the large inedible seeds.

PEACHES

The sure herald of summer, peaches taste best just off the tree, eaten over the sink with juice running down your face. They require special care to keep from bruising and deteriorating, so buy them as close to the source as you can. If you're hesitant about the over-the-sink approach, you might cover sliced peaches with a little cream or dust them with chopped pecans.

PINEAPPLES

Choose a whole pineapple by fragrance, full green leaves, and somewhat shiny skin. Big supermarkets now also sell fresh pineapple already skinned and sliced. What we have tried has been reasonably good, possibly because the pineapple was allowed to ripen on the plant more fully than those shipped whole. Cut pineapple, refrigerated, will keep for up to a week. Serve it warm or chilled, maybe with a drizzle of caramel sauce or a sprinkle of brown sugar.

PLUMS

A few years ago we were lucky to see any more than one variety of plum—usually the sweet-tart rosy Santa Rosa—and just for a month in the summer. Now some markets carry eight or more kinds extending from early summer into the fall. All are good eaten out of hand or halved, pitted, and dabbed with crème fraîche and a sprinkling of mint.

STRAWBERRIES

Strawberries are the cheeriest essence of spring, but to get great ones you may need to grow them yourself. The only other realistic option is to buy from an area grower and eat them immediately. While the finest strawberries can be relished without embellishment, they are the ultimate fruit to eat with a drizzle of cream or another dairy accompaniment. For optimum flavor and texture, take the time to remove the cottony white center so pronounced in varieties raised for shipping.

SPICED FRESH BLUEBERRIES

The blueberry is to other Maine berries what Mardi Gras is to Lent, except that this is a Mardi Gras that arrives at summer's height. . . . It's true that [the blueberry] doesn't have the panache of the raspberry or the subtle perfume of the strawberry. But its simple taste is as astonishingly bright and fresh as a dipper of cold well water. If summer has a flavor, it is blueberries eaten out of hand or, perhaps, in a cereal bowl (without the cereal, please), sugared a little and splashed with milk.

John Thorne, *Serious Pig* (1996)

Nature didn't intend for us to get fussy with blueberries, one of the most intensely flavored fruits native to North America. This is about the fanciest thing we ever do with them, especially good with the nearly marble-size blueberries under wide commercial cultivation today.   **SERVES 4**

½ cup sugar

2 teaspoons fresh lemon juice

2 cinnamon sticks

4 whole cloves

1 pint fresh blueberries

Combine the sugar, lemon juice, cinnamon, and cloves with 1 cup water in a small saucepan. Bring the mixture to a boil, then reduce to a simmer and cook for 5 minutes. Cool briefly, then pour through a strainer over the berries. Chill for at least 30 minutes and up to several hours. If the berries are refrigerated for the longer period, let them sit at room temperature a few minutes to take off the chill before you serve them in bowls with some of the liquid.

BAKED APPLES WITH SAUSAGE STUFFING

Apples aren't native to the Americas, but you might think so given the country's long love affair with them. Early colonists drank more hard cider than water and devoured apple pies throughout long winters when they had little else to eat. We take them to favorite teachers and gobble them to keep the doctor at bay. Our most populous city even promotes itself as the biggest apple of all. At the start of an autumn day, when there's just a hint of chill in the morning air, few dishes comfort as fully and elementally as baked apples. Among all the manners of stuffing them, we particularly like this savory-sweet notion that comes from German-American roots. Choose a naturally chubby apple variety such as Rome Beauty or Cortland or at least the most rotund Granny Smiths you can find.

SERVES 6

2 cups apple cider or juice

6 large, well-shaped baking apples

4 tablespoons (½ stick) unsalted butter at room temperature

1 heaping cup chopped onions

2 tablespoons dried currants

¼ teaspoon crumbled dried sage

½ pound raw full-flavored sausage, preferably a smoky or sage-scented variety, crumbled or chopped (see Ingredient Tip)

Fresh sage sprigs, optional

Preheat the oven to 375°F. Butter a baking dish large enough to hold the apples upright with up to an inch between them.

Pour the cider into a saucepan and reduce by half over high heat.

While the cider cooks, scoop out the apple cores, leaving the bottoms intact. We find that the small end of a melon baller works better for this than the apple-coring gadgets. Scoop a hole in each just a bit bigger than necessary to remove the core. Slice a thin ribbon of peel from around the top of each apple cavity, which helps keep the peel from splitting while baking. Slice off all fruit remaining on the cores and chop it.

Warm the butter in a skillet over medium heat. Stir in the chopped apple pieces, onion, currants, sage, and sausage. Cook until the sausage is brown and, in a few spots, crispy. Remove from the heat and cool briefly.

Pack equal portions of the mixture into each apple cavity, mounding it over the top a bit if necessary. Pour the reduced apple cider into the dish, drizzling a little over each apple in the process. Cover the apples and place them in the oven for 30 minutes. Uncover and continue baking for about 15 minutes longer, until the apples can be pierced easily with a knife tip but still hold their shape.

Arrange the apples in small bowls, pouring the pan juices over them. Serve warm, garnished with sage sprigs if you wish.

CLASSIC BAKED APPLES

Prepare the apples for stuffing as described, boiling down the cider as suggested. Mix together the softened butter with about ¼ cup packed light or dark brown sugar or maple sugar and stuff it in the apples' cavities. Bake as directed, enriching the pan juices before serving with a few tablespoons of cream if you wish.

EMBELLISHMENTS FOR CLASSIC BAKED APPLES

Add several tablespoons of chopped pecans or walnuts, raisins, dried currants, cherries, cranberries, dates, or granola to the stuffing mixture for Classic Baked Apples. Consider a spoonful of caramel or butterscotch sauce as a topping for a special occasion.

A NATION OF NOTIONS

Long before fresh ginger became a supermarket staple, a respected home cook in Anne Arundel County, Maryland, recommended it as an apple stuffing: "1 tablespoon chopped Canton ginger mixed with enough brown sugar to fill hole." Fannie Farmer, in her original 1896 cookbook, suggests a stuffing of cooked oatmeal, and the authors of the still-fresh 1964 *The Spice Cook Book*, Avanelle Day and Lillie Stuckey, fill their apples with two bananas mashed with a squeeze of lemon and baked with a cup of orange juice instead of cider. Not everyone thinks that baked apples are best warm. The New Orleans *The Picayune's Creole Cook Book* (1901), one of the finest and most opinionated American cookbooks ever written, declares they "are much nicer served cold, with a glass of milk."

BOILED CIDER APPLESAUCE

INGREDIENT TIP

If your area doesn't have much variety in apples, you can mail-order a nice selection of fruit from Breezy Hill Orchards in New York's Hudson Valley. Elizabeth Ryan and Peter Zimmerman grow forty-five kinds of apples, including such antique and rare varieties as the Baldwin, King Luscious, and Golden Russet. Contact them at 845-266-5967 or www.hudsonvalleycider.com.

TECHNIQUE TIP

Leaving the peel on red-skinned apple varieties will turn the sauce a dusky pink, a shade we find particularly appealing. In that case we don't bother peeling any of the apples before cooking, because we always put this sauce through a food mill to eliminate chunks of peel.

The old woman of eighty-four winters was already out in the cold morning wind, bare-headed, tripping about like a young girl, and driving up the cow to milk. She got the breakfast with dispatch, and without noise or bustle; and meanwhile the old man resumed his stories, standing before us, who were sitting, with his

Apples were much more common than sugar in the original northern states, leading to the practice of cooking apple juice down to one fourth or less of the original amount to produce a "boiled cider" sweetener. In many cases it flavored other apple concoctions, especially applesauce, an important dish then because it gave new life to old apples that were no longer crisp enough to enjoy in other ways. Using fresh fruit today, you can make an especially tasty applesauce with Gravensteins or other early-season apples. For breakfast we like to serve this with potato pancakes or latkes or in the traditional New England fashion with cottage cheese or farmer cheese.

MAKES ABOUT 4 CUPS

1 quart apple cider or juice

3 pounds apples, preferably a mix of several varieties, but avoiding Red Delicious, cored and chunked (see Ingredient Tip)

¼ to ¾ teaspoon ground cinnamon, optional

¼ to ½ teaspoon freshly grated nutmeg, ground allspice, or a combination, optional

Maple sugar or light brown sugar, optional

In a large heavy pot, cook the cider down over medium heat until reduced by half. Add the apples and the cinnamon and nutmeg if desired. Reduce the heat to low, cover, and cook gently until the apples have cooked down and are very soft, about 45 minutes. Taste and, if you wish, add a little sugar, perhaps a tablespoon or two. Depending on the varieties of apples you use, some may remain somewhat chunky after the rest have virtually dissolved. Put some or all of the apple mixture (depending on whether you want it silky smooth or a bit chunky) through a food mill or puree it in batches in a food processor. Serve warm or chilled. The applesauce will keep in the refrigerator, covered, for at least a week, and can be frozen for even longer life.

RUM-ROASTED APPLESAUCE

Our favorite alternative to classic boiled applesauce is a roasted version. Toss a baking sheet's worth of pared apple chunks with enough light or dark rum to moisten, about ¼ cup. Brandy, bourbon, and cider make good alternatives to the rum. Let the apples sit briefly, stirring a time or two so they absorb the liquor evenly. Sprinkle with about 3 tablespoons light or dark brown sugar, a few pinches of cinnamon and nutmeg or cloves, and a pinch of salt and dot with butter. Bake in a 400°F oven until soft and golden brown, about 25 minutes. Cool briefly, then puree in a food processor. If the applesauce is stiffer than you like, add a little more rum or a bit of cider or water to thin it.

back to the chimney, and ejecting his tobacco-juice right and left into the fire behind him, without regard to the various dishes which were there preparing. At breakfast we had eels, buttermilk cake, cold bread, green beans, doughnuts, and tea. . . . I ate of the apple-sauce and the doughnuts, which I thought had sustained the least detriment from the old man's shots, but my companion refused the apple-sauce, and ate of the hot cake and green beans, which had appeared to him to occupy the safest part of the hearth.

Henry David Thoreau, *Cape Cod* (1865)

APPLESAUCE WITH OTHER FRUIT

An old American tradition calls for adding a few quinces to the simmering applesauce, not a bad idea for resurrection now that these lovely fruits have been rescued from obscurity and are showing up in produce departments in autumn. The quinces should be started about an hour before the apples (see page 292 for more information on cooking quinces). Scandinavian settlers in the upper Midwest liked to toss a handful of their beloved lingonberries into the applesauce cauldron, and New Englanders did the same with cranberries.

SAVORY APPLESAUCE

The cooks in the communal kitchen of Hancock Shaker Village in Massachusetts made a savory applesauce to accompany ham, an idea that also works with breakfast sausage. To approximate the Shakers' results, sauté 1 cup minced onions in several tablespoons of butter and, when very soft, combine with 4 cups applesauce. Zip up the dish and your day with a teaspoon or two of prepared horseradish.

APPLE FRITTERS

SELECTIONS FROM THE

BREAKFAST MENU AT THE

RIGGS HOUSE HOTEL IN

WASHINGTON, D.C.,

CIRCA 1880

FRUIT

Apples and Oranges

FISH

Broiled Bass   Potomac Herring

Smelts   Fried Perch

Broiled Salt-Mackerel

Fruit fritters have a long and happy history in American home cooking. French and Spanish settlers helped make them popular in cities such as Charleston and Mobile, and African-Americans carried a similar enthusiasm for the fried treats to other areas of the South. The various cultural strands came together passionately in nineteenth-century New Orleans, where early cookbooks included as many as two dozen varieties of fritters, featuring everything from figs to elderflowers. We use apples in this preparation for the delightful contrast they provide between the warm, mellow crunch of the interior and the crispy exterior. The apples can be marinated overnight, then fried just before serving. We like them as a side with Spiced Lamb Sausage (page 140) or Corned Beef Hash (page 183).   **SERVES 4**

4 medium apples, preferably cooking apples such as McIntosh, Cortland, or Macoun

¼ cup applejack, brandy, rum, or sweet or dry white wine

3 tablespoons sugar

2 large eggs, separated

2 tablespoons almond oil, other nut oil, or vegetable oil

1 cup unbleached all-purpose flour

¼ teaspoon salt

Vegetable oil for deep-frying

Confectioners' sugar

Peel and core the apples and cut each into wedges about ½ to ¾ inch at their wider side. Arrange the wedges in a shallow nonreactive dish and sprinkle with the applejack and sugar. Toss to combine. Cover the apples and let them sit for about 30 minutes. (You can also do this step before you go to bed, then refrigerate the apples until morning. Let them sit out at room temperature for a few minutes before proceeding. It's fine for the apples to brown on the surface since it won't be visible later.)

Prepare the batter, whisking the egg yolks together with the oil until light yellow, then mixing ¾ cup water with it. Stir together the flour and salt in a medium bowl and mix the egg yolk mixture into it until well combined. Drain off the liquid from the apple wedges and stir it into the batter too. Beat the egg whites until stiff but not dry and fold them into the batter. The batter will remain somewhat thin.

Heat at least 1 inch of oil to 350°F in a deep skillet or large pot.

Pat the apple wedges lightly with a paper towel, just enough so that they're not soaking wet. Dunk the apples in the batter and coat them well. Fry them in batches until golden brown and crisp, 2½ to 3 minutes. Remove with a slotted spoon and drain on a rack, or on paper towels. Repeat with the remaining apples and batter. Serve hot, sprinkled with confectioners' sugar.

PEACH FRITTERS

The same basic batter can cloak inch-thick wedges of ripe but somewhat firm peaches (skin on or off, as you choose). Substitute peach brandy, rum, or white wine for the applejack and add a pinch of nutmeg or cinnamon to the batter if you wish. We love these with slices of salty country ham or a rasher of crisp bacon.

FRIED APPLES

This is probably the easiest and quickest way to cook apples. It's an old favorite in the mid-South, equally good as a side dish with a ham steak or as a topping for corncakes.

SERVES 4

3 large apples, such as Granny Smith or a good baking variety that holds its shape, such as Rome Beauty, peeled or unpeeled and quartered

3 tablespoons unsalted butter

Pinch of salt

3 to 4 tablespoons packed light or dark brown sugar

Ground cinnamon or freshly grated nutmeg, optional

Core the apple quarters and cut each into a few thick slices.

Warm the butter in a large skillet over medium-low heat. Add the apples and stir to coat them with the butter. Cover and cook for about 5 minutes, until very tender and liquid pools around them. Sprinkle the salt and 3 tablespoons of the sugar over the apples and turn them again to coat evenly with the sugar. Taste and add a bit more sugar if they are overly tart. Cook uncovered briefly, until the sugar has melted into the butter and formed a thick sauce.

Serve warm, topped with a dash or two of cinnamon if you wish. Avoid too heavy a hit of cinnamon, though, because it easily begins to mask rather than enhance the apple flavor.

FRIED APPLE RINGS

It's just not the same to some folks if the apples aren't cut the way their mom did it. If you grew up in the ring school of thinking, or just prefer doughnut shapes, simply core and slice the apples horizontally into rings.

FRIED MIXED FRUIT

Replace one or more of the apples with pears or add a plump fig or two, sliced into thin wedges.

AHWAHNEE CREAMED BANANAS

Creamy and silken, this banana lover's dream comes from the historic Ahwahnee Hotel in Yosemite National Park. A Sunday morning staple there, the dish now pops up on bed-and-breakfast menus throughout the Yosemite and Sequoia national parks region. Most versions call for a heavy dose of banana extract, but we prefer to enhance the flavor by mixing varieties of bananas, including perhaps chubby finger-size reds or baby Turbanas with the common Cavendish, available in every supermarket. **SERVES 4 TO 6**

6 ounces cream cheese, softened

3 tablespoons heavy (whipping) cream

3 tablespoons milk or more as needed

1 teaspoon sugar or more to taste

¾ teaspoon pure vanilla extract

¼ teaspoon pure almond extract

¼ teaspoon pure banana extract, optional

4 large bananas or 1 large and 4 to 6 small bananas, peeled and thickly sliced (2 to 2½ cups)

½ pint fresh raspberries

In a mixer or food processor, combine the cream cheese, cream, 3 tablespoons milk, 1 teaspoon sugar, and extracts. Spoon into a serving bowl, preferably of a brightly contrasting color, and gently stir in the bananas. Let the mixture stand for 10 to 30 minutes, during which the bananas will begin to soften. The mixture should be rather thick but easily spoonable. Stir in an additional tablespoon or two of milk, if needed, and a touch more sugar if you think it will enhance the bananas. Scatter berries over the bananas and serve.

BIG-LEAGUE BANANAS

Other than Carmen Miranda, the person most closely associated with the banana may be Dick Foster, whose name graces one of the richest preparations possible for the humble fruit. The famed Brennan's restaurant in New Orleans created Bananas Foster in the 1950s and christened it in honor of the distinguished patron, who was then serving on the Vice Committee charged with cleaning up the city's French Quarter. The tableside preparation features banana slices sautéed in butter, flamed with rum and liqueur, and plated on top of ice cream, making it a tad overboard for the average home breakfast.

SAUTÉED BANANAS WITH MILK PUNCH SAUCE

[My father's] special oh-so-good-peachy breakfast consisted of fried bananas, ham or Canadian bacon, and eggs. If you try this some morning, fry the ham or bacon in a separate pan and fry the bananas in plenty of butter. When they're done, set them aside on heated plates, add a little more butter, and fry the eggs in the butter and juice of the bananas. It's a superb dish and as good to go to bed on as to start the day on.

Trader Vic, *Trader Vic's Book of Food & Drink* (1946)

If you have to eat breakfast on the run, bananas on the peel are a good fruit for the purpose, like apples, but we usually prefer them cooked. The make-ahead sauce for this sauté is inspired by a favorite southern morning beverage, the innocent-sounding but potent milk punch. Serve the bananas as part of a festive weekend breakfast with Fried Quail and Andouille Sausage Bayou Style (page 152) or Country Ham with Sautéed Hominy (page 132). **SERVES 6**

MILK PUNCH SAUCE
1 cup whole milk
½ cup heavy (whipping) cream
3 large egg yolks
3 tablespoons sugar
¼ cup brandy
¼ teaspoon freshly grated nutmeg

4 tablespoons (½ stick) unsalted butter

3 large or 4 medium bananas, halved crosswise then sliced lengthwise
¼ to ⅓ cup chopped pecans, optional
1 tablespoon cane syrup or packed light or dark brown sugar

Whisk the milk, cream, egg yolks, sugar, 2 tablespoons of the brandy, and the nutmeg together in a heavy medium saucepan over medium-low heat. Cook just below a simmer, whisking frequently, until the mixture thickens lightly into a sauce that just clings to the whisk, about 10 minutes. Do not let the mixture boil. Whisk in the remaining brandy. The sauce can be used warm or covered and chilled for up to 2 days, in which case it will thicken a bit.

Shortly before you plan to serve the bananas, melt the butter in a medium skillet over medium heat. Sauté the bananas (and pecans, if you are using them) briefly until just soft, turning once gently. Stir in the cane syrup and remove from the heat. Spoon the bananas into bowls. Top with a healthy drizzle of milk punch sauce, thinned if necessary with a little milk or water, and serve. Any leftover sauce can be drizzled over ice cream or pound cake.

STRAWBERRY TOAST

SELECTIONS FROM THE BREAKFAST MENU AT THE HOTEL BRUNSWICK IN NEW YORK CITY, 1886

FRUIT

Cantaloupe   Pears

Watermelon   Plums

Blackberries with cream   Apples

Raspberries with cream   Oranges

Hot-House Grapes   Bananas

American cooks have dipped and dunked toast in innumerable liquids. We found this interesting approach, which produces something of an instant jam, in a World War II publication *New American Cook Book* (1941), edited by Lily Haxworth Wallace. Use quality strawberries only, most likely available from a "U-pick" field or a local farmer. The standard supermarket white-at-the-core fruit, raised for good shipping year-round, won't cut it here. If that's all you can find, substitute huckleberries, blueberries, or halved cherries.   **SERVES 4**

4 cups hulled and thickly sliced fresh strawberries

½ cup sugar

4 large slices good white bread

Place the berries and sugar in a medium saucepan and cover with ¾ cup water. Cook over medium heat until boiling, then remove the berries from the liquid with a slotted spoon, reserving the liquid.

Toast the bread until lightly brown and slice each piece on the diagonal. Dip the pieces into the liquid syrup just long enough to soften. Arrange 2 pieces on each plate and top with equal portions of strawberries and syrup. Serve warm.

BREAKFAST AMBROSIA

A longstanding southern holiday dessert, but a fine breakfast option then or at other times, ambrosia can be as simple as orange slices and coconut. It's even better supplemented with other fruit, but resist marshmallows, Jell-O, or anything creamy. For a special treat, use freshly cracked and shredded coconut prepared as described in the following tip, which gives you the plus of using the coconut water for extra flavoring. Ambrosia is best when made the night before.

SERVES 4 TO 6

3 medium to large oranges

2 tangerines or another orange

1 to 3 tablespoons confectioners' sugar, optional

¾ to 1 cup unsweetened shredded coconut (see Ingredient Tip)

1 cup fresh pineapple chunks or halved small fresh figs, optional

Coconut water from a fresh coconut, sweet white wine, brandy, or curaçao or other orange-flavored liqueur, optional

Set an orange on its side and slice off the top and bottom ends with a paring knife, cutting just deeply enough to expose the fruit itself. Set the orange on one of the sliced ends and peel it by slicing down and around the orange from top to bottom, following its contour all around the fruit. Repeat with the remaining oranges and tangerines. Slice the oranges and tangerines crosswise into ¼-inch rounds and combine.

Ambrosia looks prettiest layered in a crystal or glass bowl. Arrange a thick layer of oranges and tangerines in the bottom of the bowl, then add a sprinkling of sugar and enough coconut to cover lightly. If using the pineapple or figs, add half now. Continue alternating oranges, sugar, coconut, and pineapple, saving enough coconut to top off the salad with a generous layer. Pour coconut water or a healthy splash of one of the alcoholic options over the ambrosia, along with any remaining fruit juices. Refrigerate for at least 2 hours and preferably overnight.

STRAWBERRY AMBROSIA

Florida isn't as renowned for strawberries as for citrus fruit, but the state does produce a substantial commercial crop in the early spring. In season some local cooks substitute the berries for the oranges in ambrosia, creating a sprightly variation. Use about 2 pounds strawberries, thickly sliced, in place of the oranges and add a light sprinkling of confectioners' sugar to each layer. Pour 1 cup fresh orange juice over the ambrosia prior to the last coating of sugar and coconut. Eat this version within an hour or so for the best flavor and texture.

COCONUT ODYSSEY

Coconut probably originated in Southeast Asia, but the buoyant fruit managed to sail itself to other areas of the world. In one of the first commercial shipments to the United States, nineteenth-century growers sent a whole boatload of coconuts to Philadelphia as payment for a Caribbean flour shipment. The recipient was miller Franklin Baker, whose name remains today on Baker's coconut, chocolate, and other baking products. He popularized coconut nationwide by developing the grating and drying process for the shreds still sold commonly today.

HONEYED ORANGES WITH JALAPEÑOS

**SELECTIONS FROM THE
BREAKFAST MENU AT THE
SANFORD HOUSE HOTEL
IN FLORIDA, 1881**

Oranges

Hominy   Cracked Wheat

Broiled Shad

Hashed Potatoes   Fried Potatoes

Citrus and spice, a natural combination in the Southwest, has traveled the country far and wide in recent decades. This preparation makes a real eye-opener, though it's only mildly hot. We prefer it with a combination of orange cousins, including a blood orange or two, but use what you can find.

SERVES 4 OR MORE

1 large navel orange

2 medium tangerines or Satsumas

2 medium blood oranges

1 to 2 tablespoons orange-blossom
or other honey

½ to 1 fresh red or green jalapeño,
finely chopped

Slice the navel orange, unpeeled, into rounds about ⅓ inch thick. Slice the smaller citrus into rounds about ¼ inch thick. Reserve the end pieces of each fruit, then arrange the rest on a platter, more or less overlapping. Squeeze the end pieces over the fruit. Drizzle with some or all of the honey. Sprinkle with the jalapeño. Allow to sit at least 20 minutes at room temperature for peak flavor. We eat this with a combination of fork and fingers, leaving most of the peel and white pith behind.

HONEYED POMEGRANATE ORANGES

For a milder dish, replace the jalapeño with pomegranate seeds.

SPANISH-AMERICAN CITRUS

Spanish explorers and settlers introduced citrus fruits to both Florida and California early in our national history. Columbus brought oranges to the New World on his second voyage, and Ponce de León probably planted some in Florida by 1513. A freeze in 1835 killed almost every tree in the state except for some on the Indian River, a wide, long tidal lagoon on the east coast. Graftings from the surviving trees led to the expansion of groves in this more protected area and the birth of the Indian River citrus industry, still thriving today.

Spanish priests introduced citrus orchards in the West when they established missions in California in the first decades of the eighteenth century. Following the end of Mexican rule in 1848, William Wolfskill, a transplanted Kentuckian, became the first commercial grower in the region. The coming of the railroad provided a transportation link with the rest of the country, quickly stimulating orange cultivation. The first shipment of fruit from California arrived in St. Louis in 1877, still in good shape after four weeks in transit.

BROILED GRAPEFRUIT

A few Florida farms established grapefruit groves by the early nineteenth century, but the fruit didn't become well known throughout the country until the Depression, when the government gave free citrus to the unemployed. Even then, welfare agencies reported, many people remained suspicious, saying they had boiled their grapefruit for hours and it was still too tough to eat. Try this as an alternative cooking method.

SERVES 4

2 large pink or red grapefruit (we prefer Rio Star or Ruby Red), halved, at room temperature (see Ingredient Tip)

3 tablespoons sugar

1½ teaspoons unbleached all-purpose flour

¼ teaspoon ground cinnamon or freshly grated nutmeg

1½ tablespoons unsalted butter, softened

Fresh mint sprigs

Section each grapefruit half, cutting the fruit away from the skin and membranes but leaving the halves intact.

Heat the broiler.

Combine the sugar, flour, and cinnamon in a small bowl. With a fork, mash the butter into the dry ingredients. Smear equal portions of the mixture over each grapefruit half. Place the grapefruit on a baking sheet and broil at least several inches from the heat for about 5 minutes, until the topping is bubbly and light brown. Arrange each grapefruit half in a shallow bowl or on a small plate, garnish with mint, and serve.

SPICE-SCENTED BROILED GRAPEFRUIT

Anything Marjorie Kinnan Rawlings says about Florida food is worth hearing. In her *Cross Creek Cookery* (1942), the Pulitzer Prize–winning author and noted hostess topped Indian River grapefruit with a light coating of brown sugar, a pinch or two of cloves, and dots of butter before cooking as directed. The arbiters of hosting success at *Gourmet* magazine, in a 1996 brunch article, recommended a more involved idea for their topping, grinding granulated sugar with a tablespoon of chopped crystallized ginger and a good splash of pure vanilla extract in a spice grinder.

CANTALOUPE WITH COUNTRY HAM AND REDEYE GRAVY

We learned about this southern specialty from regional food authority Damon Lee Fowler. It may sound at first like an odd combination, but it's similar in many respects to the classic pairing of Italian prosciutto and melon.

SERVES 4

1 small ripe cantaloupe, cut into 8 wedges, at room temperature

1 tablespoon bacon drippings or unsalted butter

4 slices uncooked moist country ham or other smoky ham, about ¼ inch thick (about 2 ounces each)

1 tablespoon unbleached all-purpose flour

1 cup freshly brewed coffee

Salt and freshly milled black pepper to taste

Slice the skin off the cantaloupe wedges and arrange them on 4 plates.

Prepare the ham and gravy, first melting the drippings in a large heavy skillet over medium-high heat. Slash the edges of the ham's exterior fat to keep the slices from curling while cooking. Fry the ham slices in batches until lightly browned and a bit crispy on the edges, about 2 minutes per side. Arrange the ham slices over and between the cantaloupe slices.

Whisk the flour into the pan drippings. Pour in the coffee and scrape up any browned bits from the bottom of the skillet. Add at least ¼ cup water or more for a milder coffee jolt. Cook for just a couple of minutes, enough to thicken just a bit. Taste the gravy and add salt and pepper as needed. Spoon the gravy equally over the ham and cantaloupe and serve immediately.

SUMMER MELON SALAD

TECHNIQUE TIP

You can always add other summer fruits to a melon salad, chunked in sizes similar to the melon. Choose fruit that remains firm when ripe, such as plums, grapes, or nectarines, rather than peaches, raspberries, or other, softer fruits that will deteriorate in the mix.

The Picayune's Creole Cook Book (1901) declared, "Muskmelons and Watermelons are among our most common articles of food, and are within the reach of all classes, rich and poor, white and black, in season." The authors spoke of the New Orleans of a hundred years ago, but the statement is true of the entire country today. Melon salads don't really require a recipe, so use this as a general guide rather than a prescription, picking and mixing the ripest and most colorful varieties you can find. Unlike many fruits, fine summer melons are so naturally sweet that you can serve them icy cold without deadening the flavor.

SERVES 4

3 to 4 tablespoons fresh lime juice

1 tablespoon or more sugar

Pinch of salt, optional

About 3 cups cubed watermelon

About 2 cups cubed honeydew or other green-fleshed melon

About 2 cups cubed cantaloupe or muskmelon

2 tablespoons minced fresh mint, lemon verbena, or lemon balm

Fresh mint sprigs

Combine the lime juice with the sugar and the salt if desired. Arrange the melon cubes on a platter or shallow serving bowl and toss with the juice mixture. Let sit for a few minutes for the juices to combine or refrigerate, covered, up to overnight. Mix in the minced mint and garnish individual portions with mint sprigs just before serving.

POACHED DRIED FRUIT COMPOTE

Drying fruit developed as a way to preserve the bounty of summer into the winter, just like canning. Cooks rehydrated the fruit as needed, stewing or simmering it in a flavorful liquid. We still find dried fruit useful in the winter, when fresh options look peaked and tired from a journey halfway around the world. We like this compote full of contrasting shapes, colors, and textures. It keeps well, so don't hesitate to make the whole batch. **SERVES 8 OR MORE**

4 cups mixed dried fruit, such as prunes, figs, pears, apricots, peaches, apples, cherries, or cranberries (see Ingredient Tip)

½ cup packed light brown sugar

1 tablespoon chopped candied crystallized ginger

1 cinnamon stick

1 or 2 lemon slices or a squeeze or two of fresh lemon juice

About 1 cup shortbread or vanilla wafer crumbs, optional

Combine the fruit, brown sugar, ginger, and cinnamon with 2 cups water in a large saucepan. Bring the mixture to a boil over high heat, then reduce to a bare simmer and cook until the fruit is quite tender, 10 to 20 minutes, depending on the dryness of the fruit and the kinds used. Add the lemon and remove from the heat. The fruit can be served immediately but will develop a more complex flavor if steeped overnight. Serve chilled or at room temperature. When ready to serve, spoon it into bowls with a bit of the syrup, then top with shortbread crumbs if you wish and serve. The fruit keeps well for at least several days.

CURRIED FRUIT COMPOTE

Stir about 2 teaspoons curry powder into the syrup with the ginger and cinnamon. We prefer to let this steep overnight, but then warm it again before serving. Eliminate the shortbread topping.

DRIED APRICOT–CHERRY COMPOTE

Sometimes a mix of many fruits can detract from other flavors in a meal. When you want a version with a bit more restraint, try this. The colors are still festive, and the tang of the cherries enlivens the lush but blander apricots. Use about 3 cups dried apricot halves and 1 cup dried cherries, eliminating the ginger from the syrup.

CHERRY-RICE COMPOTE

TECHNIQUE TIP

A mixture of fruit in syrup, compotes range broadly in ingredients and style. Typically you make syrup by adding twice the amount of water or other liquid to the amount of sweetener, perhaps sugar, brown sugar, or honey. Common aromatics include a teaspoon or more of vanilla, orange-flower water, rose water, cinnamon, nutmeg, and allspice. For special breakfasts, use a vanilla bean or stick cinnamon. Don't overlook herbal possibilities. Lavender flowers or leaves of lemon verbena, mint, and even rosemary or thyme can contribute signature notes to a compote. A little lemon or lime juice adds pizzazz and balances the sweetness. Just choose the mix judiciously for compatibility. We especially like seedless green and red grape halves in clove syrup, papaya with lime syrup, blood orange sections with honey and orange-flower water syrup, pears in rosemary syrup, apples in cinnamon and nutmeg syrup, and peaches with vanilla and allspice syrup. Use leftover syrup to top ice cream or frozen yogurt.

Called a compote, but closer to a cherry rice pudding, this is a soothing delight by any name.

SERVES 4

¼ cup short-grain rice

1¼ cups whole milk

Pinch of salt

1 large egg yolk

¼ cup sugar

2 tablespoons heavy (whipping) cream or half-and-half

¼ teaspoon pure vanilla extract

1 cup fresh or frozen cherries, preferably sour "pie" cherries

Ground cinnamon or cardamom

Combine the rice, milk, and salt in a medium saucepan. Bring to a boil (this has a tendency to boil over), then reduce the heat to medium-low, cover, and cook for 30 to 35 minutes, until the rice is very soft and several tablespoons of liquid remain.

While the rice cooks, whisk the egg yolk, 2 tablespoons of the sugar, the cream, and the vanilla together in a small bowl. Whisk until the mixture is light yellow and thick and reserve.

Also while the rice cooks, prepare the cherries. Place them in a small saucepan with the remaining 2 tablespoons sugar and 2 tablespoons water. Simmer over medium heat briefly, just until the cherries soften and give up some of their juice, so that a light syrup forms.

When the rice is ready, and while still hot, whisk the egg yolk mixture into it, stirring constantly. There should be enough residual heat to cook the egg yolk through. Stir the cherry mixture into the rice and serve warm, dusted with cinnamon. Leftovers keep for several days and can be served chilled or rewarmed in a microwave oven or double boiler. Add a bit of milk if the compote is too thick to stir easily.

QUINCES AND CRANBERRIES IN SYRUP

English colonists introduced the country to quinces, a fall and winter fruit that prospered in the past. It fell from favor in our quest for fast preparations because long, slow cooking is required to bring out the wonderful apple-pear-berry flavor. Quinces are enjoying a well-deserved renaissance now, stimulated largely by what they add to dishes like this. The fruit turns rosy cooked by itself and is even more festively bright with crimson cranberries in the pot.

SERVES 6 OR MORE

2 cups sugar

2 pounds (3 to 4 large) ripe quinces

One 12-ounce bag fresh cranberries

Grated zest of 1 orange or 2 tangerines, minced, or 1 or 2 tablespoons fresh orange or tangerine juice, optional

Make the syrup, combining the sugar in a medium nonreactive saucepan with 1 quart water, then bringing it to a simmer over medium heat. While the syrup heats, peel the first quince, slicing it lengthwise into ½-inch chunks. Cut quinces brown quickly, so put the fruit into the simmering water as soon as it is sliced. Repeat with the remaining quinces. Reduce the heat to low, cover, and cook for about 30 minutes, until soft and dusky in color. Add the cranberries, turn up the heat to medium-high, and cook, uncovered, until the cranberries are soft, about 10 minutes longer. Add a bit more hot water if the mixture gets overly thick. The fruit can be served warm or refrigerated for up to a week. Serve in bowls or goblets with some of the syrup. Portions can be topped with orange zest or juice if you wish.

A BREAKFAST MENU SUGGESTION FROM THE NATIONAL CRANBERRY ASSOCIATION

Chilled Grapefruit Juice with Mint

Chicken à la King in Pattie Shells

Cranberry Sauce Hearts

Parsley Potato Balls

Carrot Sticks

Celery Curls

Bowknot Rolls

Strawberry Preserves

Wedding Cake

Ice Cream Molds

Black Coffee

From an undated promotional pamphlet from the National Cranberry Association

PERSIMMON AND MIXED FALL FRUIT MEDLEY

The distinctive taste of persimmon adds punch to a mixture of fall fruits. When timing the readiness of a persimmon for eating, bear in mind the comment of Jamestown founder Captain John Smith, who cautioned, "If it not be ripe it will draw a man's mouth awry with much torment, but when it is ripe it is as delicious as an apricock."

SERVES 4 OR MORE

1½ pounds (about 4) ripe persimmons (see Ingredient Tip)

1 to 2 tablespoons orange marmalade or apricot jam or preserves

A squeeze or two of fresh lemon juice

1 ripe large pear, such as Comice or Red Bartlett, cut into thin lengthwise slices

4 fresh figs, halved, or 4 dried figs simmered in water until soft, then halved

¼ teaspoon ground cardamom, optional

Slice the persimmons in half and spoon out all of the pulp into a medium bowl. Add enough of the marmalade and lemon juice to heighten the fruit's sweetness. Mix with the pear and figs and the cardamom if you wish. Let sit for about 30 minutes at room temperature. Serve spooned into bowls or goblets.

TROPICAL FRUIT PARFAIT

INGREDIENT TIP

The starfruit, or carambola, can be found in winter months in well-stocked supermarkets or in Latin markets. It looks like a little golden-ribbed zeppelin. Occasionally one is inexplicably sour, so we always buy at least two. If bought fresh, they keep in the refrigerator crisper for up to a couple of weeks. The fruit's slightly waxy skin is so thin that it needs no peeling. When sliced crosswise into the namesake stars, the fruit should be juicy and a bit crisp.

This cheery parfait starts with a pineapple base and incorporates other tropical fruits as available into a bowl of sunshine. A creamy coconut sauce tops the fruit and melds the flavors.

SERVES 4 TO 6

TROPICAL CREAM SAUCE

1 large banana, cut into chunks

One 8-ounce can cream of coconut (not coconut milk)

Juice of ½ orange, 1 tangerine, or 1 small passion fruit

1 to 2 tablespoons fresh lime juice

1 small fresh pineapple, cut into small neat chunks (3 to 4 cups with juice)

1 small papaya or mango, diced

1 small banana, ripe but still firm, diced

1 to 2 kiwis fruit, peeled and diced, or 1 tablespoon freshly grated lime zest

Minced fresh mint to taste

1 starfruit, sliced crosswise into ⅓-inch-thick stars (see Ingredient Tip), optional

Fresh mint sprigs or lime wedges

Prepare the sauce. Combine the banana, cream of coconut, orange juice, and 1 tablespoon of the lime juice in a blender until smooth. Add the rest of the lime juice if the mixture seems overly sweet. (The sauce can be made a day ahead, covered, and refrigerated.)

Spoon a small layer of pineapple into the bottom of parfait glasses, wineglasses, or glass bowls. Top with 1 or 2 tablespoons of the sauce. Mix the papaya, banana, kiwi fruit, and minced mint together, then use about half of the mixture to make another layer in the glasses. Top each again with 1 to 2 tablespoons of the sauce then divide the remaining pineapple among the glasses. Spoon additional sauce over the pineapple. If using starfruit, top each parfait with a star or two, standing the fruit up on edge. Garnish with mint or lime and serve. (Extra sauce keeps for several days, ready to dress your next fruit parfait or salad.)

TROPICAL CREAM SAUCE WITH MIXED BERRIES

Mix strawberries, raspberries, and blueberries, depending on what you have available locally. Use at least 4 cups, filling in if you wish with banana or kiwi fruit for more texture or color. With a slight adjustment the sauce is scrumptious with these more fragile fruits. Eliminate the lime juice and reduce the amount of orange juice to about 1 tablespoon.

It is morning—sunlight already brilliant on coral roadway and garden wall. . . . The patio is still shady, so put a green cloth on the old iron table, and let me bring you some chilled papaya, your morning coffee Havana style if you like, fresh Cuban bread with perhaps some carissa jelly for it, and a fluffy omelet with just a pinch of oregano in it. Work can wait . . . there is always mañana.

Key West Woman's Club, *Key West Cook Book* (1949)

THE NOBLE PINEAPPLE

The pineapple waxes and wanes in popularity, but it reached its all-time peak of fashionableness just shortly after early Spanish explorers found the fruit in the New World. It quickly became a sensation in Europe, particularly England, where aristocrats insisted on growing it in their inhospitable clime in elaborate greenhouses called *pineries*. The fruit became such a symbol of nobility, wealth, and graciousness that people rented pineapples by the night for dinner-party centerpieces. Woodworkers carved its likeness as accents in grand homes, and it returned to the New World colonies in this form as a design motif, still used today on replicas of old plantation-style four-poster beds.

POACHED GUAVAS WITH CREAMY CHEESE

INGREDIENT TIP

Guavas are picked when still firm and green and should be allowed to soften at room temperature before being used. They develop a rich, musky fragrance when ready. The fleshy skin, often called a *shell,* turns pale or deep pink when ripe and may have a yellow tinge. Peel it away only in spots that are badly blemished. We favor scooping out the seedy center before cooking, but it can be removed after cooking too. The seeds come out a little more readily then, but it's a messier process.

Though guavas can be eaten raw, it is difficult to separate the pulp from the seeds. They are more often baked or poached until tender or cooked down further into a paste or jelly. We like the fruit with several styles of cheese, from assertive choices such as manchego or even Roquefort to this mild creamy cheese blend.

SERVES 4

8 small guavas (about 2 inches in diameter), firm but ripe (see Ingredient Tip)

1 cup sugar

Zest from 1 small lemon or 1 large lime

3 whole cloves

½ vanilla bean, sliced in half lengthwise

CHEESE TOPPING

¾ cup ricotta cheese

¼ cup plain yogurt or crème fraîche (crema)

Cut the guavas in half, more or less lengthwise. Scoop out the center seeds, preferably with a serrated grapefruit knife or spoon or a melon baller.

Combine the sugar with 2 cups water in a large saucepan. Add the lemon zest, cloves, and vanilla bean. Bring to a boil over high heat. Add the guavas to the sugar syrup, then reduce the heat to a bare simmer and cook until tender, about 10 minutes. Remove from the heat and let sit until cool.

Retrieve the vanilla bean from the syrup and, with a small sharp knife, scrape out the remaining seeds. Discard the bean and, in a small bowl, stir the vanilla seeds with the ricotta and yogurt. Serve the guavas in shallow bowls with a dollop of the cheese mixture in the cavity of each.

STEEPED PRUNES

Valued for years mainly for purging properties, rather than taste, prunes are the most unfairly maligned of all breakfast fruits. Even people who love the flavorful plum, the fresh version of the fruit, often avoid the dried form because of its reputation. At their best, as in this preparation, prunes evoke their roots strongly, offering a deeply concentrated essence of plum.

SERVES 4 OR MORE

1 cup packed light or dark brown sugar

1 tablespoon cider vinegar

2 cinnamon sticks

1 teaspoon whole allspice, bruised

1 pound large pitted prunes

½ lemon, thinly sliced

6 tablespoons dark or light rum

Combine the brown sugar, vinegar, cinnamon, and allspice with 2 cups water in a large saucepan. Bring to a boil over high heat, then add the prunes, reduce the heat to a simmer, and cook until the prunes are plump and tender, about 20 minutes. Stir in the lemon and rum while still hot and let steep for 10 minutes. Serve warm or cover and keep chilled for up to several days.

ANISE AND PORT STEEPED PRUNES

Eliminate the vinegar, allspice, and rum and reduce the water to 1 cup. Add 1 cup inexpensive port and 1 teaspoon bruised anise seeds to the brown sugar, cinnamon, and water.

FRUIT NOT A DAINTY DISH

Thomas Jefferson Murrey wrote one of the first American cookbooks focused entirely on breakfast. His 1887 *Breakfast Dainties* covered foods such as fresh fruit, toast, eggs, potatoes, and much more in individual chapters devoted to those subjects. In a different, special section on "dainty dishes" for the morning, Murrey proposed artichokes, lamb chops with French peas, tripe, soft-shell crabs, sardines, smelts, and squab.

ROASTED FRUIT WITH VANILLA SUGAR

Quick, high-heat roasting of fruit concentrates and caramelizes its natural sugar. For this preparation we like to use stone fruits such as peaches, plums, or apricots and other soft-textured fruit like figs, sprinkled with aromatic vanilla sugar. Top with a drizzle of vanilla-flavored yogurt or softly whipped cream for a more special presentation.

SERVES 4

1 vanilla bean

1 cup sugar

1½ pounds soft-textured fruits of at least 2 kinds, such as peaches, plums, apricots, nectarines, plucots, and figs

1 tablespoon almond or walnut oil

Preheat the oven to 400°F.

Process the vanilla bean in a food processor until it is chopped into rough pieces. Add the sugar and continue to process until the sugar is infused with the vanilla's flavor and turns a uniform warm brown color. Pour the sugar through a strainer to sift out the vanilla bean chunks and discard them. The sugar is ready to use or can be stored airtight for weeks.

Cut the pitted fruit in half or into quarters, depending on size. Toss it gently with the oil. Arrange in a single layer on a baking sheet and sprinkle with 2 to 3 tablespoons of the vanilla sugar. Roast the fruit for 10 to 12 minutes, until soft and tender but not cooked down to mush. Serve warm.

BUTTERSCOTCH BAKED PEARS

I cannot count the good people I know who, to my mind, would be even better if they bent their spirits to the study of their own hungers. There are too many of us, otherwise in proper focus, who feel an impatience for the demands of our bodies, and who try throughout our whole lives, none too successfully, to deafen ourselves to the voices of our various hungers. Some stuff the wax of religious solace in our ears. Others practice a Spartan if somewhat pretentious disinterest in the pleasures of the flesh, or pretend that if we do not admit our sensual delight in a ripe nectarine we are not guilty . . . of even that tiny lust!

M.F.K. Fisher, *How to Cook a Wolf* (1951)

In the days of hearth cooking, kids and adults alike enjoyed skewering fruits on sticks and roasting them over the live fire, concentrating the natural sugars and enhancing the silky texture. Baking fruit in the modern oven produces a similar effect. Most cooks choose apples for oven roasting, but pears make a luscious alternative.

SERVES 4 OR MORE

4 medium to large pears, firm but ripe (see Ingredient Tip)

4 tablespoons (½ stick) unsalted butter

¼ cup packed light or dark brown sugar

⅛ teaspoon salt

¼ cup heavy (whipping) cream

½ teaspoon pure vanilla extract

2 teaspoons bourbon, rum, or Scotch whiskey, optional

Chopped walnuts, hickory nuts, or pecans, optional

Preheat the oven to 375°F.

Peel the pears and halve them vertically. With a melon baller or small spoon, scoop out the hard core of each.

Melt the butter in an 8- to 10-inch ovenproof skillet (or other pan or dish that can go from stovetop to oven) over medium heat. Stir in the brown sugar and salt, then add the pears in a single layer, cut sides down. Spoon some of the butter mixture over the pears.

Transfer the skillet to the oven and bake the pears until soft, 15 to 20 minutes, basting once with the butter mixture while they bake. Remove the pears from the skillet and arrange them on a rimmed platter or in a large shallow bowl. Return the skillet to the stovetop and mix in the cream, vanilla, and, if you wish, the bourbon. Bring to a boil and reduce by about half, until very thick, stirring and keeping a close eye on the mixture. Pour the sauce over the pears. Garnish with nuts if you wish and serve warm.

BAKED RHUBARB

INGREDIENT TIP

We've been surprised to discover lately that some cooks don't know that rhubarb leaves are poisonous, with a high concentration of oxalic acid. Use only the stalks in cooking.

———

SELECTIONS FROM THE BREAKFAST MENU ON THE PENNSYLVANIA RAILROAD, 1899

Orange Marmalade

Preserved Cherries

Broiled Spring Chicken on Toast

Baked Beans

———

A spring favorite of American cooks in past generations, rhubarb is beginning to surge in popularity once again. Used so commonly as a pie filling that it earned the nickname of "pie plant," it's also frequently made into a cooked sauce. We used to boil the sauce until thick and mushy, the usual approach, but recently found this tasty alternative in a spiral-bound Oklahoma cookbook, *Long Lost Recipes of Aunt Susan* (1989).   **SERVES 4 OR MORE**

2 pounds rhubarb, fresh or frozen   1½ to 2 cups sugar
(see Ingredient Tip)

Preheat the oven to 325°F.

Slice the rhubarb into ¾-inch chunks using a sharp knife. (Make sure you cut all the way through the stalks, without leaving strings of peel, so that the chunks will hold their shape while baking.) Arrange the rhubarb in a baking dish that lets you pile it an inch or two deep. Pour the sugar over the rhubarb and stir lightly, allowing it to trickle down between the chunks. Cover the dish and bake for 30 minutes. Stir to combine the rhubarb and melting sugar evenly and return the uncovered dish to the oven for 5 to 10 minutes longer, until tender but not mushy. Serve warm or chilled. Leftovers keep well for several days.

POACHED FIGS, OLD MARYLAND STYLE

INGREDIENT TIP

The wild black walnut, long cherished for its intense flavor, has begun to appear in specialty food stores, usually shelled. The nuts turn rancid more quickly out of their shells, so store them in the freezer to keep them at peak flavor. Black walnut pieces can be ordered by mail from Sunnyland Farms in Albany, Georgia (800-999-2488). If you don't have time to order ahead, substitute hickory nuts or pecans rather than the mild English walnuts.

Poached, stewed, and baked figs, along with fig preserves and pickled figs, used to appear regularly on American tables. The inspiration for this version comes from a classic regional cookbook, *Maryland's Way* (1963), which says the idea dates back to 1835 Annapolis. If you can't find fresh figs, you can poach dried figs in the same manner by halving the amount of fruit and doubling the amount of water used for the syrup. We prepare this the night before we plan to serve it.   **SERVES 6 OR MORE**

½ cup sugar

½ cup chopped black walnuts (see Ingredient Tip)

Minced zest of 1 large orange

1½ pounds plump ripe fresh figs, stemmed

1 to 2 tablespoons chopped black walnuts, toasted

Combine the sugar, walnuts, and orange zest with 1 cup water in a heavy pan. Bring the mixture to a boil, stirring to dissolve the sugar. Reduce the heat to a simmer, add the figs, and cook until the fruit is just tender, about 15 minutes. Scoop out the figs with a slotted spoon and place them in a bowl. (It's OK if you take a few walnuts out with the fruit. They'll all end up in the same place eventually.)

Continue simmering the cooking liquid briefly until it is reduced to about ½ cup. Pour the syrup over the figs, sprinkle with walnuts, and serve warm or chilled. Leftovers will keep for several days, refrigerated.

POACHED FIGS, NEW MARYLAND STYLE

On the PBS series "Chesapeake Bay Cooking," a modern Maryland cook, Mealy Sartori of Baltimore's Little Italy, demonstrated how she stews figs Italian-American style. She scents the cooking liquid with half a cinnamon stick and layers the cooked figs with zabaglione, a frothy stovetop custard. Prepare the zabaglione by whisking together 8 egg yolks with ½ cup sugar in the top of a double boiler over barely simmering water. When it's pale yellow and creamy, whisk in 1 cup dry Marsala. Continue whisking until foamy and thickened, about 3 to 5 minutes.

TAPIOCA FRUIT SOUP

TECHNIQUE TIP

You can, instead, prepare just the liquid fruit soup "base." Then each morning, cut fruit into your bowl and simply pour the chilled liquid over it.

———

A BREAKFAST MENU SUGGESTION FOR A "PERFECTLY NORMAL PERSON"

One Red Apple with Combination Nut Butter

One Ounce Protoid Nuts

Five or Six Black Dates

One Glass Milk

Eugene Christian and Mollie Griswold Christian, *Uncooked Foods and How to Use Them* (1904)

———

Our friend B. J. Weil spent many summer days on her maternal grandmother's farm in eastern Oklahoma. When we started working on this book, she asked if we could re-create the refreshing fruit soup that her grandmother prepared frequently for breakfast. B. J. thinks the idea came originally from a recipe on a box of tapioca but was adapted to accommodate locally available fresh fruit. A lovely way to start the day, the soup makes a fine alternative to a smoothie.

SERVES 4

⅓ cup sugar or more to taste

3 tablespoons instant or granulated tapioca

Pinch of salt

3 cups fruit juice, such as orange, tangerine, white grape, cranberry, cran-apple, watermelon, or mango

2 cups mixed soft-textured fruits such as sliced strawberries, peaches, apricots, plums, papayas, or mangoes, halved grapes, or tangerine or clementine segments

Juice of ½ lemon or lime, optional

Stir the sugar, tapioca, and salt together in a medium saucepan. Mix in the fruit juice and let stand for 5 minutes. Bring to a full boil over medium-high heat, stirring occasionally. Remove from the heat and let stand until lukewarm.

Place the fruit in a large bowl, then pour the liquid over. Add more sugar if you wish, stirring it in to dissolve. Refrigerate for at least 1 hour and up to overnight. Cover the soup if you plan to chill it longer than an hour or two. Taste before serving and add a squeeze of lemon or lime if you think either would enhance the soup.

TAPIOCA FRUIT PUDDING

You can make dairyless puddings in a similar way by reducing the amount of liquid to 2 cups and leaving out the fruit, which you can save for a garnish instead. We especially like this with frozen or bottled pomegranate juice—easiest to find in the late fall and winter months—and a topping of garnetlike pomegranate seeds, found fresh at the same time.

12

Potatoes, Tomatoes, Grits, Greens, and Beans

WHETHER YOU'RE looking for a side dish to go with eggs or a main dish for the center of the plate, American breakfast vegetables never disappoint. It's true that "never" stretches the realm of the imaginable, but so do top versions of hash browns, fried green tomatoes, and creamy grits—all among the finest food classics ever created in the country.

American cooks keep embellishing the tradition too, adding tasty new options such as chipotle potato pancakes and eggless scrambles featuring a mix of vegetables. These new favorites expand our breakfast repertoire but stay clearly within the established heritage of heartiness. From today's innovations with fresh greens to the home fries your mother used to make, we've learned a wealth of ways to veg out in the morning. Never neglect the opportunities.

HEAVENLY HASH BROWNS

TECHNIQUE TIP

If you want to rev up your enthusiasm for cooking breakfast, buy a griddle that fits over two burners on your stove, preferably a cast-iron version coated with a nonstick surface. Perfect for many preparations of potatoes, tomatoes, bacon, sausage, pancakes, and more, a griddle allows you to cook two or even three dishes side by side at the same time. You work more quickly and efficiently, simplify the cleanup, and just have more fun with the scooping, scraping, and turning.

Like other skillet-browned hash dishes, our most popular breakfast potato treat owes its genesis to lowly leftovers. Cooks reclaimed uneaten potatoes from the night before by simply cutting them up, adding butter and cream, and frying them in bacon drippings. The result is so good you wonder why you bothered with the dinner step anyway.

SERVES 4 AS A MAIN DISH, UP TO 6 AS A SIDE DISH

2¼ to 2½ pounds (about 4 large) cooked (preferably baked) russet or Yukon Gold potatoes, cooled and peeled

4 tablespoons (½ stick) unsalted butter, melted

¼ cup heavy (whipping) cream

¼ to ½ cup minced scallions

Salt and freshly milled pepper to taste

Approximately ¼ cup bacon drippings or additional unsalted butter

Either shred the potatoes on the large holes of a box grater or chop them finely but rather roughly. You want a little bit of texture. Place the potatoes in a mixing bowl. Pour the butter and cream over them, then toss to combine. Stir in the scallions and add generous amounts of salt and pepper. Melt the bacon drippings on a griddle or in a large heavy skillet over medium heat. Make 8 potato "cakes," scooping the mixture up with your fingers and patting it together loosely, no thicker than about ½ inch. Gently plop the cakes onto the griddle. Plan on a total cooking time of 5 to 7 minutes. Cook the hash browns without disturbing them for at least 2 minutes, so that the crust can develop. Check the underside of the potatoes and turn when richly brown and crusty. Repeat with the second side and serve hot.

SAGE AND CHEDDAR HASH BROWNS

Reduce the cream by half, then add ½ cup grated sharp Cheddar to the potato mixture along with fresh or dried sage to taste. We add up to 1 tablespoon minced fresh sage, but only about 1 teaspoon dried.

CHUNKY RANCH-STYLE HOME FRIES

INGREDIENT TIP

You can make home fries, hash browns, and other fried dishes with many types of potatoes. We favor the common high-starch russet, also the usual choice for baking, because the greater the starch level, the crispier the results. We also sometimes use Yukon Gold potatoes, which have a more moderate starch level but a compensating buttery glow. Don't be afraid to experiment with some of the heirloom varieties common at farmers' markets today. The vendor will be able to steer you toward higher-starch, buttery-tasting varieties that fry up great.

If you don't have leftover potatoes for hash browns, make equally good home fries from scratch. Starting with raw potatoes means a longer cooking time, but they require little more than an occasional stir while you're figuring out your weekend. If you want to double the serving, make it in two skillets. Serve the home fries with a big scoop of cottage cheese or A Simply Sublime Scramble (page 10).

SERVES 2 GENEROUSLY AS A MAIN DISH, 4 AS A SIDE DISH

2 tablespoons unsalted butter

1½ to 1¾ pounds russet or Yukon Gold potatoes, peeled and cut into ¾-inch cubes (see Ingredient Tip)

Salt and freshly milled black pepper to taste

¼ cup diced onion

¼ cup diced green bell pepper

¼ cup diced red bell pepper or additional green bell pepper

½ teaspoon chili powder, optional

Minced fresh chives or parsley, optional

Warm the butter in a 10- to 12-inch cast-iron skillet over medium-low heat. Stir in the potatoes, and when coated with a bit of butter, season them with salt and pepper and cover the skillet. Cook for 20 minutes, during which you should hear only a faint cooking sound.

Uncover the potatoes and cook for 30 minutes longer, turning them at 10-minute intervals and patting them back down. When you turn them the first time, stir in the onion, bell peppers, and chili powder if desired. As the potatoes soften, pat them down more lightly, bringing as much of their surface in contact with the skillet as possible without mashing them.

Cook the potatoes for about 20 minutes longer, turning them at 5-minute intervals. During the last 10 minutes, bring the heat up to medium and, if you wish, add more salt and pepper. The home fries are ready when the potato cubes are richly browned and clearly crisp with tender, melting centers. Plate them up immediately, scatter with chives if you wish, and serve.

EXTRA-CRISPY HOME FRIES

Replace the butter with rendered beef suet, as ranch cooks sometimes do, or with rendered duck fat or goose fat. You can also reduce the butter by half and combine it with an equal amount of lard.

HERBED HOME FRIES

Add generous amounts of fresh herbs during the last 5 minutes of cooking. Mix in up to a couple of tablespoons of parsley, thyme, chives, tarragon, summer savory, or lovage or a combination of any of the others with parsley. Substitute dill perhaps when serving the home fries with trout or other fish. Rosemary is fabulous, but a little goes a long way. Start with 1 teaspoon fresh or ½ teaspoon dried, working up from there after you've had a chance to taste the results. A generous handful of Parmesan is always a good enhancement.

RED CHILE–ONION HOME FRIES

Toss the cooked home fries with ½ cup or more of Jack or asadero cheese, ladle Red Chile Sauce (page 74) over, and sprinkle with minced onion or scallion. This makes a fine one-dish meal, particularly when topped with a fried or poached egg.

SWEET POTATO HOME FRIES

Substitute sweet potatoes for the other tubers. Using all green bell pepper (rather than sweeter red) balances the natural honeyed flavor of the sweet potatoes. We like to add a few pinches of hot red pepper flakes just before removing the home fries from the stove. These are especially good with rosemary as an herbal flavoring.

FRIES AHOY

Home fries offer an almost unlimited potential for embellishment, as many restaurant chefs have demonstrated. The popular Hi Spot hangout in Seattle serves a rambunctious version called Mexi-Fries, a virtual world tour of fry ingredients. The potatoes come mixed with sautéed onion, carrot, bell pepper, zucchini, mushrooms, tomato, olives, green chiles, feta, mozzarella, Monterey Jack, and, crowning it all, salsa. Lynn's Paradise Café in Louisville features another fabulous over-the-top variation. The BLT Fries boast bacon, spinach (the "lettuce" in the BLT) tomatoes, onions, Jack cheese, and horseradish sour cream.

OVEN-CRISPED TABASCO COTTAGE POTATOES

A BREAKFAST MENU SUGGESTION FOR OVERNIGHT GUESTS

Sherried Grapefruit

Steamed Smoked Black Cod or Sablefish

Rye Toast

Butter Steamed Potatoes

Cherry Tomatoes

James Beard, *Menus for Entertaining* (1965)

No vegetable except the potato is especially serviceable as a breakfast food, and it is much more readily digested when baked than when prepared in any other way.

Ella Eaton Kellogg, *Science in the Kitchen* (1910)

James Beard mused once about the American penchant for potatoes at breakfast, noting that no other nation eats them in the morning. Our long love of fried foods may account for some of that singular enthusiasm, but certainly not all of it since we cook our morning potatoes in many other ways as well. This baked variation is one of the most popular of the alternative approaches, partly because of its wonderful flavor and partly because it can be assembled a day ahead. Serve the potatoes with a tangy citrus accompaniment, perhaps Honeyed Oranges with Jalapeños (page 286) or just orange wedges or tangerine sections.

SERVES 4 AS A MAIN DISH, UP TO 6 AS A SIDE DISH

2 pounds Yukon Gold, russet, or other baking potatoes, unpeeled, cut into neat ¾-inch cubes

Salt to taste

6 tablespoons unsalted butter

1 large onion, diced

⅔ cup diced green bell pepper

⅔ cup diced red, yellow, or orange bell pepper

½ teaspoon Tabasco or other hot pepper sauce or more to taste

1 tablespoon paprika

1½ teaspoons seasoned salt, such as Lawry's, or regular salt, or more to taste

1 teaspoon freshly milled black pepper

1 to 1½ cups grated Monterey Jack or Cheddar cheese or a combination, optional

Bring the potatoes to a boil in a pan of well-salted water and boil until just tender, 4 to 6 minutes. Watch carefully—a few crumbly edges are fine, but you don't want mush. Drain the potatoes.

Warm the butter in a 10-inch ovenproof skillet over medium heat. Stir in the onion and bell peppers and sauté until just beginning to soften, about 2 minutes. Stir in the Tabasco, paprika, seasoned salt, and pepper and remove from the heat. Mix in the potato chunks, coating them well. Proceed with the baking if you wish or, to allow a fuller blending of flavors, cool briefly, cover, and refrigerate overnight.

If refrigerated, uncover the potatoes and let them stand at room temperature while the oven preheats to 375°F. Bake the potatoes for 25 to 30 minutes, until richly brown and crunchy in spots. If you are adding the cheese, scatter it over the top, then return the skillet to the oven for 1 minute. Serve hot.

THREE-ONION AND POTATO CASSEROLE

I have made a lot of mistakes falling in love, and regretted most of them, but never the potatoes that went with them.

Nora Ephron, *Heartburn* (1983)

Fans of twice-baked potatoes will love this casserole. We almost never use canned soup in our preparations, and rarely call for anything like canned French-fried onions, but this is an exception on both counts. Each contributes in a special way to the desired texture, though a substitution of buttered bread crumbs for the third type of onion sacrifices little in the final result. Unless you're cooking for a crowd, count on leftovers from the recipe, which keep well and taste fine reheated in the oven or on a griddle.

SERVES AT LEAST 6 AS A MAIN DISH,

8 OR MORE AS A SIDE DISH

1¾ pounds cooked (preferably baked) Yukon Gold, russet, or other baking potatoes, cooled and peeled (see Ingredient Tip)

¾ pound medium to sharp Cheddar cheese, grated (about 3 cups)

One 10¾-ounce can cream of celery soup

1 cup sour cream

1 large sweet onion, such as a Vidalia, Texas 1015, or Walla Walla, or 1 medium regular onion, finely chopped

⅓ cup minced fresh chives

1 teaspoon salt or more to taste

1 teaspoon freshly milled black pepper or more to taste

One 2.8-ounce can French-fried onions

Preheat the oven to 350°F. Grease a 9 × 13-inch baking dish.

Combine the potatoes, cheese, soup, sour cream, onion, chives, salt, and pepper in a large bowl. Spoon the mixture into the pan and pat it down evenly.

Bake for approximately 1 hour, until lightly golden and bubbly. Sprinkle the French-fried onions over the casserole and return to the oven for 5 to 8 minutes, until the onions are crisp and a darker brown in color. Serve hot.

THREE-ONION, BLUE CHEESE, AND POTATO CASSEROLE

Eliminate the Cheddar. Replace it with 6 ounces crumbled blue cheese and 6 ounces grated mild cheese, such as Fontina or Gouda.

THREE-ONION, BACON, AND POTATO CASSEROLE

Add ½ to 1 cup cooked crumbled bacon or cubed Canadian bacon to enhance the heartiness of the potatoes.

ROSEMARY RÖSTI

TECHNIQUE TIP

If you want to make rösti at another time of day, you can get by with refrigerating the cooked potatoes for as little as 3 hours. The brief cooking and chilling has an interesting effect on the potatoes and their starch. When grated, the shreds hold together well enough to form a cohesive cake, but they also retain some of their original lightness and dryness.

SELECTIONS FROM THE BREAKFAST MENU AT THE GLADSTONE HOTEL IN RHODE ISLAND, 1899

Veal Cutlets, Plain or Breaded, Tomato Sauce

Frizzled Beef

Potatoes, Fried, Baked, Lyonnaise, Sautéed, Saratoga, or Hashed with Cream

---

With an Old World name that alludes to "crisply golden," rösti was a natural for the American breakfast table. The Swiss-German immigrants who brought the dish here originally ate it later in the day, but the compelling marriage of potatoes, butter, and cheese spoke clearly of comforting morning fare to American cooks. To attain the signature texture you want with rösti, you must boil the potatoes briefly and then chill them in advance, which makes this a handy overnight dish. In the summer, try it with sliced apricot halves or, when it's colder, maybe Baked Apples with Sausage Stuffing (page 274).

SERVES 4 AS A MAIN DISH, 6 AS A SIDE DISH

2 pounds (about 3 medium to large) russet potatoes

4 tablespoons (½ stick) unsalted butter

¾ cup grated Gruyère, raclette, or Swiss cheese (about 3 ounces)

1 teaspoon salt

½ teaspoon dried rosemary

Freshly milled black pepper to taste

Minced fresh parsley

Fresh rosemary sprigs, optional

The night before you plan to prepare the rösti, bring the unpeeled whole potatoes to a boil in a large saucepan of well-salted water. Boil for 7 to 10 minutes, depending on size, until soft just under the skin but still firm at the core. Drain and refrigerate the potatoes overnight.

Peel the potatoes, then grate them on the large holes of a box grater.

Melt half of the butter in a heavy 10-inch skillet over medium heat. (If you don't have a skillet this size, choose one slightly smaller. The thicker potato layer will end up with a smaller proportion of crust to creamy insides but will still be wonderful.) Scatter half of the potatoes in the skillet followed by all of the cheese and half of the salt and rosemary. Add a few good grindings of pepper. Repeat with the remaining potatoes, salt, rosemary, and pepper and pack the mixture down with a spatula. Cover the skillet and cook for 5 minutes, then uncover and cook for about 5 minutes longer, until brown and crisp. Slide the spatula around the cake, in from the edges, to loosen the cake if necessary. Remove the skillet from the heat and place a large plate or round platter over it. Using oven mitts, invert the skillet over the plate and give it a firm shake to drop the cake onto the plate. (If it cracks a bit, don't worry. Just neaten it back up with the spatula and continue.)

Return the skillet to the stove and melt the remaining butter in it again over medium heat. Slide the cake back into the skillet browned side up and cook until the bottom is brown and crisp, 5 to 7 additional minutes. When fully cooked, nudge it from the skillet with the spatula back onto the plate. Cut into wedges and sprinkle with parsley. Serve garnished with rosemary sprigs if you wish.

You deserve something delicious to eat, but there is nothing much in the fridge. You might have egg and toast, or a glass of hot milk, or toasted cheese, but you feel your spirit crying out for something more. Here is the answer: rösti . . . an excuse for eating a quarter of a pound of butter.

Laurie Colwin, *Home Cooking* (1988)

DILLED POTATO PANCAKES

TECHNIQUE TIP

You can peel the potatoes up to the night before, cover them with water, and refrigerate, but to prevent discoloration don't grate them until shortly before you plan to make the pancakes. One of the keys to good pancakes is wringing out as much water as you can from the potatoes.

A BREAKFAST MENU

SUGGESTION FOR

"OFFICE GIRLS WHO

BOARD THEMSELVES"

Rice and Raisins

Dry Toast

Fried Potatoes   Beet Pickles

Bananas

The Inglenook Cook Book (1911)

Like rösti, European potato pancakes in the United States found their way from the dinner menu to the breakfast menu. They remain particularly popular in areas of heavy German-American settlement, from the upper Midwest down to central Texas, though we've found them everywhere from California to Florida. Preparation styles differ significantly, but this one is a classic, similar to how many Jewish cooks make latkes. If you're not a fan of dill, simply leave it out. These pancakes are fabulous with Columbia River Hot-Smoked Salmon Omelet (page 41) or as the base for poached eggs.

SERVES 4 AS A MAIN DISH, 6 OR MORE AS A SIDE DISH

2 to 2¼ pounds (about 4 medium to large) russet potatoes, peeled	2 teaspoons salt or more to taste
2 medium to large yellow onions	1 teaspoon freshly milled black pepper or more to taste
¼ to ⅓ cup finely ground cracker crumbs or unsalted matzoh meal	Peanut oil or vegetable oil for panfrying
3 large eggs	Applesauce
¼ cup minced fresh dill	Sour cream

Arrange a clean dish towel in a large bowl.

Grate the potatoes on the large holes of a box grater, holding them vertically to get the longest strands. Every few handfuls, transfer the potatoes to the bowl. After you have grated 2 potatoes, grate an onion, which may seem a little like grating a tomato. The onion will become mostly mush and juice, but persevere, then scoop it up with a spatula and toss it all with the grated potato. Combining the mixture helps keep the potatoes from discoloring. Repeat with the remaining potatoes and onion.

Gather up the edges of the towel and, holding it over the bowl, wring it out more or less lengthwise. Squeeze hard to eliminate as much water from the potatoes and onions as you can manage. Let the liquid stand for about 5 minutes. The potato starch will sink to the bottom and the water will float to the top. Pour off the water, leaving the starch in the bowl. Add the potatoes and onions to the bowl, along with ¼ cup of the cracker crumbs, the eggs, dill, salt, and pepper, and mix well to combine. The batter should be moist but not soupy. If it seems a little too wet, add more of the cracker crumbs.

Warm ¼ inch of oil in a large heavy skillet or griddle over medium to medium-high heat. Fry a mini-pancake about 1 tablespoon in size to check the seasoning. Adjust if needed.

Spoon batter into the skillet, ⅓ to ½ cup per pancake. Make as many pancakes as you can easily fit into the skillet. Work quickly, but avoid crowding the pancakes or they will become soggy. Pat each pancake down lightly with a spatula to under ½ inch in thickness. Fry on both sides, turning once, until golden to medium brown and crisp, 5 to 6 minutes per side. If they are browning too rapidly, turn down the heat a bit. They need time to cook through while they develop a crisp, richly colored crust. Repeat with the remaining batter, adding more oil to the skillet as needed. Serve at once with applesauce and sour cream.

POTATO-PARSNIP PANCAKES

For a little more bite, substitute ½ pound peeled, grated parsnips for the same quantity of potato. We like these served with sour cream and grated or prepared horseradish.

GINGERED SWEET POTATO PANCAKES

Replace the dill with ½ to 1 teaspoon ground ginger. Replace the potatoes with sweet potatoes. If you have a choice, get a red-orange sweet potato, such as Garnet or Jewel, for the most appealing color.

ZUCCHINI-ONION PANCAKES

Replace ½ pound potatoes with 10 ounces zucchini, starting with a larger quantity because of the squash's higher water content. Eliminate the dill and mix in ¼ cup minced fresh chives or scallion greens.

CHIPOTLE POTATO PANCAKES

Made with different potatoes and seasonings, these pancakes depart substantially from traditional versions. Adjust the amount of the smoky chipotle chiles as you wish, but the level in the recipe should please most fans of southwestern food. We think these are great with soft-textured Brown-Butter Scramble with Avocado (page 14) or Pan-Seared Creole Fish (page 157).

SERVES 4 AS A MAIN DISH, 6 OR MORE AS A SIDE DISH

CHIPOTLE SOUR CREAM

½ cup sour cream

1½ to 2 teaspoons ground chipotle chile powder or minced chipotles in adobo sauce

PANCAKES

1½ pounds waxy red potatoes, peeled and grated

2 teaspoons salt

2 large eggs

⅓ cup thinly sliced scallions

2 shallots, minced

2 garlic cloves, minced

3 tablespoons minced fresh cilantro

1½ tablespoons unbleached all-purpose flour

2 teaspoons ground chipotle chile powder or minced chipotles in adobo

Vegetable oil for panfrying

Prepare the sour cream, stirring together the sour cream and chipotle powder in a small bowl.

Prepare the pancakes, first placing the potatoes on a clean dish towel. Sprinkle the potatoes with the salt and let them stand for several minutes. Wrap up the potatoes in the towel and squeeze it over a large bowl, wringing out as much moisture as possible. Let the potato liquid stand for about 5 minutes. The potato starch will sink to the bottom and the water will float to the top. Pour off the water, leaving the starch in the bowl. Add the eggs, scallions, shallots, garlic, cilantro, flour, and chipotle powder and combine. Stir in the potatoes and mix well.

Warm about ¼ inch of oil in a large heavy skillet over medium heat. With a big spoon, scoop up ¼ to ⅓ cup of the potato mixture and spoon it into the hot oil in a little mound. The mixture does tend to pop and sputter a bit. Repeat with several more mounds, avoiding crowding. After the potato mounds are in the skillet, flatten each with a spatula into a little cake about ½ inch thick. Fry on each side for about 3 minutes, until richly brown and crusted. Drain on paper towels. Repeat with the remaining potato mixture, adding more oil to the skillet as needed. You will end up with about 16 cakes. Serve hot accompanied by the sour cream.

CHIPOTLE JÍCAMA CAKES

A popular southwestern and Mexican tuber, jícama makes an interesting change from potatoes in pancakes. Most often served raw, it cooks up creamy at the center and crisp on the surface, much like a potato, with texture and flavor that's something of a cross between a water chestnut and an apple. Treat it as you would a potato, peeling and grating it first. We like the juice of 1 lime added to it with the salt while it drains. Jícama holds even more moisture than potatoes, so squeeze it in the towel an extra time or two. You won't have the potato starch, so add 1½ teaspoons extra flour when stirring the batter together.

SPICED SWEET POTATO SLICES

Sweet potatoes earned a spot on southern breakfast tables generations ago because they mate wonderfully with other regional favorites such as grits and ham. We roast them in this preparation, slice them, and then reheat the rounds in a skillet with sweet spices. If you do the roasting the night before serving, you can finish them in the morning in a matter of minutes.   **SERVES 4 OR MORE**

Two 12- to 14-ounce sweet potatoes

3 tablespoons unsalted butter

2 teaspoons Asian sesame oil

¼ teaspoon ground cinnamon

¼ teaspoon freshly grated nutmeg

¼ teaspoon ground ginger

Pinch of salt

2 to 3 teaspoons sesame seeds

Preheat the oven to 400°F.

Poke the tines of a fork into the top of each sweet potato so that steam can escape while they cook. Bake the potatoes for 45 to 55 minutes for potatoes of average girth, until tender but not squishy. (The potatoes can be prepared to this point the evening before, then refrigerated overnight.)

When cool enough to handle, peel the potatoes. Slice each rather thickly into rounds or, if they are especially portly, into half-moons.

Warm the butter and sesame oil in a skillet over medium heat. Sprinkle in the cinnamon, nutmeg, ginger, and salt. Add the potato slices, turn gently to coat, and heat through. Serve warm, sprinkled with sesame seeds.

Breakfast in America is peculiarly a family meal. At this, more than any other, there is an unrestrained enjoyment of the home circle. . . . It is usually a hearty meal, consisting of coffee, meats, fish, toast, a variety of hot cakes, and in the Southern States, hominy and rice, cooked in various ways, and several kinds of hot bread.

Julie C. Andrews, *Breakfast, Dinner, and Tea* (1865)

SELECTIONS FROM THE BREAKFAST MENU AT THE NEW YORK HOTEL, 1859

VEGETABLES

Potatoes, Stewed   Potatoes, Fried

Hominy, Boiled   Hominy, Fried

Boiled Rice

TOMATO GRAVY

**A BREAKFAST MENU
SUGGESTION FOR A
SUMMER MORNING**

Strawberries without Stemming

Broiled Tomatoes, Cream Gravy

New Potatoes, Boiled

Cheese Ramakins [sic]

Rolls

Coffee

Sarah Tyson Rorer,
Philadelphia Cook Book (1886)

When you serve fried fish for breakfast in the South, grits are the traditional accompaniment, often topped with a tasty tomato gravy. Something like a morning version of stewed tomatoes, the gravy also makes a vibrant blanket for biscuits, toast, omelets, hash browns, and more. When you're starting with the finest fresh tomatoes in the summer, the topping can turn almost any breakfast into a celebration of garden goodness.   **SERVES 4 OR MORE**

3 thick slices bacon, chopped

2 large shallots, minced

2 tablespoons unbleached all-purpose flour

3 cups finely chopped peeled red-ripe tomatoes or one 28-ounce can whole tomatoes, drained with juice reserved, then chopped

Salt and freshly milled black pepper to taste

Fry the bacon in a medium skillet until golden and partially crisp, about 3 minutes. Stir in the shallots and continue cooking until they are soft and translucent, about 5 minutes longer. Sprinkle the flour over the mixture, then stir it in and cook for 1 minute. Add the tomatoes and any juice and simmer until reduced and thickened into a gravylike sauce, 8 to 10 minutes with fresh tomatoes, 3 to 4 minutes with canned. Season generously with salt and pepper. Serve warm over grits, under fried fish, or with other dishes.

SCALLOPED TOMATOES

Some American cooks broil tomatoes for breakfast, others even make them into a morning cobbler, but for oven cooking we prefer this simple layered approach. Heat stimulates the flow of tomato juice, drenching the bread crumbs in the dish in a melange of marvelous flavors. Serve alongside any omelet or with Eggs Benedict Soufflés (page 38).

SERVES 4 AS A MAIN DISH, 6 AS A SIDE DISH

2 tablespoons olive oil

2 cups fresh bread crumbs, preferably from a country-style bread

4 medium to large red-ripe tomatoes, thickly sliced

2 tablespoons minced fresh chives

2 tablespoons minced fresh parsley

Salt and freshly milled black pepper to taste

2 to 3 tablespoons freshly grated Parmesan cheese

Oil a medium gratin dish or a shallow medium baking dish. Preheat the oven to 375°F.

Warm the oil in a skillet over medium heat. Add the bread crumbs and toast them until golden, stirring occasionally, about 4 minutes.

Scatter approximately half of the bread crumbs over the bottom of the prepared dish. Arrange a single layer of tomato slices over the bread crumbs, adding any juice from the cutting board. Scatter about one third of the chives and parsley over the tomatoes, season with salt and pepper, then add another light layer of bread crumbs. Repeat with the remaining tomatoes, herbs, and seasonings, ending with a sprinkling of bread crumbs. Scatter Parmesan over all. Bake for 15 to 20 minutes, until heated through, golden, and crunchy.

SINGING FOR YOUR BREAKFAST

At the second annual breakfast banquet of the Lydia F. Wadleigh Association in New York in 1899, the printed program called for the group to come together singing the "Battle Hymn of the Republic." The celebrants ate then, starting with oysters and consommé, followed by sole, steak, sorbet, and salad, and concluding with petits fours and coffee. While they digested the food, five speakers lectured on subjects such as "Our Children," "Our Husbands," and "Our Country." For a finale, everyone sang "Auld Lang Syne."

FRIED GREEN TOMATOES

Fannie Flagg's *Fried Green Tomatoes at the Whistle Stop Café,* and the popular movie based on the book, fortified a common association of the dish with the South. In fact, people everywhere used to enjoy fried green tomatoes, but southerners have remained loyal to that and other culinary traditions longer than most of us. Firmer than their red-ripe kin, they hold up well in the skillet, and their youthful tang offsets the richness of the cooking method. Try them on the side with any breakfast meat or fish or relish them as a main dish along with Buttermilk with Crumblin's (page 67).

SERVES 2 AS A MAIN DISH, 4 AS A SIDE DISH

1 to 1¼ cups fine saltine cracker crumbs

½ teaspoon salt or more to taste

½ teaspoon freshly milled black pepper

Pinch or two of cayenne pepper

Pinch of sugar, optional

4 medium to large firm green tomatoes, sliced ¼ to ⅓ inch thick

Bacon drippings, vegetable oil, or olive oil for panfrying

Mix together the cracker crumbs, salt, pepper, and cayenne on a plate. If the tomatoes taste especially tart, add the sugar. Dredge the tomato slices in the mixture.

Warm enough drippings in a large skillet over medium heat to cover the skillet generously. Fry the tomatoes for about 2 minutes per side, until golden. Serve hot.

FRIED GREEN TOMATO SANDWICHES

Turn these into a heartier morning meal by placing several between 2 slices of soft bread spread with mayonnaise. A slice or two of mild cheese, such as fresh mozzarella, makes a good enhancement.

CREAMY GRITS

A BREAKFAST MENU
SUGGESTION FOR A
SUNNY SOUTHERN MORN

Grapefruit Cocktail

Mackerel   Hominy (grits)

Toast

Hot Cakes and Syrup

Coffee

Mrs. S. R. Dull, *Southern
Cooking* (1928)

INGREDIENT TIP

In spite of being called *hominy
grits,* and even sometimes in the
South just *hominy,* grits today are
rarely made from hominy, which
is corn that has been treated with
wood ash or lye to remove the
hull. Producers now start with
regular dried corn, often white
corn, and the best of them stone-
grind it to a coarse texture. Top
versions are usually labeled
"speckled heart" to indicate they
were ground with—and still
contain—the darker-hued
nutritious heart of the corn kernel.

You get out of grits what you
put into them in time. Always
avoid "instant grits," on a par
with instant coffee. For a
weekday morning or when you
have hungry kids to sooth,
"quick" 5- to 10-minute grits are
tolerable, with the cooking time
and water reduced according to
package directions. When you
want the genuine article, order
your grits from a mill that still

Unlike fried green tomatoes, grits are almost strictly southern in ancestry
and are only now beginning to gain a following in other areas. People who have
tried them and found them lacking have generally eaten a version made with
instant or otherwise inferior grits, which are unfortunately common even in the
South today. It takes a while to cook real stone-ground grits, but they rarely disappoint anyone. For a classic Sunday morning (or evening) feast, serve them
with Ham Steak with Redeye Gravy (page 130), with some of the gravy spooned
over the grits.   **SERVES 4**

1½ cups stone-ground grits, not
instant or quick-cooking (see
Ingredient Tip)

1 teaspoon salt or more to taste

1 cup half-and-half

4 to 5 tablespoons unsalted butter

Tabasco or other hot pepper sauce
to taste, optional

Make the grits in a large heavy saucepan, first bringing 6 cups water and
the salt to a boil. Whisk in the grits a few handfuls at a time. (They will bubble up initially.) When you have added all the grits, reduce the heat to a very
low simmer and cook over low heat for a total of 40 to 45 minutes, stirring
occasionally at first and more frequently toward the end.

After 30 to 35 minutes, or when the grits begin to seem somewhat stiff and
give a bit of resistance at the bottom, add the half-and-half, 2 to 3 tablespoons of the butter, a splash of Tabasco, and additional salt if you like.
Cook for about 5 minutes longer, until all the additions have been absorbed.
The grits should have body and thickness but still be easily spoonable. (The
grits can be covered and held briefly over low heat, with a little water or
additional milk added to keep them from getting too stiff.)

Spoon the grits into large shallow bowls. Top each with a thin pat of the
remaining butter and serve.

JUST PLAIN GRITS

Some cooks can't abide milk or cream in their grits. If that's you, or you're fresh out of dairy
products, use just water. As the grits begin to get dry, add more warm water as needed.
Leave out the hot pepper sauce if you wish. For best flavor, you'll still want to finish with
pats of butter, either stirred into the grits, topping each bowl, or both.

GRITS WITH BIG HOMINY

Stir 1 drained 15-ounce can hominy into the grits a few minutes before removing from the
heat. If available, buy yellow hominy to contrast with white corn grits or vice versa.

stone-grinds the corn, such as the venerable War Eagle Mill in Arkansas (501-789-5343) or the Old Guilford Mill in North Carolina (336-643-4783). John Martin Taylor sells another fine version, ground in Georgia, through his Charleston culinary mail-order business, Hoppin' John's (800-828-4412 or www.hoppinjohns.com). Always store stone-ground grits in the refrigerator or freezer.

TECHNIQUE TIP

The more you slow down the cooking of grits, the creamier they will be, whether your version includes any dairy or not. Cooks often use a proportion of 1 cup grits to 1 quart water, but stone-ground grits will require at least an additional cup or two of liquid. Stir with a flat-tipped utensil—we especially like a wooden spatula/spoon that stays cool while cooking. Stir up from the bottom each time. Always cook grits long enough that you have toothsome but soft bits suspended in a creamy but full-bodied liquid. As with mashed potatoes, it's hard to add too much butter.

GRITS CAKES

After the grits have cooled and begun to stiffen, form little patties of about ⅓ cup grits each. Dredge them in flour and panfry in about ¼ inch of oil, preferably peanut oil, until golden and crusty, about 2 minutes. Serve alone or with corn relish.

FRIED GRITS

In the same way you make Fried Cornmeal Mush (page 256), grits can be spooned into a pan, chilled, and fried. Start with the Just Plain Grits variation. Rather than form the grits into a loaf-shaped brick for slicing, some cooks just pour the mixture onto a greased baking sheet and smooth it. After chilling, the grits can be cut into shapes with a knife, biscuit cutter, or cookie cutter. Dust with flour or cornmeal, then fry in oil or bacon drippings or a combination of both. Serve on the side with quail, duck, or ham or alone in the style of cornmeal mush, with cane syrup, sorghum, or maple syrup. *Mrs. Porter's New Southern Cookery Book* (1871), published shortly after the Civil War, said fried grits are "a necessary accompaniment to pork."

CINNAMON-SUGAR GRITS WITH FRIED APPLES

Skip the hot sauce and instead stir into the grits 1 teaspoon ground cinnamon and 2 tablespoons or more of sugar, to taste. After the grits are spooned up, top with portions of Fried Apples (page 280).

TRUE GRIT

Keepers of southern culinary tradition would prefer that everyone stop messing with their grits. Damon Lee Fowler, in *Beans, Greens, and Sweet Georgia Peaches* (1998), laments that in recent years grits "got truffled, creamed and jalapeñoed, and infused with more garlic than a Genoa salami." Southern food authority and author Ronni Lundy swears she's seen everything in additives from peanut butter to Cheez Whiz. Ironically, all the tampering is a fine testament to the earthy goodness of grits, a form of flattery begotten by the forthright allure.

NASSAU GRITS

Grits, grits, it's
Grits I sing—
Grits fits
In with anything.
Rich and poor, black
and white,
Lutheran and
Campbellite,
Jews and Southern
Jesuits,
All acknowledge
buttered grits.
Give me two hands,
give me my wits,
Give me forty pounds of
grits.

Roy Blount, Jr., *One Fell Soup*
(1982)

This Florida favorite, now gaining fans in many other areas, boasts a Creole appeal. More robust and filling than most grits preparations, it makes a luscious main course, though many cooks serve it on the side at a big breakfast with fish, ham, or eggs.

SERVES 4 AS A MAIN DISH, 6 AS A SIDE DISH

4 thick slices bacon, chopped

1 medium onion, chopped

1 medium green bell pepper, chopped

1 garlic clove, minced

½ to 1 cup finely chopped or ground ham, preferably country ham or another smoky, full-flavored ham

3 large red-ripe tomatoes, peeled and chopped, or one 14½- to 15-ounce can tomatoes, undrained (chop or crush the tomatoes into bite-size pieces)

Freshly milled black pepper to taste

1 cup stone-ground grits

Salt to taste, optional

Fry the bacon in a medium skillet over medium heat until brown and crisp. Remove the bacon with a slotted spoon, drain it, and reserve it. To the pan drippings, add the onion, green pepper, and garlic and sauté until soft, about 5 minutes. Stir in the ham and sauté for 5 minutes longer. Add the tomatoes and a generous grinding of pepper and reduce the heat to medium-low. Cook until reduced to a thick sauce, about 15 minutes longer.

While the bacon-tomato mixture simmers, cook the grits in a large saucepan, first bringing 6 cups water to a boil. Whisk in the grits a few handfuls at a time. (They will bubble up initially.) When you have added all the grits, reduce the heat to a very low simmer and cook over low heat for a total of 40 to 45 minutes, stirring occasionally at first and more frequently toward the end. Judge whether to add salt to the grits by the saltiness of your ham. With an aged country ham, for example, you may need no additional salt. You can always add salt to taste before finishing the dish.

When the grits are cooked to your liking (grits should have body and thickness but still be spoonable), stir in the ham-tomato mixture. Continue cooking over medium-low heat for 2 to 3 minutes longer, giving the flavors a chance to mingle. Spoon into shallow bowls, sprinkle with bacon, and serve without hesitation.

A PRESIDENTIAL SEAL OF APPROVAL

Grits are an all-purpose symbol for practically anything of importance to Southerners. They stand for hard times and happy times, for poverty and populism, for the blessings and curses of a righteous God. They stand for custom and tradition, for health and humor, for high-spirited hospitality. They also stand for boiling, baking, and frying.

John Egerton, *Side Dishes* (1990)

As the last leader of Union troops in the Civil War, Ulysses S. Grant defeated the Confederacy, but he said later that the South had won his appetite. As president, he made grits a common dish at the White House. Franklin Roosevelt seconded the notion. He enjoyed grits so much that the kitchen staff at his Warm Springs, Georgia, residence had a special bowl made with a cover so that the grits would stay warm even when his breakfast was invariably interrupted. More recently, Jimmy Carter reportedly ate grits almost daily, more than any other food, and made the dish something of a down-to-earth symbol of his presidency.

BREAKFAST POLENTA SOUTHWEST STYLE

Katherine Kagel, the chef-owner of Pasqual's in Santa Fe, makes the tastiest breakfast cornmeal dish we've found anywhere. Griddle-cooked polenta topped with red chile and chorizo, it's soothing and exciting all at once, creamy throughout but toothsome too. Unlike most recipes we attribute to other cooks, we haven't adjusted this one in the least. The multiple steps may seem a bit intimidating, but each is easy to execute and can be done at least a day ahead. All that's left for you is to dazzle your family or breakfast guests by quickly assembling the vibrantly colored fiesta on a plate. **SERVES 4 GENEROUSLY**

POLENTA

2 teaspoons salt

2 cups polenta cornmeal

2 large eggs, lightly beaten

½ cup freshly grated Parmesan cheese (about 2 ounces)

½ cup mascarpone cheese

1 tablespoon olive oil

1 tablespoon unsalted butter

PASQUAL'S RED CHILE SAUCE

¾ pound (about 5 dozen whole) dried mild red New Mexican chile pods, stemmed, seeded, and rinsed

1 medium white onion, coarsely chopped

8 plump garlic cloves

2 teaspoons dried Mexican oregano or 1 teaspoon other oregano

2 teaspoons kosher salt

1 teaspoon ground cumin

Clarified butter or vegetable oil for panfrying

1 pound Pasqual's Chorizo (page 138), crumbled, fried, and kept warm

3 cups fresh or frozen corn kernels, cooked in boiling water until just tender, then drained and kept warm

12 fresh cilantro sprigs

Prepare the polenta in a large heavy saucepan, first bringing 6 cups water to a boil over high heat. Reduce the heat slightly to keep the water bubbling but not popping wildly. Whisk in the polenta a few handfuls at a time, whisking continuously. (It will bubble up initially.) When you have added all the polenta, reduce the heat to a very low simmer and cook over low heat for a total of 40 to 45 minutes, stirring frequently with a wooden spoon. The polenta is ready when it tastes of cooked corn rather than raw and it appears to "tear away" from the sides of the pan. (It should be very stiff so that it will still hold its shape well after you add the remaining ingredients. Cook a few more minutes, if needed.) Remove from the heat and mix in the eggs, Parmesan, mascarpone, olive oil, and butter. Stir vigorously to combine well.

Grease a baking sheet. Pour the polenta out onto the sheet. Dampen your hands and use them to smooth the polenta's surface. Cover and refrigerate for at least 2 hours and up to a day.

Prepare the chile sauce in a large nonreactive saucepan, first covering the chiles with warm water. Place a plate over the chiles to keep them submerged. Let them stand in the water for 20 minutes, until somewhat soft and pliable. Remove the plate and add the other sauce ingredients to the pan. Bring to a boil over high heat, reduce the heat to low, and simmer for 20 minutes. Drain the chile mixture, reserving the liquid. Working in batches, puree the chiles in a blender, filling no more than three-quarters full and adding about ½ cup of the liquid. Blend until the sauce has a ketchuplike consistency, adding a bit more liquid if needed. Pour the sauce through a fine-mesh strainer, pressing on it to extract as much of the chile flavor as you can. This process is a little messy but yields a great sauce. The sauce is ready to use still warm or can be covered and refrigerated for later use. (You will have more chile sauce than needed for the polenta. Any extra can be used with enchiladas, burritos, or soft tacos; over corn pancakes, posole, or hominy; or replacing the tomato sauce on breakfast pizzas. It keeps for 4 to 5 days refrigerated or can be frozen for up to 2 months.)

Shortly before serving, cut the chilled polenta into 6 or more large squares, then halve them diagonally to make triangles. Warm enough butter to coat a griddle or large heavy skillet with a thin film over medium-high heat. Add the polenta triangles, in batches, and fry until golden brown and crusty, 4 to 5 minutes per side. Fry the remaining polenta, adding more butter as needed. Reheat the chile sauce, if needed, warming it over medium-low heat to prevent scorching.

To assemble each portion, place 2 or more polenta triangles in a shallow bowl, then cover with one sixth of the chorizo and corn. Spoon ½ cup chile sauce over the top and garnish with cilantro sprigs. Repeat with the remaining ingredients and serve hot.

SAUTÉED GREENS

**EMBELLISHMENTS FOR
SAUTÉED GREENS**

Add extra flavor with a minced
shallot, small onion, or grated
small carrot sautéed in the oil
before adding the greens. Thyme
is a good herbal enhancement,
and a pat of butter, a spoonful of
bacon drippings, or a showering
of grated hard-boiled egg adds
richness.

Greens taste great in the morning, as our grandparents knew. They ate
them wilted sometimes, and also long simmered and topped with a fried egg. We
prefer a simple sauté, using sturdy greens such as chard, kale, escarole, or mustard greens. For breakfast eating, we blanch the greens first for a slightly milder
flavor and softer texture, and at the end of the cooking we always wonder about
adding that egg.   **SERVES 4**

2 pounds sturdy cooking greens
such as chard, escarole, dandelion
greens, kale, mustard greens,
turnip greens, or collard greens

Salt to taste

2 tablespoons olive oil

⅓ cup chicken stock

Pinch or two of hot red pepper
flakes

Freshly milled black pepper to
taste

Pepper vinegar, other vinegar, or
lemon wedges

Lop off any long, coarse portions of stems from the greens. Transfer the
greens to a large pot and add at least 4 inches of water, lightly salted. Bring
the greens to a boil over high heat, cover, then reduce to a simmer and cook
for 8 to 12 minutes, until the greens are tender but still have some body.
(They are listed in roughly the sequence of recommended cooking time,
with chard the least and collards the most.)

Pour off the cooking water and drain the greens, pressing on them lightly to
eliminate much of the liquid. When cool enough to handle, chop them
roughly. (The greens can be prepared to this point the day before you plan
to serve them. Cover and refrigerate until needed.)

Warm the oil in a shallow pan over medium heat. Stir in the greens, coating
them with the oil. Cook for about 1 minute, then pour in the stock and season with hot red pepperflakes, salt, and black pepper. Reduce the heat to
medium-low and simmer for 5 to 8 minutes, until most of the liquid is
reduced and the greens are very tender. Serve hot or at room temperature
with pepper vinegar or lemon wedges.

SAUTÉED SPINACH

Spinach can be on the table even more quickly because it doesn't need the blanching of the
sturdier greens. Warm the oil in a large pot, then add 1 to 1½ pounds of fresh spinach, the
crinkly savoy variety if available. Season as directed and cook, covered, just until the leaves
are wilted.

CREAMED MUSHROOMS ON MULTIGRAIN TOAST

**A BREAKFAST MENU
SUGGESTION FOR A
MONDAY MORNING IN
NEW ORLEANS**

Sliced Oranges

Boiled Grits, Milk or Cream

Fried Croakers   Olives

Broiled Spring Chicken

Potato Croquettes

Radishes   Watercress

Batter Cakes   Butter

Louisiana Syrup

Café au Lait

The Daily Picayune

The Picayune's Creole Cook Book
(1901)

Mushrooms are another vegetable overlooked for breakfast today but eaten regularly in the past. You may not want them simmered in Sauternes, as some old cookbooks suggest for a morning preparation, but we suspect you'll love them this way. If you're cooking for someone special—like yourself—fresh morels really shine in the dish.   **SERVES 4**

CREAMED MUSHROOMS

3 tablespoons unsalted butter

1 large shallot, minced

1¼ pounds wild or button mushrooms, sliced

¾ cup chicken stock

¾ cup heavy (whipping) cream

½ teaspoon salt or more to taste

⅛ teaspoon freshly milled white pepper

4 slices multigrain bread, toasted

Paprika

Warm the butter in a sauté pan over medium heat and add the shallot. Sauté until the shallot begins to soften, a minute or two. Stir in the mushrooms and cook until they are limp and have given up much of their liquid, 6 to 8 minutes longer. Add the stock, cream, salt, and pepper and cook until the liquid reduces by about half.

Arrange the toast on 4 plates and top each with an equal portion of the mushrooms and sauce. Dust with paprika and serve.

EVENING TEA

Early American cookbooks often presented dishes we associate with breakfast today as equally appropriate for tea. Some families served tea as a snack before supper, in the British fashion, but many others just substituted the former for the latter. In 1852, Mrs. T. J. Crowen in *The American Lady's System of Cookery* simply dismissed supper as a proper meal for "*bona-fide* Americans." She advised having tea between six and eight in the evening, and nothing after that except light cakes and lemonade, syrup water, or wine.

PORTOBELLO AND SPINACH SCRAMBLE

OTHER SCRAMBLE EMBELLISHMENTS

Eliminate the fennel seeds and add ¾ cup corn kernels, bite-size pieces of asparagus, or boiled potato chunks when you add the mushrooms. Trade out the onion for a large leek, sliced into thin half-moons. Replace the spinach with chard or more bitter dandelion greens. Use any leftovers to stuff omelets or make into a wrap.

A stir-fry of sorts, an eggless scramble can be adjusted easily in ingredients and portions to serve almost any purpose at breakfast. In this version we use mushrooms for heft and heartiness and bell pepper, onion, and spinach to brighten the plate and fill out the flavor. It goes great on the side with a Classic Cheese Omelet (page 40) and makes a splendid centerpiece with Flaky Buttermilk Biscuits (page 336).

SERVES 4

2 tablespoons olive oil

¾ pound portobello mushrooms, halved and then sliced

1 medium red bell pepper, diced

½ medium yellow onion, diced

6 ounces fresh spinach, roughly chopped (5 to 6 lightly packed cups)

½ teaspoon fennel seeds

Pinch or two of hot red pepper flakes

Salt and freshly milled black pepper to taste

Warm the oil in a large skillet over medium heat. Stir in the mushrooms, which will immediately absorb nearly all the oil. Cook, stirring occasionally, until they begin to look moist and start to turn limp, about 3 minutes. Stir in the bell pepper and onion and cook until crisp-tender, about 5 minutes longer. Add the spinach, fennel seeds, hot red pepper flakes, salt, and pepper. Cover and cook just long enough for the spinach to become limp, about 3 minutes longer. Uncover and cook for another minute or two, long enough to eliminate any liquid but short enough for the spinach to retain its vibrant emerald color. Serve immediately.

PORTOBELLO AND SPINACH SCRAMBLE WITH ITALIAN SAUSAGE

Chop a ¼-pound hot Italian sausage link into small bits and fry it first in the skillet. Remove with a slotted spoon. Use the drippings, if you wish, to replace a portion of the oil. Add the sausage back in just before you are ready to serve.

PORTOBELLO AND SPINACH SCRAMBLE WITH TEMPEH

Make the scramble heartier without adding meat. Steam ¼ to ½ pound soy tempeh, cut into bite-size cubes, for about 20 minutes. Then add it to the scramble with the mushrooms. Look for tempeh in natural foods stores, often in the freezer section.

BREAKFAST BUTTER BEANS

INGREDIENT TIP

Fresh butter beans can be a challenge to find outside the South. Baby limas make a good substitute, but when you yearn for the real thing, mail-order from King Cotton Produce in Montgomery, Alabama (334-272-1040). The beans are in season from June to September.

TECHNIQUE TIP

If you want to leave out the pork, skip the first 20 minutes of cooking, which helps season the water with the ham hock's flavor. Cook the beans and other ingredients together with about 3½ cups chicken stock instead of water.

———

A BREAKFAST MENU
SUGGESTION FOR A
SUMMER MORNING PARTY

Berries

Baked Turbans of Flounder,
White Sauce

Potato Balls, with Parsley Butter

Broiled Chicken

Green Peas   Rolls

Tomato Omelet   Pop-overs

Frozen Peaches, with
Whipped Cream

Tea   Coffee

Maria Parloa, *Miss Parloa's
Kitchen Companion* (1887)

———

In *Butter Beans to Blackberries* (1999), Ronni Lundy recalls one of her favorite childhood breakfasts as "my mother's speckled butter beans, reheated and spread atop a toasted wedge of leftover cornbread from dinner the night before." It sounded good to us and turned out even better than we suspected right out of the pan. Southerners get passionate about their speckled beans, a regional crop, but baby limas from elsewhere also work fine in the preparation. Corn bread makes a good base, as Lundy says, and so do Corn Batty Cakes and Fresh Corn Fritters.

SERVES 4

1 small ham hock or 6-ounce chunk of smoky ham

½ medium onion, finely chopped

1 teaspoon minced fresh marjoram or thyme or ½ teaspoon dried

Pinch of hot red pepper flakes

½ teaspoon salt or more to taste

4 cups fresh or frozen butter beans or baby limas (see Ingredient Tip)

2 tablespoons heavy (whipping) cream, optional

Buttermilk Breakfast Corn Bread (page 343), Corn Batty Cakes (page 192), or Fresh Corn Fritters (page 99)

Place the ham hock and the onion in a large saucepan. Pour in 1 quart water, then add the marjoram, hot red pepper flakes, and salt. Bring the mixture to a boil and boil for about 20 minutes. Add the beans and cook, partially covered, over medium-low heat for 25 to 35 minutes, until tender and buttery. (Frozen baby limas generally take at least 5 to 10 minutes less than fresh, which vary themselves a bit with the age of the bean.) If the beans begin to get dry, add more water to keep them a bit soupy. Remove the ham hock. Add the cream if you want to enhance the creaminess of the beans. Serve the beans and some of their liquid over or alongside a crunchy corn bread or corncake.

REFRIED BEANS

Dried beans come to breakfast in many forms. In the Northeast, they are likely to be Boston-style baked beans, made from Jacob's cattle, yellow-eye, or tiny round navy beans. In the Southwest, the burnished brown-red pinto remains king. For breakfast eating, whole beans from the night before are often mashed and fried. Creamy well-cooked beans and a generous hand with seasonings contribute to good "refries," but the best versions also gain a major dimension from the lard or bacon drippings used in the frying. The beans are de rigueur with Huevos Rancheros (page 26), and their company benefits many other dishes as well, from Tamale Hash (page 202) to Avocado Mash on Sourdough Toast (page 248).

SERVES 4

3 tablespoons lard, bacon drippings, or a combination (see Ingredient Tip)

½ medium onion, finely chopped

2 plump garlic cloves, minced

2 cups cooked well-seasoned pinto beans with ¾ cup cooking liquid

¼ cup heavy (whipping) cream, half-and-half, or milk

½ teaspoon chili powder or dried ground mild red chile, such as New Mexican or ancho, or more to taste

Salt to taste

Crema or crème fraîche or grated Monterey Jack, pepper Jack, or mild Cheddar cheese

Warm the lard in a medium skillet over medium heat. Add the onion and garlic and sauté them until soft and translucent, about 5 minutes. Stir in the beans and cooking liquid and mash the beans with a spatula, large fork, or potato masher. We like to leave the texture rather rough, but you can mash the beans as much as you wish. Stir in the cream, chili powder, and salt. Continue cooking, scraping up from the bottom occasionally, until most of the liquid is absorbed and the beans become a thick puree. We prefer to cook them until a little crust forms in spots but the beans are still fairly moist and creamy, 5 to 8 minutes longer, but other cooks stop short of that point. Serve hot, drizzled with crema.

REFRIED BLACK BEANS

Lots of people associate black beans with southwestern cooking, but they actually have a much longer history along the eastern seaboard, from Boston to Miami. They can be mashed and refried in a fashion similar to the southwestern pinto, though we prefer them with a few modifications. Drop the lard in favor of olive oil. Add a few tablespoons of diced red bell pepper along with the onion and garlic. Skip the cream in the beans but use crema or sour cream as the topping.

BLACK BEANS AND YELLOW RICE

INGREDIENT TIP

Annatto has been used for generations in this country to color butter and cheese, but it has now become common in supermarkets because of increased interest in Caribbean and Latin American cuisines. It stains dishes like rice a lovely yellow-orange, but be careful with it because it can also spot your clothing the same bright shade. Annatto seeds usually come in small bottles and achiote paste (ground annatto with a few other spices) in small plastic-wrapped cakes.

TECHNIQUE TIP

To make the recipe from 2 cups dried black beans, you'll want to cook them a day ahead of breakfast. You use all the same ingredients, but change their sequence in the preparation. Soak the dried beans for a few hours or overnight or add an extra hour to the cooking time above. Combine the beans with the bay leaf, oregano, and cumin and cover with several inches of water. Bring the beans to a boil, then reduce to a simmer and cook for 1½ to 2 hours, until somewhat soft. Add hot water whenever it falls to less than 1 inch over the beans. Warm the olive oil in a small skillet and sauté in it the onion, bell peppers, and garlic until very soft, about 8 minutes over medium heat. Add this mixture to the beans, along with the vinegar, sugar, and salt, and continue cooking until the beans are soft and creamy.

This Cuban-American favorite is spreading across the country today, but few of the new fans realize that it's often served at breakfast on its home turf and is just as tasty then as at other meals. We call for canned beans in the recipe, to hasten the preparation for the morning, but the dish reaches its zenith with freshly cooked dried beans, which we describe how to make in the accompanying Technique Tip. If you need anything else on the plate, a mango mates nicely.

SERVES 4

YELLOW RICE

1 tablespoon olive oil

1 tablespoon annatto seeds, 2 teaspoons achiote paste, or 1 teaspoon ground turmeric (see Ingredient Tip)

1 cup long-grain rice

¾ teaspoon salt or more to taste

BLACK BEANS

¼ cup olive oil

1 small onion, chopped

½ medium red bell pepper, chopped

½ medium green bell pepper, chopped

2 garlic cloves, minced

1 bay leaf

Two 15-ounce cans black beans, drained

2 teaspoons vinegar, preferably red wine or cider

1 teaspoon dried oregano

1 teaspoon ground cumin

¼ teaspoon sugar

Salt to taste

Minced fresh cilantro

Lime wedges

Prepare the rice, first warming the oil in a medium saucepan over medium heat. Sprinkle in the annatto seeds and sauté, stirring occasionally, until the oil turns red-gold and seeds start to crackle, about 3 minutes. Remove the seeds with a slotted spoon. (If using achiote paste, mash it into the oil with a spoon or spatula. Skip the straining step.)

Stir the rice into the oil and cook briefly until it becomes translucent. Pour in 1¾ cups plus 2 tablespoons water and the salt. Cover the pan, reduce the heat to low, and cook for about 18 minutes, until the liquid is absorbed. If a steady stream of steam is still escaping from the pan after 18 minutes, cook for an additional minute without peeking.

While the rice cooks, prepare the beans, first warming the oil in a medium saucepan over medium heat. Add the onion, bell peppers, garlic, and bay leaf and sauté until the vegetables are very soft, about 8 minutes. Reduce the heat if they begin to brown at all. Add the beans, vinegar, oregano, cumin, sugar, and ½ cup warm water. Bring to a simmer, then reduce the heat to low. Stir in salt as you wish and cook for about 10 minutes. Add a little more water if the beans seem dry.

When the rice is cooked, take the pan off the heat, remove the lid, and quickly arrange a folded clean dish towel over the pan. Cover the towel with the pan lid and let the rice steam for at least 10 minutes. Fluff the rice. Mound it on plates and then ladle the beans over it. Scatter the cilantro on top, garnish with lime wedges, and serve.

Who doesn't enjoy an omelet for lunch or pancakes and fried eggs for supper? There's a calming, easy feeling about eating breakfast for dinner, as if it doesn't really count somehow. It's backward and fun, like taking a holiday or leaving work early.

Deborah Madison, *Vegetarian Cooking for Everyone* (1997)

13

The Breadbasket

WE LIKE toast as well as anyone we know, but it's never our first choice for breakfast bread. Give us an option between it and a freshly baked biscuit, scone, popover, or muffin, and toast always loses. We suspect that's true of most Americans, though many of us don't realize it's a hereditary thing not shared with any other people on earth.

Our grandparents and their grandparents ate so much hot bread for breakfast that we've got it in our genes. We often make do now with toast—merely a rewarmed bread—but it never quite satisfies our primal yearnings.

Our favorite hot breads, as Americans used to understand, are quick and simple to make. Nothing may seem that way today, but we're going to try to entice you back to your oven and demonstrate the ease of breakfast baking. While you're there working on the hot breads, we'll sneak in some yeast breads that need a little extra time to rise and even some loaves that you can enjoy a day or two later as toast. You probably won't want to bake every morning, but if you do it once, we're sure that you'll do it again.

FARMHOUSE SODA BREAD

Many Americans today seek out rustic country breads for their hearty flavor and toothsome texture. Irish-Americans brought us this favorite, traditionally baked in the homeland in an iron pot over a live fire in a similar way to how chuck-wagon cooks made their famous Dutch-oven biscuits. Quicker and easier to assemble than almost any loaf bread, this is breakfast baking at its best.

MAKES 1 LARGE ROUND LOAF

4 cups unbleached all-purpose flour

1 teaspoon baking soda

1 teaspoon salt

4 tablespoons (½ stick) unsalted butter, cut into small bits

1 cup golden raisins, soaked briefly if stiff

2 to 3 teaspoons caraway seeds, optional

2 cups buttermilk

1 large egg

2 tablespoons molasses

About 1 tablespoon heavy (whipping) cream or half-and-half

About 1 tablespoon rolled oats

For best results, place a baking stone like that used for pizza or bread on the oven's middle shelf. If you don't have a baking stone, use a heavy baking sheet. Preheat the oven to 425°F.

Sift the flour, baking soda, and salt together in a mixing bowl. With a pastry blender, cut the butter into the flour mixture. Stir in the raisins and the caraway seeds if desired. Form a well in the center and pour into it the buttermilk, egg, and molasses. Mix with a sturdy spoon until too stiff to stir. The dough will be very moist and sticky.

Turn the dough out onto a floured work surface. Wash and dry your hands. Gently knead a few times and form the dough into a plump disk about 8 inches in diameter. Slash an X across the top with a small sharp knife. Brush with cream and sprinkle with oats. Transfer the bread to the oven with a large spatula. Bake for 35 to 40 minutes, until golden brown and hollow sounding when thumped. Serve hot or at room temperature, cut into wedges or simply torn into chunks.

FARMHOUSE SODA ROLLS

This dough makes great rustic rolls for breakfast too. Form the dough into oversize golf balls and slash the top of each, dividing the cream and oats toppings evenly among them. It will probably be easier to move the hot baking stone from the oven, arrange the rolls on it, and return it to the oven than to try to arrange the rolls on the stone while standing at the open oven door. In either case, be cautious with the hot stone. The baking time will be closer to 20 minutes.

FLAKY BUTTERMILK BISCUITS

INGREDIENT TIP

Lard gives biscuits a flakiness that you cannot obtain from any other fat. Despite its reputation as coarse and outmoded, lard is a wonderful ingredient for biscuits, pie crusts, and doughnut frying. If you refuse to use it, substitute vegetable shortening, but please understand that you're missing something special.

That innocent and new-born crispness when you break a hot biscuit, the savory, steaming substance of its two halves between the teeth, those are experiences as soul-stirring as falling in love, and can be indulged in much oftener without serious consequences.

George Rector, *Dine at Home with Rector* (1934)

From the chuck-wagon "doughgods" that fueled cowboys on the range to the fat "catheads" of the Appalachians, biscuits boast a heritage much more American than apple pie. We may have started with versions of crisp, crackerlike British biscuits, but we ended up with a new notion altogether, an ethereal hot bread that makes any breakfast a special occasion regardless of what else is on the plate. Americans have probably eaten more biscuits in our history than any other single homemade food. Isn't it your turn for a little of the bliss?

MAKES ABOUT EIGHT 3-INCH BISCUITS OR TWELVE 2-INCH BISCUITS, SERVING 4 TO 6

2 cups low-gluten biscuit or pastry flour or 1¾ cups unbleached all-purpose flour plus ¼ cup cake flour or, less desirably, 2 cups unbleached all-purpose flour

2 teaspoons baking powder

¾ teaspoon salt

½ teaspoon baking soda

3 tablespoons lard, well chilled (see Ingredient Tip)

2 tablespoons unsalted butter, well chilled

¾ cup plus 2 tablespoons buttermilk, well chilled

Preheat the oven to 475°F.

Sift the flour, baking powder, salt, and baking soda into a large shallow bowl. Cut the lard and butter into small chunks and add them to the dry ingredients. Combine with a pastry blender just until a coarse meal forms. Make a well in the center and pour in the buttermilk. With your fingers and a few swift strokes, combine the dough just until it's a sticky mess. Turn out onto a lightly floured board or, better, a pastry cloth. Clean, dry, and flour your hands. Gently pat out the dough and fold it back over itself about a half-dozen times, just until smooth. (A dough scraper helps greatly with this.) Pat out again into a circle or oval about ½ inch thick. Cover the dough lightly and refrigerate it for about 20 minutes.

Remove the biscuit dough from the refrigerator. Cut it with a biscuit cutter, trying to get as many biscuits as possible since they will toughen if the dough is rerolled. You should be able, with practice, to get about eight 3-inch biscuits or twelve to fourteen 2-inch biscuits from the dough. Make your biscuits with a quick, clean straight-down push on the cutter, taking care to avoid twisting the cutter, which results in an uneven biscuit. Bake the biscuits in the center of the oven, turning the baking sheet around once halfway through the baking time. Bake 3-inch biscuits for 8 to 10 minutes total and 2-inch biscuits for 7 to 9 minutes, until raised and golden brown.

CORNMEAL BISCUITS

Replace ¼ cup flour with stone-ground cornmeal. If you are using the combination of all-purpose flour and cake flour, the cornmeal should replace 2 tablespoons of each.

VERMONT SOUR CREAM BISCUITS

Eliminate the baking soda and increase the baking powder to 2½ teaspoons. Replace the buttermilk with ¾ cup sour cream and 2 tablespoons heavy (whipping) cream, half-and-half, or milk.

CHEESE BISCUITS

Reduce the lard by 1 tablespoon. When the lard and butter are added to the flour, mix in ⅓ cup finely grated sharp Cheddar cheese.

PINWHEEL BERRY BISCUIT PIE

This is something of a cross between a shortcake and a cobbler, cooked in a pie dish. Roll out a batch of the biscuit dough into a rectangle about 10 × 18 inches. Spread ¾ cup Sunshine Strawberry Jam (page 404), Blackberry-Raspberry Jam (page 406), or other berry jam or preserves (not jelly) over the dough. Roll up from one of the long sides and cut into a dozen even spiral-sliced biscuits. Mix together 1 to 1¼ pounds of the same berry as your jam (fresh or frozen), about ¼ cup sugar and 2 tablespoons instant or granulated tapioca and pour the mixture into a 9-inch pie plate. Top with the biscuits, arranged evenly with cut sides up. Bake, covered, at 400°F for 10 minutes, then uncover and continue cooking for 15 to 20 minutes, until the biscuits are golden brown. Brush with butter while still hot, then let stand for a few minutes before serving warm. A little moat of cream around each serving is a luxuriant touch.

BISCUIT BOUNTY

You could probably fill an entire cookbook with the many different versions of American biscuits, particularly if you included all the toppings and fillings that cooks use. Beaten biscuits, one of the oldest types and the closest perhaps to the British progenitor, take their name from a long pounding of the unleavened dough, work once performed by slaves on southern plantations. Angel or bride's biscuits, with double leavening, occupy the opposite end of the spectrum in lightness and labor both. In between you find variations made with cream, cheese, fruit, nuts, vegetables, and more. Gravy toppings range from a thin redeye (page 130) to a thick sawmill (page 137), and fillings run the gamut of salty to sweet from country ham (page 130) to strawberry jam (page 404).

GINGER CREAM SCONES

TECHNIQUE TIP

Scone dough is quick to prepare but can also be made ahead, cut into wedges, reassembled into disks, and frozen. It's not actually necessary to thaw the dough before baking. Just add a few more minutes to the cooking time.

Scones seem to have replaced muffins as the trendy bread of the day, particularly in popular coffee shops. Hardly any of the people buying scones in these establishments would think of making a better version at home, however fast and easy that is. It would take the same time and effort, after all, as brewing a pot of good coffee for yourself. These ginger-enriched little triangles are a great accompaniment for fresh fruit and perhaps a tall glass of Iced Chai (page 430).

MAKES 1 DOZEN

2¼ cups unbleached all-purpose flour

⅓ cup sugar

1 tablespoon baking powder

2 teaspoons ground ginger

12 tablespoons (1½ sticks) unsalted butter, well chilled and cut into small bits

¾ cup heavy (whipping) cream, well chilled, plus 1 to 2 tablespoons for brushing

½ cup chopped candied crystallized ginger

Preheat the oven to 400°F. Butter a cookie sheet.

In a food processor, whir together the flour, sugar, baking powder, and ground ginger. Scatter the butter over the dry ingredients and pulse the mixture just until it resembles coarse meal. Pour in the cream and pulse the mixture just until combined. Turn the dough out onto a floured work surface and scatter the crystallized ginger over it. Gently pat out the dough and fold it back over itself about a half-dozen times, until smooth. (A dough scraper helps with this.) Use a light hand and don't overmix. Divide the dough in half and pat it out again into two ¾-inch-thick disks. Cut each disk into 6 plump pie-shaped wedges.

Transfer the scones to the prepared cookie sheet and brush with cream. Bake for 16 to 18 minutes, until light brown. Serve warm or at room temperature.

MAPLE OAT SCONES

Eliminate the crystallized ginger. Reduce the sugar to ¼ cup and add ⅔ cup old-fashioned rolled oats to the dry ingredients in the food processor. After pouring in the cream, pour in 6 tablespoons maple syrup. Once the dough is formed into disks, refrigerate it for 20 to 30 minutes. After cutting the individual scones, glaze by brushing on 1 to 2 tablespoons maple syrup instead of cream and sprinkle with 1 to 2 tablespoons additional rolled oats.

RASPBERRY-HAZELNUT SCONES

Add in place of the crystallized ginger ¾ cup fresh raspberries and ¼ cup chopped hazelnuts. Sprinkle with additional chopped nuts after brushing the scones with cream.

DATE-WALNUT SCONES

Add in place of the crystallized ginger ½ cup finely chopped fresh or dried dates and ⅓ cup chopped walnuts. Sprinkle with additional chopped nuts after brushing the scones with cream.

GALISTEO INN'S CORNMEAL SCONES

SELECTIONS FROM THE BREAKFAST MENU AT THE METROPOLITAN HOTEL IN NEW YORK CITY, 1859

BREAD

Hot Rolls   Corn Bread

Graham Bread and Rolls

Boston Brown Bread

Stale Bread   Plain Bread

A lovely ranch hacienda in the New Mexico village of the same name, the Galisteo Inn has earned a solid reputation for its cooking. The kitchen sometimes includes these currant-plumped scones, laced with yellow or blue cornmeal, among the array of breakfast breads. Not quite as rich as the previous scones, they are still seductive, with an enhanced texture and moistness.

MAKES 1 DOZEN

2 cups unbleached all-purpose flour

1 cup yellow or blue stone-ground cornmeal

⅓ cup sugar

1 tablespoon baking powder

1 teaspoon ground cinnamon

⅓ teaspoon salt

½ teaspoon baking soda

12 tablespoons (1½ sticks) unsalted butter, well chilled and cut into small bits

1 cup buttermilk

¾ cup dried currants

Turbinado sugar or other crystallized sugar, optional

Preheat the oven to 400°F. Butter a cookie sheet.

In a food processor, whir together the flour, cornmeal, sugar, baking powder, cinnamon, salt, and baking soda. Scatter the butter over the dry ingredients and pulse the mixture just until it resembles coarse meal. Pour in the buttermilk and pulse the mixture just until combined. Turn the dough out onto a floured work surface and scatter the currants over it. Gently pat out the dough and fold it back over itself about a half-dozen times, until smooth. (A dough scraper helps with this.) Use a light hand and don't overmix. Divide the dough in half and pat it out again into two ¾-inch-thick disks. Cut each disk into 6 plump pie-shaped wedges.

Transfer the scones to the prepared cookie sheet and sprinkle with sugar if you wish. Bake for 12 to 14 minutes, until golden. Serve at room temperature.

CHEESE-CORNMEAL SCONES WITH PEPPER JELLY

Eliminate the currants. Add 3 ounces grated Cheddar (about ¾ cup) to the dough when you add the butter. Serve with pepper jelly, either a mild version from bell peppers or one heated up with red or green chiles, such as Orange Pepper Jelly (page 403).

SAVORY CHEESE–CORNMEAL SCONES

Eliminate the cinnamon and currants. Add 2 ounces freshly grated Parmesan (about ½ cup) when you add the butter, along with ½ cup minced fresh chives and 1 teaspoon freshly cracked black pepper. If you want to distinguish these from sweeter scones in a breadbasket, shape the dough into 2 squares rather than disks and then cut the scones into small squares rather than triangles. You can also brush the tops before baking with a little buttermilk or milk and then sprinkle with more cracked pepper.

HERBED POPOVERS

An airy steam-powered savory quick bread related to Yorkshire pudding, popovers look impressive, taste heavenly, and go great with an array of other breakfast dishes, from softly scrambled eggs to Creamed Finnan Haddie (page 164). Some cooks beat the batter mixture much longer than we do, and others swear by starting in a cold oven, but the simple steps that follow yield terrific results for us.   **SERVES 4 OR 8**

1 to 2 tablespoons finely grated fresh Parmesan or dry Jack cheese

1 cup unbleached all-purpose flour

¾ teaspoon salt

2 large eggs

1 cup whole milk

1 tablespoon minced fresh chives or scallion greens

1 tablespoon minced fresh parsley, thyme, sage, or summer savory

1 tablespoon unsalted butter, melted

Preheat the oven to 450°F. Grease 8 ramekins or a popover pan or a muffin tin with at least 8 cups. Dust each cup lightly with cheese.

Stir together the flour and salt in a medium bowl. In another bowl, whisk the eggs with the milk, chives, and parsley. Whisk the egg mixture gradually into the dry ingredients, stirring well but only until combined. Add the butter and give the batter another stir or two. Pour the batter into the prepared cups. Bake for 15 minutes. Reduce the oven temperature to 350°F and bake for 12 to 15 minutes longer, until the popovers are golden brown, crusty, and well puffed. Avoid opening the oven door any time before what you think will be the last 2 to 3 minutes of cooking. Unmold the popovers, slit each with a knife to release the steam, and serve warm.

A BREAKFAST MENU SUGGESTION FOR A MAY MORNING IN NEW ENGLAND

Sliced Oranges

Fried Brook Trout

Country Fried Potatoes

Popovers

Coffee

Ella Shannon Bowles and Dorothy S. Towle, *Secrets of New England Cooking* (1947)

All the countryside folk and half the city folk once counted hot breadstuffs twice a day as part of the pattern of living, and if you could have persuaded the beneficiaries of that usage that a day was at hand when all the hot bread would come out of a toaster, they would have thought you were describing a world gone to pot.

Sidney W. Dean, *Cooking American* (1957)

BUTTERMILK BREAKFAST CORN BREAD

INGREDIENT TIP

Out of season, or whenever corn on the cob is not easily available to you, replace the fresh corn with 1½ cups frozen kernels, chopped lightly in a food processor with 1 tablespoon half-and-half or milk.

Southern traditionalists won't abide a hint of sugar in corn bread. Others make the bread into a cloying cake. This version tries to bridge the chasm, offering a subtle sweetness derived mainly from fresh corn, which we add for extra moisture and flavor. For us at least, it's good enough to enjoy on its own with apple or pumpkin butter and a scoop of Creamy Cottage Cheese (page 53). If you want to rev up the natural richness, serve a poached or fried egg on top.

SERVES 6 OR MORE

About 2 large ears of fresh sweet corn (see Ingredient Tip)

3 tablespoons unsalted butter

1 tablespoon bacon drippings or vegetable oil

1½ cups stone-ground yellow or white cornmeal

½ cup unbleached all-purpose flour

2 tablespoons sugar

2 teaspoons baking soda

½ teaspoon baking powder

1 teaspoon salt

Pinch of cayenne pepper

3 large eggs

1½ cups buttermilk

Stand an ear of corn upright for handling. With a medium knife, slide down the ear, slicing off the top half of the kernels. Rotate the ear and repeat the motion until you've trimmed the entire ear. Turn the knife over to the dull top side of its blade and scrape down the ear again, pressing against the cob to release the thick semiliquid milk. The process is a little messy but worth it. Repeat with the remaining ear until you have 1½ cups kernels and runny scrapings. Melt the butter in a medium saucepan over medium heat. Add the corn kernels and scrapings and cook until the corn kernels are just tender, about 3 minutes. Set aside to cool briefly.

Preheat the oven to 400°F. Place the drippings in a 9- to 10-inch cast-iron skillet and put the skillet in the oven.

Stir the cornmeal, flour, sugar, baking soda, baking powder, salt, and cayenne together in a large bowl. In another smaller bowl, whisk the eggs together, then mix in the buttermilk. Pour the liquid ingredients into the dry ingredients and stir until barely combined, with a few dry streaks remaining. Add the corn mixture, mixing just to incorporate. Take the hot skillet from the oven and spoon the batter into it. You should get a good sizzle when the batter hits the skillet. Smooth the batter and return the skillet to the oven. Bake for about 18 minutes, until lightly browned and a toothpick inserted in the center comes out clean.

The corn bread is scrumptious served piping hot right from the skillet. If you plan instead to serve it at room temperature, let it cool in the skillet for about 10 minutes before turning it out onto a baking rack, where its surface will stay the crispest. Cut into wedges just before serving.

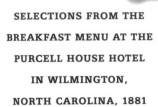

MORNING STARS

Individual corn bread portions are often cooked in muffin tins or cornstick pans. Star-shaped cast-iron pans, increasingly common, form especially radiant servings of yellow corn bread. If you can't find the pans locally, you can mail-order from Lodge Manufacturing in South Pittsburg, Tennessee (423-837-7181 or www.lodgemfg.com). Request their "All-Star" pan. Be sure to season the cast iron as directed before using it. Reduce the baking time to about 15 minutes.

CORN MUFFINS WITH SAGE AND SMOKY HAM

The corn flavor shines in this more savory muffin. Reduce the sugar to 1 tablespoon. Stir 1 teaspoon crumbled dried sage into the batter with the dry ingredients and ½ cup minced smoky ham in with the corn. Make a dozen muffins from the recipe batter, reducing the baking time to 16 to 18 minutes.

CORN AND TOASTED MILLET MUFFINS

Add even more crunch with underutilized millet, a grain available in natural foods stores and well-stocked supermarkets. First soak ¼ cup millet in hot water for about 10 minutes, then drain it and toast it in a dry skillet over medium-high heat until it begins to pop, a minute or two. Stir all but 1 tablespoon into the batter. Form as a dozen muffins, sprinkling the remaining millet evenly over the muffins. Reduce the baking time to 16 to 18 minutes.

MAPLE BRAN MUFFINS

It is an old tale that the South is known as the land of the hot biscuit and the cold cheek. Yet a part of the placidity of the South comes from the sense of well-being that follows the heart-and-body-warming consumption of breads fresh from the oven. We serve cold baker's bread only to our enemies, trusting that they will never impose on our hospitality again.

Marjorie Kinnan Rawlings,
Cross Creek Cookery (1942)

With lots of encouragement from the makers of bran cereals, bran muffins evolved from "Graham gems," named for Sylvester Graham, a nineteenth-century dietetic reformer who railed against the sinfulness of eating for pleasure. Like the foods Graham touted, bran muffins were reputed to be healthy, even when commercial versions bulged with sugar and fat. This rendition, gently flavored with maple syrup, is lighter and fluffier than most, but we can't guarantee it's more healthy. We eat these muffins as contented sinners, just because they taste good.

MAKES 1 DOZEN

1¼ cups unbleached all-purpose flour

1 teaspoon baking powder

½ teaspoon baking soda

1 teaspoon salt

2 tablespoons wheat bran

2 tablespoons wheat germ, raw or toasted

6 tablespoons unsalted butter, cut into small chunks, softened

½ cup packed brown sugar, preferably dark

2 large eggs

1 cup buttermilk

¼ cup real maple syrup (darker Grade B syrup, sometimes called "cooking maple," if available)

1 teaspoon pure vanilla extract

1¾ cups raisin bran cereal

⅓ cup dark raisins

Preheat the oven to 375°F. Grease a muffin tin for 12 muffins.

Stir the flour, baking powder, baking soda, and salt together in a medium bowl. When combined, mix in the wheat bran and wheat germ. With an electric mixer, cream together the butter and brown sugar on medium speed until light and somewhat fluffy. Add the eggs, one at a time, mixing well after each addition. Mix in the buttermilk, maple syrup, and vanilla. Add half of the dry ingredients and beat just until combined. Stop the mixer, add the rest of the dry ingredients, and stir them in by hand. When just a few streaks of the dry ingredients remain, add the cereal and raisins, mixing just until combined. The batter will be somewhat thin compared to many muffin batters. The wheat bran, wheat germ, and cereal absorb the extra liquid as the muffins cook.

Spoon out the batter equally among the muffin cups. Bake for about 20 minutes, until light brown and a toothpick inserted into a muffin comes out with just a crumb or two still attached. Cool the muffins briefly, then turn out onto a baking rack. They can be eaten immediately or later at room temperature. Wrapped tightly, the muffins remain tasty for up to 2 days.

VERY BLUEBERRY MUFFINS

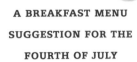

**A BREAKFAST MENU
SUGGESTION FOR THE
FOURTH OF JULY**

Red Raspberries and Cream

Fried Chicken

Scrambled Tomatoes

Warmed Potatoes

Tennessee Muffins

Toast   Coffee

**Hugo Ziemann and Mrs. F. L.
Gillette,** *The White House
Cook Book* (1898)

Early versions of muffins, which date back to British hearth cooking, contained fruit only occasionally and then usually in dried forms such as raisins. The indigenous American blueberry became one of the first fresh fruits used in breads, and it remains among the best. We add them with gusto to this cakey muffin.   **MAKES 1 DOZEN**

1¼ cups unbleached all-purpose flour

2 tablespoons toasted wheat germ or stone-ground cornmeal

¾ teaspoon baking powder

½ teaspoon baking soda

½ teaspoon salt

6 tablespoons unsalted butter, cut into small chunks and softened

¾ cup plus 2 tablespoons sugar

1 large egg

½ cup plus 2 tablespoons sour cream

2 teaspoons minced fresh lemon zest

½ teaspoon pure vanilla extract

2 cups fresh or thawed frozen blueberries

Preheat the oven to 375°F. Grease a muffin tin for 12 muffins.

Stir the flour, wheat germ, baking powder, baking soda, and salt together in a small bowl.

With an electric mixer on medium speed, cream together the butter and sugar until fluffy and light yellow. Mix in the egg, sour cream, lemon zest, and vanilla until well combined. Pour the dry ingredients into the wet ingredients and mix by hand with just enough strokes to combine. Fold in the blueberries while streaks of flour remain.

Spoon out the batter equally among the muffin cups, using an ice cream scoop if you have one. Bake for 20 to 23 minutes (or 1 to 2 minutes longer if using frozen berries), until light brown and a toothpick inserted into a muffin comes out with just a crumb or two still attached. Cool the muffins for 5 to 10 minutes, then turn them out onto a rack to cool further. They can be eaten immediately or later at room temperature. Wrapped tightly, the muffins remain tasty for up to 2 days.

VERY HUCKLEBERRY MUFFINS

Substitute fresh huckleberries for the blueberries.

VERY PEARY MUFFINS

Substitute 2 heaping cups chopped ripe pear for the blueberries and replace 2 tablespoons sour cream with pear nectar or Poire William liqueur.

CHERRY CREAM MUFFINS

These may look modest, but there's nothing modest about their forthright flavor. The creamy almond-scented batter brings out the best of the sour-cherry tang. We use local fresh fruit in season, usually from our own trees, but even frozen cherries give excellent results.

MAKES 1 DOZEN

2 cups fresh or frozen sour cherries, pitted

2 cups unbleached all-purpose flour

1½ teaspoons baking powder

½ teaspoon salt

8 tablespoons (1 stick) unsalted butter, softened

2 ounces almond paste

1 cup sugar

2 large eggs

½ cup heavy (whipping) cream

½ teaspoon pure vanilla extract

½ teaspoon pure almond extract

Turbinado sugar or other crystallized sugar, optional

Preheat the oven to 375°F. Grease a muffin tin for 12 muffins. Puree ½ cup of the cherries in a food processor or blender.

Stir the flour, baking powder, and salt together in a medium bowl. In the bowl of a mixer, cream together the butter, almond paste, and sugar until light and well combined. (Small bits of almond paste may still be evident.) Mix in the eggs, cream, vanilla and almond extracts, and pureed cherries. Pour the dry ingredients into the wet ingredients and mix by hand with just enough strokes to combine. Fold in the remaining cherries, again keeping strokes to a minimum.

Spoon out the batter equally among the muffin cups, mounding it slightly in the center, or use an ice cream scoop if you have one. Sprinkle lightly with turbinado sugar if you wish. Bake the muffins for about 20 minutes, until golden brown and a toothpick inserted into a muffin comes out clean. Cool the muffins briefly, then turn out onto a baking rack. They can be eaten immediately or later at room temperature. Wrapped tightly, the muffins remain tasty for up to 2 days.

The first meal was many times the heartiest. When our family was growing up near Greenville and later in Lancaster County—and with a healthy gang of six children—our mother would cook up an amazing breakfast batch of forty-five biscuits. . . . In addition to that, of course, Mother cooked up at least a dozen scrambled eggs, fried sausage, and fixed hot coffee and milk. For breakfast dessert, we had a generous helping of sorghum syrup that we stirred with butter and then sopped with the biscuits.

Joseph E. Dabney, *Smokehouse Ham, Spoon Bread & Scuppernong Wine* (1998)

CAKE DOUGHNUTS

INGREDIENT TIP

When you're ready to make the doughnuts, invest in whole nutmegs to grate fresh if you haven't done so before. We call for freshly grated nutmeg throughout this book, because nutmegs are easily grated on the fine holes of any grater, and the resulting ground spice is headily fragrant. Freshly grated nutmeg adds a citruslike undertone to the doughnuts and other dishes.

TECHNIQUE TIP

The original fat for frying doughnuts was lard, which yields a very crisp surface and an elusive hint of flavor. Try it for a special occasion.

SELECTIONS FROM THE BREAKFAST MENU AT THE CONGRESS SQUARE HOTEL IN PORTLAND, MAINE, 1902

BREAD

Plain   Home Made   Biscuit

Doughnuts   Graham Gems
Corn Muffins

Griddle Cakes—Maple Syrup

Early Dutch settlers in New York probably introduced the other colonists to doughnuts, a fried bread called *olie-koecken* in their homeland. Later American cooks added the hole, perhaps as a way of eliminating soggy dough in the center. Cake doughnuts, unlike the original yeast-raised variety, are a baking powder–and–soda–fueled quick bread, a style that developed after those commercial leavenings appeared more than a century ago. These came from home kitchens and still taste best there fresh out of the pan. You need to control the temperature of the cooking oil with a thermometer, but the rest of the preparation is a breeze. **MAKES ABOUT 1½ DOZEN 3-INCH DOUGHNUTS**

4 cups unbleached all-purpose flour

2 teaspoons baking powder

1½ teaspoons freshly grated nutmeg (see Ingredient Tip)

1 teaspoon salt

½ teaspoon baking soda

½ cup plus 2 tablespoons buttermilk

2 large eggs

1 large egg yolk

¾ cup sugar

3 tablespoons molasses (not blackstrap)

Peanut oil for deep-frying

Sugar

Sift the flour, baking powder, nutmeg, salt, and baking soda together into a large mixing bowl. In a smaller bowl, whisk the buttermilk, eggs and yolk, sugar, and molasses. Pour the wet ingredients into the dry and mix together with a minimum of strokes until you have a soft, slightly sticky dough.

Lightly flour a work surface. Turn the dough out onto it and gently pat to about an inch-thick circle. Roll the dough to exactly ½-inch thickness. (Thicker results in doughy doughnuts and thinner in too much crispy surface and too little cakey middle.) Use a doughnut cutter to cut out the doughnuts. (Or use a 3-inch biscuit cutter and cut the center holes with an apple corer. The center holes can also be cut free-form with a small knife. Cut the holes 1¼ to 1½ inches across.) Reroll the dough gently as needed to form all of it into doughnuts.

Warm 3 to 4 inches of oil to 370°F in a deep heavy skillet or Dutch oven (preferably cast iron for best heat retention). Spoon out several tablespoons of sugar onto a plate. Add 3 or 4 doughnuts to the oil, which will drop the oil temperature to about 360°F. Adjust the heat as needed to keep the heat at 360°F. The doughnuts will first sink to the bottom. As soon as they rise to the top, in seconds, turn them gently with tongs and cook for 40 to 45 seconds, then turn again and cook for another 45 seconds or so. They will brown because of the molasses in the dough. Drain on paper towels and immediately sprinkle with sugar on the top or both sides. Serve hot.

BOW-KNOTS

Cut the doughnut dough into rounds, then pull gently to elongate them and twist figure-eight style before frying.

CIDER DOUGHNUTS

A Massachusetts friend, Ruth Bauer, introduced us to cider doughnuts. Replace ¼ cup of the buttermilk with apple cider and add ½ teaspoon ground cinnamon to the batter with the nutmeg. Wash down the doughnuts, of course, with warm cider.

DIETETIC DOUGHNUTS

For great doughnut lore, get a copy of *The Donut Book* (1987) by Sally Levitt Steinberg, the granddaughter of Russian immigrant Adolph Levitt, who invented the "Wonderful Almost Human Automatic Donut Machine." Among other marvelous stories, she tells how doughnut companies tried in the past to sell the fried treat as a health and diet food. One business even funded a Yale University study in the 1930s and promoted the conclusions in an ad campaign with an illustration of a muscle man and copy that read "Digestible! In a test 6 doughnuts were consumed daily for 6 consecutive days and digestion and health were found to be normal." "Dr. Crum's Famous Donut Reducing Diet," developed a decade later, went further in its claims, billing a daily ration of doughnuts as "a common-sense way to take off pounds."

CROQUIGNOLES

What did children eat at those breakfasts of meat and potatoes and pancakes? Why, we ate meat and potatoes and pancakes. We drank quantities of milk, ate acres of bread, consumed butter by the pound, and we also ate doughnuts and cookies by the dozen. . . . And some of us, at least, lived and throve.

Della Lutes, *The Country Kitchen* (1936)

Just as British biscuits differ substantially from ours, the crunchy French croquignoles bear little relation other than a name to this Cajun specialty. Marcelle Bienvenu, a delightful Louisiana food writer, turned us on to these diamond-shaped little fried breads, a cousin to New Orleans beignets. Serve them with steaming cups of New Orleans Café au Lait (page 425).

SERVES 4 OR MORE

3 cups unbleached all-purpose flour

1 tablespoon baking powder

1¼ teaspoons salt

½ teaspoon freshly grated nutmeg

¼ teaspoon ground cinnamon

3 large eggs

⅓ cup granulated sugar

2 tablespoons unsalted butter, melted and cooled briefly

1 tablespoon milk

1 tablespoon pure vanilla extract

Vegetable shortening or vegetable oil for deep-frying

Confectioners' sugar

Stir the flour, baking powder, salt, nutmeg, and cinnamon together in a large bowl. In a second large bowl, whisk the eggs with the granulated sugar until the sugar dissolves and the eggs are frothy and a light lemon yellow. Add the butter, milk, and vanilla and continue to whisk for a full minute. Switch to a sturdy spoon and mix in the flour mixture, about 1 cup at a time. The dough will be somewhat stiff.

Flour a work surface lightly, then pat out the dough into a ½-inch-thick rectangle and let it rest for 15 minutes. Roll the dough out into a large ⅛-inch-thick square, then trim off any ragged edges. Using a pastry cutter or sharp knife, slice the dough into diamond shapes. We make them as small as 3 × 3 inches or up to twice that size, depending on the number of diners and what else we're serving.

Heat enough shortening in a large deep skillet or saucepan to measure several inches in depth, bringing it to 375°F. Transfer several dough diamonds to the shortening. After sinking briefly, the breads will rise to the surface. Fry them for about 1 minute, until puffed, crisp, and golden brown on both sides. Remove with tongs and drain. Repeat with the remaining dough. Dust with confectioners' sugar and serve immediately.

FRENCH QUARTER CALAS

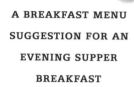

A BREAKFAST MENU
SUGGESTION FOR AN
EVENING SUPPER
BREAKFAST

Fine Hominy   Buttered Toast

Beefsteak

French Rolls

Potatoes à la Crème

Buckwheat Cakes

Tea   Coffee   Chocolate

Marion Harland, *Breakfast,*
Dinner and Supper (1889)

Another of the special fried breakfast breads of Louisiana, this Creole delicacy gained popularity as street food in nineteenth-century New Orleans. African-American women made the fritters at home and then sold them out of baskets balanced on their heads. Business got particularly lively after mass because churchgoers had to fast in the morning in order to take Communion. Enjoy that sweet reward yourself, serving the calas with cane syrup or jam and a Billie Holiday CD.

SERVES 4 OR MORE

¾ cup long-grain rice

1 teaspoon active dry yeast (about ½ envelope)

½ cup plus 2 tablespoons unbleached all-purpose flour

1 large egg

6 tablespoons granulated sugar

½ teaspoon salt

Scant ½ teaspoon freshly grated nutmeg

½ teaspoon minced fresh orange zest, optional

Vegetable oil for deep-frying

Confectioners' sugar

Combine the rice in a saucepan with 2¼ cups water and bring it to a boil over high heat. Reduce the heat to medium-low and cook for 25 to 28 minutes, until very soft and still a bit soupy. Uncover the rice and let it cool to lukewarm. Mash the rice lightly with a large fork or spoon. Stir the yeast into the rice, then add the flour. Set the mixture aside for at least an hour at room temperature (or cover and refrigerate overnight, bringing it back to room temperature before proceeding). The mixture doesn't rise like a yeast-bread dough, but it does become softer and lighter in color.

Add to the rice-flour mixture the egg, sugar, salt, nutmeg, and, if you wish, the orange zest. Beat with an electric mixer for about 1 minute. The batter will be somewhat runny. Set the batter aside to rest for about 30 minutes.

Heat several inches of oil to 375°F in a heavy saucepan. Drop the batter by rounded tablespoons and fry about 1 minute, until richly golden, turning once. Drain the fritters, then arrange them on a platter. Dust lightly with confectioners' sugar and serve.

CINNAMON ROLLS

Puffy pull-apart pillows of cinnamon, butter, and sugar, these breakfast rolls are fabulously decadent—as any homemade version should be. We generally assemble them to the point of the last rise the evening before we're serving them, then bake them fresh in the morning to eat right out of the oven.

MAKES 1 DOZEN LARGE ROLLS

ROLLS

2 teaspoons active dry yeast (most of 1 envelope)

½ pound (2 sticks) unsalted butter

⅔ cup granulated sugar

1 cup milk

1½ teaspoons salt

1½ teaspoons pure vanilla extract

4 large eggs

6 to 7 cups unbleached all-purpose flour

FILLING AND TOPPING

1 cup granulated sugar

½ cup packed light or dark brown sugar

3 tablespoons ground cinnamon

1 pound (4 sticks) unsalted butter

3 tablespoons corn syrup

1 heaping cup pecan pieces, toasted in a dry skillet

GLAZE

2 cups confectioners' sugar

1 tablespoon unsalted butter, melted

1 teaspoon pure vanilla extract

Begin to prepare the rolls, first sprinkling the yeast over ½ cup lukewarm water.

In a heavy-duty electric mixer with a dough hook on medium speed, cream together the 2 sticks butter and ⅔ cup sugar until the sugar is dissolved and the mixture is light and fluffy. Beat in the yeast mixture, milk, salt, 1½ teaspoons vanilla, eggs, and 5½ cups of the flour. Beat for several minutes, adding flour ¼ cup at a time until a cohesive but very sticky dough forms. Beat in no more flour than necessary to avoid hopeless stickiness. Beat for 5 minutes longer, until the dough becomes smooth and satiny and only a bit tacky. Pat the dough into a fat disk, transfer it to an oiled bowl, and turn to coat it with oil. Cover the bowl and set it aside in a warm, draft-free spot until the dough doubles in bulk, 1 to 1½ hours.

Begin the filling and topping. You will need 2 baking pans for the rolls, one a 9 × 12- or 13-inch size and the other an 8- or 9-inch square. Combine the granulated and brown sugars and the cinnamon in a small bowl. Melt the 4 sticks butter in a small saucepan with the corn syrup. Spoon out ½ cup of the butter mixture, pouring 5 tablespoons of it into the large baking pan and 3 tablespoons into the small pan. Tilt the pans to coat evenly. Sprinkle 3 tablespoons of the cinnamon sugar evenly over the large pan and 2 table-spoons over the small pan.

Punch the dough down and roll it out into a 12 × 18-inch rectangle. Turn the edges up just the tiniest bit, to keep the butter you will be topping the dough with from running off. Brush the dough with the remaining butter mixture, then sprinkle with the remaining cinnamon sugar and the pecans. Roll up the dough from one of the rectangle's longer sides, snugly but not too tightly. Cut the dough with a sharp knife into 1 dozen slices. Arrange the slices, one of the cut sides up, in the 2 pans, placing 7 or 8 of them in the large pan and 4 or 5 in the small pan. Cover the pans loosely and let the dough rise until doubled again, about 1 hour longer. (Alternatively, the rolls can be placed in the refrigerator to rise much more slowly overnight, for 8 to 10 hours. Let the rolls sit at room temperature for 20 minutes before baking.)

Near the end of the dough's rising time, preheat the oven to 350°F. Bake the rolls for 25 to 30 minutes, until puffy and golden brown. Let them sit in the pans on a baking rack for 5 to 10 minutes. Run a knife around the inside edges of both pans and invert the rolls onto one or more baking sheets. If any of the gooey topping remains stuck in the pans, scrape it out and plop it onto the rolls.

Prepare the glaze, mixing the ingredients with 1 tablespoon warm water. Add up to 1 tablespoon more water if the mixture is too thick to drop easily from a spoon. Drizzle the glaze over the warm rolls and serve.

HONEY BUNS

For these incredibly sticky wonder-buns, reduce the amount of granulated sugar in the filling and topping mixture by ¼ cup. Replace the corn syrup with ¼ cup mild-flavored honey.

RUM-RAISIN ROLLS

Soak ½ cup raisins in rum to cover for 10 to 20 minutes, then drain, and use them to replace ½ cup of the pecans. Add 1 tablespoon of the drained rum to the batter. Use 1 to 2 tablespoons of the drained rum instead of water in the glaze.

CARDAMOM-DATE ROLLS

In the filling, eliminate 2 tablespoons of the granulated sugar and replace ½ cup pecans with ½ cup chopped dates. Cut the cinnamon down to 2 tablespoons and add 1 teaspoon ground cardamom.

CHICAGO-STYLE BREAKFAST PAN PIZZA

TECHNIQUE TIP

To save effort, some cooks break the eggs on top of the pizza to bake with the bread. We don't do that because the high temperature that produces a proper pizza crust overcooks the eggs for our tastes.

No Neapolitan would start the day with pizza, but Americans have long taken tremendous liberties with the imported bread. You can start with a pound of frozen bread dough if you like, thawed overnight in the refrigerator, but we describe how to make a better crust from scratch. This pizza is skillet cooked, in the time-honored thick-crusted Chicago style, and makes a full meal on its own. We suggest several tasty toppings, but use your imagination with other family favorites.

SERVES 4 TO 6 AS A MAIN DISH, 6 TO 8 AS A SIDE DISH

PIZZA CRUST

1 envelope active dry yeast

½ teaspoon sugar

About 2 cups bread flour or unbleached all-purpose flour

¼ cup stone-ground cornmeal

1½ teaspoons kosher or other coarse salt

2 tablespoons olive oil

CHEESE TOPPING

1½ cups grated mozzarella cheese

6 tablespoons freshly grated Parmesan cheese

3 tablespoons minced fresh basil

1 garlic clove, minced

1 teaspoon hot red pepper flakes or more to taste

¾ teaspoon dried oregano

2 small red-ripe tomatoes, such as plum, thinly sliced

6 to 8 ounces fried bulk sausage, such as Sage Farm Sausage (page 136)

2 to 4 large eggs

Grease a heavy 10-inch skillet, preferably cast iron.

Prepare the crust, first combining the yeast and sugar with ⅔ cup lukewarm water in a small bowl. Let it sit until foamy, about 10 minutes. In a heavy-duty electric mixer with a dough hook or in a food processor, mix the yeast mixture with a scant 2 cups flour and the rest of the dough ingredients for several minutes, until the dough becomes smooth and elastic.

Transfer the dough to a floured work surface and knead for at least 2 more minutes, adding another tablespoon or two of flour if needed to get a mass that is no longer sticky. Dough on the dry side is a bit more challenging to work with but yields a crisper crust. Form the dough into a ball, place it in an oiled bowl, turn to coat it, and cover it. Set the dough in a warm, draft-free spot and let it rise until doubled in size, about 1 hour. Punch the dough down and let it rest for 10 minutes. Roll out the dough to a disk 11 to 12 inches in diameter. Transfer the dough to the skillet and pull or prod the edges with your fingers to make a lip about ½ inch high. The dough is ready to use at this point but can be covered and refrigerated overnight. If you chill it, let the dough skillet sit for about 20 minutes at room temperature before proceeding.

Preheat the oven to 400°F. Combine the cheese topping ingredients in a medium bowl. (This too can be made a day ahead and refrigerated, if you wish.) Arrange tomatoes and sausage over the crust, then sprinkle on the cheese mixture. Bake the pizza for 18 to 20 minutes, until the topping is bubbly and the crust crisp and light brown.

While the pizza bakes, scramble the eggs or fry them sunny side up, as you wish. When the pizza is done, top with the eggs. Slice the pizza into wedges and serve immediately.

BISCUIT BREAKFAST PIZZAS

These are quick and tasty little morsels, especially fun for children. You even get to cheat the clock with these by starting from a packaged base. Separate the biscuits in a tube of Pillsbury Corn Grands refrigerated biscuit dough. Roll out each into a ¼-inch-thick round. Top as you like, with grated cheese, a bit of tomato sauce, and anything else compatible. Bake at 400°F for 8 to 10 minutes and serve.

CRANBERRY-NUT BREAD

INGREDIENT TIP

We buy extra bags of cranberries when they come out after the fall harvest. They are difficult to find after the holiday season but freeze extremely well.

SELECTIONS FROM THE BREAKFAST MENU ON THE GREAT NORTHERN RAILWAY, 1943

Number 3—One Dollar

Fruit or Juice and Cereal

Ham or Sausage or Bacon with Two Eggs

Three Slices Dry Toast or

Muffins, Wheat Cakes or G. N. Health Cakes

Quick fruit breads made without yeast became prominent in American cooking by the mid–twentieth century. People add to their batter bananas, rhubarb, apricots, dates, strawberries, mangoes, muscadines (scuppernong grapes), persimmons, papaws, and more, to bake fresh in a loaf and eat warm when possible. Of all the fruit options, we're partial to tart cranberries, which contrast smartly here with astringent walnuts and a mildly sweetened batter.

MAKES 1 LARGE LOAF, SERVING 8 OR MORE

2 cups unbleached all-purpose flour

¾ cup plus 2 tablespoons sugar

2½ teaspoons baking powder

½ teaspoon freshly grated nutmeg

½ teaspoon salt

2 large eggs

8 tablespoons (1 stick) unsalted butter melted and cooled briefly

½ cup fresh orange juice

1 tablespoon chopped fresh orange zest

1¾ cups coarsely chopped cranberries (see Ingredient Tip)

1 cup chopped hickory nuts, black walnuts, or English walnuts

Preheat the oven to 350°F. Grease and flour a 9 × 5-inch loaf pan.

Stir the flour, sugar, baking powder, nutmeg, and salt together in a large mixing bowl. Make a well in the center of the ingredients. Whisk the eggs, butter, orange juice, and zest together in a small bowl and pour the mixture into the well in the dry ingredients. Combine lightly, then stir in the cranberries and nuts. Do not overmix.

Scrape the batter into the prepared pan, mounding it up in the center. Bake for 55 to 60 minutes, until browned and a toothpick inserted into the center comes out clean. Cool in the pan for 10 minutes, then turn out onto a rack covered with a clean dish towel, to prevent indentations. Let the bread cool for at least 10 minutes more before slicing. The bread can be served warm or at room temperature. It keeps well and makes good toast too.

CRAN-APRICOT-NUT BREAD

Soak ¾ cup chopped dried apricots until plump, then discard the water. Replace ¾ cup cranberries with the apricots.

RHUBARB BREAD

For spring we turn to another tangy red ingredient. Substitute an equal amount of chopped rhubarb for the cranberries and use pecans for the nuts.

BROWN SUGAR–ZUCCHINI BREAD

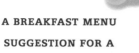
Sometimes in August, another loaf of zucchini bread is as welcome as
that fourth Christmas fruitcake. In spite of that, we guarantee you won't have any
problems in giving away slices of this dense, moist loaf.

MAKES 1 LARGE LOAF, SERVING 8 OR MORE

2 cups unbleached all-purpose
flour

½ cup packed light or dark brown
sugar

6 tablespoons granulated sugar

1¼ teaspoons ground cinnamon

½ teaspoon ground ginger

1 teaspoon baking soda

½ teaspoon baking powder

1 teaspoon salt

1 cup old-fashioned rolled oats

3 large eggs

¾ cup vegetable oil or ½ cup
vegetable oil plus ¼ cup walnut oil

2 teaspoons pure vanilla extract

2 cups grated zucchini
(about 2 medium zucchini)

Turbinado sugar or other
crystallized brown sugar, optional

Preheat the oven to 350°F. Grease and flour a 9 × 5-inch loaf pan.

Stir the flour, brown sugar, granulated sugar, cinnamon, ginger, baking
soda, baking powder, and salt together in a large mixing bowl. When combined, mix in the oats. Make a well in the center of the ingredients. Whisk
the eggs, oil, and vanilla together in a small bowl and pour the mixture into
the well in the dry ingredients. Combine lightly, then stir in the zucchini. Do
not overmix.

Scrape the batter into the prepared pan, mounding it up in the center.
Sprinkle with the turbinado sugar if you wish. Bake for 60 to 65 minutes,
until a toothpick inserted into the center comes out clean. Cool in the pan
for 10 minutes, then turn out onto a rack covered with a clean dish towel to
prevent indentations. Let the bread cool for at least 10 minutes longer
before slicing. The bread can be served warm or at room temperature. It
keeps well and makes good toast too.

BROWN SUGAR–CARROT BREAD

Replace the zucchini with 2 cups grated carrot. Because the carrots are a little starchier,
reduce the oats to ¾ cup.

WONDER-FULL WHITE BREAD

Anyone who grew up in the 1950s and '60s will remember the TV commercials that promoted softness as the most important quality for good bread. This is a white American loaf, like the ones of that era, but it's a toothsome and tasty version that has nothing in common with marshmallows. You can do most of the preparation the night before you plan to serve it, simply bringing the dough back to room temperature in the morning before slipping it into the oven. The aroma will arouse the most determined late sleeper.

MAKES 2 MEDIUM LOAVES

1 envelope active dry yeast

2 tablespoons sugar or honey

1¼ cups buttermilk

3 tablespoons plus 2 teaspoons unsalted butter

1 tablespoon salt

About 5 cups bread flour or unbleached all-purpose flour

Combine the yeast with the sugar and 1 cup lukewarm water in the work bowl of a heavy-duty electric mixer with a dough hook. Set aside until foamy, about 10 minutes. Heat the buttermilk and 3 tablespoons of the butter to lukewarm in a small pan.

Add the buttermilk mixture, salt, and 4½ cups of the flour to the yeast mixture and mix together on medium speed. Beat for about 3 minutes, then add flour a tablespoon at a time until you have a soft, supple dough. It will feel tacky but should no longer be sticky. (This may take a little more than 5 cups of flour, but don't use any more than needed to get the dough to the soft and smooth stage.) Pat the dough into a fat disk, coat it lightly with oil, and return it to the bowl. Cover the bowl and set it aside in a warm, draft-free spot until the dough doubles in bulk, 1 to 1½ hours.

Punch down the dough, kneading it a few times. Pat it back into a disk and return it to the bowl. Cover and let it rise until doubled again, another 1 to 1½ hours. Divide the dough in half and shape into 2 loaves. Grease two 9 × 5-inch loaf pans and place a loaf in each. Let the bread rise until doubled again, 45 to 60 minutes. (This is the step we usually let the refrigerator retard for us, allowing the bread to rise slowly in the pans overnight. Bring it back to room temperature before proceeding.)

Near the end of the rising time, preheat the oven to 375°F. Slash the top of each loaf with a small sharp knife. Transfer the bread to the middle shelf of the oven. Bake for 40 to 45 minutes, until the bread is richly browned and sounds hollow when tapped. If it thuds rather dully, it's not ready. In the last

5 to 10 minutes of baking, brush the top with the remaining 2 teaspoons butter. When done, cool in the pan for about 10 minutes and then remove. You can eat the bread still hot from the oven, but for best slicing, cool the loaves on a baking rack for at least 30 minutes. The bread will keep for several days and makes wonderful toast.

CINNAMON-RAISIN SWIRL BREAD

This starts with a simple enrichment of the dough, adding 1 large egg yolk when you combine the initial ingredients in the mixer. The cinnamon mixture and raisins are added just before you shape the loaves. Combine ¼ cup sugar with 1 tablespoon ground cinnamon. When you divide the dough after the first rise and before forming the loaves, roll each section into a rough rectangle about 8 × 12 inches. Sprinkle half of the cinnamon mixture evenly over each, then scatter each with ½ cup plump raisins (try a combination of dark and light). Roll up each from one of the short sides into a fat cylinder, pressing down lightly as you roll to prevent air pockets but not hard enough to squeeze the filling through. Place in the prepared loaf pans and continue.

TOAST FROM WONDER-FULL WHITE BREAD

Toast any bread right before you're going to eat it, or if you're making a big batch, keep it warm in a low oven (no baking sheet necessary). Aim for the golden-brown range of doneness for optimum flavor. One of us favors dry toast, and the other loves a bold brush of melted butter. We often slice the bread rather thickly. If you don't have a toaster that can take extra-thick slices, it's easy to make toast on a dry griddle over medium-high heat or in a 400°F oven. Just keep an eye on it to avoid burning.

CINNAMON TOAST

Our tiny grandkids love this and even volunteer to help us make it. For 4 pieces, stir up 2 tablespoons sugar with about 1 teaspoon ground cinnamon, more or less to taste. Sprinkle it over 4 slices of buttered white toast. It can be eaten as is, but it's even better with a quick minute under the broiler. Watch it carefully and serve immediately, sliced into fingers or triangles for pint-size eaters. We sometimes replace the sugar with fragrant maple sugar and other times use ¼ teaspoon cinnamon and ¼ teaspoon five-spice powder. Serve with a mug of hot chocolate.

MILK TOAST

This is soothing and gentle in flavor, not the ho-hum dish you might expect. For each diner, arrange 2 slices of warm white toast in a shallow bowl. Bring just to a boil 1 to 1½ cups milk (not skim), 1 to 2 tablespoons butter, and 1 to 2 teaspoons sugar. Pour over the toast and let it stand for several minutes before serving. A pinch or two of cinnamon, nutmeg, or anise is a good addition. We've come across a Cajun version of this suggested as a Sunday morning hangover cure, using molasses or cane syrup as the sweetener and a good dash of Tabasco sauce. No guarantees come with that one.

CIDER TOAST

For a twist on milk toast, try this variation from the apple-orchard region of New York's Hudson Valley. For each diner, arrange 2 slices of warm white toast in a shallow bowl. Bring just to a boil 1 to 1½ cups of cider, 1 to 2 tablespoons butter, 1 to 2 teaspoons brown sugar, and a good pinch ground ginger. Pour it over the toast and let it stand for several minutes before serving.

MULTIGRAIN LOAF

TECHNIQUE TIP

To store bread, it's best to keep it uncovered at room temperature, with the cut side down, or in a paper bag. Plastic is generally an enemy of bread, turning a good crust soft and giving mold a better chance to flourish. The only place you should use it is in an extremely dry climate, such as the area where we live. We have to wrap bread overnight in plastic to keep it from becoming as hard as a log by the morning. Day-old bread makes great toast, croutons, stratas, French toast, and bread puddings, which is how many of these things developed in the first place.

A BREAKFAST MENU

SUGGESTION FOR A

SEPTEMBER MORNING

Hominy Snowflakes

Lamb Chops   Baked Potatoes

Boiled Eggs

Entire-Wheat Rolls   Toast

Maria Parloa, *Miss Parloa's Kitchen Companion* (1887)

Despite our long affection for plain white bread, Americans have also always eaten loaves with more complexity and substance, sometimes for health reasons more than for flavor. This yeast-raised version provides plenty of fiber, but the focus is on taste.

MAKES 1 LARGE LOAF

1 envelope active dry yeast

2 tablespoons honey

1 cup buttermilk

1 cup Grape-Nuts or other corn-barley nugget cereal

1 cup whole wheat flour

½ cup stone-ground cornmeal

2 teaspoons salt

2 tablespoons sunflower, corn, or other vegetable oil

About 2 cups bread flour or unbleached all-purpose flour

¼ cup hulled pumpkin seeds (pepitas)

¼ cup hulled salted sunflower seeds (sunflower kernels)

1 tablespoon poppyseeds

1 egg yolk, lightly beaten

Combine the yeast with the honey and 1 cup lukewarm water in a small bowl. Set aside until foamy, about 10 minutes. Heat the buttermilk to lukewarm in a small pan. Remove from the heat and stir in the Grape-Nuts.

In a heavy-duty electric mixer with a dough hook on medium speed, mix together the whole wheat flour, cornmeal, and salt. Add the yeast mixture and the Grape-Nuts mixture, followed by the oil. Mix in about 1¾ cups of the bread flour. Beat for several minutes, adding ¼ cup or more flour as needed if the dough is remaining hopelessly sticky. Stir the seeds together in a small bowl. Reserve about 4½ teaspoons of the mixture and add the rest to the dough. Beat for approximately 5 minutes, until the dough becomes smooth and supple but is still a little tacky. Pat the dough into a fat disk. Rinse out the bowl, dry it, coat it with oil, and return the dough to it. Turn the dough to coat it with oil. Cover the bowl and set it aside in a warm, draft-free spot until the dough doubles in bulk, 1 to 1½ hours.

Punch down the dough, kneading it a few times. Pat it back into a fat disk and return it to the bowl. Cover and let it rise until doubled again, another 1 to 1½ hours. Shape the dough into a loaf. Grease a 9 × 5-inch loaf pan and place the bread in it. Let it rise until doubled again, 45 to 60 minutes longer.

Near the end of the rising time, preheat the oven to 375°F. Place an empty heavy skillet on the lowest rack of the oven. Slash the top of the bread with a sharp knife. Transfer the bread to the middle shelf of the oven. Before closing the oven, pour ½ cup water into the skillet to create steam in the oven. Close the oven immediately.

After 30 minutes, brush the loaf with the egg yolk and sprinkle the reserved seeds over it. Continue baking for about 25 minutes, until the bread is deeply brown on top and sounds hollow when thumped. If it thuds rather dully, it's not ready. Cool the bread in the pan for 10 minutes, then unmold and transfer to a baking rack, letting it cool completely to room temperature for best slicing. The bread keeps for a couple of days and makes great toast.

GRANOLA BREAKFAST LOAF

Replace the Grape-Nuts cereal in the bread with 1 cup Crunchy Granola (page 263) or other granola.

DAKOTA CRACKED-WHEAT BREAD

The inspiration for this comes from Peter and Linda Quinn, owners of Café Latté in St. Paul, which specializes in breads. For our interpretation of their Dakota bread, replace the Grape-Nuts with ½ cup cracked wheat or medium bulgur, soaking it in the buttermilk as described. Add 1 tablespoon raw sesame seeds to the seed mixture. We use a little more bread flour, about 2¼ cups.

ANADAMA BREAD

Early New England breads frequently combined scarce wheat flour with cornmeal or other grains to stretch it, creating classics such as Boston brown bread and "thirded" breads that contain equal proportions of wheat, corn, and rye. For toasting in particular, we're partial to this yeasted cornmeal and wheat-flour bread, mellowed with a bit of molasses. Legends abound about the "damned Anna" who was behind it, but given the cornmeal mush base and other common ingredients, many a cook may have come up with something like the moist, dark-crusted loaf. The bread freezes well if you'd like to double the recipe and save a loaf for another morning. **MAKES 1 LARGE LOAF**

½ cup stone-ground cornmeal, preferably yellow

3 tablespoons unsalted butter, in several chunks

2 tablespoons dark molasses

1 cup boiling water

1 envelope active dry yeast

1 large egg

1½ teaspoons salt

½ cup whole wheat flour

2 to 2¼ cups bread flour

Place the cornmeal in the work bowl of a heavy-duty mixer with the butter and 1 tablespoon molasses. Pour the boiling water over the mixture, beat on lowest speed just long enough to combine, and cool to lukewarm. Sprinkle in the yeast and again let the mixture sit, this time for 5 to 10 minutes while the yeast begins to work. Add the egg, salt, whole wheat flour, and 2 cups of the bread flour and beat on medium speed for a minute. Continue beating for about 3 minutes longer, adding more of the remaining flour, a tablespoon at a time, until the dough is smooth and elastic. It will remain a bit tacky, but if really sticky, it needs more flour.

Pat the dough into a fat disk, coat lightly with oil, and return to the bowl. Cover the bowl and set it aside in a warm, draft-free spot until the dough doubles in bulk, 1 to 1½ hours.

Punch down the dough, kneading it a few times. Shape it into a loaf. Grease a 9 × 5-inch loaf pan and place the dough in it. Let the bread rise until doubled again, 45 to 60 minutes. (This is the step we usually let the refrigerator retard for us, allowing the bread to rise slowly in the pans overnight. Bring it back to room temperature before proceeding.)

Preheat the oven to 400°F.

Combine the remaining tablespoon molasses with 1 tablespoon warm water. Brush about half of it over the bread, reserving the rest. Bake for 20 minutes, then reduce the oven temperature to 350°F. Brush with the remaining molasses mixture. Continue baking for 25 to 30 minutes longer, until richly browned and hollow when tapped. If it thuds rather dully, it's not ready. Cool in the pan for about 10 minutes and then remove. Let the bread cool to room temperature for best cutting, preferably into rather thick slices. The loaf is best for eating as is the day it's made but makes fine toast on successive days.

ANADAMA-CURRANT BREAD

Work about ½ to ¾ cup dried currants into the dough after you have added the initial 2 cups flour.

CUBAN-AMERICAN CORNMEAL BREAD

Families of Cuban descent sometimes prepare a similar bread with brown sugar rather than molasses. Substitute an equal amount of the sugar for the liquid sweetener.

RUSTIC PUEBLO SAGE AND CHEESE BREAD

A BREAKFAST MENU

SUGGESTION FOR

THANKSGIVING MORNING

Grapes   Oat Flakes

Broiled Porterhouse Steak

Codfish Balls   Browned Potatoes

Buckwheat Cakes, Maple Syrup

Wheat Bread

Coffee

Hugo Ziemann and Mrs. F. L. Gillette, *The White House Cook Book* (1898)

The Pueblos who live along the Rio Grande in New Mexico continue to bake bread in the beehive-shaped adobe *horno* ovens first brought to the region several centuries ago by the Spanish, who acquired the idea from Moors. The most common Pueblo bread is an uncomplicated crusty round, often called *adobe bread*. This feast-day style, also crusty and chewy, uses more ingredients but is no more difficult to prepare. We thank Lucy Zamora of Taos Pueblo and Lucille Hummingbird Flower King of San lldefonso Pueblo for demonstrating how they bake their bread, which encouraged us to develop this version for the conventional home oven.

MAKES ONE 1-POUND LOAF

1 teaspoon active dry yeast (about ½ envelope)

2 teaspoons molasses

1 tablespoon lard or vegetable shortening

2 teaspoons salt

¼ pound creamy fresh goat cheese, crumbled

½ cup cottage cheese

1 teaspoon dried sage or more to taste

3 to 3¼ cups bread flour

Combine the yeast with the molasses and 2 tablespoons lukewarm water in the work bowl of an electric mixer. Set aside until foamy, about 10 minutes. Heat 1 cup water with the lard to lukewarm in a small pan.

Add the water mixture, salt, cheeses, sage, and 2½ cups of the flour to the yeast mixture, mix together with the dough hook on medium speed. Beat for about 3 minutes, then add flour ¼ cup at a time until you have a smooth, elastic dough, no longer sticky but with a satiny sheen. Pat the dough into a fat disk. Wash out the bowl, coat it with oil, transfer the dough back to it, and turn the dough to coat it with the oil. Cover the bowl and set it aside in a warm, draft-free spot until the dough doubles in bulk, 1 to 1½ hours.

Punch down the dough, kneading it a few times. Pat it back into a fat disk and return it to the bowl. Cover and let it rise until doubled again, another 1 to 1½ hours. Shape the dough into a 7- to 8-inch round loaf. Let it rest briefly while you finish preparations for its baking.

Place an empty heavy skillet on the lowest rack of the oven and, for best results, a baking stone like that used for pizza or bread on the middle shelf. If you don't have a baking stone, use a heavy baking sheet. Preheat the oven to 400°F.

Transfer the bread to the heated baking stone or sheet, using a large spatula. Before closing the oven, pour ½ cup water into the skillet to create steam in the oven. Close the oven immediately. Bake for 15 minutes, then reduce the heat to 375°F and continue baking for 40 to 45 minutes, until the bread is brown on top and sounds hollow when thumped. If it thuds rather dully, it's not ready. Cool the loaf on a baking rack, letting it cool completely to room temperature for best slicing.

This is probably the place to pay my respects to the notion that hot bread is a menace to life and limb. I'm no doctor, you understand, but there are two sides to every question, and I once knew an old doctor, a Kentuckian by birth and rearing, who not only ate hot biscuits for breakfast every morning but swore it was the best way to keep young. A colleague of his who watched him packing away biscuits and strawberry jam one morning said he'd never seen a man so set on digging his grave with his teeth. "I know, Hank," says the doctor, ringing the bell for another batch, "but when I do get into my grave, I want plenty of room to turn over."

George Rector, *Dine at Home with Rector* (1934)

ENGLISH MUFFINS

Despite the name, English muffins are an American invention, a twist on English and Scottish griddle-baked yeast breads such as bannocks and crumpets. Samuel Thomas, a British-American baker, introduced them to New York by pushcart in the late nineteenth century. Many home recipes suggest a soft dough that has to be corralled with a collection of cleaned-out tuna cans, but this yeast dough is stiff enough to stand on its own, making the muffins easier to prepare. When done, be sure to pull them apart with a fork rather than cut them with a knife, to give you the nooks and crannies that capture melted butter or hollandaise so spectacularly.

MAKES 1 TO 1½ DOZEN 3-INCH MUFFINS OR
TEN 4½-INCH MUFFINS

1 envelope active dry yeast

2 teaspoons sugar

¾ cup milk

3 tablespoons vegetable shortening

3 to 3¼ cups bread flour or
unbleached all-purpose flour

1½ teaspoons salt

1 to 2 tablespoons coarsely ground
yellow cornmeal

Combine the yeast with the sugar and ¾ cup lukewarm water in the work bowl of an electric mixer. Set aside until foamy, about 10 minutes. Heat the milk and shortening to lukewarm in a small pan, stirring to melt the shortening.

Add the milk mixture, 2 cups of the flour, and the salt to the yeast mixture and beat with the dough hook on medium speed, for about 1 minute, until thick and rather hopelessly sticky. Add more flour, about ½ cup at a time, just until a cohesive, somewhat sticky dough forms, and beat for about 1 minute longer. Remove the dough from the bowl and wash and dry the bowl. Form the dough into a ball, coat it lightly with oil, and return it to the bowl. Cover the dough and set it aside in a warm, draft-free spot until it doubles in size, about 1 to 1¼ hours. (You can also cover and refrigerate the dough overnight, letting it rise more slowly. Bring it back to room temperature before proceeding.)

Knead the dough several times, then pat it out on a floured surface to just under ½ inch in thickness. Cut into rounds with a large biscuit cutter, patting the dough back into shape to cut more muffins as needed. Press cornmeal lightly onto both sides of each muffin, then transfer to a baking sheet to rest 20 to 30 minutes. (Don't wait much longer than this or they begin to balloon up rather than holding their disk shape.)

Near the end of the rising time, warm a griddle over medium heat. Remove the muffins from the baking sheet and transfer to the griddle. Griddle-cook for about 15 minutes, turning 3 times, until well browned on the flat sides and still white on the edges and somewhat crisp and hollow sounding on top. Transfer to a rack and cool for at least 10 minutes. Split with a fork to halve. The muffins will be chewy on the surface and tender inside. Toast or use in other dishes, as you wish.

BAGELS AND BIALYS

A difficult bread to make at home, the bagel became one of America's most popular breakfast breads a few decades ago. Now the bialy is catching on across the country, partly perhaps because of a presumed association with the bagel. Both come from a Jewish heritage, but the bialy is really closer in character to an English muffin. Bakers stretch the dough while proofing, indent it to add a little onion paste, and cook it to a bubbly texture. Bagel dough, in contrast, is very stiff and boiled before baking, leading one wag to call the treat "a doughnut with *rigor mortis.*"

GOLD RUSH SOURDOUGH

Before the development of commercial leavenings, American cooks in many areas practiced the sourdough technique for leavening bread. Gold prospectors carried the method to the western frontier and used it so commonly that people began calling them "sourdoughs." They often made the crusty, pleasantly tangy bread in a campfire, baking it between two of their gold pans, but we suggest an easier way to get the same result with a modern oven and a quick sourdough starter. If you want to create a more complex starter like the miners kept and reused regularly, see page 90. Even with the shortcut method, you need to start the preparation at least a day ahead, but the steps can be worked around your schedule or even spaced out over several days.

MAKES 2 LARGE LOAVES

QUICK SOURDOUGH STARTER

1½ teaspoons active dry yeast (about ¾ envelope)

1 cup unbleached all-purpose flour

4 to 5 cups bread flour (see Ingredient Tip)

1 tablespoon kosher salt

Prepare the starter, first mixing the yeast in a bowl with 1 cup lukewarm water. When dissolved, in about 10 minutes, stir in the flour and mix until well combined. Cover the mixture, place in a warm spot, and let sit overnight or up to 12 hours. (Longer is fine—the starter will just develop more tang. Knead in more water if the mixture is not easily pliable.) It will look like sticky, bubbly goo. Divide and place half in a glass or ceramic jar (it corrodes metal) for later use. The other half is ready to be used for your bread.

The bread is made in stages, or *refreshments* as professional bakers know them. It's a slow process but one that allows natural fermentation to work at its best, slowly developing a distinctive and tasty tang.

Place the starter in a heavy-duty electric mixer with a dough hook. Pour in ¾ cup lukewarm water and begin to mix slowly. The starter should dissolve partially, becoming soupy. This mixture will fill only the very bottom of the mixer bowl, so you may need to stop and stir it up from the bottom by hand. Pour in 1 cup of flour gradually while mixing, then increase the speed to medium. Mix for about 5 minutes, adding another ¼ cup to ½ cup flour after several minutes as needed to get a very wet, stretchy, sticky dough. (You can get similar results by mixing the dough by hand, kneading it for about 10 minutes.)

Yeast has a mind of its own, but
that doesn't mean it can't be
manipulated to serve your needs.
You can speed up its action by
using a rapid-rise variety,
modifying our recipes according
to the packager's directions. Our
preferred method of control,
however, is to slow the rising to
fit better into our schedule.
Simply stash the dough in the
fridge between steps, bringing it
back to room temperature before
continuing. We frequently let the
bread rise its final time chilled
overnight, so that we can just slip
it into the oven at daybreak, for
hot fresh bread with minimum
morning fuss.

Remove the dough from the mixer bowl, wash the bowl, and dry it. Grease the bowl with oil, then return the dough to the bowl and turn to coat it evenly with oil. Cover the bowl with a damp cloth and let the dough rise in a warm, draft-free spot until doubled in size, 4 to 6 hours. Alternatively, refrigerate the dough for up to a day, then let it return to room temperature before proceeding.

Punch the dough down, divide it in half, and form it into 2 free-form oblong or round loaves. Place them on a floured cookie sheet, cover with large inverted bowls, and let them rise in a warm, draft-free spot until larger by half, about 2 hours longer. This rise can also be done overnight on the night before you plan to bake the bread.

Near the end of the rising time, or the following morning, preheat the oven to 425°F. Place an empty heavy skillet on the lowest rack of the oven and, for the best results, place a baking stone on the middle shelf. Transfer the bread to the oven, using a large spatula to place it directly on the heated baking stone if you are using one. Otherwise leave the bread on the cookie sheet. Before closing the oven, pour ½ cup water into the skillet to create steam in the oven. Close the oven immediately.

Bake for 35 to 40 minutes, until the bread is deeply brown on top and sounds hollow when thumped. If it thuds rather dully, it's not ready. Cool the loaf to room temperature on a baking rack. Eat it within several hours for the best flavor, though the bread keeps for days and makes fine toast.

SOURDOUGH RYE

Replace 1 cup of the wheat flour with rye flour, adding it after the first rise. The loaves will be more dense than bread made completely from wheat flour, but not as hearty and heavy as the rye bread we would choose for sandwiches later in the day. The dough will be stickier but still manageable. We like slices of this slathered with butter and then covered with a layer of paper-thin radish slices.

BLACK OLIVE BREAD

Of the many artisanal breads that have become available commercially in recent years, olive is one of the best to our tastes. To make a version at home, reduce the salt by 1 teaspoon and add to the bread dough following its first rise ¼ cup halved pitted oil-cured black olives, mashed lightly, and the same quantity of halved, pitted Kalamata olives.

14

Morning Cakes, Cobblers, and Other Sweet Treats

KUCHEN CAME and kuchen conquered. Central and eastern European immigrants brought to the United States a cherished tradition of yeast-raised breakfast cakes and sweet rolls. They called them kuchen back home and persisted in using the time-honored name for years after they had adopted English terms for most things.

Other Americans quickly embraced the treats, which they christened "coffee cakes."

Now prepared usually with quick leavenings rather than yeast, the extended family of kuchen has continued to instill craving in fans and an old sense of pride in cooks. The varied children of the clan, however, have never lacked compatible company at the breakfast table. Gingerbread, pie, and shortcake took a seat even earlier, and more recently other sweets such as cobblers and empanadas have joined the party. Any of them can make a routine day into a holiday for both the baker and the feaster.

CINNAMON WALNUT CRUMB CAKE

When someone says "coffee cake," the first image that pops to mind is usually this variety, always spare but also a crumbly delight when made well. It's simple to prepare but doesn't keep especially well. Try to finish the cake within a day after you bake it, a task you won't find taxing.

MAKES A 10-INCH CAKE, SERVING ABOUT 8

CRUMB TOPPING

¾ cup unbleached all-purpose flour

½ cup walnut pieces

⅔ cup packed light or dark brown sugar

1 teaspoon ground cinnamon

¼ teaspoon freshly grated nutmeg

8 tablespoons (1 stick) unsalted butter, chilled and chopped into several chunks

CAKE

2¼ cups unbleached all-purpose flour

1 teaspoon baking soda

1 teaspoon baking powder

¾ teaspoon salt

¼ teaspoon ground cinnamon

8 tablespoons (1 stick) unsalted butter, softened

½ cup granulated sugar

¼ cup packed light or dark brown sugar

3 large eggs

1¼ cups buttermilk

2 teaspoons pure vanilla extract

Butter a 10-inch springform pan. Preheat the oven to 350°F.

Prepare the topping in a food processor, first whirring together the flour, walnuts, brown sugar, cinnamon, and nutmeg. Scatter the butter over the flour mixture and process until crumbly. Reserve.

Prepare the cake, first combining the flour, baking soda, baking powder, salt, and cinnamon in a medium bowl. Cream together the butter and both sugars with an electric mixer on high speed until light and fluffy. Reduce the mixer speed to medium and add the eggs, one at a time, the buttermilk, and the vanilla, mixing well after each addition. Add the dry ingredients and mix just until combined. Pour the batter into the prepared pan and smooth the surface. Scatter the crumb topping over it.

Bake for 40 to 45 minutes, until the top is crisp and a toothpick inserted into the center of the cake comes out clean. Cool for 10 to 15 minutes. Unmold, first running a knife around the edge of the cake and then unlatching the spring to remove the pan's rim. Cool for at least 20 minutes more before serving warm, or cool to room temperature and serve later.

RASPBERRY–CREAM CHEESE COFFEE CAKE

You don't typically frost a coffee cake, but you can gild one in many other ways. We start here with a buttery batter and add a luxuriant mixture of almonds and almond paste, cream cheese, and raspberry preserves. The result is as richly silky as a crumb cake is crunchy.

MAKES A 10-INCH CAKE, SERVING 8 OR MORE

**A BREAKFAST MENU
SUGGESTION FOR A HUNT
BREAKFAST**

Stewed Figs and Rhubarb

Codfish Balls and Tomato Sauce

Broiled Bacon

Baked Hominy Grits

Pineapple Coffee Cake

Coffee   Milk

Ruth Berolzheimer, ed.,
*Culinary Arts Institute
Encyclopedic Cookbook* (1948)

CAKE

2¼ cups unbleached all-purpose flour

½ cup plus 2 tablespoons sugar

12 tablespoons (1½ sticks) unsalted butter, softened

½ teaspoon baking powder

½ teaspoon baking soda

½ teaspoon salt

¾ cup sour cream

1 large egg

1 large egg yolk

½ teaspoon pure almond extract

FILLING

½ pound cream cheese, softened

3 ounces almond paste, crumbled

3 tablespoons sugar

1 large egg

½ cup raspberry preserves (avoid particularly sugary varieties)

½ cup sliced almonds

Preheat the oven to 350°F. Butter a 10-inch springform pan.

Prepare the cake batter, first combining the flour, sugar, and butter in a mixing bowl with a pastry blender until softly crumbled. Scoop out 1 cup of the flour mixture and reserve it. Stir the baking powder, baking soda, and salt into the rest of the mixture. Then mix in the sour cream, egg, egg yolk, and almond extract. Spread the batter in the pan, smoothing it as well as you can. (It will be sticky.)

Prepare the filling, stirring the cream cheese and almond paste together in another mixing bowl. The almond paste will stay a bit nubbly, but when otherwise well combined, mix in the sugar and egg. Drop the filling over the batter by spoonfuls. It will cover much of the surface but isn't intended to cover it all. Drop dollops of the preserves over the filling. Scatter the reserved flour mixture over the preserves and top with the almonds.

Bake for 40 to 45 minutes, until the center feels lightly set and the edges are golden brown. Cool for at least 10 minutes. Run a knife around the inside edge of the pan and unlatch the spring to remove the pan's rim. Eat warm or at room temperature.

ALMOND-SCENTED APRICOT KUCHEN

Sometimes kuchen is cooked in a pie pan and served in wedges. To try this style, first butter a deep 9- to 10-inch pie plate. Spoon the batter into it, reserving the flour mixture as before. Eliminate the filling. Instead mix 4 cups quartered unpeeled apricots with about 2 tablespoons sugar and a drop or two of almond extract and spoon the mixture over the batter. Whisk together ¾ cup sugar and 1 tablespoon cornstarch, then mix in ¾ cup sour cream, 2 large eggs, and another drop or two of almond extract. Pour over the apricots, then top with the reserved flour mixture and bake as instructed.

SOUR CREAM COFFEE CAKE

Sour cream and butter-enriched cake batters are a legacy from Hungary and Austria, the early capitals of fine and fanciful pastries. Generous use of sour cream yields a tender, fine-textured, and moist cake, in this case complemented by ribbons of nutty streusel over and through the batter. Accompany with sliced peaches, quartered figs, or orange or mandarin sections and steaming New Orleans Café au Lait (page 425).

MAKES A 10-INCH CAKE, SERVING 8 OR MORE

STREUSEL

½ cup pecan pieces

6 tablespoons packed brown sugar

2 teaspoons ground cinnamon

½ teaspoon freshly grated nutmeg

CAKE

2 cups sour cream

2 large eggs

4 teaspoons pure vanilla extract

2 teaspoons minced fresh orange zest

3 cups unbleached all-purpose flour

1 tablespoon baking powder

¾ teaspoon salt

½ pound unsalted butter, softened

2 cups granulated sugar

Preheat the oven to 350°F. Butter a 10-inch Bundt pan, or use walnut or almond oil to grease it well.

Scatter the pecans evenly in the bottom of the Bundt pan. Combine the brown sugar, 1½ teaspoons of the cinnamon, and the nutmeg in a small bowl. Sprinkle half of the streusel mixture evenly over the pecans, reserving the rest.

Whisk the sour cream, eggs, vanilla, and orange zest together in a bowl. In another bowl, stir together the flour, baking powder, salt, and remaining cinnamon.

With an electric mixer on medium speed, cream the butter and granulated sugar together, beating until fluffy and light. Pour in the sour cream mixture about ½ cup at a time, beating well after each addition. Beat in the flour mixture, about one third at a time, stopping to scrape the bowl after each addition and beating only until combined. The batter will be thick. Spoon a third to half of the batter into the prepared pan. Leave its surface rather uneven. Sprinkle with the remaining streusel mixture and then spoon in the remaining batter, smoothing the surface.

Bake on the oven's middle rack for 55 to 60 minutes, just until a toothpick inserted in the center comes out clean. Cool the cake in the pan for about 10 minutes. Then run a knife around the edges, invert it, and remove it from the pan. Finish cooling, top side up, on a greased baking rack. Cool for at least 10 minutes more before slicing. Serve warm, if you wish, but the cake keeps well for several days when it's tightly covered.

COFFEE COFFEE CAKE WITH ESPRESSO GLAZE

Some of the earliest American references to "coffee cake" are for cakes and cookies laced with coffee. This contemporary update of that variety, marbled with a coffee batter, owes its inspiration to the late food writer and cooking teacher Richard Sax, who included a version in his *Classic Home Desserts* (1994).

Eliminate the struesel. Dissolve 2 tablespoons instant espresso powder in 1 tablespoon of hot water. When you have mixed the batter, spoon out about a third of it into another bowl and stir the espresso mixture into it. Spoon a third of the plain batter into the prepared pan, then spoon the coffee batter over it. Top with the remaining plain batter. Pull a knife through the center of the batter, turning it gently from side to side as you round the pan, to marble the batter a bit. Bake and unmold as directed. Prepare the glaze, stirring together 2 tablespoons strong brewed coffee with 2 teaspoons instant espresso powder in a medium bowl. When the powder is dissolved, stir in approximately ¾ cup confectioners' sugar, enough to make a pourable but not runny glaze. (Add a bit of water if it's too thick.) When the cake is cool, pour the glaze over it slowly. Let set briefly before slicing.

PEAR CARDAMOM COFFEE CAKE

For the streusel, replace the pecans with an equal amount of walnuts and the cinnamon and nutmeg with ¾ teaspoon ground cardamom. Scatter the walnuts and half of the spice mixture in the bottom of the pan as before, but combine the remaining streusel with 1 peeled and chopped large Comice or Barlett pear. Scatter the pear streusel mixture over the first third to half of the batter and top with the remaining batter.

YEASTED COFFEE CAKE HORSESHOE WITH RHUBARB FILLING

Before the introduction of commercial leavenings in the mid–nineteenth century, cooks made coffee cakes with yeast. They enriched bread dough with sugar, egg, and other flavorings and used that as a foundation for scores of sweet treats that varied in shape, toppings, fillings, and fruity essence. In this case we start with the dough from our Cinnamon Rolls (page 352), but end up with a strikingly different dish, a cake filled with tangy rhubarb, scented with anise, and decoratively molded. The action of the yeast also produces a lighter texture and more complex taste than you get with quick batters, resulting in a distinctive style of coffee cake. As with yeast-raised breads, most of the preparation can be done a day ahead of your breakfast. This makes a beautiful and bountiful presentation for a morning party.

MAKES AN 18- X 6-INCH HORSESHOE-SHAPED CAKE,

SERVING 10 OR MORE

CAKE

2 teaspoons active dry yeast

½ pound (2 sticks) unsalted butter, softened

⅔ cup granulated sugar

1 cup milk

1½ teaspoons salt

1½ teaspoons pure vanilla extract

4 large eggs

6 to 7 cups unbleached all-purpose flour

FILLING

1½ pounds fresh or frozen rhubarb, chopped into ½-inch pieces (about 3 cups)

¾ cup granulated sugar

2 teaspoons ground anise seeds

1 tablespoon cornstarch

EGG WASH

1 large egg yolk

1 tablespoon heavy (whipping) cream, half-and-half, or milk

GLAZE

1 cup confectioners' sugar

1 tablespoon unsalted butter, melted

2 teaspoons Pernod or other anise liqueur

Begin to prepare the cake, first sprinkling the yeast over ½ cup lukewarm water. Let it sit until foamy, about 10 minutes.

This makes a lot of cake. Halve the recipe portions if you wish or make the whole amount of dough and filling, divide them in half, and keep one half refrigerated to use within a few days. The dough will keep frozen for a month, but thaw it overnight in the refrigerator before using.

In a heavy-duty electric mixer on medium speed, cream the butter and granulated sugar together until the mixture is light and fluffy. Using the mixer's dough hook, beat in the yeast mixture, milk, salt, vanilla, eggs, and 5½ cups of the flour. Beat for several minutes, adding more flour ¼ cup at a time until a cohesive but very sticky dough forms. Beat in no more flour than necessary to avoid hopeless stickiness. Beat for 5 more minutes until the dough becomes smooth, satiny, and only a bit tacky. Pat the dough into a fat disk, transfer it to an oiled bowl, and turn to coat it with oil. Cover the bowl and set it aside in a warm, draft-free spot until the dough doubles in bulk, 1 to 1½ hours. (This step we usually let the refrigerator retard for us, allowing the dough to rise slowly overnight. Bring it back to room temperature before proceeding.)

Prepare the filling. Simmer the rhubarb in a saucepan with the granulated sugar, anise, and ½ cup water over medium heat, until the rhubarb softens and begins to melt into the liquid. Stir occasionally. Depending on the rhubarb, expect this to take 10 to 20 minutes. Whisk the cornstarch together with 1 more tablespoon water and then whisk it into the rhubarb. Bring to a boil, then reduce the heat and continue cooking briefly, until very thick and jamlike. Set aside to cool. (The filling can be prepared a day ahead, covered, and refrigerated. Use it cold.)

When the dough has risen, punch it down and roll it out into a 12 × 18-inch rectangle, the longer sides running parallel to the counter's front edge. Spoon the filling over the dough, leaving a border of about ½ inch on all sides. Roll up the dough from one of the rectangle's long sides, snugly but not too tightly. Pinch at the seam to secure it. Arrange on a baking sheet in a smiley-looking U, seam side down. With a sharp thin knife, cut slashes along the outside of the U at 2-inch intervals, slicing only about half of the way through the dough. Pull apart a bit at the cuts to expose the inside pinwheel appearance more. Cover the horseshoe loosely and let the dough rise until doubled again, about 1 hour. (Alternatively, the cake can be placed in the refrigerator to rise more slowly overnight. Let the cake set at room temperature for 20 minutes before baking.)

Near the end of the dough's rising time, preheat the oven to 350°F. Whisk together the egg wash in a small bowl and brush it lightly over the top. Bake the cake for about 35 minutes, until puffy and deeply golden brown. Let it cool on the baking sheet.

Prepare the glaze, mixing together the confectioners' sugar with the butter and liqueur. Add 1 to 2 teaspoons water or as much as needed to make it pourable but not runny. Drizzle the glaze over the cake and let set briefly before slicing and serving.

YEASTED COFFEE CAKE TWIRLS

When the dough has been rolled up around the filling, cut the cake in half. Place each half on the baking sheet in a straight line rather than a U. Make the cuts two thirds of the way down directly through the top (instead of on the side) at 2-inch intervals. Pull the cut portions of the dough lightly in alternating directions, starting at one end. Pull the first piece toward the left, the next to the right, and so forth, exposing the pinwheel effect a bit with each pull. Glaze and bake as directed.

OLD SALEM MORAVIAN SUGAR CAKE

Though this North Carolina classic is traditionally made from a yeast dough enriched with mashed potatoes, our dough—minus the filling, egg wash, and glaze—yields a good approximation. After the dough's first rise, press it into a 9 × 13-inch pan. After it has risen again about double, punch deep indentations with your thumb into the surface at about 2-inch intervals. Prepare the topping, warming 6 tablespoons butter, 3 tablespoons heavy (whipping) cream or half-and-half, ½ cup packed light or dark brown sugar, and 1½ teaspoons ground cinnamon together in a small saucepan over medium heat. When melted, brush the topping over the surface, allowing it to pool up in the indentations. Bake the cake on the middle rack of the oven for 30 to 35 minutes, until the topping glistens and the cake is a deep golden brown. Cool briefly, then cut into squares.

MORAVIAN STREUSEL CAKE

Skip the thumbprints in the preceding sugar cake variation. Replace the topping with the crumb cake streusel mixture on page 373. Before sprinkling the topping over the cake, brush the dough with 2 tablespoons melted unsalted butter.

RISE AND DINE

Though you find it in other places, Moravian sugar cake is closely associated with Old Salem, North Carolina, where many Moravians first immigrated after leaving their eastern European homeland. It's traditionally a Sunday morning treat, with the yeast working its magic while the cook attends church. Winston-Salem's Moravian Home Church serves the sugar cake at its annual Easter breakfast, which starts in the middle of the night to accommodate thousands of diners prior to the popular sunrise service.

STRAWBERRY SHORTCAKE

As the sun lights the sky on a late spring morning, what could be more blissful than biting into biscuitlike shortcakes layered with syrupy strawberries and crowned with a creamy topping? As the season progresses, change the fresh fruit and maybe the dairy as well, using mascarpone cheese on a fig shortcake or sweetened cream cheese on a guava variation. We deviate from the traditional whipped cream even in this classic strawberry version, substituting sour cream brightened with brown sugar.

SERVES 6

BERRIES

5 generous cups halved strawberries, measured after cutting out the cottony white cores

3 tablespoons sugar or more to taste

SHORTCAKES

2¾ cups unbleached all-purpose flour

2 tablespoons sugar

1½ tablespoons baking powder

¾ teaspoon salt

3 tablespoons unsalted butter, well chilled

3 tablespoons vegetable shortening, well chilled

1 cup milk

1 teaspoon pure vanilla extract

TOPPING

1 cup sour cream

3 tablespoons packed light or dark brown sugar or a bit more to taste (see Ingredient Tip)

½ teaspoon pure vanilla extract

Stir the strawberries together with the 3 tablespoons sugar, mashing them very lightly with a fork to help release the juice. Let the berries sit at room temperature while you prepare the shortcakes and topping.

Preheat the oven to 450°F.

Sift the flour, sugar, baking powder, and salt into a large shallow bowl. Cut the butter and shortening into small chunks and add them to the dry ingredients. Combine with a pastry blender just until a coarse meal forms. Make a well in the center and pour in the milk and vanilla. With your fingers and a few swift strokes, combine the dough just until it's a sticky mess. Turn out onto a lightly floured board or, better, a pastry cloth. Clean, dry, and flour your hands. Gently pat out the dough and fold it back over itself about a half-dozen times, just until smooth. (A dough scraper helps greatly with this.) Pat out again into a circle or oval about ¾ inch thick. Cover the dough lightly and refrigerate it for about 20 minutes.

After removing the dough from the refrigerator, cut it with a biscuit cutter, trying to get as many shortcakes as possible since the dough toughens if it's rerolled. With practice you should be able to get about six 3½-inch biscuits from the dough. Make your shortcakes with a quick, clean, straight-down push on the cutter. Twisting the cutter twists the dough, resulting in an uneven shortcake. Bake the shortcakes in the center of the oven, turning the baking sheet around once halfway through the baking time. Bake for 12 to 14 minutes total, until raised and golden brown.

Prepare the topping, whisking together the sour cream with the brown sugar and vanilla in a small bowl.

Split a shortcake in half and place the bottom portion in a broad shallow bowl or on a dessert plate. Spoon several tablespoons of berries and juice over it. Spoon on a dollop of the flavored sour cream. Place the shortcake top over the cream and add another layer of berries and sour cream. Repeat with the remaining shortcakes, berries, and cream and serve immediately.

A BOUNTIFUL TABLE

One of the most popular American cookbook authors in the second half of the nineteenth century, Maria Parloa didn't skimp at breakfast. The many varied dishes she recommended in an 1880 tome included Vegetable Hash made with leftovers from a traditional New England boiled dinner, Minced Veal and Eggs, Mutton Réchauffé, Chicken in Jelly, Curry of Liver Hominy Muffins, Squash Griddle-Cakes, and Sweet Strawberry Short-Cake.

The biscuits, hot as a poker, were split the instant they came from the oven and simply baptized in butter. Then the strawberries, taken from the cold room—and were they cold! Cut or lightly mashed, sugared and clapped between those steaming hot biscuit halves, then more berries and juice all around—oh my! And cream. Not whipped cream. Cream from a jug, a very fat jug with a nozzle just meant to spill and not retard cream from joining those shortcakes in an indissoluble union which should not fade from memory while memory remains! That, my dears, is a breakfast dish.

Sidney W. Dean, *Cooking American* (1957)

GINGERBREAD CAKE

Crisp gingerbread—the kind that you cut into little people and use as construction material for tiny Christmas houses—came from Europe with the early colonists. The soft cakey variety we make here began to pick up in popularity later after the development of reliable commercial leavenings. Few things perk up a morning more than a pan of the bread loaded with ginger. This keeps well for several days but rarely lasts that long. Try it topped with Creamy Vanilla Breakfast Spread (page 59) or with a side of Ahwahnee Creamed Bananas (page 281) or Honeyed Oranges with Jalapeños (page 286).

MAKES A 10-INCH CAKE, SERVING 8 OR MORE

3½ cups unbleached all-purpose flour

2 tablespoons ground ginger

2 teaspoons baking soda

1 teaspoon salt

½ teaspoon ground allspice or cloves

½ teaspoon freshly grated nutmeg

14 tablespoons unsalted butter, softened

1 cup packed light brown sugar

1 cup granulated sugar

2 large eggs

1 cup boiling water

1 cup cane syrup, Lyle's golden syrup, or ⅔ cup molasses plus ⅓ cup light corn syrup (see Ingredient Tip)

Confectioners' sugar

Preheat the oven to 350°F. Butter a 10-inch Bundt pan or tube pan.

Sift together the flour, ginger, baking soda, salt, allspice, and nutmeg.

With an electric mixer on high speed, cream together the butter and both sugars until light and fluffy. Reduce the speed to medium and add the eggs one at a time, beating well after each addition. Continue beating and drizzle in the syrup. Add the dry ingredients and the boiling water, alternating about one third of each at a time, stopping the mixer, and scraping down as needed. Beat only until the flour is just incorporated. Mix in the last portion of the dry ingredients and water by hand, again mixing until just combined.

Spoon the batter into the prepared pan and bake on the middle rack of the oven for 50 to 55 minutes, until a toothpick inserted into the center comes out with just a few moist crumbs adhering. The gingerbread should be just starting to pull away from the side of the pan. Cool on a rack for 20 minutes. Run a knife around the outside of the cake and invert it onto a plate. Serve warm or at room temperature, sliced with a serrated knife.

OATMEAL CAKE

SELECTIONS FROM THE BREAKFAST MENU AT THE BEVERLY HILLS HOTEL, 1914

Oranges as you like them

Stewed Strawberries

Sliced Bananas

Clam Broth in Cup

Zwieback

Popovers   Rice Hot Cakes

Let your breakfasts be of wholesome and substantial food. The system needs nourishment in the morning after the long, unbroken fast of the night. The practice of taking only a cup of tea or coffee with hot biscuit, and possibly pie or doughnuts, gives a very poor foundation for the morning's labor, which is and should be the hard labor of the day. Milk, coffee, or chocolate, mushes, fruits, potatoes or bread, meat, fish, or eggs, in some of their

This moist confection, chock-full of oats in the batter and topping, is the only frosted cake we would serve for breakfast. The nubbly topping, broiled until crunchy in spots, strikes us as something of a cross between cream-topped granola and the nutty icing used on German chocolate cake.

MAKES A 9-INCH CAKE, SERVING 8

CAKE

1 cup old-fashioned rolled oats

1¼ cups boiling water

1½ cups unbleached all-purpose flour

1 teaspoon ground cinnamon

¾ teaspoon salt

½ teaspoon baking powder

½ teaspoon baking soda

8 tablespoons (1 stick) unsalted butter

½ cup plus 2 tablespoons packed brown sugar

½ cup granulated sugar

2 large eggs

2 teaspoons pure vanilla extract

TOPPING

½ cup evaporated milk

4 tablespoons (½ stick) unsalted butter

½ cup packed light or dark brown sugar

½ cup old-fashioned rolled oats

½ cup shredded coconut, preferably unsweetened

½ cup black walnut or English walnut pieces

½ cup pecan pieces

Preheat the oven to 350°F. Butter a 9-inch springform pan.

Place the oats in a heatproof bowl and pour the boiling water over them. Stir and set aside until lukewarm. Stir together the flour, cinnamon, salt, baking powder, and baking soda in a medium bowl.

With an electric mixer on medium speed, cream together the butter and both sugars, beating until fluffy and light. Add the eggs one at a time, beating well after each addition. Beat in the vanilla. Alternately beat in the flour mixture and the oat mixture in thirds, stopping to scrape the bowl after every addition and beating only until combined. Spoon the batter into the prepared pan.

Bake on the oven's middle rack for 32 to 35 minutes, just until a toothpick inserted in the center comes out clean. Cool the cake in the pan for about 10 minutes. Then run a knife around the edges and unlatch the spring to remove the pan's rim. Transfer the cake (on the springform pan base) to a baking sheet.

Prepare the topping, first combining the milk, butter, and brown sugar in a medium saucepan. Bring to a boil over medium heat. Remove from the heat and stir in the oats, coconut, and both nuts. Spoon the topping evenly over the top of the cake.

Heat the broiler. Broil the cake on the baking sheet at least several inches from the heat source for about 2 minutes, until the topping darkens a shade or two and gets a bit brown and crunchy in spots. Watch it carefully so that you crisp it but don't burn it.

Cool at least 10 minutes before slicing. Serve warm or store the cake tightly covered for up to a couple of days.

simple and digestible combinations should form the basis of the breakfast. The morning meal should be taken as soon as possible after rising. Any prolonged bodily exertion or exposure to the early morning air, before the stomach is fortified by food, is now condemned by the majority of physicians.

Mary J. Lincoln, *Boston Cooking School Cook Book* (1884)

BROWN-BUTTER APPLE CAKE

It used to be common, especially in New England, to start the morning with a savory or sweet apple pie. Most people won't make pies for breakfast today— even those who will sneak a slice from a previous dinner—but this simple apple cake sounds more acceptable to contemporary sensibilities and tastes just as good. Browned butter and toasted nuts enhance the fruit subtly, and the optional caramel sauce dresses up the dish seductively. We like using a combination of Winesap and Wolf River apples, but you get similar results with other baking apples such as Cortland, Rhode Island Greening, Idared, or the ubiquitous Granny Smith. Serve the cake with chilled cider or apple juice.

MAKES A 10-INCH CAKE, SERVING ABOUT 8

3 cups unbleached all-purpose flour

1 teaspoon baking soda

1 teaspoon salt

½ teaspoon freshly grated nutmeg

1 cup slivered almonds, toasted in a dry skillet

¾ pound (3 sticks) unsalted butter

2 cups sugar

3 large eggs

Zest of 1 medium orange, minced

3 cups chopped peeled apples

CARAMEL SAUCE, OPTIONAL

4 tablespoons (½ stick) unsalted butter

¾ cup sugar

¾ cup heavy (whipping) cream

Confectioners' sugar

Preheat the oven to 350°F. Butter a 10-inch springform pan.

Sift the flour, baking soda, salt, and nutmeg together in a small bowl. Grind the almonds in a food processor until uniformly fine textured but short of almond butter.

Brown the butter in a small skillet over high heat, stirring frequently until toasty brown and smelling of popped corn, about 5 minutes. Remove from the heat and let the butter cool to very warm room temperature, still liquid but viscous. With an electric mixer on high speed, cream the butter together with the sugar. (It gets a bit mealy in texture, not quite as fluffy as butter simply softened.) Reduce the mixer speed to medium and beat in the eggs one at a time, followed by the orange zest. Mix in the flour one third at a time, stopping to scrape the bowl after each addition. Beat in the almonds and then the apples. The batter will be quite thick. Spoon into the prepared pan and smooth the top as well as you can.

Bake for about 1¼ hours until golden brown and a toothpick inserted in the center comes out clean.

If you plan to prepare the caramel sauce, make it while the cake bakes. First combine the butter and sugar in a small saucepan over medium-high heat and cook until golden brown. Stir as needed to color evenly. Reduce the heat to medium-low and stir in the cream, watching out for the steam. Some of the mixture will harden initially but will liquefy within a couple of minutes. Cook for about 5 minutes longer, until thick but still easily spooned. (Refrigerate the sauce, if you wish, to use later. Reheat before proceeding.)

Cool the cake for 10 to 15 minutes. Unmold, first running a knife around the edge of the cake and then unlatching the spring to remove the pan's rim. Cover tightly and store at room temperature if you wish. Otherwise cut into wedges with a serrated knife and serve warm with a dusting of confectioners' sugar and maybe the caramel sauce.

A BREAKFAST MENU SUGGESTION FROM THE CHAUTAUQUA SCHOOL OF COOKERY

Strawberry Shortcake

Broiled Chicken

Creamed Hashed Potatoes

Vienna Rolls   Butter

Coffee

Emma P. Ewing, *The Art of Cookery* (1896)

DROPPED-BISCUIT CHERRY COBBLER

Bed-and-breakfast inns frequently feature cobblers these days. The fruit-filled treats provide the same nurturing comfort as old-time breakfast pies with a lot less fuss. Some cooks even use a pie-crust covering, but we opt for a biscuit or cakelike batter in our cobblers, bursting in this case with cherry flavor.

SERVES 8

FILLING

6 cups fresh or frozen pitted sour cherries (see Ingredient Tip)

¾ cup sugar, plus another tablespoon or two if the cherries are quite tart

1 teaspoon pure vanilla extract

1 or 2 drops red food coloring, optional

BISCUIT TOPPING

1¼ cups unbleached all-purpose flour

2 tablespoons sugar

1½ teaspoons baking powder

½ teaspoon salt

6 tablespoons unsalted butter, well chilled and cut into bits

⅔ cup heavy (whipping) cream or half-and-half

½ teaspoon pure vanilla extract

Preheat the oven to 400°F. Butter a shallow medium baking dish.

Prepare the filling, combining the ingredients in a mixing bowl. If you use the food coloring, go easy with it to avoid a stop-sign hue. Let sit for about 10 minutes to draw out the cherry juices.

Prepare the biscuit topping, first stirring the flour, sugar, baking powder, and salt together in a mixing bowl. Add the butter and combine with a pastry blender just until a coarse meal forms. Make a well in the center and pour in the cream and vanilla. With a few swift strokes, combine the dough just until it's cohesive and sticky.

Pour the filling into the prepared dish. Drop the topping by heaping tablespoons over the filling, leaving some of the cherries exposed. Bake in the center of the oven for 30 to 35 minutes, until the topping is golden brown. Serve warm.

DROPPED-BISCUIT BERRY COBBLER

Replace the cherries with seasonal berries, skipping the food coloring and reducing the sugar by a couple of tablespoons. We especially like blueberries, raspberries, or a combination of blackberries, such as marionberries and tangier loganberries.

BROWN-BUTTER SPICED PEACH COBBLER

In this cobbler the batter starts out under the fruit but bubbles up around and over it while it bakes. As with our apple cake earlier in this chapter, the quick step of browning the butter before combining it with the other batter ingredients gives the whole dish greater depth. The mellowed smokiness of bourbon accentuates the effect. The liberal spicing, reminiscent of southern preserved peaches, complements rather than overwhelms the fruit. This and other fruit cobblers and crisps go great with any ham steak or with Pan-Seared Iowa Breakfast Chops (page 127).

SERVES 8

FILLING

3 to 3¼ pounds (about 12 medium) ripe juicy peaches, peeled, pitted, and thickly sliced

6 tablespoons sugar

2 to 3 tablespoons bourbon or brandy

Juice of ½ medium lemon

½ teaspoon ground cinnamon

¼ teaspoon freshly grated nutmeg

¼ teaspoon ground ginger

¼ teaspoon ground allspice

Pinch of salt

BATTER

8 tablespoons (1 stick) unsalted butter

1¼ cups unbleached all-purpose flour

3¼ cup sugar

½ teaspoon baking powder

½ teaspoon baking soda

Pinch of salt

1 cup buttermilk

1 teaspoon pure pure vanilla extract

Heavy (whipping) cream or half-and-half, optional

Preheat the oven to 350°F.

Prepare the filling, stirring the ingredients together in a large bowl, and reserve it.

Prepare the batter, first melting the butter in a flameproof 9 × 13-inch baking dish or pan. Place the dish on a stovetop burner over medium-high heat, stirring frequently until toasty brown and smelling of popped corn, about 5 minutes. Immediately remove from the heat.

Stir the flour, sugar, baking powder, baking soda, and salt together in a bowl. Mix in the buttermilk and vanilla and pour the batter over the butter in the baking dish. Pour it throughout the dish, but don't worry if you have a few holes or a bit of unevenness. (Don't stir the batter, which would make it turn out with fewer of the desirable crunchy edges.) Spoon the peach filling over the batter.

Bake the cobbler for about 45 minutes, until the crust has oozed up through the fruit and is golden brown, lightly raised, and still moist. Serve the cobbler warm, accompanied by cream if you wish.

CORNMEAL-TOPPED PEACH COBBLER

Add a little more crunch to the topping by replacing ¼ cup of the flour with an equal amount of cornmeal.

WHITE PEACH COBBLER

If you are lucky enough to find white peaches in their fleeting summer season, use some in a cobbler. Cut back on the spice, though, to allow their more delicate flavor to shine through. Replace the bourbon with 1 teaspoon pure vanilla extract and eliminate the cinnamon, ginger, and allspice. If you wish, toss, in a handful of raspberries with the peaches. Scrumptious.

BROWN-BUTTER SPICED PEAR COBBLER

The cobbler is equally good with Comice, Bartlett, or Bosc pears replacing the peaches.

PLUM-ALMOND CRISP

Crisps impress guests with little effort. As with cobblers, their fruit bottoms and pastry tops can be assembled in about the time it takes to heat the oven. What typically defines a crisp is the crunchy streusel—sometimes enriched with nuts, sometimes with oats, and sometimes neither.   **SERVES 8 TO 10**

FILLING

3 pounds red or purple plums, such as Santa Rosa or Italian prune

¼ cup packed light or dark brown sugar

¼ cup granulated sugar

2 teaspoons cornstarch or up to 1 teaspoon more if the fruit is especially ripe and juicy

2 teaspoons minced fresh orange zest

¼ teaspoon freshly grated nutmeg

Pinch of salt

1 tablespoon unsalted butter, cut into bits

TOPPING

1 cup slivered almonds

1 cup old-fashioned rolled oats

1 cup packed light brown sugar

1½ cups all-purpose unbleached flour

Pinch of salt

12 tablespoons (1½ sticks) unsalted butter

Preheat the oven to 375°F. Butter a 9 × 13-inch baking dish.

Prepare the filling, first pitting and quartering the plums. Pile the pieces into the prepared dish. Mix the remaining filling ingredients into the plums.

Prepare the topping, combining the almonds, oats, brown sugar, flour, and salt in a food processor. Add the butter and pulse until the mixture becomes a crumbly meal. (There will be quite a bit of topping.) Spoon it over the plums evenly, packing it down lightly. Bake the crisp for 40 to 45 minutes, until the topping is crunchy and the plums tender. Serve warm.

INDIVIDUAL PLUM HAZELNUT CRISPS

It looks truly special when everyone's crisp comes to the table in its own ramekin. We use shallow 4-inch-wide versions to serve 8, dividing the filling and topping equally among them. Bake for about 25 minutes.

APPLE-MINT CRISP

Peel, core, and chop 3 pounds tart apples and toss them with 1 to 2 tablespoons minced fresh mint. Eliminate the orange zest and add 1 teaspoon pure vanilla extract. Substitute walnuts for the almonds in the topping. Serve with perky mint sprigs for garnish.

CHEESE DANISH

Many people think of any morning sweet roll as a "Danish." According to master baker Nancy Silverton, co-owner of La Brea Bakery in Los Angeles, a true Danish is made with a particular style of yeasted dough, richly layered with butter and fragrant with cardamom and nutmeg. As with doughnuts, a home-made version is a revelation, well worth the bother for special occasions. The multiple steps can be slowed down over several days to better fit into your schedule.

MAKES SIXTEEN 5-INCH PASTRIES

PASTRY

1 envelope active dry yeast

½ cup whole milk, heated to lukewarm

1 large egg at room temperature

¼ cup granulated sugar

2½ cups unbleached all-purpose flour

1 teaspoon salt

¼ teaspoon ground cardamom

¼ teaspoon freshly grated nutmeg

½ pound (2 sticks) unsalted butter, well chilled and cut into ½-tablespoon pats

FILLING

½ pound cream cheese, softened

½ cup confectioners' sugar

1 large egg yolk (save the white for the egg wash)

1 teaspoon minced fresh lemon zest

1 teaspoon pure vanilla extract

¼ teaspoon salt

Several tablespoons thick fruit preserves, optional

EGG WASH AND TOPPING

1 large egg white

Crystallized sugar such as sanding sugar or turbinado sugar

Prepare the pastry. If you've ever made croissant dough, this is somewhat similar, but with less butter and more sugar, resulting in a softer pastry. Combine the yeast, milk, egg, and sugar in a large mixing bowl and let stand for a few minutes, until the yeast foams.

Place the flour, salt, cardamom, and nutmeg in a food processor, and pulse twice briefly to combine. Scatter the butter bits over the flour. Pulse quickly, in about 8 little bursts, just enough to submerge the butter and break it into chunks about half the size of what you started with. Spoon the flour-butter mixture into the yeast mixture and gently and quickly combine the two, just enough to moisten the dry ingredients. Stop while you still have a very lumpy mixture. Cover and refrigerate for at least 4 hours and up to a couple of days.

You'll need a ruler for the next steps of rolling and turning and rolling some more. A dough scraper is helpful too. The steps are a little finicky but not as difficult as often portrayed and should be executed without hesitation. Lightly flour a work surface, marble if you have it, and spoon the dough out on it. Sprinkle the dough and your hands lightly with flour. Pat the dough into a thick square, then roll it out into a square of about 16 inches. Fold the dough over itself in thirds, like a business letter being prepared for an envelope. Turn it so that the closed fold is on your left.

Roll the dough back out again (add a bit of flour to the surface or rolling pin as needed), this time into a long narrow rectangle about 10 × 24 inches. Again, fold the dough over itself in thirds. Position again so that the closed fold is on your left. Roll this time into a 20-inch square, then repeat the folding and positioning. Roll again into a long narrow 10 × 24-inch rectangle. Fold in thirds one more time. Wrap in plastic and return to the refrigerator for at least 45 minutes and up to a couple of days. (If you prefer, the dough can be double-wrapped and frozen for up to a month. Thaw overnight in the refrigerator before proceeding.)

When you are ready to shape and fill the pastry, prepare the filling. Combine the cheese and confectioners' sugar in a medium bowl, stirring until smooth. Mix in the egg yolk, lemon zest, vanilla, and salt.

Cut the dough in half and keep one portion chilled. Flour a work surface and the top of the dough you'll work with first. Roll the pastry out into a 10 × 20-inch rectangle. Use your ruler again. Exactness counts here. With a pizza cutter or sharp thin knife, trim off any uneven edges, then cut the rectangle into eight 5-inch squares.

Turn the first square so that you have a diamond. Spoon about 2 tablespoons of filling from the top point down to the bottom point. (Don't take the filling quite to the edge.) If you wish, dribble a teaspoon or two of preserves over the cheese filling. Bring the left and right sides up over the filling, pressing gently to seal them at the center. You will have a little open-ended tube. Repeat with the remaining dough and filling. Arrange on two greased baking sheets spaced about 2 inches apart.

Make the egg wash, whisking together the egg white with 1 teaspoon water. Brush the mixture over the dough. Sprinkle with sugar crystals. Set aside to rise in a warm, draft-free spot until soft and puffy, about 30 minutes.

Preheat the oven to 400°F. Bake the Danish for 20 to 23 minutes, until golden brown and crisp. Cool on the baking sheet for about 5 minutes, then carefully transfer to a rack to cool further. Serve warm or at room temperature.

BEAR CLAWS

New shapes get new names. Once the pastry has been cut into 5-inch squares, spoon a generous tablespoon of the filling across the center of one from side to side. Fold the bottom half of the square up over the top half. Repeat with the rest of the dough. Along the bottom side of each formed rectangle, cut ½-inch-deep incisions about ½ inch apart. Transfer the pastries to the baking sheet and shape gently into a curve so that the slashes fan out, creating the "claws."

PINWHEEL DANISH

Once the pastry has been cut into 5-inch squares, cut a slit from each outside corner to within one-half inch of the center. Spoon a couple of teaspoons of filling into the center of the first square. Brush the egg wash over every other corner. Bring one of the egg-washed corners of the dough up to the center and repeat with the next 3 egg-washed corners in sequence until you've formed a pinwheel. Press gently at the center and repeat with the remaining dough. (The pinwheels use less filling than other shapes. If you plan to form all the pastry into pinwheels, you can halve the amount of filling. We usually make some pinwheels along with other shaped pastries, adding a little extra filling to the others.) These take up more space on baking sheets. Use an extra sheet rather than crowd them.

DANISH BRAIDS

These are easier to form than a true braid and come out spectacular looking. Divide the dough in half and refrigerate one portion. Roll out the other into a rectangle about 8 × 12 inches, with the long side running across the work surface. The actual size of the rectangles is not critical, but you do want even edges. Trim off any uneven areas.

Think of the rectangle as a letter again. This time you will be turning the left third and right third over the center after making a series of slits in the two outer sides to simulate the braided effect. Starting on the right third of the pastry, cut a dozen even ¾-inch slits angled somewhat downward. Repeat on the left third of the pastry, keeping the spacing even with the slits on the right side. The dough will look something like a fringed jacket.

Spoon half of the filling down the middle, keeping it ¼ to ½ inch away from where the slits begin. Starting at the bottom, bring the strips from each side up over the center, crisscrossing them alternately where they meet in the center. Tuck the pastry ends in neatly when done, pressing lightly and trimming off any excess that doesn't neatly fold under the rest. Transfer to a baking sheet. Repeat with the remaining dough and filling. Brush with the egg wash, sprinkle with sugar, and let rise as the recipe instructs. Bake for about 5 minutes longer than the small pastries.

FUSION BAKING

Danish and other Scandinavian immigrants popularized the pastry for Danish in the United States, but their forebears picked up the idea originally from the Viennese, the old masters of the art who also developed the first croissant. Swedish-American cooks sometimes refer to their version of the pastry as "Swedish," but the name associated with it in their mother country is Wienerbrod, or Vienna bread. The next thing you know, someone will be calling a wiener a frankfurter.

CHOCOLATE BREAD PUDDING

From the earliest years on the Virginia frontier, [breakfast] was an important meal, probably the most important of the day. It was a heavy meal then—pork and beef, fowl and fish, game meats, hot breads, cheese, eggs, fruit, ale and other drinks, cakes and pies. It made sense nutritionally, providing as it did the body fuel for long days of hard physical labor. Such heartiness was also hospitable to the guests who often came and went in the wildness and stayed overnight.

John Egerton, *Southern Food* (1987)

We ignored the first three friends who brought up this dish as a favorite breakfast indulgence. By the fourth mention, we began wondering if we were being stuffy about the idea. When a fifth chocoholic said that it reminded her of eating French *pain au chocolat,* a personal favorite, we had to try it. Purely American in sunrise decadence, it starts out with store-bought croissants—and day-old will do. Serve with plain or vanilla yogurt. **SERVES 6 TO 8**

6 to 6½ cups lightly packed bite-size croissant pieces (approximately 6 medium croissants)

6 ounces bittersweet or semisweet chocolate, chopped (see Ingredient Tip)

2 large eggs

2 large egg yolks

1¼ cups heavy (whipping) cream

1¼ cups whole milk

½ cup sugar

2 teaspoons pure vanilla extract

Preheat the oven to 350°F. Butter a medium baking dish.

Arrange the bread in the baking dish and scatter the chocolate over the bread. Whisk the eggs, yolks, cream, milk, sugar, and vanilla together and pour evenly over the bread and chocolate. Lightly pat the bread down in the custard. Let sit for 5 to 10 minutes; then stir and pat back down again, keeping the chocolate well distributed. A bit of the bread should remain above the custard.

Bake the pudding for about 35 minutes, until slightly puffed and golden, with oozing chocolate. Serve warm, spooned onto plates.

BLUEBERRY TURNOVERS

INGREDIENT TIP

If you want the turnovers on the table even faster, substitute good-quality blueberry preserves or jam for the fresh fruit mixture. Stonewall Kitchen's Wild Maine Blueberry Jam is a good one to try, available from many gourmet food retailers and by mail order (800-207-JAMS or www.stonewallkitchen.com).

TECHNIQUE TIP

Puff pastry should indeed puff, and puff high, when it bakes. To help it reach optimum height, cut it cleanly and sharply and try to crimp only the outside edge of the pastry when forming the turnovers. Avoid dripping the egg wash down onto the pan, where it can cause the pastry to stick and retard the rising.

Americans love pastry wrapped fruits, whether in the form of a baked or simmered apple dumpling, fried peach or apricot "hand" pie, or pillowy berry turnover. A particular favorite of Cheryl and her sisters as kids, these turnovers begin with frozen puff pastry to expedite the preparation. The young Cheryl relished everything about them—folding the pastry diamonds around the juicy filling, watching them poof miraculously in the oven, drizzling the glaze over the warm flaky crust, and then finally biting into shattering crust and oozing berries. The resulting blue lips seemed pretty fun too.

MAKES 4 LARGE TURNOVERS

FILLING

2½ cups fresh blueberries or one 14-ounce bag frozen blueberries (see Ingredient Tip)

2 to 3 tablespoons sugar

1 teaspoon fresh lemon juice

1 teaspoon instant or granulated tapioca

One ½-pound sheet frozen puff pastry, thawed but chilled

1 large egg

½ cup confectioners' sugar

Preheat the oven to 400°F.

Stir the blueberries, sugar, lemon juice, and tapioca together in a saucepan. Simmer over medium heat long enough for the berries to release their juice and then to get very thick and syrupy, 10 to 15 minutes, depending on the juiciness of the berries. Cool to lukewarm or cover and refrigerate overnight.

Roll the puff pastry out on a floured surface into a 10-inch square. Cut into four 5-inch diamonds, preferably with a floured pizza cutter or pastry wheel. Don't worry about precise measurements, but you want to be in this range. Whisk the egg together with 1 teaspoon water.

Spoon a quarter of the berries onto the center of each pastry square, then brush a bit of the egg around the edge. Fold one half over the other to make a triangle and pinch the edges securely closed using the tines of a fork. Repeat with the remaining pastry and filling. Arrange the turnovers on a baking sheet, leaving at least an inch between them on all sides. Cut 2 small slashes in the top of each turnover, then brush lightly with the egg. Bake for 10 to 12 minutes, until puffed and golden brown.

While the turnovers bake, prepare the glaze. Mix the confectioners' sugar with about 2 teaspoons water. After the turnovers have cooled for about 5 minutes on the baking sheet, drizzle the glaze over them, zigging and zagging it. The sheet will collect your dribbles. Transfer to a baking rack and let cool for at least 10 minutes longer, so that the filling is no longer molten. Eat slightly warm or at room temperature.

CHERRY TURNOVERS

Substitute an equal quantity of pitted sour "pie" cherries for the berries and use 3 to 4 tablespoons sugar. Add just a drop or two of red food coloring if you like.

LEMON TURNOVERS

Use store-bought lemon curd for the filling, using 2 to 3 tablespoons per turnover. For the glaze, mix the confectioners' sugar with fresh lemon juice instead of water.

RICE PUDDING EMPANADAS

Mexicans immigrants began arriving in Chicago in the early decades of the twentieth century to work in the city's railroad and meatpacking businesses. These crusty empanadas blossomed from the cultural ferment, combining tastes of the homeland with the American talent for speed and convenience. The empanadas start from store-bought tortillas that encase a cinnamon-scented pudding whipped up the evening before you plan to serve them. We like these with a side of Pasqual's Chorizo (page 138), a papaya wedge, and Breakfast Lemonade (page 435).

SERVES 4 OR MORE

TOPPING

2 tablespoons sugar

¾ teaspoon ground Mexican cinnamon (*canela*), or other cinnamon

EMPANADAS

¾ cup short-grain rice

One 2-inch Mexican cinnamon (*canela*) stick or other cinnamon stick

¼ teaspoon salt

1½ cups milk

¼ cup heavy (whipping) cream, half-and-half, or additional milk

¼ cup sugar

¼ teaspoon pure vanilla extract

4 to 6 thin flour tortillas, 6 to 7 inches in diameter, at room temperature

Vegetable oil for panfrying

Prepare the topping, stirring together the sugar and ground cinnamon in a small bowl.

Prepare the empanadas, first bringing the rice to a boil in a medium saucepan with 1½ cups water and the cinnamon stick and salt. Cover, reduce the heat to medium-low, and cook for about 18 minutes, until the rice is tender. Mix in the milk, cream, sugar, and vanilla and cool, uncovered, for 10 to 15 minutes longer, until quite thick, frequently stirring up from the bottom. When the spoon leaves a wide solid trail across the bottom of the pan, it is ready. (The pudding can be made to this point the night before, cooled, covered, and refrigerated. Reheat before proceeding, adding a bit of milk or water if too thick to stir.)

You can make either 4 plump or 6 thin empanadas. Use 4 tortillas with ½ cup of the pudding each or 6 tortillas with ⅓ cup each. Spread the pudding over one half of each tortilla. Fold the other half over the filling and press down lightly so that both sides of the tortilla stick to the rice.

Warm ¼ inch of oil in a heavy skillet over medium heat. Fry the empanadas, a few at a time, until crisp and golden brown, about 1 minute per side. Drain and immediately sprinkle with cinnamon-sugar topping. Serve warm.

15

A Brimming Breakfast Pantry

MAPLE SYRUP DESERVES a prominent place in any American breakfast pantry, and most of us also want honey and maybe molasses and sorghum. We personally require Tabasco and a few other hot sauces, while other people need soy or Worcestershire sauce, horseradish, or lemon curd.

Those make a good start on a well-rounded breakfast pantry, but your shelves won't be complete without some homemade specialties of your own.

We offer jellies, jams, fruit syrups, a margarita marmalade that will zest up any morning, a ketchup that makes a regal crown for fried potatoes, and even a chocolate gravy for your biscuits. Many of the condiments originated as a way to preserve the bounty of summer through a barren winter, but at this point we enjoy them year-round for the striking accents they add to morning foods. When your pantry is full, your breakfasts burst with flavor.

CONCORD JELLY

TECHNIQUE TIP

Homemade jellies and jams rarely will set as firmly as commercial versions. If yours come out extra-runny on occasion—which is usually caused by a lower-than-expected pectin content in the fruit—call it "homemade fruit syrup" and everyone will be impressed. You can also choose to add a bit of commercial liquid pectin, such as Certo, though many experienced jelly makers eschew this. Bring the thin jelly back to a boil with a teaspoon or 2 liquid pectin, and boil for 1 minute.

Using fruit from mesquite beans to mayhaws, roselles to rose hips, Americans have made jellies, jams, and related condiments from an extraordinary array of edibles. Now that we prepare them for pleasure instead of "wintering up," we can work with small batches, allowing for solid control of sweetening and thickening. Because Concord grapes contain a great deal of pectin, the natural substance that makes jelly gel, they are an easy and reliable place to start. More important, they make a wonderfully tasty jelly that boasts a royal purple sheen.

MAKES 2 CUPS

3 pounds Concord grapes, preferably about 2½ pounds ripe and ½ pound a little underripe

About ¾ cup sugar

½ teaspoon unsalted butter

Sterilize 2 half-pint (1-cup) canning jars.

Stem the grapes, discarding any that are bruised. Place in a heavy nonreactive saucepan and crush lightly with a potato masher or pastry blender. Bring to a full rolling boil over high heat, then remove from the heat and let stand for 2 minutes.

Place a jelly bag or a colander layered with a double thickness of damp cheesecloth over a bowl and spoon the fruit over it. Let the jelly drip undisturbed until no more juice drains. Do not press the fruit solids to coax out more juice, because it will cloud the jelly. Discard the solids.

Rinse out the saucepan. Chill a saucer in your freezer. Measure the juice, which will likely be about 2 cups. For every 2 cups of juice, measure ¾ cup sugar. Add the juice, sugar, and butter to the pan and bring to a rapid boil. Boil until the jelly gels, generally about 10 minutes. Begin to test for gelling after 8 minutes, spooning a teaspoon of the mixture onto the cold saucer. Let the mixture sit for about 10 seconds, then tip the saucer a bit. If the liquid separates and runs like water across the plate, it is not yet done. Test every minute or so, until the jelly holds a soft shape. Skim off any foam, though the butter should help decrease its formation.

Pour the jelly into the jars, leaving at least ¼ inch of headspace. Cover, cool, and refrigerate, or process in a boiling-water bath for longer storage. It can take up to a day for the jelly to set. It keeps, refrigerated, for several weeks.

SCUPPERNONG OR MUSCADINE JELLY

These two related wild grapes, old favorites for jellies, are generally tarter than Concords. For every 2 cups of juice, use 1 cup of sugar.

PRICKLY PEAR JELLY

The prickly pear cactus sprouts an electric-red fruit, tempting otherwise sane people to deck out like beekeepers and do battle with forbidding spines and stickers. The reward for the effort is a lush berrylike juice and pulp, as bright as the fuchsia in a desert sunset. In love with the taste and hue, we developed a much easier way to enjoy the fruit.

MAKES 2 CUPS

1½ cups prickly pear syrup (see Ingredient Tip)

¾ cup sugar

2 tablespoons fresh lemon juice

¼ teaspoon unsalted butter

3 ounces liquid pectin, such as Certo (measure out half of one 6-ounce pouch, using the rest for a second batch or discarding it)

Sterilize 2 half pint (1-cup) canning jars.

Combine the syrup, sugar, lemon juice, butter, and 6 tablespoons water in a medium saucepan. Bring to a rolling boil over high heat. Pour in the pectin, stir well, and continue boiling for 1 minute or whatever length of time is specified by the pectin manufacturer, stirring constantly. Skim off any foam, though the butter should decrease its formation.

Pour the jelly into the jars, leaving at least ¼ inch of headspace. Cover, cool, and refrigerate, or process in a boiling-water bath for longer storage. It can take up to a day for the jelly to set. It keeps, refrigerated, for several weeks.

ORANGE PEPPER JELLY

Born among the cacti and orange groves of Southern California, I went the wrong direction when I grew up—East, trading sunshine for the caverns of Wall Street. But every spring I was reminded of my desert roots, and my betrayal of them, by a package my folks sent from Riverside. Hidden in a carton bandaged in brown paper, tape and string, in a nest of newspaper and kitchen towels, were a dozen paraffin-topped jars of deep-rose cactus jelly. . . . Each jar held the smell and taste of spring in the desert and the miracle of blossoming sands.

Betty Fussell, *Williams-Sonoma Taste,* Summer 2001

Many people assume that pepper and chile jellies originated in the Southwest, but they are actually a southern specialty. In this version we pair the peppers with Florida oranges, combining sweet, heat, and citrus zip all in one brightly colored package.

MAKES 6 CUPS

6 medium red bell peppers, chopped

6 to 8 fresh red jalapeño chiles, or 1 to 2 fresh New Mexican or Anaheim red chiles, seeded and chopped

6 cups sugar

1 cup white vinegar

½ cup fresh orange juice

1 tablespoon grated orange zest

½ teaspoon unsalted butter

6 ounces liquid pectin, such as Certo

Sterilize 6 half-pint (1-cup) canning jars.

Combine the bell peppers, jalapeños, sugar, vinegar, orange juice, zest, and butter in a large saucepan and bring to a boil over high heat. Boil until the pepper mixture is tender, about 15 minutes. If it threatens to overflow the pan at any time, reduce the heat a bit. Pour the mixture into a food mill or through a coarse strainer and press the liquid through. Discard the remaining solids. Rinse the pan, return the liquid to it, and bring the liquid back to a rolling boil over high heat. Pour in the pectin, stir well, and continue boiling for 1 minute or whatever length of time is specified by the pectin manufacturer. Skim off any foam with a clean spoon, though the butter should decrease its formation.

Pour the jelly into the jars, leaving at least ¼ inch of headspace. Cover, cool, and refrigerate, or process in a boiling-water bath for longer storage. It can take up to a day for the jelly to set. It keeps, refrigerated, for several weeks.

SUNSHINE STRAWBERRY JAM

TECHNIQUE TIP

The level of pectin in fruit varies considerably. Apples, grapes, quinces, and blackberries contain pectin in abundance. Peaches, nectarines, pears, and raspberries have little. Weather plays tricks too, lowering the content in wet seasons. Slightly underripe fruit has more pectin than the ripest fruit, so experienced jam makers often toss in some of both for the best balance of flavor and thickness. They may also try to avoid using a commercial pectin product, feeling that it weakens the results. Generally, we go for the natural gel with high-pectin fruits, but don't hesitate to add Certo or a similar product when making other preserves.

Fruits such as strawberries are so delicate that the boiling time needed for them to gel into a cooked condiment compromises their quality. In those cases, try the uncooked sunshine method, simply letting fruit mixed with sugar sit in the sun for a couple of days. Some cooks boil the mixture very briefly to speed up the process, but we think the jam comes out better with a more gradual evaporation to concentrate the fruit's fragrance and juices. The sugar and natural acidity retard spoilage while the strawberries transform themselves. We ignored this technique for years because it just seemed too easy to work well, but sometimes real simplicity is really best.

MAKES ABOUT 2 CUPS

2 pounds strawberries

2 to 3 cups sugar

2 to 3 tablespoons fresh lemon juice

Make sure you and your utensils are scrupulously clean. Discard berries that are bruised or otherwise ailing. Stem the berries and halve them, cutting out any cottony white cores. This can easily eliminate ½ pound of the berries. Weigh the berries and combine them with ¾ cup sugar per ½ pound of berries. Mash lightly with a potato masher or pastry blender until you have a goopy strawberry soup of sorts, a thick liquid with small but distinct berry nuggets.

Pour into a shallow dish. Cover with cheesecloth secured with rubber bands. Set out in the sun for the day. Bring back inside and refrigerate overnight and repeat the following day. If you live in a warm, dry, sunny climate, you'll probably have jam by the end of this second day, without doing another thing. In a more humid or cloud-covered setting, it will likely take another full day of sitting out (and overnight refrigeration) to get the proper gelled texture, less thick than commercial versions, but with definite body. It will help speed the evaporation if you stir the jam a time or two during the day. If rain is anticipated, leave the jam in the refrigerator rather than putting it out.

When the jam is ready, sterilize 2 half-pint (1-cup) canning jars. Spoon the jam into the jars, leaving about ¼ inch of headspace, and refrigerate for up to several weeks. Freeze for longer storage.

ABBY FISHER

> The first thing I remember tasting and then wanting to taste again is the grayish-pink fuzz my grandmother skimmed from a spitting kettle of strawberry jam. I suppose I was about four. . . . Grandmother, saving always, stood like a sacrificial priestess in the steam, "skimming" into a thick white saucer, and I, sometimes permitted and more often not, put my finger into the cooling froth and licked it. Warm and sweet and odorous. I loved it, then.
>
> **M.F.K. Fisher,** *The Gastronomical Me* (1943)

The first African-American cookbook author, Abby Fisher established herself in the culinary field by making award-winning pickles and preserves. Probably born a slave in South Carolina around 1832, she eventually made her way to San Francisco and started a home-based condiment business. Patrons encouraged her to write *What Mrs. Fisher Knows About Old Southern Cooking* (1881), which remains a remarkable work. Look for a recent facsimile edition and check out what she has to say about goodies such as strawberry jam, one of her specialties.

BLACKBERRY-RASPBERRY JAM

We relish the flavor of raspberries, but they contain little pectin for jam making and quickly lose their heady perfume when cooked. To overcome these obstacles, we pair them with sturdier pectin-rich blackberries and loganberries.

MAKES 4 CUPS

2 cups red raspberries

4 cups wild or domestic blackberries, preferably mixed half and half with loganberries

2 cups sugar

2 tablespoons fresh lemon juice

½ teaspoon unsalted butter

Sterilize 4 half-pint (1 cup) canning jars.

Look the berries over carefully, discarding any that are bruised or disintegrating. Place the berries in a heavy saucepan. Mash the berries lightly with a pastry blender or large fork. Stir in the sugar and let sit for from 1 to several hours.

Add the lemon juice and bring the mixture to a boil over medium-high heat. Cook for about 10 minutes, until thick and somewhat gelled looking on a clean spoon. Begin to test for gelling after 8 minutes, spooning a teaspoon of the mixture onto a chilled saucer. Let the mixture sit for about 10 seconds, then tip the saucer a bit. If the liquid separates and runs like water across the plate, it is not yet done. Test every minute or so, until the jelly holds a soft shape. Remove from the heat and skim off any foam, though the butter should help decrease its formation.

Pour the jam into the jars, leaving at least ¼ inch of headspace. Cover, cool, and refrigerate for up to several weeks, or process in a boiling-water bath for longer storage. The jam will require at least several hours to set.

BLACKBERRY JAM

Cookbook author Janie Hibler makes the best version of this jam we've ever tasted. She uses a half and half combination of wild or domestic blackberries with loganberries.

PEACH PRESERVES

I ordered breakfast for dinner. There's nothing so comforting as scrambled eggs at night; soft cheery yellow, bright with butter, flecked with pepper. I had three strips of crisp bacon, a pile of hash browns sautéed with onion, and two pieces of rye toast, drenched in butter and dripping with jam. I nearly crooned aloud as the flavors blended in my mouth.

Sue Grafton, *N is for Noose* (1998)

Every summer our longtime friend Susie Gonzales makes wonderful peach preserves that taste like golden sunshine in a jar. Despite the complexity of flavor, they aren't difficult to make. Susie starts with the best peaches in our region of the country, from Colorado's "Western Slope," and you should do the same in your area, shopping at a peach shed, farm stand, farmers' market, or U-pick orchard.

MAKES 4 CUPS

2 generous pounds peaches, mature and fragrant but not overly ripe

2½ cups sugar

¼ cup to ½ cup fresh lemon juice

½ teaspoon unsalted butter

Sterilize 4 half-pint (1 cup) canning jars.

Dunk the peaches in boiling water for a few seconds, just long enough to loosen the skins. Peel, pit, and slice them thinly. Place in a large heavy saucepan with the sugar and chop up with a pastry blender. You want to have lots of bite-size bits of peach. Stir in the lemon juice, using up to the greater amount if the peaches are especially sweet. Let sit for about 10 minutes, long enough to draw out the juices but not long enough for them to begin to brown.

Add the butter and bring the mixture to a boil over high heat. Boil until the jam gels, generally about 10 minutes. Begin to test for gelling after 8 minutes, spooning a teaspoon of the mixture onto a chilled saucer. Let the mixture sit for about 10 seconds, then tip the saucer a bit. If the liquid separates and runs like water across the plate, it is not yet done. Test every minute or two, until the liquid holds a soft gelled shape. Skim off any foam, though the butter should help decrease its formation.

Pour the preserves into the jars, leaving at least ¼ inch of headspace. Cover, cool, and refrigerate, or process in a boiling-water bath for longer storage. Susie initially turns the jars upside down for several hours to help distribute the peach pieces thoroughly. It takes at least several hours for the jam to set. It keeps, refrigerated, for weeks.

PEACH MELBA PRESERVES

Add a ½-pint basket of raspberries to the peach mixture after you have mashed it.

MARGARITA MARMALADE

Marmalades are generally citrus-based fruit preserves, characterized further by the inclusion of fruit peel. Americans adopted marmalade from the British, but you're not likely to find this tequila-laced version on the Queen Mum's tea table. Try it on Galisteo Inn's Cornmeal Scones (page 340) or with warm flour tortillas.

MAKES ABOUT 3 CUPS

6 to 7 medium limes

About 3 cups sugar

3 tablespoons tequila, preferably silver

1 tablespoon Triple Sec or Cointreau

Zest the limes, measuring 6 tablespoons to ½ cup lightly packed peel. (The strips of peel should be no wider than about ¼ inch.) Using a sharp knife, peel off the white pith from the limes and discard it. Chop the lime fruit, eliminating seeds, and measure 1⅓ cups of pulp.

Place the zest in a heavy nonreactive saucepan and cover with water. Bring to a boil over high heat, boil 1 minute, and pour off the water. Add the chopped pulp and 3 cups water to the pan and let the mixture stand, lightly covered, for at least 4 hours or up to 24 hours.

Sterilize 3 half-pint (1-cup) canning jars.

Bring the mixture to a boil and boil until the fruit and zest are tender, about 10 minutes. Measure the fruit and its liquid and add an equal amount of sugar. Bring the mixture back to a full rolling boil and boil until it gels, which may be as little as 3 minutes more since it is already hot. Spoon a teaspoon of the marmalade onto a chilled saucer. Let the mixture sit for about 10 seconds, then tip the saucer a bit. If the liquid separates and runs like water across the plate, it is not yet done. Test every minute or two, until the marmalade holds a soft shape. Stir in the tequila and Triple Sec.

Pour the marmalade into the jars, leaving at least ¼ inch of headspace. Cover, cool, and refrigerate, or process in a boiling-water bath for longer storage. Store upside down for the first few hours to help distribute the fruit evenly. It takes at least several hours for the marmalade to set. It keeps, refrigerated, for several weeks.

MEYER LEMON MARMALADE

Replace the limes with these extra-fragrant extra-sweet Western lemons. (You may need 1 or 2 fewer fruits, though, because of their typically larger size.) Leave out the tequila. Keep the Triple Sec, which adds an interesting orange note.

OGEECHEE LIME MARMALADE

This is a specialty of the Carolina Low Country, where these wild limes thrive. Since they are as small (and tangy) as key limes, which can be substituted, you may need to double the number of limes called for in the recipe. Leave out the tequila and Triple Sec.

THE BUZZ ABOUT HONEY

Much of the honey in supermarkets continues to be the mild, golden blended variety associated with bear squeeze bottles, but it's getting easier to find versions with real character. Depending on the nectar that bees drink, their honey can run from colorless to dark amber in hue and from mild to bold in sweet flavor. Clover and orange blossom honeys are gentle and floral in character, for example, and buckwheat and eucalyptus varieties are assertive. In some cases, companies also infuse their honeys with additional flavors, using everything from herbs to chiles. Honeycomb, with the chewy beeswax comb, used to be popular and seems to be coming back. Producers harvest honey all over the country, from the Beehive State of Utah to the tops of New York City skyscrapers.

PARADISE PRESERVES

Paradise jelly, preserves, and conserves became something of a rage in the 1930s and '40s. Some canning authorities speculate that the name derives from a belief that the quince (rather than the apple) may have been the fateful fruit in the Garden of Eden. Still fresh in spirit and taste today, the condiment is a real beauty, a rosy mix of fall fruits. Because these fruits peak shortly before the winter holiday season, consider canning the preserves in a boiling-water bath and making them in ample quantity to give as gifts. Spread it on bread or just eat it like applesauce.

MAKES 4 CUPS

2 cups apple juice or 1½ cups apple juice plus ½ cup dry red wine

1 cup sugar

1½ pounds (about 3 medium to large) fragrant ripe quinces

¾ pound apples, preferably a tart variety

1½ cups cranberries

Sterilize 4 half-pint (1 cup) canning jars.

Combine the juice and sugar in a heavy saucepan over low heat. Peel and core the quinces and apples and cut them into small bite-size pieces, placing them in the juice as they are cut. Bring to a boil over high heat, then cover and continue cooking at a boil until the quinces are crisp-tender, 30 to 35 minutes. Stir in the cranberries and continue boiling, uncovered, until they pop and all the fruit is very soft and suspended in thick soupy liquid, about 20 additional minutes. Add a little water if the fruit begins to get dry before it is soft enough.

Spoon the preserves into the jars, leaving at least ¼ inch of headspace. Process the jars in a boiling-water bath according to the manufacturer's directions, generally about 10 minutes. Let the preserves sit for at least a day before serving. Refrigerate the jars after opening.

RHUBARB CONSERVE

2 p rhubarb add 4 cups sugar let stand over night in morning cook sloly till soft then add five slices pineapple just before removing from fire add one cup wallnuts all so little lemon peal

Eliza Willmore's kitchen shorthand in her manuscript cookbook

In most definitions, conserves differ from other preserves by the inclusion of nuts. The inspiration for this one comes from the manuscript cookbook of Eliza Willmore, maternal grandmother of our friend Susan Curtis. Remembered fondly by her granddaughter as high-spirited and full of fun, Mrs. Willmore's family ran a bar in the Mormon town of Evanston, Wyoming. Her sense of celebration routinely extended to the breakfast table, where she would preside daily over a groaning sideboard. The meal always included fluffy biscuits made with water she saved from cooking loads of potatoes for hash browns and home fries. She accompanied the biscuits with her home-canned preserves and jellies or this conserve, made from rhubarb harvested each spring on the family farm.

MAKES 4 CUPS

1½ pounds rhubarb, neatly chopped

2 cups sugar

1 cup chopped or crushed pineapple

Zest of 1 large lemon, minced

¼ teaspoon salt

1 cup chopped walnuts, toasted in a dry skillet

Combine the rhubarb and sugar in a heavy nonreactive saucepan and set aside for at least several hours or up to overnight to draw out the juices.

Sterilize 4 half-pint (1-cup) canning jars.

Bring the mixture to a boil over medium heat. Reduce the heat to a simmer and cook for about 20 minutes, until the rhubarb is quite tender but still holds its shape. Add the pineapple, lemon zest, salt, and walnuts and continue cooking until thick and syrupy, about 5 minutes longer.

Pour the conserve into the jars, leaving at least ¼ inch of headspace. Cover, cool, and refrigerate, or process in a boiling-water bath for longer storage. The conserve keeps, refrigerated, for several weeks.

FIG CONSERVE

In the later summer, trade out the rhubarb for figs. To the same quantity of figs (we use Missions), add the crushed or chopped pineapple, 1 cup sugar, the salt, and a whole lemon, halved and thinly sliced rather than just the zest. Cook for about twice as long as the rhubarb, until thick and syrupy. Replace half of the common English walnuts with pungent black walnuts if available or skip the walnuts and use pecans instead.

APPALACHIAN APPLE BUTTER

German immigrants brought the country a harvest tradition of long-cooked fruit butters. They used almost any fruit that produced a bumper crop, including peaches, pears, persimmons, crabapples, quinces, and cherries. This classic rendition, enriched with sorghum, comes from the apple orchards of western North Carolina. Families and friends got together to make it outdoors in an enormous copper pot or enameled dishpan, cooking down bushels of apples over a day and a night. Participants took turns stirring the apple butter continuously to prevent scorching, using a long-handled perforated paddle. For this manageable home kitchen version, we use handfuls rather than basketfuls of apples, mixing at least one tart kind with other varieties. Spoon the butter over a bowl of oatmeal or cottage cheese or serve it alongside a ham steak or Sage Farm Sausage (page 136).

MAKES ABOUT 4 CUPS

2 quarts apple cider, preferably unfiltered

4 pounds apples, peeled and cored

¼ cup sugar

¼ cup sorghum syrup or molasses or more to taste

½ teaspoon ground cinnamon or more to taste

¼ teaspoon freshly grated nutmeg or more to taste

Sterilize 4 half-pint (1-cup) canning jars or freezer containers.

Pour the cider into a large heavy pan and bring to a boil over high heat. Cook the cider down by about one third. While the cider reduces, slice the apples in a food processor, using the thinnest slicing blade. (This can be done by hand too but takes a good bit more time.)

When the cider is ready, add the apples, reduce the heat to medium, and cook until the apples begin to disintegrate, about 1 hour. Reduce the heat to low and continue cooking until very thick, spreadable, and nearly smooth, 3½ to 4 hours longer. Stir the apple butter every 10 to 15 minutes during the last 1½ hours. In the last hour, add the sugar, sorghum, and spices, working up in quantity if desired. Using more sugar or sorghum makes the final spread softer and more syrupy but less redolent of apples. Spoon into the jars, leaving at least ¼ inch of headspace.

For long shelf life, the apple butter can be processed in a boiling-water bath according to the jar manufacturer's directions. Given the small yield, we typically freeze it or just refrigerate and eat it within a couple of months.

PEACH BUTTER

Start with 4 pounds peaches, dunked in boiling water until the skins are easy to remove. Peel them, then puree in a food processor. Combine the peaches with 2 cups sugar and 1 cup water in a large heavy saucepan and cook over low heat for about 3 hours, stirring frequently toward the end. If you wish, add ½ teaspoon ground ginger, a tablespoon or two of bourbon or brandy, or 1 teaspoon pure vanilla extract. Cook for at least 10 minutes longer. This makes about 6 cups.

PEAR BUTTER

Peel 4 pounds of pears, core them, and slice them very thin in the food processor. Combine the fruit in a large heavy saucepan with 2 cups sugar and either 1 cup water or 1 cup Gewürztraminer or Riesling wine. Cook over low heat for about 3 hours, stirring frequently toward the end. If you wish, add a teaspoon of vanilla or ½ to ¾ teaspoon of ground ginger or cardamom. Cook at least 10 minutes longer. This makes about 6 cups.

GREEN TOMATO–MINT CHUTNEY

**SELECTIONS FROM THE
BREAKFAST MENU AT THE
HOTEL IMPERIAL IN NEW
YORK CITY, 1905**

RELISHES

Anchovy Toast   Pickled Onions

Indian Chutney Sauce

Caviar on Toast

Chili Sauce   Pickled Walnuts

Celery   Stuffed Mangoes

A tangy savory condiment works much better than a sweet one at many meals. Green tomato preparations are associated with the end of the growing season, as a way to use up immature tomatoes before a freeze, but we also like them earlier in the season. If you don't have a garden of your own to raid, just ask a local grower at a farmers' market or produce stand to pick some green tomatoes for you. We like this chutney as a counterpoint to rich dishes such as Eggs Benedict (page 32) or biscuits covered in Appalachian Sawmill Gravy (page 137). It's also great on a plain or Cheddar-topped English muffin.

MAKES ABOUT 3 CUPS

2 pounds green tomatoes, chopped
(see Ingredient Tip)

1 cup chopped onion

½ cup dried currants

Juice and minced zest of
1 medium lemon

½ cup sugar

6 tablespoons cider vinegar

2 teaspoons yellow mustard seeds

1 teaspoon salt

¼ teaspoon ground ginger

¼ teaspoon ground cinnamon

⅛ to ¼ teaspoon cayenne pepper

¼ cup minced fresh mint

Sterilize 3 half-pint (1-cup) canning jars or freezer containers.

Combine all the ingredients except the mint with ½ cup water in a large heavy saucepan and bring to a boil over high heat. Reduce the heat to medium-low and cook until thick, about 1 hour. Stir frequently toward the end of the cooking, adding the mint in the last 5 to 10 minutes. Cool the chutney, then spoon it into the jars, leaving at least ¼ inch of headspace. The chutney can be used the following day, refrigerated for up to several weeks, or frozen for several months.

STARFRUIT IN SPICED SYRUP

In the morning they rose in a house pungent with breakfast cookery, and they sat at a smoking table loaded with brains and eggs, ham, hot biscuits, fried apples seething in their gummed syrups, honey, golden butter, fried steaks, scalding coffee. Or there were stacked buttercakes, rum-colored molasses, fragrant brown sausages, a bowl of wet cherries, plums, fat, juicy bacon, jam.

Thomas Wolfe, *Look Homeward, Angel* (1929)

Bananas, coconuts, pineapples, and oranges once aroused excitement as exotic fruits. Today the starfruit or carambola attracts similar attention, always eliciting a smile for its namesake sliced shape and pleasant crispness. Rather than cooking them down for a condiment, which would alter the appearance and texture, we simply bathe them in syrup. Eat immediately or freeze them for up to a couple of months. A festive morning fillip, the starfruit goes with Sour Cream Coffee Cake (page 376) and vanilla yogurt or can garnish a chilled breakfast beverage.

MAKES 4 CUPS

2 pounds (4 to 6) medium starfruit (see Ingredient Tip)

1½ cups sugar

½ vanilla bean, cut into 2 pieces

½ teaspoon whole allspice

Sterilize two 1-pint canning jars or a freezer container.

Cut any brown edges from the ribs of the starfruit. Slice across the fruits into ⅓-inch-thick stars. Place in a heatproof bowl. Combine the sugar, vanilla bean, and allspice in a saucepan with 1 cup water and bring to a boil over high heat. Reduce the heat to a simmer and reduce by about one quarter. Pour the hot syrup over the fruit and let stand at room temperature for about 1 hour. (If the fruit floats, place a small plate directly on it to help keep it submerged.) Freeze with the syrup and the vanilla bean in a covered container. If you want to keep it in 2 jars, divide the spices between them and leave at least ½ inch of headspace.

RUM-RAISIN SYRUP

As full-bodied as real maple syrup, this is a fine homemade substitute for the natural product. Drizzle it over plain yogurt, fresh or sautéed bananas or pineapple spears, or serve with Bishop Hill Cottage Cheese Pudding (page 72), New England Brown–Bread Griddle Cakes (page 85), or Swedish Pancakes (page 94).

MAKES 2 CUPS

½ cup raisins

½ cup dark rum

¼ cup light corn syrup

¼ cup packed light or dark brown sugar

Pinch of ground allspice or freshly grated nutmeg, optional

Sterilize 2 half-pint (1-cup) canning jars unless you intend to use all the syrup immediately.

Combine the raisins and rum in a medium saucepan and let them sit for 10 to 15 minutes. Stir in ¾ cup water and the remaining ingredients and bring to a boil over high heat. Reduce the heat to a simmer and cook for about 5 minutes, until melded into a thin sauce. Use the syrup immediately or pour into jars, cover, cool, and refrigerate. The syrup keeps for weeks.

THE MAGNIFICENT MAPLE

Maple syrup shouts "American breakfast." Canadians share our love for it, but few other people in the world are aware of its existence. From the upper Midwest to New England, people have long collected the sap from sugar maples when it begins to run, a condition brought on in March and April by sunny warm days, melting snows, and frigid nights. Some fans still use a galvanized steel pail hung on trees, but the commercial producers connect all the trees in the "sugarbush" with plastic tubing. Since the sap is perishable, it must be cooked down immediately, yielding 1 gallon of syrup for 40 gallons of sap.

Real maple syrup varies in shades and intensity of flavor. It's graded in Vermont according to a strict code. The industry there calls the early-season light syrup Fancy grade, followed by Grade A Medium Amber (the most common store variety), Grade A Dark Amber, and the ultra-dark and strong Grade B. We like fancy or medium amber on French toast and delicate pancakes. For buckwheats, brown-bread pancakes, and other hearty dishes, we prefer the deeper strength of dark amber or Grade B. For peak flavor, serve maple syrup slightly warmed. A couple of our favorite mail-order sources are Green Mountain Sugar House (800-643-9338) and Highland Sugarworks (802-479-1749 or www.highlandsugarworks. com).

The manufacture of maple syrup is not a process, but a ritual—a ritual of mysticism that has all the appurtenances of paganism and the Black Arts. The very metamorphosis of a thin, colorless, insipid, sweetish liquid of no particular character into a rich and delicate flavor, a distinctive table personality, partakes of alchemy. It could not be more marvelous were it done with the aid of unicorn horn, mummy dust, and bezoar stone.

Sydney Woolridge writing in Imogene B. Wolcott's *The New England Yankee Cook Book* (1939)

CITRUS SYRUP

More gently flavored than maple or our Rum-Raisin Syrup, this makes a better match for fresh fruit or subtle dishes such as Ethereal Cloud Cakes (page 96).

MAKES 2 CUPS

1 cup sugar

½ cup sweet dessert-style white wine or water

Minced zest and juice of 1 large orange or 2 medium tangerines or Satsumas

Sterilize 2 half-pint (1-cup) canning jars unless you intend to use all the syrup immediately.

Combine the ingredients in a small nonreactive saucepan and bring to a boil over high heat. Reduce the heat to a simmer and cook, stirring occasionally, until the sugar has dissolved, about 5 minutes. Use the syrup immediately or pour into jars, cover, cool, and refrigerate for several weeks. The syrup is good chilled, at room temperature, or reheated.

LAVENDER SYRUP

Like prickly pear cactus, lavender makes impressively colored syrups or jellies. Even if you love the herb, be a little stingy with it as a flavoring. A little goes a long way. Just as you remove the syrup from the heat, stir in about 3 tablespoons of fresh or dried buds and let the mixture sit at room temperature to infuse, at least 1 hour. Pour the syrup through a strainer before serving. Serve with Sweet Fried Ricotta (page 78) or over sliced honeydew, cantaloupe, or white peaches. We learned recently from lavender enthusiast Randy Murray that white chocolate and lavender is a remarkably good combination. Make Chocolate Chip Pancakes (page 96) substituting chunked white chocolate for the chocolate chips and serve them with the lavender syrup.

BIRCH SYRUP

A red-gold syrup made from the sap of the lovely birch tree often usurps the spot of maple syrup on the breakfast table in Alaska, Minnesota, and other far northern areas. The spring collection, which sometimes takes place by dogsled, requires twice the effort necessary for the better-known rival because a hundred gallons of sap produce only a single gallon of syrup. The lightly fruity syrup can be used judiciously on sourdough pancakes or steel-cut oats, fried apples or fresh fruit, or even to sweeten coffee or black tea. The Cameron Birch Syrup company in Wasilla, Alaska, provides more information and takes mail orders at www.birchsyrup.com and 800-YO-BIRCH.

WATERMELON SYRUP

The most popular watermelon preserve is pickled rind, but this style of syrup from the pulp of the fruit also has legions of fans in the northern prairie states. Midwest food authority Judith Fertig suggests pouring it over coffee cakes or pancakes or using it as a sweetener in baked dishes. It also makes the base for a refreshing beverage, stirred into soda water and topped with a sprig of mint. When melons are plentiful, you can prepare the syrup by cooking down the pulp of a whole watermelon. For quicker work for morning meals, we start from the watermelon juice readily available in our local Hispanic groceries and natural foods stores.

MAKES 2 CUPS

1 quart unstrained watermelon juice

2 tablespoons corn syrup

Sterilize 2 half-pint (1-cup) canning jars unless you intend to use all the syrup immediately.

Combine the ingredients in a heavy saucepan and bring to a boil. Reduce the heat to medium-low and simmer, stirring occasionally, until reduced by half, 15 to 20 minutes. Serve immediately or cool, transfer to the jars, and store in the refrigerator for up to several weeks. We prefer it warmed again before topping pancakes or other dishes.

COOKING THE COB

If watermelon syrup sounds unusual, you probably haven't had a corncob version. In times and places of scarcity, cooks made syrups and jellies from almost anything that wasn't poisonous, including peach leaves, violets, and the cobs left over from fresh corn. One of Cheryl's great-grandmothers in Illinois gained local renown for her cob preparations. Starting with cobs that would yield a rosy hue (such as "Tennessee Red"), she simmered a half-dozen in a quart of water until 3 cups of nearly purple liquid remained. She then removed the cobs and added 1 cup sugar, along with pectin if she wanted jelly. A tattered recipe card we have says to strain the liquid through cheesecloth or "an old curtain." Gayle and Ron Ice, farmers in Alcalde, New Mexico, still make corncob jelly with the sheen of rose quartz, which they sell at area farmers' markets and by mail from 505-852-2589.

CAJETA

A *dulce de leche* that moved north from Mexico, the goat's milk caramel called *cajeta* dresses up many dishes in the Southwest. We particularly like it in the breakfast pantry to provide a richly creamy and tangy topping for waffles, baked apples, sautéed bananas, toasted wheat cereal, and more. It's simple to make and keeps well in the refrigerator. When we first experimented with *cajeta* a couple of decades ago, we actually had to go to a pet store to get the goat's milk. It's much easier to find today, especially at natural foods stores.

MAKES 2 CUPS

1 quart fresh goat's milk, or 2 cups canned evaporated goat's milk plus 2 cups water

1 cup sugar

1 tablespoon light corn syrup

¼ teaspoon baking soda

Sterilize one 1-pint (2-cup) canning jar unless you intend to use all the *cajeta* immediately.

Combine the milk, sugar, and corn syrup in a large heavy saucepan and cook over medium heat. When the mixture boils, stir in the baking soda, which will cause it to bubble up merrily. Lower the heat so that bubbles just break occasionally at the edge. Cook until rich golden brown, syrupy, and reduced by at least half, 1 to 1½ hours. The *cajeta* can be used immediately or poured into a jar, cooled, covered, and refrigerated for months.

COFFEE CARAMEL SAUCE

Make the caramel with ½ cup less milk than usual. When thick and reduced, stir in ½ cup strong coffee.

CHOCOLATE GRAVY

Recently, when a *Dallas Morning News* reader asked the paper's "recipe swap" column for a version of southern chocolate gravy, she received forty suggestions for the preparation. Some people snicker at the idea, but the first cook who boiled down maple sap into syrup probably got a few guffaws too. The gravy traditionally goes on Flaky Buttermilk Biscuits (336), but you might also want to try it on Chocolate Chip Pancakes (page 96) or New Orleans Pain Perdu (page 116). It's not a keeper condiment, like the others in the chapter, but you can make it easily from ingredients routinely on hand.   **MAKES ABOUT 2 CUPS**

½ cup sugar

3 tablespoons unsweetened cocoa powder

2 tablespoons unbleached all-purpose flour

Pinch of salt

1¾ cups whole milk

2 tablespoons unsalted butter

½ teaspoon pure vanilla extract

Stir together the sugar, cocoa, flour, and salt in a saucepan. Place the pan over medium heat and whisk in ¼ cup water. Cook for 2 minutes, then whisk the milk slowly into the cocoa paste mixture. Bring the mixture just to a boil and cook until thick and smooth, stirring frequently, 5 to 7 minutes. Stir in the butter and vanilla and remove from the heat. Serve immediately.

ROASTED RED PEPPER AND TOMATO KETCHUP

We usually cringe when we see someone in a café cover breakfast in candy-sweet commercial ketchup. We realize that tomato flavor can enhance corned beef hash, a simple scramble, or hash browns, but an excess of sugar ruins the impact. This less cloying version is sweetened naturally in part by mellow red bell peppers.

MAKES ABOUT 3 CUPS

2 large red bell peppers

½ medium onion, quartered

Two 15-ounce cans tomato sauce

6 tablespoons inexpensive red wine vinegar

3 tablespoons sugar

3 tablespoons corn syrup

1½ teaspoons salt

1 teaspoon paprika

½ teaspoon ground cinnamon

Pinch or two of cayenne pepper

¼ teaspoon ground allspice

¼ teaspoon ground cloves

Preheat the broiler. Cover a small baking sheet with foil for easy cleanup.

Place the peppers on the baking sheet. Broil about 6 inches from the heat for about 15 minutes, turning occasionally, until the peppers are soft and the skins dark and split in spots. (Alternatively, hold the peppers with tongs over a high gas flame.) Cool the peppers in a plastic bag so that their skins loosen further from the steam. When cool enough to handle, pull the charred skins from the peppers and stem and seed them.

Puree the peppers with the onion in a food processor.

Combine the pureed mixture and the remaining ingredients in a large heavy pan. Bring the mixture to a boil over high heat, then reduce the heat to low and cook for 45 minutes to 1 hour, reducing the mixture by about half. Stir up from the bottom frequently during the last few minutes of cooking.

While the ketchup cooks, sterilize 3 half-pint (1-cup) canning jars.

The ketchup can be processed in a boiling-water bath for long-term preservation. We prefer to spoon it into jars and refrigerate it for use over a few weeks.

SALSA FRONTERA

Everyone should have an easily prepared, all-purpose salsa to quickly enliven fried or scrambled eggs, stratas, makeshift morning sandwiches, breakfast burritos and tacos, and savory corn cakes. This border style, with roasted tomatoes, is our favorite. The quick high heat burnishes the tomato skins and adds complexity, deepening the flavor of the less-than-perfect fruits often available. It keeps, refrigerated, for several days to serve cold. If you'd prefer a warm spicy sauce, try Diablo Breakfast Salsa (page 76), Red Chile Sauce (page 74), or Mesilla Valley Green Chile Sauce (page 40).   **MAKES ABOUT 2 CUPS**

1½ pounds small tomatoes, such as plum

½ medium onion, cut into chunks

¼ cup chopped fresh cilantro

2 to 3 serrano or jalapeño chiles

2 plump garlic cloves

1½ teaspoons salt

2 to 3 tablespoons white or cider vinegar

Pinch of sugar, optional

Preheat the broiler. Cover a small baking sheet with foil for easy cleanup.

Place the tomatoes on the baking sheet. Broil about 6 inches from the heat for 15 to 18 minutes, turning occasionally, until the tomatoes are soft and the skins dark and split in spots. Cool the tomatoes briefly.

Puree the tomatoes, with their skins and cores, with the remaining ingredients, adding the sugar if you think it would round out the flavor. The salsa can be served warm but is usually chilled. It keeps for several days in the refrigerator and can be perked up quickly with another teaspoon or two of minced cilantro or an extra splash of vinegar.

SALSA FRONTERA EMBELLISHMENTS

Minor changes can give you a whole new salsa. Leave one tomato unbroiled and dice it and the onion to add at the end, creating a chunkier style. Or replace the tomatoes with tangy green tomatillos, removing their papery husks before broiling. Try canned chipotles in adobo sauce in place of the fresh chiles for a smokier taste or add a bit of crumbled Mexican oregano or substitute lime juice for vinegar. For a more festive note, mix in a diced avocado after pureeing the tomatoes.

16

Wake-Up Drinks

AMERICANS HAVE always liked a bracing drink to get themselves moving in the morning. In the early years, when we didn't much trust our water supply, people often got their spark from a mug of ale or hard cider or even a tumbler of rum or whiskey.

We still favor spirits on special occasions, but generally today we're amply satisfied with a jolt of caffeine from coffee or tea or, in other cases, a kiss of sunshine from a zestful juice.

Many of us won't forsake our drink of choice—particularly when it's coffee—but almost everyone is open to extras, including new and unfamiliar possibilities. Americans continue to experiment with beverages at breakfast in the way we used to with edibles. The happy result is a broad array of bright and sprightly morning drinks sure to open your eyes and lift you to your toes.

NEW ORLEANS CAFÉ AU LAIT

A good cup of Creole Coffee! Is there anything in the whole range of food substances to be compared with it? And is there any city in the world where coffee is so delightfully concocted as in New Orleans? . . . The Creole cuisinières succeeded far beyond even the famous chefs of France in discovering the secret of good coffee-making, and they have never yielded the palm of victory.

The Picayune's Creole Cook Book
(1901)

Until recent decades, few Americans knew much about making good coffee. We often started with mediocre beans and then boiled or percolated out most of their meager taste. To find a full, flavorful cup on a consistent basis, you had to travel to New Orleans, a city that has long taken pride in its café noir and café au lait. The latter, with milk, is the traditional breakfast favorite, but both brews blend superior, dark-roasted beans with chicory. The chicory mellows the strong coffee while adding aroma, body, and depth of color.

MAKES THREE 8-OUNCE CUPS OR TWO 12-OUNCE CUPS

3 tablespoons freshly ground dark-roasted arabica coffee beans, ground as appropriate for your coffee maker

1 tablespoon ground roast chicory (see Ingredient Tip)

1½ cups heavy (whipping) cream, half-and-half, or milk, warmed

Sugar, optional

Mix the coffee and chicory. Using your favorite coffee maker (traditionally in New Orleans a manual drip model), brew the coffee mixture with 1½ cups water heated to the point just below boiling. Pour the coffee equally into 2 or 3 cups and fill each with the same amount of cream. Serve immediately, with sugar if desired.

CAFÉ NOIR

For a stout black morning brew, leave out the cream and double the portions of coffee, chicory, and water.

A CUSTOM CUP OF JOE

To tailor coffee to your taste, experiment with different beans and roasts, topics discussed on the following pages. Prepare them like Café Noir, but replace the chicory with the same amount of additional coffee. If you plan to add milk, you can reduce the quantities of coffee and water proportionately.

PERFECTING YOUR BREW

KNOWING YOUR BEANS

Seeds from a fruit native to Africa, coffee beans come from two different species of tree. Arabica is the prized variety, named for the original Arab connoisseurs who popularized coffee in the fifteenth century. They imported their beans from East Africa, where the fruit flourished at high altitudes in a subtropical climate. Some of the finest coffees in the world still originate in Ethiopia and Kenya, but growers cultivate the bean today in mountainous, equatorial regions around the globe. The second species, robusta, is a major step down in flavor but easier to raise and harvest, making it less expensive. Big commercial producers have long used it as the primary bean in canned coffees.

The best specialty coffee companies feature arabica beans, which they roast themselves and sell whole as fresh as possible. Using a professional process called *cupping,* they select their raw beans when they are green and have little coffee taste. Roasting brings out the flavor. Cooks used to do it at home, which is still possible, but the process requires expert finesse to achieve the desired results on a consistent basis. Like winemakers, "roastmasters" turn a simple fruit into a complex drink that varies in flavor according to their skill and vision. They sometimes roast a blend of beans from different places, creating a signature coffee, and at other times they start with a batch of beans from one distinctive growing area, such as Costa Rica, Colombia, Guatemala, Yemen, Indonesia, or Kona, Hawaii.

The length of the roasting time affects the taste of beans, which makes it a source of controversy in the craft. Some experts favor a longer, deeper roast, while others prefer a lighter result. "French" and "Italian" roasts are darker than most, but other blends and single-origin beans will vary in depth of doneness according to the preferences of roastmasters and their customers. Ultimately you must decide for yourself what you like. Sample different styles of beans from local roasters, or if those choices are limited, mail-order from one of the many high-quality specialty companies across the country. For a full-bodied dark roast, one good source is Peet's Coffee and Tea (800-999-2132 and www.peets.com), a pioneer in the field. Distant Lands Coffee (888-262-5282 and www.dlcoffee.com) specializes in light roasting of premier beans, including ones from its own coffee estate in Costa Rica.

BREWING TIPS

- Most coffee connoisseurs brew with either a manual drip coffeemaker or a French press (aka plunger pot), both of which require more attention than an electric machine but generally make a better cup. The proponents of the drip method often say they get too much sediment from a French press, while the advocates of the plunger system claim that the paper filters common in drip methods rob the coffee of flavor. If you like the drip system, as we do, try it with a gold instead of paper filter.

- To avoid staleness, buy beans as freshly roasted as possible, purchase only as much as you will use in one week, and grind the beans just before brewing. Use the grind suggested by the manufacturer of your coffeemaker, which may range from coarse for a French press to medium or fine for some drip systems. Inexpensive propeller grinders work well, but as a guide in using one you may want to ask a professional roaster to grind one batch for you to your specifications to get an idea of your target range of coarseness or fineness.

- Start with fresh, cold water. If your tap water is hard, heavily chlorinated, or off-tasting for any other reason, use bottled or filtered water. The ideal water temperature for brewing is right under 200°F. We bring it to a boil and then let it cool for a moment. Some electric drip machines never reach the proper water temperature.
- Measure your water and coffee, sticking usually to the classic proportion of 2 tablespoons coffee for 6 ounces water. If you want a stronger or weaker brew, try changing beans before adjusting measurements. You can also add hot water to dilute coffee that's too stout for your taste.
- Leaving water in contact with the grounds too long can make coffee bitter and harsh tasting, what the experts call "overextracted." The optimal brewing time is 4 to 6 minutes.
- Aficionados brew only what they plan to drink immediately. If you brew more, store it in a Thermos for up to several hours rather than leave it on a hot plate, which undermines the flavor quickly.

ESPRESSO, CAPPUCCINO, AND LATTE

The recent explosion of interest in specialty coffees has driven American tastes to the doorsteps of Europe, particularly Italy. Many people now love espresso, both as a morning and an after-dinner drink, and millions more have learned ways to make it palatable with lots of milk and sometimes sweeteners too.

It's a bit of a challenge to make fine espresso at home, but it can be done. The brewing process is the key difference from other coffee, and it requires special equipment that quickly forces hot (but not boiling) water at high pressure through beans that are finely (but not too finely) ground. The type and even the quality of the bean make somewhat less difference than the process of extracting its flavor. The most visible sign of success is *crema,* a brown foam that forms on top of good espresso as it flows into the cup.

In *The Joy of Coffee* (1997), Corby Kummer thoroughly surveys the styles of espresso makers on the American market. He finds advantages and disadvantages in most models but ultimately recommends going high-end with an expensive pump machine or low-tech with an old-style moka pot. If you want to make latte as well as espresso, and you're not willing to spend hundreds of dollars, he suggests supplementing a moka with an inexpensive electric milk steamer rather than buying one of the popular moderately priced steam espresso makers with a built-in milk nozzle. In Italy, a latte usually contains two to four parts milk to one part espresso, but coffee shops in this country frequently double the amount of milk.

To make cappuccino, you need both steamed and foamed milk, combining equal portions of each with the same amount of espresso in the classic Italian formula. Foaming derives from aeration of steamed milk, a process generally accomplished easily in the most powerful espresso makers. If your milk steamer doesn't have an aeration device, you can achieve much of the effect by releasing the milk just above the cup rather than inside it.

MORNING TEA

Tea is an older beverage than coffee—dating back at least a couple of millennia in China—and is consumed in much greater amounts worldwide. Americans began drinking it in the colonial period but then cut back consumption for patriotic reasons after dumping a shipload of it in the Boston Harbor in 1773. We later learned to love it iced, but only recently, paralleling the boom in specialty coffees, have we developed much of a discriminating palate for fine tea served warm. This is a classic cup, worth the slight fuss of the soothing ritual.

MAKES TWO 6-OUNCE CUPS

2 teaspoons whole black or oolong tea leaves or premium tea bags

Milk, optional

Sugar and thin lemon slices, optional

Fill a small teapot with hot water. Let it stand briefly to warm the pot. Bring 1½ cups cold water just to a boil over high heat in a teakettle or saucepan. Pour the warm water out of the pot and add the loose tea leaves or bags to the bottom of the pot. Immediately pour the boiled water over the tea and cover it. Let the mixture steep for about 4 minutes. If you want milk, add just a bit now to 2 empty cups. Pour the tea equally into the cups, using a tea strainer if needed to capture the leaves. Serve immediately, with sugar or lemon or both on the side if you think they would enhance the particular tea you have chosen. (If you plan to drink both cups yourself, remove the tea leaves from the pot when you pour your first cup). Sit down, relax, and enjoy.

PERFECTING YOUR TEA

All true teas—which exclude herbal varieties more properly called *tisanes* or *infusions*—are black, oolong, or green. The three types start out from the same leaves but are processed differently. With green tea, the leaves are steamed immediately after being picked to stop fermentation and then dried. Black leaves are fermented for long periods before steaming, and oolong for a shorter time.

Sample the staggering variety of teas available today to pick a personal favorite. You can buy rare white tea from China, tea leaves tied to open like chrysanthemums when infused, and nineteen grades of jasmine tea, topping out at what is called "Silver Jasmine." If you like a milder tea, Ceylon tea from Sri Lanka might be just your cup, and if you favor a more robust, almost malty flavor, try an Assam tea from northeast India. Some teas have additional flavoring, such as the aromatic pine smoke of exotic Lapsang Souchong or Earl Grey's hint of bergamot, from a small acidic orange native to Italy. For iced tea, we especially like Paradise

Tropical Tea (800-221-2674 or www.superiorcoffeeshop.com), a blend of Chinese and Sri Lankan teas with a light tropical fruit nectar and flower petals.

Republic of Tea (800-711-8768 or www.republicoftea.com) and Honest Tea (800-865-4736 or www.honesttea.com) have substantially enhanced the quality and variety of tea available in supermarkets, especially in natural foods and specialty foods stores. Our favorite general source for tea is Ten Ren Tea Company (800-543-2885 or www.tenren.com) in San Francisco's Chinatown, which has now expanded to other locations around the city. Cecilia Chang, San Francisco's grand lady of Chinese food and drink, recommends it highly, providing a much better endorsement than ours.

A PROPER POT OF TEA

- Use a teapot of china, ceramic, glass, or cast iron with a patina. Other metals can alter the flavor. Some pots come with a wire mesh insert that holds loose tea leaves. A tea ball can accomplish the same thing, though some connoisseurs avoid them because they don't necessarily allow for a full flow of water through the leaves. If you use a ball, fill it no more than half full so that the leaves have room to expand. You can also put the leaves loose in the pot and filter them with a tea strainer placed over each cup as your pour.
- Connoisseurs generally frown on tea bags because they are often filled with poor-quality tea leaves and the bag can interfere with the proper flow of water through the leaves. Many premium teas now are available in better-designed bags, however, so use your own judgment. The convenience is hard to resist. If you use a tea bag, it should be placed in the bottom of the cup, not dangled from the side, so that the water can flow through effectively.
- To avoid staleness, buy tea frequently and store it tightly closed, preferably in a metal canister, to seal out moisture. Keep it away from heat, but don't store it in the refrigerator.
- Pour hot water into the teapot, allow it to warm the pot, and then pour it out and add the tea. Cover the pot while you bring the brewing water to a boil.
- Start with fresh, cold water. If your tap water is hard, heavily chlorinated, or off-tasting for any other reason, use bottled or filtered water. Bring the water to a quick but unequivocal boil, then pour it over the leaves immediately.
- Measurements for water and tea vary, depending on the tea, but the classic proportion is 1 teaspoon leaves for 6 ounces water, plus 1 teaspoon "for the pot." It should steep for 3 to 4 minutes in most cases or sometimes up to 5 if recommended by the tea company. You can add more hot water to dilute tea that's too stout for your tastes, but you may want to change to a different, milder tea if this is consistently the case. If a tea seems too weak, add more leaves to the pot rather than infuse it longer.
- Leaving water in contact with the leaves for longer than recommended makes the tea too tannic and harsh tasting, which isn't remedied by simple dilution. Aficionados brew only what they plan to drink immediately or remove the leaves from it and place the tea in a Thermos to keep warm.
- A touch of milk is fine with many black teas, and some oolongs, but virtually never with green tea. Properly, it should be added to the cup before the tea. Most connoisseurs eschew sugar. Try tasting before adding sugar or honey, then add it minimally if at all.

ICED CHAI

A black tea simmered with spices, then sweetened and cut with milk, chai became one of the trendiest beverages in the country in the last decade. Some marketers push it as tea latte, a name that reflects both its preparation style and its popular status. Many commercial blends are hopelessly sweet and one-dimensional, sometimes loaded with cheap cinnamon and little other spice, but at home you can correct those deficiencies and add savory undertones such as bay and black pepper that give real chai its character. On a simmering summer day, we like it iced in the morning.

SERVES 2

5 quarter-size slices fresh ginger

One 2-inch cinnamon stick

2 bay leaves

1 teaspoon black peppercorns

4 whole cloves

3 black tea bags, preferably Darjeeling

½ cup milk or more to taste

2 tablespoons packed brown sugar, granulated sugar, or honey or more to taste

Ice cubes

Place the ginger, cinnamon, bay leaves, peppercorns, and cloves in a medium saucepan. Bruise the spices with a pestle or meat-tenderizing mallet. Add 1½ cups cold water and bring to a boil over high heat. Place the tea bags in a heatproof pitcher or bowl and pour the water and spices over them. Let the tea steep for 4 to 5 minutes. Remove the tea bags and let the mixture continue to steep for at least 10 minutes longer or, if you have time, let it cool to room temperature. Strain into 2 tall glasses, add milk and sugar, and fill the glasses to the top with ice.

HOT CHAI

You can always just serve the chai warm, the usual way, following the initial steeping. You may want to dilute it with a little more milk.

EMBELLISHMENTS FOR CHAI

Good chai can be as complex in seasoning as a good curry. Use the preceding recipe as a starting point, experimenting if you like with the addition of a star anise or two, or teaspoons of bruised cardamom pods, fennel, or coriander seeds.

MINTED GREEN TEA

Rather than an infused herbal tea, made solely with herbs, this is tea with herbal accents. We start with gentle green tea and add fresh mint, producing a heady but subtle brew.

MAKES 2 CUPS

1 cup lightly packed fresh mint leaves

2 teaspoons green tea leaves or 2 premium green tea bags

Sugar or honey, optional

Fill a small teapot with hot water. Let it stand briefly to warm the pot. Bring 2 cups water just to a boil over high heat in a teakettle or saucepan. Pour the warm water out of the pot and add the mint leaves and loose tea leaves or bags to the bottom of the pot. Immediately pour the boiled water over the leaves and cover it. Let the mixture steep for 4 to 5 minutes. Pour the tea equally into the cups, using a tea strainer if needed to capture the leaves. Serve immediately, with sugar if you like. (If you are planning on drinking both cups yourself, remove the leaves from the pot when you pour your first cup.)

ICED MINTED GREEN TEA

This is equally refreshing in an iced variation. Make the tea with just 1 cup water, pour it over tall glasses filled with ice, and garnish with a mint sprig and an edible blossom.

LEMON VERBENA GREEN TEA

We also like this herb and tea brew, with a floral lemon scent and taste. Substitute an equal quantity of lemon verbena for the mint.

COMFORTING COCOA

The first connoisseurs of chocolate, the Aztecs, served it as a beverage, and that remained the most common way of enjoying it in Europe and the United States until a century ago. Technically, cocoa starts with dried powder and hot chocolate with melted chocolate, but most people blur the terms today. Either drink makes a good pick-me-up, but for an optimal cup of comfort, we like using both, cocoa for its deeper flavor and chocolate for its silky richness.

MAKES 2 OVERSIZE CUPS

3 tablespoons premium-quality unsweetened cocoa powder (see Ingredient Tip)

2 tablespoons sugar

Minuscule pinch of salt

1 ounce bittersweet chocolate, finely chopped (see Ingredient Tip)

1½ cups milk

2 tablespoons half-and-half

¼ teaspoon pure vanilla extract

A few mini-marshmallows, a spoonful of marshmallow creme, sweetened whipped cream, or crème fraîche, optional

Whisk the cocoa, sugar, and salt together in a saucepan, then add the chocolate. Whisk in ½ cup water and cook over low heat for 1 to 2 minutes, giving the cocoa time to release its full flavor. Whisk in the milk and half-and-half and cook over medium-low heat just until piping hot with tiny bubbles steadily forming around the edge. Do not boil. Stir in the vanilla and remove from the heat. Pour into 2 mugs. Top sparingly with marshmallows or whipped cream if you wish and serve immediately.

QUICKER COCOA

This is almost as good, and you avoid chopping chocolate. Just add 1 tablespoon more cocoa and eliminate the bittersweet chocolate.

HOT MOCHA

Substitute hot strong coffee for half of the milk.

HOT WHITE CHOCOLATE WITH MINT

Eliminate everything but the milk and half-and-half. Warm them in a saucepan along with 3 ounces chopped good-quality white chocolate and 1 tablespoon crushed peppermint candy (the red-and-white striped variety). For grown-ups, add a splash of white crème de menthe or peppermint schnapps if you like.

MEXICAN HOT CHOCOLATE

Replace the cocoa and chocolate with about 3 ounces fine Mexican chocolate, such as Ibarra. Its texture is a little gritty, because the chocolate typically contains bits of almond and cinnamon and doesn't go through the process called *conching* that silkens American chocolates. Chop it up in a blender before starting the recipe. Use heavy cream rather than half-and-half and whisk until very frothy before pouring into cups. Dust cups with cinnamon and serve.

EMBELLISHMENTS FOR A CUP OF COCOA

Add a teaspoon or more of flavored syrup, especially vanilla, hazelnut, or almond. For a fruity fragrance, try a bit of cherry or raspberry syrup or a big strip of orange zest. On the weekend or at the end of the day, put in a splash of brandy, cognac, amaretto, Tuaca, Kahlúa, or Irish whiskey. If using whipped cream or crème fraîche, sprinkle shaved chocolate curls or slivered almonds over the top. For silliness, use a peppermint stick for a stirrer or, for real decadence, a halved vanilla bean.

GARDEN-FRESH TOMATO JUICE

INGREDIENT TIP

We like the pulpiness that comes from skin-on tomatoes. If you prefer juice completely silky, or are serving it to picky children, you may want to peel the tomatoes first.

In the memory of the passing generation, Nutmeggers, like other New Englanders, ate formidable breakfasts. They commenced a summer day with a light menu of broiled steak, or ham and boiled eggs, with wheat battercakes, or boiled or baked potatoes, graham or Boston brown bread, and baked apples or applesauce. The meal that broke the fast in winter was more heating—fried sausages and potatoes, and cold boiled tongue or other cold meat, fried "Indian" mush, buckwheat battercakes, and pickled cucumbers. . . . Those were the days that have

No other savory juice rivals tomato as a breakfast favorite, but few people ever serve it fresh. It's simpler to make than a smoothie and doesn't even require a juicer.

SERVES 1

2 medium red-ripe tomatoes, stem and any white core removed (see Ingredient Tip)

Salt and freshly milled black pepper to taste

Pinch of cayenne pepper or dash or two of Tabasco or other hot pepper sauce, optional

Place the tomatoes in a blender with 2 tablespoons cold water and blend until smooth, with tiny bits of skin suspended in liquid. Add seasonings to taste and blend again. Pour into a tall glass and drink up.

GARDEN-PARTY TOMATO JUICE

Deck out glasses of fresh juice as you would a Bloody Mary, with a celery stick, pickled okra or asparagus spear, or a lemon or lime wedge.

HOT TOMATO JUICE COCKTAIL

The first thing Cheryl's junior-high home economics class ever cooked was a hot juice drink called Tomato Twizzlers. It involved lacing hot canned tomato juice with a drop of Tabasco, a shake of black pepper, a dusting of powdery Parmesan from the green can, and a jaunty breadstick swizzle stick. The idea actually isn't bad if you use high-quality unprocessed ingredients. Just be sure to call it something different.

BREAKFAST LEMONADE

Given a choice every day of any restaurant in the country to have breakfast, we would end up at Irma's in downtown Houston as much as half the time. For her signature drink, Irma Galvan serves this inspired cross between a Mexican *agua fresca* and an American lemonade, chock-full of bits of fresh seasonal fruit. This is how we make it at home for ourselves. Irma gives you a bottomless glass at breakfast, but we guarantee that this pitcher will go fast.

MAKES APPROXIMATELY 2 QUARTS

One 12-ounce can frozen lemonade concentrate, thawed

1½ cups watermelon juice (great for its color), other melon juice, or mango juice

2 to 2½ cups finely chopped mixed fresh fruit, such as strawberries, mangoes, apple (skin on), red grapes, peaches, apricots, lychees, pears, honeydew melon, or pineapple (at least 3 kinds)

Combine in a large pitcher, preferably a clear one to show off the fruit, the lemonade concentrate, watermelon juice, and 2 cups cold water. Stir in the fruit. Taste and add a bit more water if you wish. Serve in tall glasses immediately or cover and refrigerate to serve later in the day.

NO NUKES WILL RUIN MY BREAKFAST

In 1955, during one of the hottest periods of the cold war, the Texas State Defense and Disaster Relief Control agency published an optimistic little leaflet describing how to survive "enemy action." It urged families to store sufficient food for three or four days and offered sample menus for emergency planning. For the first day, the state officials suggested a breakfast of frozen citrus juice, scrambled eggs, bread, butter or margarine, jelly, frozen coffee, cream and sugar, and milk. The cook, they said, might prepare the eggs "in a large frying pan set on a frame of a chafing dish."

SUNRISE

The tequila sunrise, laced with orange juice and grenadine syrup, inspired this alcohol-free morning beverage, as strikingly lovely as it is tasty. If you make a bunch of these for a party, garnish with Starfruit in Spiced Syrup (page 415).

SERVES 1

¾ cup freshly squeezed tangerine or orange juice

Lime slice

3 to 4 ounces pomegranate juice, fresh, from concentrate, or bottled, or grenadine (see Ingredient Tip)

Place 3 or 4 ice cubes in an oversize wineglass. Pour the tangerine juice over the ice, then top with the pomegranate juice, which will sink in slowly. Serve garnished with lime.

SUNRISE SPRITZER

Add ½ cup sparkling mineral water or club soda and serve in a tall glass.

DRINK AN ORANGE

Why do we drink orange juice with breakfast more than any other beverage except coffee? Partly at least because of clever marketing by Florida citrus growers, who launched an advertising campaign in *The Saturday Evening Post* in 1916 offering readers a ten-cent fruit squeezer to encourage them to "Drink an Orange." In later decades, the industry even promoted itself through shipping crates—effectively touted for use as end tables and toy chests—and the colorful crate labels bearing names such as Breakfast Belle, Moonbeam, Florigold, and Hearts Delite. The large Indian River Sub Exchange employed "Flo," a dark-haired Florida beauty, as its marketing symbol from the 1920s through the 1950s, a period during which her trademark bathing suit became increasingly skimpy. Orange juice tastes great, of course—particularly when freshly squeezed—but it's lovable for other reasons as well.

PINEAPPLE SLUSH

This may remind you a bit of an alcoholic drink, the piña colada, but this is neither as syrupy sweet nor as lethal.   SERVES 2

1½ cups chopped fresh pineapple, placed in the freezer for 30 minutes to 1 hour

1 cup canned coconut milk

1 to 2 tablespoons cream of coconut or sugar to taste

1 tablespoon fresh lime juice or more to taste

Toasted coconut shreds, fresh pineapple slices, or both

Combine the chopped pineapple, coconut milk, coconut cream, and lime juice in a blender and puree. Pour into 2 tall glasses, sprinkle coconut on top, add the pineapple slices to the rims if you wish, and serve. Tiny paper parasols are optional.

CRANBERRY SLUSH

Replace the pineapple with ½ cup cranberries (again, partially frozen) and ½ cup cranberry juice. Increase the amount of cream of coconut or sugar a bit, but keep the drink refreshingly tangy. Float a few whole cranberries on top and garnish with a lime slice.

MANGO SLUSH

Treat voluptuously ripe mango in the same way, garnishing with the coconut or a lime slice.

HONEYDEW-MINT SLUSH

Trade out pineapple for juicy honeydew melon chunks and add 2 tablespoons packed fresh mint leaves. Replace the coconut milk and cream of coconut with ½ cup sweetened condensed milk and ½ to ¾ cup of still or sparkling water. You may want a little extra lime juice. Garnish with mint sprigs.

ALMOND-VANILLA SODA

———

Sometimes now, out here, we will rise in the cool breezes of a spring dawn, needing no further goading than the prospect of Aunt Ida's egg pancakes or Rosalie's veal cakes. Or a party has lasted too long, and hash made from last night's roast or fowl seems the perfect greeting to the rising sun, before we separate for sleep. Taken before or after sleeping, it is a happy thing, a friend has said, that breakfasts were designed for the morning hours.

Edward Harris Heth, *Wisconsin Country Cookbook and Journal* (1956)

Hand in hand with espresso, Italian drink syrups have surged in popularity in the United States in the last couple of decades. In combination with soda or mineral water, they provide possibilities for myriad beverages. It's fun to play with the flavor options, but for breakfast we usually limit ourselves to simple pairings such as this almond and vanilla blend, finished off with a splash of cream. If you have the two syrups handy for this drink, you can also use them together or individually to top pancakes or fruit. **SERVES 1**

About 2 teaspoons almond syrup

About 2 teaspoons vanilla syrup

1½ teaspoons to 2 tablespoons heavy (whipping) cream or half-and-half (see Ingredient Tip)

¾ cup sparkling mineral water or club soda, chilled

A few ice cubes, optional

Combine the syrups in a medium glass with cream to taste. Pour the water over, stir, and serve, maybe adding ice on a hot morning.

PURPLE COW

Use blackberry or blueberry syrup to replace the almond and vanilla varieties, then add a couple of fresh blackberries or blueberries.

STRAWBERRY BREAKFAST SODA

Use strawberry syrup to replace the almond and vanilla varieties, then add a fresh strawberry or two.

RAINBOW MIMOSAS

For a festive breakfast sip, nothing matches a flute of champagne or sparkling wine. The classic mimosa combines equal parts of champagne and orange juice, but the idea is ripe for experimentation. For a breakfast party, we like to offer several fruit juices, nectars, or freshly pureed fruits as alternatives, along with a few fruit liqueurs or eau de vies. **SERVES 4 OR MORE**

Fruit juices, nectars, or pureed fruit such as blood orange, mango, apricot, strawberry, raspberry, peach, honeydew melon, or passion fruit

Fruit liqueurs such as Grand Marnier or Cointreau (orange), Grand Passion or Alizé (passion fruit), Midori (melon), or framboise (raspberry)

Small strawberries or raspberries

One 750-milliliter bottle moderately priced champagne or sparkling wine, well chilled

Let everyone fill a flute about one-third to one-half full of fruit juice and, if desired, a splash of a companionable liqueur. Encourage them to pop in a berry if they wish. Pour champagne to fill, serve, and toast. Repeat.

I used to think, in my Russian-novel days, that I would cherish a lover who managed through thick and thin, snow and sleet, to have a bunch of Parma violets on my breakfast tray each morning—also rain or shine, Christmas or August, and onward into complete Neverland. Later, I shifted my dream plan—a split of cold champagne, one half hour *before* the tray.

M.F.K. Fisher, *With Bold Knife and Fork* (1968)

BLOODY MARY

Even during the recent white wine era, when serious cocktails fell out of favor, the bloody Mary never lost its standing as a breakfast libation. The rising popularity of both brunch and hot sauces in the same period may have even fanned the flames of ardor.

SERVES 1

½ medium lime or lemon

Celery salt

¾ cup tomato juice

¼ cup vodka (pepper or lemon versions are good too)

2 to 3 dashes Worcestershire sauce

2 to 3 dashes Tabasco or other hot pepper sauce

Freshly grated or prepared horseradish

Freshly cracked black pepper

Several ice cubes

Celery stalk or pickled asparagus spear or okra

Lime or lemon wedge, optional

Rub the lime half around the rim of an old-fashioned glass. Place a thin layer of celery salt on a saucer and dip the lime-rubbed glass into the salt. Shake off excess salt to leave just a light sprinkling on the rim. Squeeze the rest of the lime half into a cocktail shaker or lidded jar and add the tomato juice, vodka, Worcestershire sauce, Tabasco sauce, and enough horseradish and black pepper to tingle your nose. Shake together, add several ice cubes to the prepared glass, and pour the drink over the ice. Garnish with celery, asparagus, or skewered okra. Add a lime wedge to the rim if you like and serve.

DIRTY GERTIE

This Baltimore version of a bloody Mary comes from the family of John Shields, cookbook author and PBS host. Eliminate the celery salt. Use only 2½ to 3 ounces tomato juice, replacing the rest with clam juice. Trade out the lime for a lemon and add ¼ teaspoon Old Bay seasoning with the other seasonings. Garnish with celery.

MORE THAN ONE WAY TO QUENCH A THIRST

In *Fried Coffee and Jellied Bourbon* (1967), William C. Roux argues that breakfast is a manly meal. He describes the morning choices of notable men, from Carl Sandburg to Dr. Spock, and then suggests a range of morning entrees sufficient for "a year of Saturdays and Sundays, a two week vacation and a couple of holidays." Roux's favorites include shirred eggs with shad roe and bacon, lamb chops and sausages with fried hominy, ham hash, and rum omelets.

One morning he went into Donovan's saloon to get his usual stiffener, to which every patron of the house was entitled free of charge. The theory was that a man who spent his money in a saloon had a right to at least one cocktail to start the day with. Some took advantage of this, of course, and went to 12 or 13 saloons for their morning nips, but as a general thing, I think, the respectable ones didn't extend their routes to more than seven places.

Comstock Lode quoted in Helen Evans Brown, et al., *The Virginia City Cook Book* (1954)

MINT JULEP

Mint juleps enjoy an even longer breakfast legacy than bloody Marys, dating back to the plantation era in the South. They remain a big favorite in Kentucky on Derby Day, traditionally served in a silver goblet, but they're also wonderful on any other leisurely summer Saturday. We always serve them with Derby Day Turkey Hash with Corn Batty Cakes (page 192) and sometimes with ham and biscuits.   **SERVES 1**

1 teaspoon, more or less,
granulated or confectioners' sugar

4 to 8 fresh mint leaves

3 to 4 ounces bourbon or other
American whiskey

Fresh mint sprig

In the bottom of a medium glass, combine the sugar and mint leaves with 1 teaspoon cold water. Crush the mint lightly with a spoon or bar muddler and dissolve the sugar. Fill with crushed ice. As soon as frost forms on the glass, pour in the bourbon slowly, then top the julep with a mint sprig. Avoid touching the sides of the glass if possible to preserve the regally frosted presentation. Serve immediately.

MINT JULEP QUENCHER

The julep is a stout beverage for the morning. To make sure you see noon, you can add ½ cup still or sparkling mineral water and more ice, which makes 2 servings.

MARDI GRAS MILK PUNCH

A BREAKFAST MENU

SUGGESTION FOR

CHRISTMAS MORNING

Pan-Fried Oysters

Eggs Sunny-Side Up

Liver Pudding

Pork Sausage

Skillet-Fried Potatoes

Biscuits

Butter

Wild Strawberry Preserves

Bourbon

Coffee

Edna Lewis, *The Taste of Country Cooking* (1976)

According to New Orleans lore, French Quarter apothecaries concocted the milk punch in the late eighteenth century as a morning pick-me-up. It still serves that purpose in the Creole city, particularly during Mardi Gras, when celebrants drink it by the gallon.

SERVES 4

1¼ to 1½ cups bourbon

1½ cups milk

½ cup heavy (whipping) cream

6 tablespoons sugar, superfine if available

1 tablespoon pure vanilla extract

Freshly grated nutmeg

Combine the bourbon, milk, cream, sugar, and vanilla in a large pitcher. Whisk vigorously. Pour into old-fashioned glasses and dust with nutmeg.

BRENNAN'S ABSINTHE SUISSESSE

SELECTIONS FROM THE

BREAKFAST MENU AT

BARNUM'S CITY HOTEL IN

BALTIMORE, 1875

BREAKFAST WINES

	PTS.	QTS.
Medoc, Brandenburg Frères	$.30	$.50
St. Julien, Brandenburg Frères		1.00
Chateau la Rose, Brandenburg Frères	1.25	2.50
Chateau Bouiliac, Cruse & Fils	.75	1.50
Pontet Canet, Cruse & Fils	1.00	2.00
Chateau Margaux, Cruse & Fils		3.50
Sauternes, Cruse & Fils	.75	1.50
Chateau Yquem, Cruse & Fils		3.50

"Now you take a town like New York; they don't even serve drinks before noon," Ella Brennan once chided a New York–based food magazine. America's foremost restaurateur and a vigorous defender of New Orleans traditions, Brennan particularly enjoys this morning drink, which she and her delightful daughter Ti shared with us at their Commander's Palace restaurant during our breakfast research.

SERVES 1

1¼ ounces Pernod or other anise-flavored liqueur

2 tablespoons heavy (whipping) cream or half-and-half

1 tablespoon orgeat syrup (see Ingredient Tip)

1 medium to large egg white

3 to 4 ice cubes, cracked

Place the ingredients in a cocktail shaker or lidded jar and shake vigorously. Pour into a chilled old-fashioned glass and serve.

BREAKFAST AT BRENNAN'S

Hermann B. Deutsch in *Brennan's New Orleans Cookbook* (1964) tells the story of how Brennan's Restaurant began to specialize in the morning meal. Famed gastronome Lucius Beebe came to visit Owen Brennan in New Orleans in the early 1950s, when Frances Parkinson Keyes's *Dinner at Antoine's* was riding high on the best-seller lists and boosting business at the rival restaurant. As Brennan bemoaned his fate, Beebe suggested that he fight back by touting "Breakfast at Brennan's." The two sat down immediately and started conjuring elaborate morning menus featuring dishes such as Absinthe Suissesse, eggs Sardou, and bananas Foster. Breakfast at Brennan's quickly appealed to locals and soon attracted busloads of tourists, far eclipsing the fame of dinner at Antoine's.

Index